Music and Narrative since 1900

MUSICAL MEANING & INTERPRETATION

Robert S. Hatten, editor

Music and Narrative since 1900

EDITED BY MICHAEL L. KLEIN AND NICHOLAS REYLAND

INDIANA UNIVERSITY PRESS

Bloomington & Indianapolis

This book is a publication of

INDIANA UNIVERSITY PRESS
601 North Morton Street
Bloomington, Indiana 47404-3797 USA

iupress.indiana.edu

Telephone orders 800-842-6796
Fax orders 812-855-7931

Manufactured in the
United States of America

Library of Congress
Cataloging-in-Publication Data

Music and narrative since 1900 / edited
by Michael L. Klein and Nicholas
Reyland.
    pages cm. – (Musical meaning and
interpretation)
    Includes bibliographical references and
index.
    ISBN 978-0-253-00644-8 (cloth :
alkaline paper) 1. Narrative in music.
2. Music – Philosophy and aesthetics.
3. Music – Semiotics. 4. Musical analysis. 5. Music theory. I. Klein, Michael
Leslie, editor. II. Reyland, Nicholas W.,
editor. III. Series: Musical meaning and
interpretation.
    ML3849.M933 2013
    780.9'04 – dc23

                                    2012025523

1 2 3 4 5   18 17 16 15 14 13

"We're two academics in an intellectual environment. It's our duty to examine currents of thought, investigate the meaning of human behavior. But think how exciting, to come out a winner in a deathly struggle, to watch the bastard bleed."

"Plot a murder, you're saying. But every plot is a murder in effect. To plot is to die, whether we know it or not."

"To plot is to live," he said.

Don DeLillo, *White Noise*

Contents

Preface

When approaching musical narrative, the conventional place to start is with Jean-Jacques Nattiez's famous question, "Can one speak of narrativity in music?" Nattiez's equally famous answer was "no." Music simply lacks the semantic specificity to identify and tell us about the characters and actions in its putative narratives. True as Nattiez's objection might be, though, it does not form an effective strategy in keeping us from pursuing the very speech it hopes to curtail. As soon as we are urged not to speak about something, we feel compelled to deny the interdiction and speak about it anyway. The 1990s thus saw a "narrative turn" in musicology that abated early in the new century but that has come back like the return of the repressed. A long list of articles about musical narrative, many of which will inform the essays collected here, has grown in recent years. We have also seen the publication of the first book-length studies of the topic in Byron Almén's *A Theory of Musical Narrative* and Vincent Meelberg's *New Sounds, New Stories.* Arguably, as well, James Hepokoski and Warren Darcy's *Elements of Sonata Theory,* with its emphasis on the sonata as a "perfect human action," is a book that illustrates how to read any eighteenth- or nineteenth-century sonata as a musical narrative. To Nattiez's famous statement that we cannot properly speak of narrativity in music, then, musicologists and theorists have responded with the (now) equally famous statement "yes, we can." As if to illustrate one of Lacan's cherished aphorisms, Nattiez's message came back to him in inverted form.

Nattiez's question was not the right one to ask, although it certainly spurred a large literature of responses. Among the more productive questions one might ask instead are: *How* can we speak of narrativity in music? What do we gain from a narrative understanding of music? How is a narrative reading different from a hermeneutic one or from a formalist one? Does musical narrative take on the same kinds of ordering/societal functions as narratives in other media? Is musical narrative always extrinsic and interpretive, or are there musically intrinsic forms of narrativity? Some of the answers to these kinds of questions have already come from Carolyn Abbate, Lawrence Kramer, Fred Maus, Robert Samuels, Alan Street, and many others, even when those answers have sought to confine the range of musical narrative in the first place. Speaking about music as narrative has long been a productive enterprise.

Since we know it is productive to speak about musical narrative, the primary question asked in this collection concerns what has happened to musical narrative since 1900. The date is somewhat arbitrary, of course. We could just as well ask what happened to musical narrative after functional or common-practice tonality. But this question ignores the extent to which tonality still holds sway in some repertoires of the twentieth and twenty-first centuries. The question also risks confusing musical narrative for tonality itself, thus masking one ideology (tonality) with another (narrative). We could ask what happened to music since modernism, but this question risks writing modernism large as the predominant mode of artistic thought in the last century, when it was only one of several -isms in our recent past. We could ask what happened to music after the rise of cinema, of psychoanalysis, of relativity, or of technology, all of which made their marks on music, and all of which revolve uneasily around the year 1900 (and many of which are topics of essays in this collection). So the editors remain content to hold on to 1900 as an uncomfortable date from which to start our inquiry into musical narrative.

Keeping the year 1900 in our sights, we see that most work on musical narrative has focused on music before modernism. Once we turn our attention to music across that illusory boundary into the twentieth century, studies of musical narrative drop off dramatically. Historical forces do make a case for connecting the nineteenth century in particular with the rise of narrative paradigms in music: the emergence of program music, the emphasis on music as personal communication, the polemics around the New German School, and so on. But when we look at particular arguments for narrative in that century, it is not always the historical forces that receive attention, but tonality itself. Susan McClary, for example, claims that functional tonality allowed for the development of musical narrative in ways that post-tonal techniques do not. And the narrative impact of sonata form in Hepokoski and Darcy's work is tied to tonal processes. The implication of all the work on narrative in nineteenth-century music is that tonality invites narrative, while post-tonal music is less open to narrative interpretation.

The editors of this collection disagree with this notion. Having written separately about the music of Witold Lutosławski in narrative terms, the editors have concluded that although music since modernism poses special problems *vis-à-vis* narrative, musicology would deny a rich set of historical, analytical, and ideological issues if it were to forgo narrative as one of the perspectives from which to understand this music. For us, the question is not whether music since modernism is open to narrative analysis: we think it is. Instead, we think that more meaningful questions include, among others: What happened to musical narrative after 1900? How do composers cue narrative in this music? How do composers treat narrative elements such as agency, temporality, plot, and the contested notion of the narrator itself? What do modern musical narratives tell us about culture, subjectivity, and the crises of recent history? How do listeners make narrative sense of this music?

In an effort to see if others shared our point of view, Nicholas Reyland organized narrative workshops and paper sessions for the Sixth International Conference on Music since 1900, which was held at Keele University in Staffordshire, England, in July 2009. The editors personally invited a number of musicologists and theorists to attend these workshops. The response and number of participants far exceeded our expectations. The workshops involved freewheeling discussions among internationally recognized scholars (Lawrence Kramer, Márta Grabócz, Fred Maus, Philip Rupprecht, among others) and younger academics, as well. Although different perspectives were expressed regarding the nature of narrative in music after 1900, there was virtual unanimity that the topic was a timely one. Those narrative workshops and paper sessions at Keele marked the inception of this volume of essays, the editors having witnessed the exciting ideas that could come from careful thinking about music and narrative since modernism. At the conference, Lawrence Kramer gave a keynote address on the topic of literary and musical narratives in modernism, and by good fortune he agreed to publish a version of that material in the present collection (chapter 8, "Narrative Nostalgia: Modern Art Music off the Rails"). We were off to a good start. During the conference, as well, many of the other contributors to this volume expressed keen interest in writing an essay.

The editors realized that to cover the vast territory of twentieth- and twenty-first-century musical narrative in one volume was impossible. But we hoped to offer a large enough survey of the issues to spur future work on this enormously fascinating topic. Thus we gave the writers a tall order. We wanted essays of modest length so that the collection could include as many voices as possible and touch on a large number of issues in a diversity of repertoires. We also asked the contributors to eschew long digressions in endnotes in order to focus on tightly wrought arguments. We think that the writers of these essays rose to these challenges admirably.

The collection is divided into three parts: "Framing the Narrative," "Theorizing Modern Musical Narrative," and "Interpreting Modern Musical Narrative." The first part includes introductory essays by the editors, which serve as preludes not only to the problems of narrative since modernism but also to the notion of musical narrative itself. In his "Musical Story," Michael Klein examines the classic division of narrative into discourse/story and argues that previous work on musical narratives (tonal and post-tonal) has tended to focus on discourse at the expense of story. The essay concludes that the way to musical story is through hermeneutic analysis: thus narrative analysis is a form of hermeneutics. In "Negation and Negotiation: Plotting Narrative through Literature and Music from Modernism to Postmodernism," Nicholas Reyland explores works by artists, composers, novelists, poets, and theorists in order to problematize style histories of music since modernism predicated on the idea of a denial of narrative. Drawing on recent narratological theory, he considers analogous evolutions in the plot strategies of modern and postmodern compositions and novels, plus the broader implications of such strategies for theories of musical narrativity before modernism. Reyland argues that adopting a narrative approach remains a useful, sometimes necessary, critical and polemical option for studies of music since the turn of the twentieth century.

The second part of the collection includes six essays that theorize musical narrative. As is always the case, the distinction between theory and analysis is an uncomfortable one; as with any opposition, it falls apart with careful scrutiny. But the essays in this part tend to take a broader look at the problems and possibilities of modern musical narrative or particular repertoires therein, even if analysis is part of the discussion. The first two essays in the collection, furthermore, demonstrate the spirit of enquiry at the heart of the volume and the editors' desire that contributions herein should offer a broad range of opinions on the collection's contested topic. Byron Almén and Robert Hatten's "Narrative Engagement with Twentieth-Century Music: Possibilities and Limits" surveys twentieth-century musical style history through the lens of narrativity, focusing on styles in which narrative, or its absence, becomes marked. Building on Almén's adaptation of James Jakób Liszka's semiotic approach to narrative, Almén and Hatten offer a preliminary outline of the ways in which post-1900 musical styles address issues such as agency and temporality. The essay then clarifies the continuing role of "transvaluation" (a temporalized shift in a narrative's hierarchy of values) in the absence of traditional forms of conflict, presenting analyses of works by Krzysztof Penderecki, Olivier Messiaen, and Arvo Pärt. Arnold Whittall's "Optional Extra? Contextualizing Narrative in the Critical Interpretation of Post-Tonal Composition" then addresses the challenges arising when concepts such as Liszka's "transvaluation" are applied to post-tonal and modernist repertoires in which ideas about victory and defeat, for instance, might continue to resonate even when decisive endings and resolutions are no longer present. Whittall addresses his theoretical concerns through analytical commentaries on music by Arnold Schoenberg, Anton Webern, Pierre Boulez, James Dillon, and Harrison Birtwistle, framing those concerns within a broader consideration of the critical implications of reading modern music as narrative.

In her "Archetypes of Initiation and Static Temporality in Contemporary Opera: Works of François-Bernard Mâche, Pascal Dusapin, and Gualtiero Dazzi," Márta Grabócz looks to Carl Jung and his followers to find narrative paradigms of ritual, and rites of passage, that promise to make whole the fractured self. She hears parallels to these rituals in the static and sometimes minimalist sections of several contemporary operas and oratorios. Joshua Mailman picks up the minimalist theme in his "Agency, Determinism, Focal Time Frames, and Processive Minimalist Music," an essay that wonders where the agent might be in music whose processes are pre-determined. If agency implies freedom, must determinate music lack an agent? Ultimately, Mailman does find an agent in minimalist processes while making a plea to hear mechanical determinism, with its implications of technology, in more humanist terms. Elisheva Rigbi's "Musical Prose and Musical Narrativity in the *Fin de Siècle*" argues that the disparity between story and discourse central to many theories of literary modernism was effected musically, at the turn of the twentieth century, through musical prose: a phenomenon of rhythm, melody, and form for which the period was noted, paradigmatically associated with Arnold Schoenberg and Max Reger. Her study thus offers original perspectives on narrativity in early modernism, but also on musical rhythm, temporality, and structure, and Rigbi draws on a rich diversity of music and thought to exemplify musical prose's role in sustaining the possibility of musical narrativity through the *fin de siècle*'s emergent aesthetics of plurality. Completing the second part is Lawrence Kramer's "Narrative Nostalgia: Modern Art Music off the Rails," which begins by arguing that modernism in literature questioned the possibility of narrative itself. Kramer finds a correlate to the fragmentation of modernist literary narratives in Debussy's *Jeux* before concluding with an extended reading of songs from Benjamin Britten's cycle *Winter Words*.

The third part of the collection involves close readings of individual musical works. The first four essays all approach modern British music. In his "Agency Effects in the Instrumental Drama of Musgrave and Birtwistle," Philip Rupprecht examines the instrumental-drama movement in British art music of the 1960s. Taking on the difficult questions of whether agency lies in the music, the individual lines, the performer, or even the performer as onstage actor, Rupprecht interprets Thea Musgrave's Chamber Concerto No. 2 and Harrison Birtwistle's *Verses for Ensembles* as musical reenactments of social rituals. In Emma Gallon's "Narrativities in the Music of Thomas Adès: The Piano Quintet and *Brahms*," the issues move from agency to temporality, with Gallon arguing that the conflicting temporal cues in Adès's Piano Quintet and *Brahms* suggest multiple narratives unfolding simultaneously. From temporal conflict the collection moves to moral conflict in Sumanth Gopinath's "Britten's *Serenade* and the Politico-Moral Crises of the Wartime Conjuncture: Hermeneutic and Narrative Notes on the 'Nocturne,'" which finds that the pastoral topic in the music covers a deeper anxiety that subtly forecasts the darker songs to come in Britten's song cycle. Moving from narrative in art song to popular song, Fred Maus's "Identity, Time, and Narrative in Three Songs about AIDS by the Pet Shop Boys" examines the relationship between archetypal narratives of gay male identity and songs responding to the HIV/AIDS crisis – articulations of sexual identity and politics in which time and narrative prove crucial structuring factors. The nuances of the music and lyrics in the relevant Pet Shop Boys songs (Maus offers especially detailed readings of "It Couldn't Happen Here" and "Being Boring") remind us of the role musical narratives can play in specific cultural communities, but also of the different readings that may develop from listeners with varying degrees of appropriate contextual knowledge.

In the four "British" essays, and those that follow in part 3, the theory-analysis conflict noted above continues to pertain, as the authors consider problems and possibilities of modern musical narrative in the context of sustained close readings. Vincent Meelberg's "A Story of Violence: A Guitar Improvisation as a Narrative about Embodied Listening" extends his existing work on narrativity in post-tonal music. Meelberg reads Kevin Eubanks's guitar improvisation in "Nemesis" as a narrative foregrounding the fact that listening is embodied and that the embodied nature of listening is often violent. Meelberg also outlines his concept of "sonic strokes," thereby demonstrating music narratology's potential for productive engagement with theories of musical affect, emotion, kinesthetics, and embodiment. Matthew McDonald's "Ives and the Now" directs our attention to the problem of time in early modernism, when technological developments like those in early cinema threatened to fragment temporal experience. McDonald focuses his argument on Charles Ives's "The Things Our Fathers Loved," which both enacts temporal fractures and looks nostalgically to an imagined unbroken time from the past.

The next two chapters deal with vocal/theatrical and operatic works. In "Narrativity, Descriptivity, and Secondary Parameters: Ecstasy Enacted in Salvatore Sciarrino's *Infinito nero*," Rebecca Leydon examines texture, timbre, and density as narrative cues. Leydon's argument relies on the assumption that the loss of tonality does not correlate to a loss of narrative potential in Salvatore Sciarrino's music. Yayoi Uno Everett takes a post-Lacanian approach in "The Tropes of Desire and *Jouissance* in Kaija Saariaho's *L'amour de loin*." Her method involves understanding Lacan's Imaginary register, one in which the subject hopes for a wholeness that he or she can never achieve.

The final essays begin with a pair devoted to music by Soviet composers. In "Expressive Doubling and the Narrative of Rebirth in Dmitri Shostakovich's String Quartet No. 3, op. 73," Sarah Reichardt Ellis discusses the inescapable brutality and intense sorrow of Shostakovich's Third String Quartet. Ellis shows how thematic and harmonic returns in pairs of movements (expressive doubling) undercut the directional narrative of the quartet. Gregory Karl's "Afterlife of an Archetype: Prokofiev and the Art of Subversion" turns to Sergei Prokofiev's Violin Sonata in F Minor and argues that the heroic narrative archetype common to Beethoven's middle-period music is subverted and transformed into a sense of hopelessness through the course of Prokofiev's sonata. The last essay of the collection returns to the Second Viennese School and the post-tonal modernism that marks one of the historical end points of the book. Alan Street's "Identity Formation in Webern's Six Pieces for Large Orchestra, op. 6" considers the complex array of associations, both personal and cultural, that gives this work a sense of multiple identity formations. The problem of the self in early modernism is the backdrop to the problems of Webern's musical style.

In curating this collection on music and narrative in music since ca. 1900, it has not been the intention of the editors to legislate new rules for speaking of music and narrative before or since modernism, although a number of recurring principles do emerge across the volume – absolutely unforced, yet suggesting reliable and broadly applicable concepts now emerging at the top of the theoretical pile. It has certainly been our intention, however, to form a collection of narrative-oriented music criticism demonstrating new ways of hearing and thinking about music from modernism onward and, more broadly, about art, life, and culture in the twentieth and twenty-first centuries. The truth, we would argue, can only take you so far; speaking of musical narratives, though, can set you free.

Acknowledgments

A collection of essays like this one cannot reach publication without the help of more people than we can thank properly. The editors would like to begin, though, by thanking the contributors to this collection, who have offered their invaluable insights about contemporary music and narrative to the essays herein. We very much appreciate their hard work, flexibility, and talents as musicians, scholars, and writers.

This collection would not have been possible without the support of Robert Hatten, the editor of the Musical Meaning and Interpretation series at Indiana University Press. Robert took a keen interest in this project from the moment Nick pitched the idea to him at CarMAC, the 2008 Music Analysis Conference held at Cardiff University in Wales. Robert's ever-capable hand led us through the long journey from conference workshops, to the book proposal, and through to publication. We cannot thank him enough.

Spurred on by Robert's support, Nick wove a strand on music and narrative into the Sixth International Conference on Music since 1900 at Keele University in July 2009, with a view to gathering together (for papers, roundtables, keynotes, and what turned out to be a series of invaluable and memorable discussion workshops) scholars with an interest in this topic and recent repertoires. The editors would therefore like to thank everyone who participated in the narrative-related events at that conference: the groundswell of enthusiasm carried us through this task. We also wish to thank the Research Institute for the Humanities, Keele University, for its support of the conference; the staff and students of the Music and Music Technology programs at Keele; and particularly Diego Garro, who co-organized the conference with Nick. We must also thank the following for their generous support of ICMSN 2009: Cambridge University Press, *twentieth-century music*, the *Music*

& *Letters* Trust, the Keele Key Fund, the Society for Music Analysis, and the Institute of Musical Research.

The editors would also like to thank Jane Behnken, Music and Humanities Editor, and Sarah Wyatt Swanson, Assistant Sponsoring Editor at Indiana University Press at the time that the manuscript was ready to begin the production process. Putting together a collection of essays is a process complicated by the many writers involved. Jane and Sarah were always ready to answer the countless questions and problems that arose as we brought this project to completion. As the book moved into later stages, we were helped by Raina Polivka, Music, Film, and Humanities Editor; and in the area of production we were led ably by June Silay, Angela Burton, Mary M. Hill, and Bernadette Zoss. We thank the entire team at Indiana University Press for their attention to detail. The editors thank Rosendo Reyna of musicprinting .org for his assistance in locating the image used on the front jacket, and thank Philip Blackburn, David Gilbert, Robert Messenger, and other readers of AMS-List for their music typewriting advice.

Finally, we thank the Society for Music Theory, which granted us a publication subvention to complete this collection of essays. And we express gratitude to the Board of the *Music Analysis* Development Fund for so generously supporting this publication.

Turning to individual thanks on the parts of the editors, Michael would like to thank Robert Stroker, the Dean of the Boyer College of Music and Dance at Temple University, for several Dean's Grants that reduced his teaching load, allowing him to pursue this project. On a more personal level, I would like to thank Nicholas (okay, Nick) Reyland, who, at first, had to drag me kicking and screaming into this project (I know what it's like to put together a collection of essays). But this whole experience, beginning with the conference at Keele, has been highly rewarding, in no small part thanks to Nick. On the most personal level, I would like to thank my wife, Yu-Hui Tamae Lee, and my daughter, Michelle Lee Klein, for putting up with many nights and weekends when editing had to take the fore at the expense of more appealing family activities. I could not have finished this collection, which was so important to me, without your sacrifice of things that were important to you. You will always have my love and loyalty.

Nick would like to thank the Research Institute for the Humanities, and my colleagues throughout Keele University, for their continuing support of my work. My wife, Deborah, and my children, Harrison, Albert, and William, have been like gravity during the past three years as I ran the conference and then finished two books. I love you comprehensively. Finally, I would like to thank Michael Klein for all of the incredibly hard work he has put into this project over the last two years, taking any number of batons from me and carrying them over the finish line . . . I mean, this is the kind of fool thing a reader might suppose I just said. It never even occurred to me to say it. I know the conventions that govern who should and should not be thanked in the acknowledgments. That was merely a brief disnarration.

The editors would like to thank the following publishers and composers for their kind permission to reprint portions of the following:

Piano Quintet
By Thomas Adès
© 2007 by Faber Music Ltd., London
Reproduced by kind permission of the
    publishers

Brahms
By Thomas Adès
Music © 2009 by Faber Music Ltd.,
    London
Text © 1996 by Alfred Brendel
Reproduced by kind permission of the
    publishers

Verses for Ensembles
By Harrison Birtwistle
© 1972 Universal Edition (London) Ltd.,
    London/UE 15331
© Renewed
All rights reserved
Used by permission of European Ameri-
    can Music Distributors LLC, U.S. and
    Canadian agent for Universal Edition
    (London) Ltd., London

Serenade, op. 31
By Benjamin Britten
© 1944 by Hawkes & Son (London), Ltd.
Reprinted by Permission

La rosa de Ariadna
By Gualtiero Dazzi
With kind permission from the
    composer

Medeamaterial
By Pascal Dusapin
© Éditions Salabert / Universal Music
    Publishing Classical
With kind permission

La melancholia
By Pascal Dusapin
© Éditions Salabert / Universal Music
    Publishing Classical
With kind permission

Temboctou
By François-Bernard Mâche
With kind permission from the
    composer

Chamber Concerto No. 2
Music by Thea Musgrave
© 1967 Chester Music Limited
All Rights Reserved. International
    Copyright Secured.
Reprinted by Permission.

L'amour de loin
Music by Kaija Saariaho
Libretto by Amin Maalouf
Music © 2002 Chester Music
    Limited.
Libretto © 2002 Amin Maalouf.
All Rights Reserved. International
    Copyright Secured.
Reprinted by Permission.

PART ONE

Framing the Narrative

I

Musical Story

Michael L. Klein

❧

A STORY ABOUT DISCOURSE

Rightly heard all tales are one.

CORMAC MCCARTHY, *THE CROSSING*

Imagine that once upon a time the Muse of storytelling – a curious amalgam of Calliope, Melpomene, and Thalia – granted our wish, so that all the subjects in the land agreed that music is narrative (or narrative-like). Henceforth, those tiresome arguments about music's failures of diegesis, representation, temporality, agency, and causality are rendered moot with the wave of a wand. Gone are the classic opening arguments, those cases of special pleading, reminding us that music cannot tell literal stories: no real characters nor actions, just virtual ones. Gone is the necessity to make careful distinctions between program music as a subspecies of musical narrative and absolute music, which (all now agree) was always narrative-like, despite its apparent failures of diegesis, representation, and so on. Gone is the urgency to argue that musical processes are plot-like, their motives agential, their temporalities multiple. Gone is the caveat that the story we tell on the page is not the same as the story we hear in the music.

While she's at it, the Muse grants us a second wish of exuberant ecumenical thought. Instantly and magically, we all happily accept multiple views of musical narrative as an unfolding of affective states (Tarasti, Maus, Klein), or the tracking of hierarchical relationships (Almén, Grabócz, Tarasti), or the response to music's unruly surface (McDonald, Klein), or simply as an intentional act of perception (Maus, Reyland). Further, we never invoke narrative simply to resuscitate a lost and enchanted form of structuralism (Kramer, McClary), except when we do (Meelberg, Grabócz, Almén). Despite the granting of our first wish, we all agree that music is only rarely narrative-like (Abbate, Nattiez), except when we find it especially useful to think of music as undeniably narrative through and through (Tarasti, Almén, Reyland, Samuels, and, well, everybody else). Anything goes in this new narrative world.

But wait! There's more. Our Muse is on a roll and promptly inquires if we have any other wishes. What about narrative in music after 1900? (we ask). The Muse ponders this for a while. Well (she starts), I am a big fan of Susan McClary – she tells such good stories – and like McClary (the Muse opines), I have always felt that musical narrative depends most heavily on tonality. At best, I think, music after 1900 is anti-narrative, a critique of narrative. And look (she continues), although endnotes and parenthetical citations can be antithetical to a well-wrought story – they break the plot so abruptly – I will provide you with one that cites McClary right here.[1] But this will not do (you reply), I can understand how Cage's *Atlas Eclipticalis* or Stockhausen's *Carré* makes anti-narrative appeals, but what about Debussy, Rochberg, Shostakovich? Surely Shostakovich is a narrative composer, for God's sake! I think (you continue) Nicholas Reyland's essay in this collection tells a much richer story about musical narrative. But if you're not familiar with that story, you might at least look over Jann Pasler's alternatives to narrative post-1900, which I cite with my own plot-breaking citation (Pasler 1989). Settle down (the Muse tells us), although I am not a fan of meta-anything – I'd rather tell a story than a story about a story – let me think this through (long pause: ellipses needed) . . .

(The Muse begins again.) How about this? I will grant you a range of possibilities for narrative discourse in music after 1900. And I will give you a way of structuring this discourse in a neat box. We'll call it a *map of narrative discourse*. Here it is. (With a wave of the wand, our Muse of storytelling produces a curious little map, reproduced as Figure 1.1.)

In the top left corner (she explains), we have music that largely accepts the tonal, topical, and thematic premises of the nineteenth century, including moments of thematic transformation, crisis and catastrophe, transcendence and apotheosis. This music is undeniably *narrative* (or narrative-like in our newly made world): think Rachmaninoff's *Symphonic Dances*. Down to the right in the opposing corner, we have the contrary: *non-narrative*. Here we find music with no tonality, no themes, no sense of causality or transformation, no organizing principle whatsoever, in fact: just a set of independent sound

Map of Narrative Discourse

Narrative   Anti-narrative

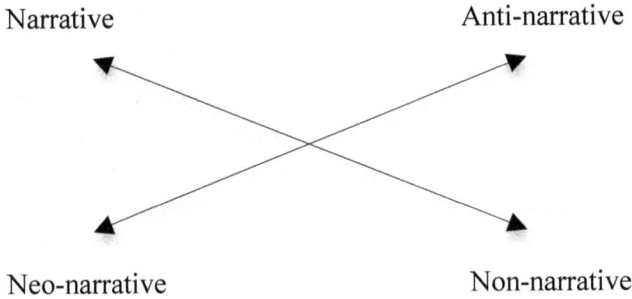

Neo-narrative   Non-narrative

FIGURE I.I. The storyteller's first map.

worlds, textures, or blips of acoustic matter. Feldman's *Projection 4* and Earle Brown's *Folio* are found here.

Now (the Muse continues), here's the important part. If we open up this map, we find two more corners. Just below the narrative one we find a category for any new narrative discourse: let's call this corner *neo-narrative*. Here is music in search of new ways to tell stories. Sometimes the rhythmic drive of this music is enough to give us a sense of musical plot, or the ever-changing timbres of orchestral color stand in for transformation, or the gradual motion through register lends us a sense of musical agency. Listen to how we strive to reach the top of the keyboard in György Ligeti's "The Devil's Staircase" only to experience a series of vertiginous falls. And once we reach the top, the refusal of the musical agent to move away makes us question our proposed narrative of success: make it stop! In the light of this kind of narrative discourse, we can reconfigure Boulez's complaint – postmodernists might say misread it – and argue that Schoenberg was too content with the neo-narrative position on the map. When Boulez writes that Schoenberg's ambition was "to create works of the same nature as those of the old sound-world which he had only just abandoned" (1991: 212), might we say that Schoenberg was confirming musical narrative albeit with a new discourse, where Boulez would have preferred to find a new position on the map, a position away from narrative? Was it really Schoenberg who was dead to Boulez, or was it narrative itself that had perished?

Finally, above the non-narrative corner, we find a fourth possibility for music that serves as the critique of nineteenth-century narrative discourse, or what Pasler calls *anti-narrative*. Here composers take on the conventions of musical narrative discourse in order to deny our expectations for their continuation. We hear the oddly compelling repetitions without transformation and the collages and interruptions of Stravinsky's *Petrushka*. We find the odd juxtapositions in Debussy's late style, the "wrong-note" music of Shostakovich and Prokofiev, and even the disruptive whack that opens Witold Lutosławski's *Jeux vénitiens*. Perhaps you have seen a performance of Theodore Antoniou's *Parastasis*? At the back of the ensemble is a giant gong that remains silent until the end of the piece, when one of the percussionists picks up a great mallet to make a climactic wallop. But just as the percussionist is about to make a hit . . . (the Muse pauses), well . . . I don't like to give away the ending of a story you may not have heard. Let us just say that *Parastasis* ends with an anti-narrative gesture. In any case, here is your map, which, I think, fulfills your third wish. (She hands the map to you with a flourish and a bow.)

(The Muse was done. You stare at her for a moment before speaking.) I confess that I'm a bit disappointed (you whisper). This is just a semiotic square, a structure, a categorical map that ultimately will fail us. I hesitate to say this, but you really do live in the past tense, because this kind of structuralist gesture is not what people are looking for these days. Structures are so contingent and pseudo-scientific. And this is not a very good square anyway: I can think of pieces that might fit into more than one category. Is *Petrushka* really an anti-narrative, or is it a neo-narrative? I'm also surprised that you, the Muse of storytelling, would include a category for non-narrative. I would think you could make a narrative out of anything. To you, a single soft *staccato* from a bassoon must be an epic.

(Our storytelling Muse takes a deep breath.) Well (she begins, slightly annoyed), I am astonished that you forget the semiotic square comes to us from Greimas, who, I admit, can be rather prickly – we view his alluring charts and symbols from afar with puzzlement, as one looks upon the alphabet of Ge'ez or the graphs of music theory (yes, a trope on Jameson 1987: vi). As you should know, the corners are just far points in the discursive space. A piece of music can find a place between these corners: as you suggest, *Petrushka* mediates the anti- and neo-narrative positions. But the Greimasian square is more than a simple grid on which to plot a point: it is the promise of narrative action in, around, and through the square's possibilities. Often a musical narrative refuses to rest at one place, preferring to move about in a plot-like sequence. Let me show you. Listen again to the opening of Ligeti's

Cello Concerto. That lonely, quiet E in the cello makes a nineteenth-century gesture, announcing the coming narrative while creating it *ex nihilo*, like a tremolo in a Bruckner symphony. But soon our little E has gone on too long, as if to renounce its first narrative convention. The concerto has moved along the semiotic square from narrative to anti-narrative. But now the E takes a different shape: the changing bow position on the cello and the entrance of the strings lend the E an anxious energy, as if a once-imploded sun prepares to burst out. We suspect that our friend E has become a musical agent with a propulsive potential that it nonetheless cannot unleash. Our suspicions are confirmed when the clarinet and harp make the barest intimation of motion to F4, *fast unhörbar*, as Ligeti writes in the score. There will be some musical progress after all. The concerto has moved along the square again from anti-narrative to neo-narrative: a story about storytelling, which is made in a new discourse outside of tonality.

These shifting musical narratives are all around you (the Muse continues). Nicholas Reyland (2008) has written such a story about Lutosławski's *Livre pour orchestre*. If we believe Lutosławski – though I confess I find composers to be unreliable narrators – he had every intention of writing non-narrative music when he sketched out *Livre*. And the piece begins as a non-narrative, with its breaks, non sequiturs, and intermezzi. Or perhaps the piece toggles between non-narrative and anti-narrative, navigating in the space between these two options. In any case, by the end of *Livre*, the anti-narrative forces have come together to make a neo-narrative with a trajectory and a climax to make any storyteller proud.

Before you interrupt (the Muse was speaking ever quicker now), let me tell you, travel around the square belongs to the province of tonal music after 1900, too. Listen to the opening of Shostakovich's Sixth Quartet, which is perfectly tonal and Haydnesque in its droll first theme, as if the quartet announces: "I accept the premise of tonality and sonata form as the basis of musical narrative discourse." A repeated D in the viola sends us on our way. But just before the first cadence, a troubling E♭ disturbs the happy surface of the music, which the viola's D ignores completely. Perhaps all will be well, except E♭ begins to accumulate: an E♭-minor chord darkens the music just before the transition, a persistent E♭ in the first violin clashes horribly with the rest of the quartet in the development, the second theme of the recapitulation enters off-tonic in E♭ minor. Always, always, the music tries to ignore the problem, moving on to the next section without tonal or topical adjustments to the insolent E♭. The music wavers from narrative to anti-narrative, both reaffirming and denying its tonal-structural premise. (The Muse was speaking so quickly now, we could barely keep up.) And how shall we read the closing passage, whose cool exterior settles on the tonic, G, even in the face of a final E♭, as if nothing unusual has happened? Has the music reaffirmed tonality? Denied it? Left the question open? Or maybe at this point the music has emptied both the tonal center and its sardonic opponent, E♭, of all signification, leading us to consider the possibility of a non-narrative conclusion. (The Muse now spoke more slowly and softly, as if parenthetically.) By the way, I refer you to an analysis of this movement by Sarah Reichardt (2008) if you want to read another story about it.

(The Muse had stopped to catch her breath.) So (you summarize), music after 1900 moves around this semiotic square of narrative discourse. But (you ask) is it really the music that moves, or is it we who move? Your descriptions seem less like ontological statements and more like phenomenological ones: the stories of how we experience narrative discourse in the midst of its unfolding. I suspect (the Muse replied), that your question is really a rhetorical one, as is my very presence here. You already know the answer. We are in dialogue with the narrative discourse of the music, an esthesic and poietic dance around the semiotic square, if you will. If and when we and the music find a fixed point on the square, the story will be over. But that is an eventuality that gives me a shiver, especially since that time long ago when Walter Benjamin first guessed the site of my authority.[2]

If you will permit me (the storyteller went on), I will turn to your other complaints about our little square by letting you in on the secret of its making. As you are aware, following a narrative theme that we find in Claude Lévi-Strauss, A. J. Greimas, James Jakób Liszka (whom we know through Byron Almén), and Fredric Jameson, and implicit in the work of Lawrence Kramer, Susan McClary, and much current musicology, one of the functions of a story is to order and reorder, affirm or question an ideology, a cultural value. Our map of narrative discourse, then, adheres to an ordering opposition that I'll call *confirm or deny*. On the square's western hemisphere – this irony will not escape you – the positions for narrative and neo-narrative fall on the side of a confirmation that upholds musical narrative discourse. And on the square's eastern hemisphere, the positions for anti-narrative and non-narrative fall on the side of a denial that questions or abolishes musical narrative discourse. Nor will it escape you – and how could it? since you have co-opted my narrative voice in order to tell your tale – that Northrop Frye's narrative archetypes, which we find in the work of Hayden White, Liszka, Almén, and Kevin

Map of Narrative Discourse (2)

Meta-Narrative

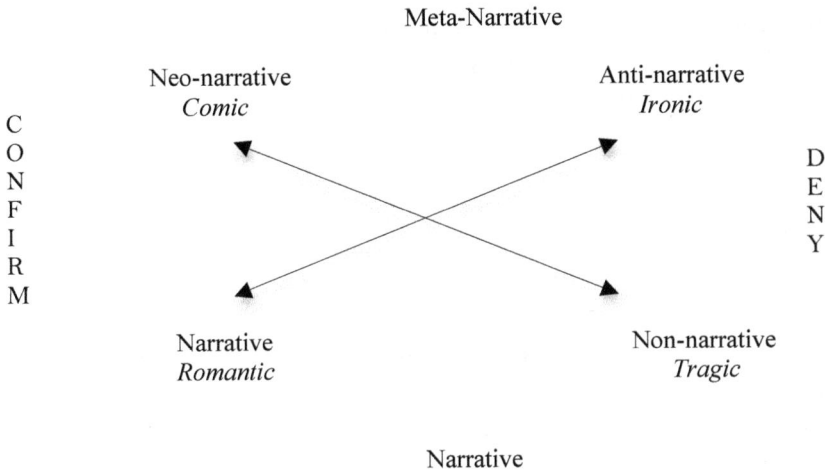

Neo-narrative
Comic

Anti-narrative
Ironic

C O N F I R M

D E N Y

Narrative
Romantic

Non-narrative
Tragic

Narrative

FIGURE 1.2. The storyteller's second map.

Korsyn, nicely map onto the narrative categories. Thus a narrative discourse is a romantic one, a neo-narrative is comic (a confirmation through new means), an anti-narrative is ironic (to use one discourse while meaning another), and to a storyteller like me a non-narrative can only be tragic.

With Frye's archetypes in place (the storyteller was coming close to the end now), we might reorient our map of discourse. You see, it matters very much where you place the corners of your semiotic square, because, as Jameson (1987) has shown, these squares are pictures of ideology; or, more properly, they are pictures of the possibilities within an ideology. As such, we must ask ourselves what the central opposition really is in the narrative discourse of music after 1900. I would venture that although music of the early modernist period took a position against romantic narrative discourse, the real ideological opposition for most of the past century has involved neo-narrative and anti-narrative. These are the two positions, in short, that modernist music has sought since 1900. Thus by convention, we place neo-narrative and anti-narrative discourses at the top of our semiotic square, leaving narrative and non-narrative to take the lower positions. Here, then, is a picture of our new square. (With a wave of the wand, the Muse refashioned our map to look like Figure 1.2.) With everything in its new place (the Muse appeared quite satisfied), we now see that narrative discourse in music after 1900 has tried to mediate the positions between comic and ironic possibilities. That is, this music is most often meta-narrative in its questioning and refashioning of narrative itself. Revising Marx's famous statement, we might say that all the history of musical narrative since 1900 has been a comedy whose every moment is ironic.

So much more I could tell you (the Muse appears preoccupied with other matters), but every story is incomplete. I could tell you how to open up each of the corners into its own semiotic square, filled with narrative possibilities. I could tell you about the ten possible positions on the square. But let me leave you with a different observation. The non-narrative corner that concerns you so much is the surprising possibility that threatens to unmake the narrative world, because not even chaos itself can be left outside the tapestry of storytelling. I remind you that once you have decided on narrative discourse as a problem, the ideological possibilities are already set before you, including the eventuality of a non-narrative position, which would require another narrative for its explication. Referring you to Jameson once more, I, the teller of tales, recount his claim that a culture never really synthesizes the poles of an opposition: it only sets aside one problem to take up another. We will not settle the problem of narrative discourse after the loss of tonality; we can only set aside narrative to take up another issue.

Well (the Muse said with new energy), I'm off. I have helped you too much already. Now that you have this handy map of narrative discourse, you should do what I did with Wittgenstein's ladder and set it aside. You have plenty to keep you occupied with the problem of musical story. One word before I go, though: you'll find that the classic division between discourse and story is not so easy to uphold when it comes to music. Sometimes the discourse *is* the story.

With those last words, the Muse is gone, leaving you as the survivor.

A DISCOURSE ABOUT STORY

For this world also which seems to us a thing of stone and flower and blood
is not a thing at all but is a tale.

CORMAC MCCARTHY, *THE CROSSING*

Now what? Without the benefit of the Muse, perhaps it would be best to return to first principles before taking up the fraught topic of musical stories.

Starting again in search of a suitable ending is a conventional narrative strategy, after all. Here goes, then.

Setting aside music for a moment, if we hope to find consensus in literary theory on a definition for narrative, we will only be disappointed. As J. Hillis Miller complains, narrative theories have become so abundant and diverse that "it makes the mind ache to think of them all" (1995: 67). Martin McQuillan (2000) lists eight influential definitions of narrative, including any simple recounting with at least one narrator, a set of transformations on a limited set of actions (Greimas), a form of aporia that challenges the taxonomies of genre (Derrida), a form of knowledge that articulates a community or society (Lyotard), and so on. About the best we can say, then, is that there is no shortage of definitions for narrative nor of scholars who find each one inadequate. In the end, it is easy to agree with Lawrence Kramer, who claims that while there are many narratives, there is no narrative (with a capital N).[3] A transcendental concept, narrative cannot be defined, only told.

Once we turn to music, the problem of narrative only becomes more difficult. As the first part of this introduction has intimated, musical narrative has invited a broad range of definitions and theories, usually adapted from literary theory. Since theories of narrative usually include some notion of its function (promoting ideologies, challenging genres, forming cultural values, making sense of time, etc.), definitions of musical narrative have taken on one or more of these functions as well. In one of the most recent contributions, for example, Almén defines narrative as "the transvaluation of culturally meaningful differences through a sequence of action" (2008: 230). This definition falls within a tradition of structural-semiotic theory, beginning with the work of Lévi-Strauss and working through Greimas and, later, Liszka. The theory views narrative as a means by which a culture places value on one pole of an opposition. As such, narratives emplot cultural values (those oppositions) in a crisis whose outcome promotes or denies the very values at stake. Almén nicely shows how musical narratives perform a similar function. But, as with any theory of narrative, we might wonder whether this one tells the whole story. Is every narrative about crisis? What happens when aporia hits the scene? Where are the other narrative functions (making time human, understanding suffering, performing a culture, etc.)? Rather than settle on *a* theory of musical narrative, we might acknowledge that no single theory will tell the whole story. Broadly, then, narrative theories approach music with a constellation of metaphors, including agency, temporality, plot, and some notion of a narrating voice, all of which are open to scholarly inquiry in their own right. The reader will note that I have yet to mention the problem of story. That part is coming. First, I'll turn to a brief review of musical narrative's common metaphors.

Agency involves hearing music's motives, rhythms, melodies, textures, and so on unfolding with an inner urgency or an act of will rather than from some mechanistic or determinate compositional process. The musical agent strives or yields, seeks goals or disavows them, persists or retreats. Current work on agency often begins with Edward T. Cone's now famous notion of musical personae (1974). But Eero Tarasti has shown that agency had an earlier development in Ernst Kurth's ideas about music's "state of forces" (*Kräftevorgang*), or *energetics* (1994: 98–111).[4] This earlier work may give the impression that agency is bound inextricably with voice leading and tonal function. But as Fred Maus (1989) has demonstrated, it is no easy task to disentangle musical agents even from simple textures in tonal music. As powerful as tonality may be in giving music a sense of purposeful direction, tonality alone cannot answer all the questions we might ask about musical agency. As such, it is better to disentangle agency from tonality and view it as an intentional act of listening that creates what Roger Scruton called a "virtual causality" in music, giving us "an unparalleled glimpse of the reality of freedom" (1997: 79, 76). Before or after modernism, agency brings in critical questions involving its cuing, subjectivity, and ethos. What does prompt us to pursue musical agency as an act of intention, and what new strategies do composers after 1900 develop to uphold or deny that intention? To what extent do musical agents transcend simple models of being and doing, aligning themselves with affects, goals, and desires that prompt us to consider them as forms of subjectivity, selfhood? And if we are willing to hear musical agents anthropologically, what ethical questions must we face? If we refuse to seek a subjectivity in agency, does our refusal signal an alignment with the ideology of absolute music, or do we rather seek "to think the essence of humanity outside the domain of subjectivity," to imagine agency beyond the will to power (Žižek 2005: 15)?

Temporality asks us to consider the possibility that music not only unfolds in time but also signifies time. We are alert to musical moments when time-as-meant rushes forward or stands still, flows or breaks, previews the future or recalls the past. Music's signifiers – its rhythms, motives, textures, timbres – may advance through time without pause, but music's temporal signifieds include more than an unceasing course through the present tense. Of the metaphors involved in musical narrative after 1900, temporality has perhaps been the focus of the most attention, with Jonathan D. Kramer's *The*

Time of Music (1988) often serving as the first point of order. Like many good books, Kramer's text opens new possibilities while serving as an example of the way not to go. As Raymond Monelle has argued, for example, the confusion in *The Time of Music* is the misapprehension that the time of the signifier is also the time of the signified (2000: 83–84). Paraphrasing Monelle, when we see a period in Proust, it is not our sense that time stops; instead, we sense that time-as-meant flows beyond the closure of syntax. Analogously, "musical syntax does not *necessarily* carry semantic weight" (83, emphasis in original). Thus the impulse to map temporal motion/stasis solely onto musical linearity/nonlinearity places all of music's signifying power in the unfolding of its syntactic structures while failing to recognize that even within the heavily linear tonal system, composers have developed signifiers for nonlinear time. What is required, then, are more of the temporal varieties that Kramer begins to enumerate – moment time, vertical time, multiply directed time – and less adherence to the musical structure itself as the sole signifier of time. Then the types of questions we might ask of musical temporality – what is my experience of time? how did I know? why is the music playing with time here? – are no less pressing for music before or after 1900.

As for musical plot, it is easy to consider this concept as analogous to functional tonality and form, where phrase and cadence types, thematic design, and key structure take the place of an economical but logical chain of events. Leonard Meyer has shown how nineteenth-century composers and critics tended to make narrative analogies in their descriptions of sonata forms (1989: 203). Here, for example, is one of Carl Czerny's accounts of the diachronic unity of music: "Just as in a romance, a novel, or a dramatic poem, if the entire work shall be successful and preserve its unity, the necessary component parts are: first, an exposition of the principal idea and of the different characters, then the protracted complication of events, and lastly the surprising catastrophe and the satisfactory conclusion" (1979: 34, quoted in Meyer 1989: 203). One is struck by how easily Czerny moves from formal to narrative categories. A piece of music begins with an exposition of a principal idea (formal) and of different characters (narrative), which go through protracted events and a catastrophe (narrative), leading to a satisfactory conclusion (formal and narrative). What we have is a Deleuzian assemblage whose disentanglement into separate strands would render feeble the musical imagination at play. What is needed, then, is an understanding of the discourse running through tonal and formal structures. Kofi Agawu's *beginning-middle-end* paradigm, with its allusion to Aristotelian poetics, acknowledges the discursive level of music within the first practice of functional tonality, allowing that listeners can find their place in the musical plot through an understanding of the conventions of musical openings, transitions/developments, and closings (1991: 51–79). And in Agawu's later work (2009), the discourse of musical high points, periodicity, and parentheses lends itself to plot devices such as denouement, crisis, peripeteia, parenthetical remarks, and all the ways that a plot often swerves away from the straight line that would lead to a quick conclusion of the musical tale.

Even when tonality and form do serve as the central determinates for musical plot, as in Hepokoski and Darcy's *Elements of Sonata Theory* (2006), interpretive acts need to do the plot-making work. Thus the satisfactory confirmation of the tonic key during the recapitulation's secondary theme signifies the "clearly determined graspable goal" of every sonata plot; the introduction signifies the present order of things, or a landscape behind the coming action, or an assemblage of forces, and so on; and the introduction–coda frame of some works sometimes makes strong implications for an external narrator, the very signal of music as narrative (252, 300, 305). The point is that tonality and form will not do the work of generating a narrative plot on their own. They require acts of intention. A focus on tonality as the principle of continuity in music after 1900, therefore, will not produce a concept adequate for musical plot. Instead, what we might seek are musical narrative's plot objects, like character transformation, crisis, catastrophe, lyrical evocation (landscape), action, peripeteia, and so on.

Which brings us to the problem of the narrator. So much has been written about the fragile teller of tales in music that it is best to avoid rehearsing the various arguments here. Even among those who hold that music rarely signifies a narrator, though, there is consensus that shifts in musical discourse have the potential to cue a narrating voice (Abbate 1991; Hatten 1991; Klein 2004; L. Kramer 1990; Webster 1991). As with the other narrative metaphors, though, tonality is no prerequisite to signifying a musical narrator. Vincent Meelberg argues, for example, that Helmut Lachenmann's Second String Quartet often highlights the labor necessary to produce itself, such that the "constant self-reference" is like a narrator of sounds "telling the story of their own making" (2006: 58). Careful listening and study will surely uncover other instances of telling in music after 1900. One suspects, though, that the act of narration remains the rare exception in music. Hearing music as told is another act of intention. As Lawrence Kramer reminds us, these voices, however attenuated, speak with us and through us (1995: 121). Thus the questions we might ask about narrators in music before or after 1900 involve, first, deciding whether it is productive to distinguish musical drama from musical narrative, and second, whether we have missed some voices in our quest to construct a narrating one.

Running through the discussion of these four narrative metaphors is a caveat against considering functional tonality as the sole determinate for any of them. It is too easy to mistake tonal logic for narrative logic or to miss the historical development of musical narrative as separate from, though dependent on, a tonal background. McClary claims that the "music that narrates by itself" is precisely the music of "the European canon from 1700 to 1900," because the tonality of this repertoire lends itself to teleological models (2000: 168). Here, tonality and narrative appear to be analogous, as our storytelling Muse intimated earlier. But McClary later refines this claim, arguing that the mechanics of tonality gave eighteenth-century composers a "confidence in musical expostulation" that allowed them to develop "other elements usually associated more strongly with literary practices," including a notion of themes as characters, or plots that ironically might "overwhelm the certainty promised in advance by the tonal contract" (168–69). This argument is more nuanced than a simple analogy between tonality and narrative. Tonality may have allowed composers to pursue musical narrative, and tonality may be a powerful force in signifying the metaphors associated with narrative, but tonality cannot signify narration on its own.

Picking up from McClary's idea about the "tonal contract," I want to say that functional tonality is less like the analog of narrative and more like the reigning ideology of music in the eighteenth and nineteenth centuries: even in the face of disjunction and disarray, its hegemonic power imposes a unity that we can mistake for the economical weaving of a tale. The potential of such a force is already evident in the topical riot that rides the surface of Mozart's music. If we accept the premise of Agawu's *Playing with Signs* (1991), then our listening experiences of this music oscillate between the dispersive topics at the foreground and the deeper teleological drive of harmony and voice leading that hold those topics together. But what if we re-imagine this music without its tonal ideology? Listening again to part of Mozart's Sonata in F Major, K. 332, the *locus classicus* of musical topoi, we hear how difficult the musical surface would be to pull together without the thread of tonality running through it. As every schoolchild knows, from the staid nobility of its musette-inflected minuet, the opening of this sonata moves dramatically to a *Sturm und Drang* topic, shattering the court's calm demeanor. After this strenuous passage, ending with the conventional hammer blows, our minuet returns with barely a scratch, as if oblivious to the previous storm. The storm falls in its normative location, functioning as a transition that nicely prepares the second tonal area with a move to the dominant of the dominant, while the *medial caesura* after the storm underscores the success of the tonal maneuver. Nothing wrong here: all is in its proper place.

But if we rehear the exposition without its unifying tonality, a different plot emerges in which the *Sturm und Drang* poses a greater threat. How did we get there exactly? Is the disjunction of the storm a temporal cue? A new agency? A new landscape? The move from inner court to outer countryside? The move from outward demeanor to inward psychology? Or are the minuet and storm happening simultaneously, merely presented in this particular order on the basis of a narrative decision on the part of the musical teller of tales? Finally, more difficult to answer: How can the minuet return with so little outward sign at first that it has experienced the storm? Without the indexicality of the tonal maneuver, the return of the minuet is high comic-irony, with the dancing nobility maintaining their composure heedless of the passion outside their courtly walls. Or, in a more psychological reading, the opening persona tries to hold on to its cool demeanor, while a menacing thought boils underneath. The minuet in the second half of the exposition soon loses its decorous consideration with disturbing triplet figures followed by a passage with disrupting accents and a hint of *ombra*. A final effort from the minuet finds more success with a turn to the brilliant style and an unequivocal cadence in the major mode: essential expositional closure! Triumph! But if we are alert to the conventional harmonic and formal procedure here, we may not be so sure. Hearing the passage without those conventions, we suspect that the reclaimed order is only contrivance. Far from narrative functions, then, the ideology of the tonal frame in this music keeps at bay the narrative-hermeneutic questions we might ask. Without the tonal plan, we hear a new comic-ironic story with a critical stance concerning the aristocratic minuet. We hear a tale of a societal order that uses the ruling ideology to hide its weaknesses.

Tonality as ideology may have strong implications for a narrative order in music, but tonality alone is not narrative. To pursue an understanding of musical narrative, one would need to disarticulate it from tonality to show that musical agency, temporality, plot, and the narrator, while often relying on tonal-formal structures, also have conventions apart from those structures. With the conventions of agency, temporality, plot, and narrator strongly embedded in our experiences and understanding of music before 1900, it would seem to be a simple matter to study their extension, denial, or transformation in music after 1900. Anyone who wishes to pursue these lines of research already has a small but important body of work on which to draw. I have already mentioned Jonathan Kramer's seminal *The Time of Music*, which develops a vocabulary for understanding the new temporal possibilities of contemporary music. Vincent Meelberg's *New Sounds, New Stories* (2006) offers important strategies for understanding agency, plot, affect, time, and tale in recent music. And Márta Grabócz's deep knowledge of the electroacoustic repertoire informs her thoughts on constructions of time and spatial development in that music (1993).

Given the compelling nature of listening to music as if it were a narrative, we can see the attraction of its study. Those who hear music as narrative identify with themes as characters and witness them launching into meaningful action, or pausing to remember the past, or standing firm in the face of crisis, or stepping away from the action to tell us their story. We cheer their success or mourn their passing. Turning to music after 1900, one hopes to find narrative strategies, old and new, heightening our experiences of this music as well. The unspoken assumption is that subjectivity, plot, catastrophe, and triumph, though perhaps sedimented (to borrow a word Alastair Williams [1997] uses to understand Adorno), might come to the fore to explain our deeply satisfying responses to this music. In addition to understanding those responses, a narrative project serves interpretation in the way that performers think of it. McClary has recalled being "flabbergasted when good technical musicians failed to notice struggle or miraculous arrivals or anything other than just . . . notes on the page" (2000: 169), and Meelberg has developed the idea of *focalization* as the means by which a performer brings to life a musical narrative (2006: 66–71). Study of musical narrative may tell us much more about a good performance than do the staid accounts from the classic performance-and-analysis paradigms. But as we'll see in later sections of this essay, there is even more at stake than performing or listening strategies in the study of music as narrative.

❧

We still have not approached musical story. If exploration of narrative in music after 1900 rests happily in metaphors for agency, temporality, plot, the narrator, and all of their implicit notions of setting, mood, character, crisis, and denouement, then one would have to face the fact that such a project divests narrative of story to concentrate on discourse. Put another way, such a project collapses story into discourse, leaving us with what now passes for modernism: "history without narrative; individuals without identity; discourse without meaning; art without representation; science without truth" (Anderson 1992: 48). Imagine how such a project might look in a study of literature. Describing Faulkner's *Absalom, Absalom!*, for example, we could detail how the narrators and characters intermingle: character becomes narrator becomes character again. We could point out the temporal shifts: past becomes present and morphs into future. We could focus on the lapses of emplotment, the shifting agencies, the unclear temporalities. We conclude that *Absalom, Absalom!* is about the difficulty of telling, the impossibility of getting the story straight. And there is a truth to our conclusion, based, as it is, on the novel's discourse: narrating *is* difficult, and we never *do* seem to get the tale right. But a reader not versed in narrative theory might well ask us what happened to the story about slavery, incest, plantations, greed, murder, memory, and regret. Where's the moment when Wash Jones kills Thomas Sutpen with a scythe? Where's a discussion of Rosa's father nailing himself in the attic? In short, where are all the good parts?

This brief look at a literary narrative illustrates at least two problems with musical narrative: first, our study of music often focuses on discourse at the expense of story; and, second, we cannot hope to draw a path that will lead us from discourse directly to story. Taking the second problem first, one does not uncover discursive techniques and strategies to discover the content of a story. One does not realize that there are shifting narrators in *Absalom, Absalom!* as a prerequisite to understanding that the story is about slavery, incest, and madness. One simply jumps into the story. While it is true that the discourse is part of our reading, and while it is true that we may shift our attention from story to discourse, even making an assemblage of the story and the discourse to deepen our understanding, it is not true that the discourse gets us to the story. Thus, with music we are left with the same vexing problem that Jean-Jacques Nattiez (1990) pointed out long ago: if music is like a narrative, what is the story that it is trying to tell? More particularly for the project at hand, what stories are told in music after 1900?

A good place to start is with the stories that music told before 1900. Surveying the narrative readings of this repertoire, we see that music finds its master signifiers in the sustenance of history both personal and social. One imagines that musical stories will find correlates in psychologies, social structure, ideology, and contemporaneous tales in other media. Hepokoski and Darcy tell us, for example, that sonata form is "a response to aspects of

the world view of the Enlightenment" and "an abstract metaphor for disciplined, balanced action in the world, a generalized action involving different
types of idealized mid- and late-eighteenth-century personalities" (2006: 15).
How could it be otherwise? We expect musical narrative in the eighteenth
century to take up the ideology of disciplined and balanced action within the
social sphere, whether to confirm or deny its models for success. Turning to
another musical narrative, Brahms's First Symphony, Monelle interprets it
as "a nostalgic *Eroica*," "grave and elegiac," about a "victory for bourgeois society like the universal franchise or the abolition of slavery" (2000: 126–27).
Again, contemporaneous signs whisper the possible content of music's story.
In developing one of three narratives for another nineteenth-century work,
Mahler's Sixth Symphony, Robert Samuels interprets it as "the story of the
protagonist struggling with forces that crush his or her individuality" (1995:
150). We often hear it told that music signifies both too much and too little.
Something has to point the way for musical stories, and it is no shock to see
history or (dare I write that overused phrase?) *cultural context* performing
that indexical function. To be clear, the master signifiers of a culture do not
function to pin down musical stories; rather, in the Lacanian sense, they
reorganize music's signifiers toward what really matters.

Before turning directly to what really matters after 1900, we can venture
that music before that time was preoccupied with the narratives of success.
Enlightenment values show the path to victory within which the few tragic
tales are only personal failures, not societal ones. Once the promise of these
values becomes suspect, musical narrative in the nineteenth century turns
from confirmation to utopian vision, redemption, or ironic denial. But even
as failure becomes more endemic, the possibility of success is still the aura
within which nineteenth-century narratives surround themselves. Looking
closely at Almén's semiotic appropriation of Frye's narrative archetypes, we
see that victory and defeat are the central opposition that organizes the narrative possibilities.[5] Romance, then, is the victory of order; comedy, the victory
of transgression; tragedy, the defeat of transgression; and irony, the defeat
of order. Within the semiotics of Frye's archetypes, success (victory), as the
unmarked term, is the unspoken value of all narrative. One wants to conclude
that stories after 1900 question success as the foundation of narrative and seek
new terms for storytelling. We do not transcend success as that foundation,
we simply set it aside for something else.

And nothing clues us more into the problem of success as a foundation for
stories after 1900 than the granddaddy of all modern music: Stravinsky's *Rite*

of Spring. So, what is *The Rite*? A romance – the pre-literate Russian society re-establishing its ritual of renewal through a human sacrifice? A comedy – the idea of renewal itself? A tragedy – the chosen one dancing her death because she lacks the inner will to escape her sacrifice? Surely, *The Rite* is irony – the very foundations of society are so riddled with contradictions that heroic action is rendered impossible. But to ask these questions shows how inadequate the narratives of success are to an understanding of musical stories after 1900. Even when modernist music accepts success as the premise of its narrative, we have to ask what kind of blindness is involved when we hear victory: either the composer was blind to the impossibility of success, or we are blind to some ironic level in the music that secretly denies its outward appearance. Returning to *The Rite* – we have violence to time, violence to people, violence to dance, violence to music. Every cultural and artistic convention is placed in a crisis without resolution. Irony for sure: a musical manifesto for what Harold Bloom (1994) calls *the chaotic age*. But there is a sense of disappointment in organizing all the musical stories after 1900 as ironic responses to success. It is like Žižek's pronouncement, following Brecht's lead, that atheism "is a miserable, pathetic stance of those who long for God but cannot find him" (2005: 15). If there is something sentimental about *The Rite*, it may lie in the final bassoon solo at the end of the introduction: looking back, farewell. But after that, atheism (read as the long good-bye to narratives of success) must be a positive choice if it is to be anything but pathetic.

If we are to set aside the narratives of success and turn to what matters in music after 1900, we might expect to see musical stories fulfilling the same functions as other stories: performing a culture, promoting and denying ideologies, making time human, making sense of catastrophe. An exceptional model among the few overtly narrative readings of music after 1900 is Alan Street's (1994) article on Schoenberg's Five Orchestral Pieces, op. 16. Although careful to point out the thorny problems of narrative, Street still offers three stories for Schoenberg's Five Pieces. The first of these is about musical discourse: the Five Orchestral Pieces tell of the stylistic transition from tonal destruction to reflections of past practice to an exploration of post-tonal possibilities.[6] The second story is more story-like: Schoenberg's Five Pieces play on the modern myth of eternal crisis, which, nonetheless, has "so far stopped short of a descent into meaninglessness" (171); the last two pieces in particular "hint at the slide into lawlessness threatened by the crisis of modernism" (172). Finally, the third story turns from social-cultural history to personal psychology: the music is a Freudian autobiographical narrative about

Schoenberg's mourning and melancholia. Regarding this last story, Street underscores one of the deeply humane functions of narrative "to reinscribe the necessary fictions through which the human subject itself is constituted and thereby enabled to map its symbolic place in existence" (180). Question modernity, respond to alienation and dysphoria, ironize the past, model the human psyche. Those who venture into telling modern music's stories are bound to come to grips with these themes. It is understandable, then, to see Sarah Reichardt's recent book on Shostakovich take the title *Composing the Modern Subject* (2008) or to see Lawrence Kramer write a chapter titled "The Alienation Effect from Weill to Shostakovich" (2002: 216–41). Life is messy, and we expect the stories our music tells to be messy ones too.

If we take on this larger narrative project around music's involvement in the symbolic order, then we need to know how to get at those musical stories. One place to start is with topics. It is easy to follow an aesthetic ideology that views modernism's break with the past as a repudiation of all convention, so that music after 1900 signifies only through what Umberto Eco called *ratio difficilis* – a semiotics in which the signifier and the signified are one, and conventions simply do not exist (1976: 183).[7] But this ideology is flat-out indefensible. Joseph Straus has demonstrated that even in his late music, Stravinsky was a topical composer (2001: 183–248). Grabócz (2002) lists topics in the music of Bartók. And referring to an unpublished article by Danuta Mirka, Agawu offers a list of forty-one topics in music after 1900 (2009: 48–49). Many of the topics we hear in music after 1900, of course, play on a tradition of musical convention that is centuries old. The famous *funèbre* section of Lutosławski's Quartet, for example, expands the *pianto* figure into an unbearable infinity of overlapping *glissandi*. But we also find topics peculiar to the period after 1900: its trains, planes, and automobiles. These new topics are worthy of their own studies to uncover musical signifiers, signifieds, and the ideologies within which they operate.

More broadly, Street shows us a way to go while introducing his three narrative readings for Schoenberg's Five Orchestral Pieces. Drawing on Frank Kermode ("stories as we know them begin as interpretations" [1981: 81]) and Peter Brooks ("any narrative from the very simplest is hermeneutic in intention" [1984: 34]), Street reminds us that narrative "is a form of understanding" (1994: 170). This connection between narrative and interpretation forms a theme in much narrative theory. Among Roland Barthes's five codes of reading, for example, is a hermeneutic one that concerns "an enigma . . . held in suspense, and finally disclosed" (1974: 19). Beyond the enigmas solved at the end of a tale, though, all narratives have some level of indeterminacy, gaps in the story that require work on the part of the reader to fill. The reader's work begins at the moment she tries to figure out what the story is all about. As Seymour Chatman claims, it is not that interpretation comes into play after story and discourse are set in the reader's mind but that "interpretations, variable as they may be, play an important role in narrative analysis, not only in determining plots, characters, and setting, but also in shaping our understanding of discourse itself" (2001: 217).[8] Reading a story, literary or musical, is already a hermeneutic act.

Music, what is your story? This question is a hermeneutic one, requiring of us the same set of cognate questions involved in any interpretive endeavor. What are my expectations of this music? Where does the music veer from those expectations? Where are the strange details that invite responses beyond the conventional ones? Where is there too much or too little information? Where do I stand vis-à-vis the horizon of this music's first telling? Do I inspect only my own responses, or do I hope to revive those of the dead? What was the music's cultural impact? Does the music still have a voice in the culture? To what cultural and historical problems does the music respond? We could extend this list of questions, but the point is that a narrative analysis of music is a form of hermeneutics. For that hermeneutic analysis to take on its peculiarly narrative aura, the questions will move to issues of character (agency), plot, temporality, crisis and catastrophe, suffering and transfiguration, and so on. The larger question of music as narrative, then, is not whether or not music *is* a narrative but whether it is productive to our hermeneutic understanding of music to invoke those narrative metaphors and to tell music's story.

There are plenty of reasons to be wary of this kind of narrative project. Anyone who has studied socialist realism knows how easy it is to get the story wrong: to read the dissonant idiom of Zbigniew Turski's "Olympic" Symphony as a sign for a lack of optimism, as did Polish Deputy Minister of Culture Włodzimierz Sokorski in 1949; or to miss the irony of Shostakovich's Fifth Symphony and hear only its "enormous optimistic lift," as did Alexei Tolstoy in 1937. Outside the cautionary tale of socialist realism, it is easy to imagine the narrative turn in musicology and music theory as a move toward what Bloom indelicately called the "School of Resentment" (1994: 4), in this case reading stories *into* the music, as is often claimed, in order to tear down cultural monuments as a response to an awakening guilt. To these issues, we can add the belief that telling musical stories is an easy path away from the kind of hard facts and verifiable claims we ought to be making. Since these kinds of problems have been part of hermeneutic study even outside of music, answers are easy to find and rehearse, from Jacques Derrida's "there is no outside-the-text" (1976: 158) to Jonathan Culler's pragmatic suggestion that we learn to trust our own interpretive competency.[9] One does not escape the problems of hermeneutics by denying music's lure to interpretation.

The cure for dreaming is more dreaming, Proust tells us. If hermeneutic-narrative readings of music are dangerous, the cure for them is not to interpret less but to interpret more. Interpret all the time. Making sense of music is a delicate task, requiring nuanced thinking, careful study, attention to detail, and the steady acknowledgment that texts can resist our interpretations. Proceed with caution, then, but still proceed. Anticipating resistance to reading stories in music, Samuels suggests that we view our musical stories as performances of the music. As with performances, we will consider some narratives as more or less true to the score, the history, and the range of issues around the music. Some of the stories we posit will seem willful and others tame. And like performances, no single narrative we hear can possibly tell the whole story of the music. While we can imagine many stories for a piece of music, we can never imagine a singular *story*. But a discourse without a story is a sad excuse for a narrative.

Well. I'm back (the storyteller announces). Returning to you at the end of this essay is a conventional plot device, I know, but I am all about convention. Having left our essayist perched in front of a concluding point, it would be good to summarize the main developments before we end this introduction with a hopeful thought. Here, then, is what has happened so far, all tidied up in a neat list:

1. Narrative lends us a set of metaphors for understanding music.
2. We can study each of these metaphors on their own, or we can put them together into something like a narrative.
3. These metaphors may use tonality as a signifier, but tonality alone does not signify narrative.
4. Tonality is more like the reigning ideology of musical narrative before 1900.
5. These metaphors only make up narrative discourse.

6. One cannot get from discourse directly to story; one simply jumps into the story.
7. A narrative without a story is no narrative (amen, sisters and brothers).
8. Music after 1900 often turns away from the narratives of success in order to tell the stories we expect of modernism: question modernity, respond to alienation, ironize the past, and so on.
9. Topics can get us into the musical story.
10. In the end, though, finding the musical story is a hermeneutic act.
11. Tell stories.

Yes (the Muse continues), that's a list of eleven items about musical narrative post-1900. Once upon a time, Gérard Genette joked that it is easy to make our theories conform to our favorite numbers. In response to André Jolles's enumeration of simple forms, Genette wrote: "Nine simple forms? No kidding! Like the nine muses? Because of three times three? Because he forgot one?" (1992: 49). Despite Genette's warning not to let the numbers do the thinking for us, I admit that I find eleven to be an unappealing number. We are just shy of twelve, which would be like reaching the hours of the clock or the magic number of Pythagoras. We need another point about narrative, which is why I stopped our essayist before he was finished.

Here is point number twelve: Always historicize! (Okay, I stole that from Fredric Jameson: it's the opening line of *The Political Unconscious*; but it is worth repeating.) Mentioning history may be a quaint maneuver more than two decades after the inception of new historicism and new musicology, but the study of narrative has a nasty tendency to veer toward form over content, the signifier over the signified, the object over the subject. Although the form, the signifier, the object, the structure, the discourse of narrative are also historical, through and through, these sides of the narrative equation are adept at presenting themselves as trans-historical or beyond the reach of the social. But content and form are both historical, and to forget that fact is to risk sending musical narrative back to empty formalism.

One quick example will have to suffice. I adapt this example from an article by the essayist as a form of shameless plug for him (Klein 2007). We can claim that Debussy's late music often makes narratives with a discourse that favors disjunction. In this claim, disjunction is like a Platonic object, floating around Debussy's head until the moment he decides to grasp it. No real history to see here. We can open our claim by noticing that disjunction is also a property of the cinema, which was just reaching an early blush of excitement when Debussy was writing his late music. Disjunction in this case is a weak historical claim, like an asterisk on a timeline in a middle-school classroom: 1896, George Méliès discovers "stop trick," disjunction born. We might remember that Henri Bergson was concerned about cinema and the violence he thought its disjunctions perpetrated on time. Now disjunction opens issues that are phenomenological. We might wonder if the great move toward homogeneous time in the late nineteenth century, the coordination of train schedules and time zones, had a social impact that influenced Bergson's concerns. And the entire disjunctive enterprise appears conveniently tied to Enterprise, as the working day becomes focused on an hourly wage and the clock-time of industry. Now we approach something like a social problem, an issue in modernity involving power, psychology, phenomenology, culture, modes of production, and the political. So, which is it? Did the Platonic object of disjunction strike Debussy's fancy one day, apropos of nothing in particular? Or does Debussy's late music insinuate itself into the time-space problem of modernism? At the very least, we can argue that the second possibility entails an enlargement of resonances undreamt in the first possibility. But I am arguing more strongly that the notion of disjunction as a discursive narrative device in Debussy's music is already historical. Point number twelve: Always historicize!

Forget music after 1900 for a moment. Life after 1900 is hard, and it ain't gettin' any easier. We all struggle with the vertiginous problems of modern life. The ambiguities and contradictions, the tensions and ironies, the exhilaration and despair, the wish for the return of a stable past and the anticipation of a changing future (I know; that's not a sentence). And with this catastrophe upon catastrophe hurled at our feet, what is a storyteller to do? For a start, we can do a lot worse than to try to make sense of this messy world by telling histories of the social, the political, the psychological, the cultural, and on and on. We might recognize that this crazy world is made up of stories and that music is one of the storytellers. Then we have a choice. We can fall into the music, shut out the chaotic world, click our heels three times, ignore the story around us, and live in a universe of sound away from the problem of history. Or we can find a way to give the music a voice, listen as it tells us the story of the world that it too heard as a jumble, wonder at secret histories to which the music bore witness, and find the strength to tell the stories of the music. You are a free agent. You can choose to forgo music's stories. But I am a storyteller. I already know which choice I would make.

NOTES

1. McClary writes: "Beginning with Debussy, Stravinsky, and Schoenberg and extending to the experiments of John Cage, the avant-garde music of the twentieth century has been self-consciously ANTI-narrative" (2000: 167).

2. "Death is the sanction of everything that the storyteller can tell. He has borrowed his authority from Death" (Benjamin 1969: 94).

3. Kramer made this claim during remarks at a panel discussion on music and narrative at the Sixth International Conference on Music since 1900, held at Keele University, July 2–5, 2009.

4. Tarasti is referring to Kurth's *Grundlagen des linearen Kontrapunktes* (1922). As Tarasti notes, musical energetics also informs Heinrich Schenker's work and the writings of French music philosophers Gisèle Brelet and Vladimir Jankélévitch.

5. Almén borrows this semiotic structure for the narrative archetypes from a portion of Liszka's *The Semiotic of Myth* (1989: 129–34). See particularly the chart on p. 133 of Liszka's book, which organizes the archetypes according to victory

and defeat. Almén's use of Liszka's work appears throughout his *A Theory of Musical Narrative*, but see particularly the discussion on pp. 64–67.

6. For this first story, Street borrows from Philip Friedheim's (1963) dissertation on Schoenberg's early music.

7. Monelle discusses Eco's *ratio difficilis* in music, explaining that through habit, even the most difficult sign can be conventionalized (2000: 16).

8. In this passage, Chatman is summarizing a thesis in David Herman's *Narratologies*, but it is clear that Chatman is in agreement with Herman in assigning the reader an important role in determining a story.

9. The French reads: "Il n'y a pas de hors-texte." Spivak offers two translations, each of which has a slightly different nuance from the original French: "*There is nothing outside of the text*" (italics in original) and "there is no outside-text." Culler's plea that we trust our interpretive competency is underscored by the observation that we develop that competency "in commerce with others" (1981: 52–53).

WORKS CITED

Abbate, Carolyn. 1991. *Unsung Voices: Opera and Musical Narrative in the Nineteenth Century*. Princeton: Princeton University Press.

Agawu, Kofi. 1991. *Playing with Signs: A Semiotic Interpretation of Classic Music*. Princeton: Princeton University Press.

———. 2009. *Music as Discourse: Semiotic Adventures in Romantic Music*. Oxford: Oxford University Press.

Almén, Byron. 2008. *A Theory of Musical Narrative*. Bloomington: Indiana University Press.

Anderson, Perry. 1992. *A Zone of Engagement*. London: Verso.

Barthes, Roland. 1974. *S/Z*. Translated by Richard Miller. New York: Hill and Wang. First published 1970.

Benjamin, Walter. 1969. "The Storyteller." In *Illuminations*, edited by Hannah Arendt, translated by Harry Zohn, 83–109. New York: Schocken Books.

Bloom, Harold. 1994. *The Western Canon: The Books and School of the Ages*. New York: Harcourt Brace.

Boulez, Pierre. 1991. "Schoenberg Is Dead." In *Stocktakings from an Apprenticeship*, collected by Paule Thévenin, translated by Stephen Walsh, 209–14. Oxford: Oxford University Press.

Brooks, Peter. 1984. *Reading for the Plot*. Oxford: Oxford University Press.

Chatman, Seymour. 2001. "'Soft Filters': Some Sunshine on 'Cat in the Rain.'" *Narrative* 9(2): 217–22.

Cone, Edward T. 1974. *The Composer's Voice*. Berkeley: University of California Press.

Culler, Jonathan. 1981. *The Pursuit of Signs: Semiotics, Literature, and Deconstruction*. Ithaca: Cornell University Press.

Czerny, Carl. 1979. *School of Practical Composition*. Translated by John Bishop. New York: Da Capo. First published in 1848.

Derrida, Jacques. 1976. *Of Grammatology*. Translated by Gayatri Chakravorty Spivak. Baltimore: Johns Hopkins University Press.

Eco, Umberto. 1976. *A Theory of Semiotics*. Bloomington: Indiana University Press.

Friedheim, Philip. 1963. "Tonality and Structure in the Early Works of Schoenberg." PhD diss., New York University.

Genette, Gérard. 1992. *The Architext: An Introduction*. Translated by Jane E. Lewin. Berkeley: University of California Press. First published in 1979.

Grabócz, Márta. 1993. "Narrativity and Electroacoustic Music." In *Musical Signification: Essays in the Semiotic Theory and Analysis of Music*, edited by Eero Tarasti, 535–40. Berlin: Mouton de Gruyter.

———. 2002. "'Topos et dramaturgie': Analyse des signifiés et de la stratégie dans deux mouvements symphoniques de Béla Bartók." *Degrés* 30(109–10): j1–j18.

Hatten, Robert S. 1991. "On Narrativity in Music: Expressive Genres and Levels of Discourse in Beethoven." *Indiana Theory Review* 12: 75–98.

Hepokoski, James, and Warren Darcy. 2006. *Elements of Sonata Theory: Norms, Types, and Deformations in the Late-Eighteenth-Century Sonata*. Oxford: Oxford University Press.

Jameson, Fredric. 1981. *The Political Unconscious: Narrative as a Socially Symbolic Act*. Ithaca: Cornell University Press.

———. 1987. Foreword to *On Meaning: Selected Writings in Semiotic Theory*, by A. J. Greimas, translated by Paul J. Perron and Frank H. Collins, vi–xxii. London: F. Pinter.

Kermode, Frank. 1981. "Secrets and Narrative Sequence." In *On Narrative*, edited by W. J. T. Mitchell, 79–98. Chicago: University of Chicago Press.

Klein, Michael L. 2004. "Chopin's Fourth Ballade as Musical Narrative." *Music Theory Spectrum* 26(1): 23–55.

———. 2007. "Debussy's *L'Isle joyeuse* as Territorial Assemblage." *19th-Century Music* 31(1): 28–52.

Kramer, Jonathan D. 1988. *The Time of Music: New Meanings, New Temporalities, New Listening Strategies*. New York: Schirmer.

Kramer, Lawrence. 1990. *Music as Cultural Practice, 1800–1900*. Berkeley: University of California Press.

———. 1995. *Classical Music and Postmodern Knowledge*. Berkeley: University of California Press.

———. 2002. *Musical Meaning: Toward a Critical History*. Berkeley: University of California Press.

Liszka, James Jakób. 1989. *The Semiotic of Myth: A Critical Study of the Symbol*. Bloomington: Indiana University Press.

Maus, Fred Everett. 1989. "Agency in Instrumental Music and Song." *College Music Symposium* 29: 31–43.

McCarthy, Cormac. 1994. *The Crossing.* New York: Vintage International.

McClary, Susan. 2000. "The Impromptu That Trod on a Loaf: or How Music Tells Stories." In *The Narrative Reader,* edited by Martin McQuillan, 166–70. London: Routledge.

McQuillan, Martin, ed. 2000. *The Narrative Reader.* London: Routledge.

Meelberg, Vincent. 2006. *New Sounds, New Stories: Narrativity in Contemporary Music.* Amsterdam: Leiden University Press.

Meyer, Leonard B. 1989. *Style and Music: Theory, History, and Ideology.* Chicago: University of Chicago Press.

Miller, J. Hillis. 1995. "Narrative." In *Critical Terms for Literary Study,* 2nd ed., edited by Frank Lentricchia and Thomas McLaughlin, 66–79. Chicago: University of Chicago Press.

Monelle, Raymond. 2000. *The Sense of Music: Semiotic Essays.* Princeton: Princeton University Press.

Nattiez, Jean-Jacques. 1990. "Can One Speak of Narrativity in Music?." *Journal of the Royal Musicological Association* 115(2): 240–57.

Pasler, Jann. 1989. "Narrative and Narrativity in Music." In *Time and Mind: Interdisciplinary Issues,* edited by J. T. Fraser, 233–57. Madison: International University Press.

Reichardt, Sarah. 2008. *Composing the Modern Subject: Four String Quartets*

by Dmitri Shostakovich. Burlington: Ashgate.

Reyland, Nicholas. 2008. "*Livre* or Symphony? Lutosławski's *Livre pour orchestre* and the Enigma of Musical Narrativity." *Music Analysis* 27(2–3): 253–94.

Samuels, Robert. 1995. *Mahler's Sixth Symphony: A Study in Musical Semiotics.* Cambridge: Cambridge University Press.

Scruton, Roger. 1997. *The Aesthetics of Music.* Oxford: Oxford University Press.

Straus, Joseph. 2001. *Stravinsky's Late Music.* Cambridge: Cambridge University Press.

Street, Alan. 1994. "The Obbligato Recitative: Narrative and Schoenberg's Five Orchestral Pieces, op. 16." In *Theory, Analysis, and Meaning in Music,* edited by Anthony Pople, 164–83. Cambridge: Cambridge University Press.

Tarasti, Eero. 1994. *A Theory of Musical Semiotics.* Bloomington: Indiana University Press.

Webster, James. 1991. *Haydn's "Farewell" Symphony and the Idea of Classical Style.* Cambridge: Cambridge University Press.

Williams, Alastair. 1997. *New Music and the Claims of Modernity.* Aldershot: Ashgate.

Žižek, Slavoj. 2005. *Interrogating the Real.* Edited by Rex Butler and Scott Stephens. New York: Continuum.

2

Negation and Negotiation:
Plotting Narrative through Literature and
Music from Modernism to Postmodernism

Nicholas Reyland

Amid the myriad stories scholars of Western art music tell about the interface between Romanticism and everything after, modernism's presence is often defined through the assertion of a notable absence: the desire (of composers) or ability (of post-tonal instrumental music) to represent narrative. Even if one harbors lingering hopes about speaking of musical narrativity in earlier repertoires, modernist music will apparently dispel them. The *New Grove's* entry on the topic is emblematic in this regard. While productively identifying modernism as "a multi-faceted but distinct and continuous tradition within twentieth-century composition," Leon Botstein nests modernism's skepticism toward tonality, generic formal structures, traditional modes of expression, and so on within an encapsulating critique: "The link between music and narration particularly came under scrutiny. Modernity demanded the shattering of expectations, conventions, categories, boundaries and limits as well as empirical experimentation . . . and the confident exploration of the new" (2001: 869). That inspection and consequent rejection of music's "story-telling properties" (869) was primarily focused, Botstein suggests, on rebutting the employment of programs. Yet the "shattering of expectations" in many modes of modernism can be argued to have undermined a more fundamentally plot-like aspect of prior music: tonality's presentation of sequences of events implying causation, teleology, and a marked degree of change over time. Consequently, even scholars supportive of the notion of musical narrativity in tonal music, such as Susan McClary, have declared that the "great era of narrative in music" ends alongside common-practice tonality (2004: 281). Music lost the plot after modernism – or so the story goes.

Accounts of modernism's emergence being founded, in part, on narrative's erasure are not unique to music criticism. Botstein's perspective, for instance, highlights a musical potential for innovation, discontinuity, and fragmentation allied to what Christopher Butler identifies as a more general, early twentieth-century failure of belief "in the project of representing the world through the narrative of historical development" – the artistic consequent of which was a widespread embrace of "language [that] becomes more and more elliptical, and turns to juxtaposition and the alogical, to the simultaneous and the collaged" (1994: 10). Discussing Mallarmé's sacrifice of "plot for mood" (11), for instance, Butler cites poems in which typographical inventiveness gave "new values" to a text's signifiers through "defamiliarizing juxtaposition," suggesting freshly "complicated networks of metaphoric association" (5). Similarly, Rosalind Krauss locates anti-narrativity in modernist visual art – from Picasso's cubism and Piet Mondrian through Agnes Martin and Robert Ryman – through the use of grid-like patterns. The grid, as an icon of modernism, "announces . . . modern art's will to silence, its hostility to literature, to narrative, to discourse" (Krauss 1986: 9); it resists teleological development and the will of perceivers to impose such readings on a text, thanks to its "antinatural, antimimetic, antireal" juxtapositions and lack of hierarchical structuring (9). As Krauss argues: "This structure, impervious both to time and to incident, will not permit the projection of language into the domain of the visual, and the result is silence" (158). Within such silences, however, new voices began to make themselves heard – novel languages, unencumbered by the ideologies and institutions of earlier narrative forms and thus better able to reflect the experience of late modernity and, in time, the postmodern condition, while (consciously or otherwise) reflecting new ideologies, new institutional allegiances, new sociocultural networks of metaphorical association.

Like all style histories, this one is problematic in its sanitization of reality's messy complexity. It is obviously implausible, for example, to declare just one modernism, one postmodernism, or one anything else in music, poetry, painting, or elsewhere, whatever the internationalizing intentions of specific artists, critics, or movements. Contrast, for instance, Krauss's grid-enforcers to the "Romantic Moderns" Alexandra Harris (2010) identifies in her recent study of British artists who fall between the cracks of grander art-historical narratives. John Piper might have turned away from what he termed "under-nourished" abstraction and back toward "the tree in the field," but his re-velatory paintings of churches, ruined buildings, and above all the British landscape "involved mapping a strikingly modern cubist sensibility on to the much older romantic tradition of Gilpin and Girtin."[1] The obvious point such studies suggest for scholars of recent music is that, through hermeneutic criticism such as a narratological approach, the mainstream could prove more modernist, in story rather than discourse, than has often been suggested; the composers of *Peter Grimes* and *Fantasia on a Theme by Thomas Tallis*, say, might be revealed as "Romantic Moderns" sharing modernist aesthetics with the composer of *Silbury Air* and *Down by the Greenwood Side*, and not only through their mutual inheritance of the weirdness of British pastoral. The more subtle point suggested, however, is that just as forms of realism survive and productively counterpoint more recent techniques in Piper's paintings,[2] in music one could investigate whether, rather than being stopped in its tracks by modernism, musical narrativity instead became a stream within it – neither dominant, perhaps, nor unimportant.

To consider this possibility – an obvious motivation of this collection of essays – is nonetheless to move against tendencies as much enshrined in serious scholarly discourse surrounding music since ca. 1900 as in "the music itself." Might such a move, then, profitably revise more familiar critical stories while telling new tales of its own? Comparable ideas to Butler's and Krauss's theorizing of grid-like structures, juxtapositions, discontinuities, and collage form tropes within the musicological literature that are often deployed to define aspects of modernist music through an anti-narrative turn. Writing on Stravinsky, for example, Jonathan Cross locates a "non-developmental, non-narrative objectivity" (1998: 16) in works such as *Symphonies of Wind Instruments* through the composer's "exploration of block construction" (10). Representing "the very antithesis of symphonic argument," Stravinsky's alter-nating yet unchanging grid of blocks creates, for Cross, "no sense of a directed (linear) motion": even when foreground voice-leading suggests continuities, "deeper (middleground) level discontinuities" are achieved "through fragmen-tation, opposition, disruption" (10–11). Some sense of structural continuity remains, not least because these events occur in succession over a finite period of time rather than on a temporally static canvas, and Cross cites Edward T. Cone's notion of "interlock" to emphasize the manner in which Stravin-sky found novel ways of "balancing these powerfully contradictory elements" but without evoking, amongst other things, a symphonic narrative (7–8, 19).[3]

Jonathan Kramer, writing earlier on the "profound musical experience" of discontinuity in some modern music, draws an anti-narrative line from the "extreme expression of discontinuity" in *Symphonies of Wind Instruments* through mid-twentieth-century music, including John Cage's anti-teleological chance works ("static, endless Nows"), Steve Reich's early process pieces ("a desperate attempt to recapture continuity?"), and Karlheinz Stockhausen's moment forms ("self-contained sections that do not relate to each other in any functionally implicative manner") (1978: 179).

When discussing music from the century that saw the rise to global prominence of a new narrative medium (cinema), the block-like juxtapositions of which (montage editing) highlighted narrativity's ability to intensify rather than collapse at moments of rupture – thereby demonstrating, in turn, Paul Ricoeur's conception of plot as a "synthesis of the heterogeneous" (1984: ix), triggering acts of perceiver emplotment that leap across "the boundaries of disjunction, hiding lapses in predictive logic, and binding different types of discourse" (Klein 2005: 116) – one might nevertheless feel further tempted to weigh perspectives like Cross's and Kramer's against the possibility that the story here is somewhat more complex.[4] As Richard Taruskin has argued, *Symphonies of Wind Instruments* – a memorial *tombeau* to Debussy – "demonstrably mimics the liturgical content of a Russian Orthodox *panikhida* or funeral service" (2010: 469). In spite of its extreme discontinuities, could the piece also be heard to enact a ritual of mourning with a plot-like trajectory? If so, one might even liken the music's gradual shifting of weight (from continuously rupturing materials to the ambivalent solace of its closing chorale) to the movement from loss-oriented grieving (a traumatic period punctured by interrupting visions and a sense of consciousness splintering) to more continuous forms of lament enacting restoration-oriented mourning.[5] The piece navigates tensions between fragmentation and coherence that are every bit as central to many experiences of grief-work as they are to experiences of the late-modern condition.

Revisionist possibilities thus emerge. In some pieces, musical expressions of discontinuity (or of parallel continuities), far from irrevocably damaging music's potential to invoke acts of emplotment, might actually *enhance* music's capacity to do this – just so long as some of the events articulated can be heard to approximate, without too much critical strong-arming, contributions to a *fabula*-like musical structure or, as discussed below, to recent variations on what a musical story might be. Plot, after all, is always an experience of discontinuity; stories are disunity over time. Wolfgang Iser stated that, when the flow of a text is interrupted and the discourse heads in unexpected directions, perceivers "bring into play [their] own faculty for establishing connections – for filling in the gaps left by the text itself"; modernist and postmodernist texts, furthermore, "are often so fragmentary that one's attention is almost exclusively occupied with the search for connections between the fragments" (1974: 280). Ricoeur makes a similar argument, claiming that a plot's diversions and delays intensify the urge to connect its elements into a comprehensible, if metaphorical, whole. "By means of the plot," he writes, "goals, causes, and chance are brought together within the temporal unity of a whole and complete action" (Ricoeur 1984: ix), that is, his "synthesis of the heterogeneous."

On the one hand, therefore, a piece like *Symphonies of Wind Instruments* can act as an icon of anti-narrative modernism and even as a talisman (as Stravinsky himself clearly recognized when meddling in his own reception history) for one modernist style-history written by a certain set of victors – including some who would argue, against narrativity and so much else, that music (and especially post-tonal music) is too semantically imprecise to represent anything much at all, save for its refusal to represent. On the other, the piece's avowedly modernist discourse cannot mask (and may intensify) its simultaneous provocation of the perceiver to emplot an affecting, even programmatic, representation of change over time that suggests, among other symbolic traces, a defining feature of narrative: "transvaluation," that is, a significant shift in a text's hierarchical ranking of values (see Almén 2008; see also Almén and Hatten's essay in this volume), such as the emergence in the *Symphonies* of the chorale as a structural counterbalance. It can therefore be within the "expressive potential" of post-tonal pieces – "the wide but not unrestricted range of possible expression" (Cone 1974: 166) that hermeneutic interpreters actualize in response to a composition's temporal structuring of sensuous, congeneric, and extrageneric elements – to lead one into the temptation of considering what "kinds of human situations," including those typically framed as narrative, "present themselves as congruous with its structure" (Cone 1982: 239). Alternatively, recent music may lead one away from that temptation, with equally rich results. The shock of some musical modernisms may in part be predicated on their constant invoking and rebutting of the desire to read for a plot created by a piece's juxtapositions, superimpositions, or fragmentations; in other pieces, it may be the tension *between* emergent forms of narrativity and their semi-enabling, semi-negating modernist and postmodernist discourses that suggests the more nourishing site for criticism.

Hayden White (1987) encouraged scholars to consider narrative history writing as storytelling and thus to analyze, for instance, essentializing tales of modernism's anti-narrativity via narratological means. A plot archetype emerges between the retellings of this tale – an epic, no less – in which modernism is a revolutionary hero, engaging in a just war against the reactionary forces of narrativity (allied, no doubt, along an axis of evil with other forms of "extra-musical" monstrosity). Like Gandalf facing down the fiery Balrog at the end of *The Fellowship of the Ring,* Modernism sets itself against the rampaging beast Narrativity to proclaim: "You cannot pass!" Yet as Michael Klein has argued in the preceding chapter and as I have suggested here, blithely dismissive accounts of narrative's musical fate since common-practice tonality are ripe for revision, partly through the uncovering of narrative readings of later repertoires and their surrounding critical discourses. A key critical concern must therefore be to identify what continued and what changed, once one entertains the possibility that narrativity remained a live aesthetic issue in some music since modernism. To adapt Jonathan Kramer's (1999) terminology in a different essay theorizing the transition from musical modernism to postmodernism – a nuanced view of progression that has parallels to Klein's Greimasian square in the previous chapter – it is not simply a matter of repudiation or continuation (although there is music that does both of these things) but a process with aspects of both break and extension.

Returning briefly to Gandalf's epic battle with the Balrog, it will be recalled that their fight did not end in simple victory/defeat. In fact, Gandalf dies as a result. And then he is reborn and sent back to Middle Earth, no longer Gandalf the Grey but a new entity with far greater powers named Gandalf the White. Gandalf is returned, Tolkien writes, to continue "until his task is finished." Revising my epic metaphorical conceit, therefore, one might instead suggest that Gandalf was not Modernism after all but was Narrativity all along; the Balrog must also be recast, in turn, in the role of Narrativity's adversaries. Neither story, however, will suffice: this is not a tale of binary oppositions. Narrative's influence, on music as elsewhere, did not perish in the flames of the early twentieth century: it continued its as yet unfinished tasks. So must scholars with an interest in this topic.

My small contribution to that work in the remainder of this essay is in two parts. Having surveyed examples of post-Classical narratology that theorize the transformation of other narrative media (principally literature) after modernism, I will suggest ways in which plot continued to evolve by "extension" in recent music, developing the "Narrative" cell of Klein's grid in ways that send individual pieces sliding along anti-, neo-, or non-narrative trajectories. Putative musical examples of narrative negation (disnarration, denarration, bifurcating narration, subjunctive narration) are offered here as enticements to future analysis and criticism. In the same spirit, the section also responds to ideas about music's role in literature after realism – a rise in music-inspired structuring is often linked to a problematization of plot in the modernist novel – in order to suggest further avenues one might follow when considering music's limits and potential as a narrative medium, not only since modernism but also before music crossed that interminably smudgy start line. In the final section, branching outward to the wider implications of these negations and negotiations, I suggest why narrative readings of music remain a valuable tool for critics of recent music, and in spite of the philosophical objections of some scholars to such a move – indeed, as part of the kind of critical projects within which such concerns have been articulated.

NEGATIONS

In his contribution to the volume *A Companion to Narrative Theory*, Brian Richardson notes with surprise the broad agreement, when it comes to discussions of plot, among narrative theorists who otherwise have little in common. Distilling a range of these statements (from Peter Brooks, Vladimir Propp, Ricoeur, and others) permits Richardson to present an apparently uncontroversial description of plot: "An essential element of narrative, plot is a teleological sequence of events linked by some principle of causation; that is, the events are bound together in a trajectory that typically leads to some form of resolution or convergence" (2006a: 167).

This definition begins to suggest why the notion of "purely musical" plot is probably the least controversial application of narrative-related ideas to instrumental music, to the extent that it is often implicit in theoretical approaches making no explicit reference to narrativity – recall, for instance, Heinrich Schenker's descriptions of motives living out their fates like personae in a drama (see Rothfarb 2002: 929).[6] Even the Polish modernist Witold Lutosławski, who came out in a Hanslickian rash at the merest suggestion of "extra-musical" content in his compositions, claimed a central role for pitch-related plots in his music (see Reyland 2007). The apparent ease of speaking about plot in music is facilitated, most obviously, by the dynamics of tonal harmony, but music in many styles and periods (and theories thereof) emphasizes the role (to recall Richardson's definition) of "events . . . bound together in a trajectory that typically leads to some form of resolution or convergence." This may begin to explain, then, why composers as divergent as Brian Ferneyhough, Lutosławski, and Judith Weir have discussed aspects of their post-tonal music in terms of narrative (Reyland 2009: 255). Musicians, it turns out – and contrary to expectations arising from objections to narrative approaches to music, especially since modernism – do not always lose the plot.

As Richardson moves on to document, though, the problem with generalized notions of plot "is that many narratives resist, elude, or reject this model of plot and its explicit assumptions of narrative unity, cohesion, and teleology," particularly from the twentieth century onward. He proceeds to trace forms of "narrative progression" in texts exploring "nonplot-based" methods and charts a journey away from "the most familiar to the most outrageous orderings, that is, from those that almost invisibly accompany the movement of story to those that most spectacularly overthrow it" (2006a: 168). That trajectory will be considered near the end of this section in order to highlight the role of musically inspired structural metaphors in some of these literary strategies – strategies with intriguing implications, when reversed, for thinking about musical narrativity before modernism. Eric Prieto has argued that, as part of "one of the central quests of literary modernism[,] the ever more accurate representation of psychological states and processes," writers from the symbolists onward derived literary structures from musical styles and forms to enhance what he calls "listening in": an "inwardly directed mode of mimesis . . . where the primary object of representation is not the outside world but the subtly modulating interactions between consciousness and world" (2002: x). A new link between literature and music was being constituted, "and that link was thought," that is, "abstract principles of pattern and proportion . . . in competition with the grammatical rules that govern normal linguistic statements" (10–11) like plot-based narratives. That competition, however, was already present in music before modernism.

Richardson's cataloging of such strategies forms part of his important contribution to one focus of post-Classical narratology: theorizing ways in which narrative elements continued to evolve through modernism and postmodernism, and critically analyzing the hermeneutic impact of these changes on individual texts. Byron Almén (2008) has usefully argued that the literary-narrative-to-musical-narrative relationship is sibling rather than descendental. Some of the innovations that theorists have conceptualized in literature nonetheless seem to me to have analogues in recent music – much of which, it goes without saying, was created by musicians fluent in modern developments in drama, the novel, and poetry.

In his book on "extreme narration," *Unnatural Voices*, Richardson posits a "continuum of narrative negation" from disnarration (an idea developed by Gerald Prince) to his own theory of denarration (2006b: 88); related concepts include subjunctive narration (Martin Fitzpatrick) and bifurcated narration (Alan Soldofsky). Somewhere within this spectrum of negations – which runs from almost straightforwardly plot-oriented narratives to explicitly anti-narrative strategies of progression – a slippage occurs that is typical, Richardson asserts, of postmodern narrative: contradictions in a text can no longer be contained epistemologically, and certainties cede ground to "a postmodern overturning of the fictional world" (93). As Patricia Waugh has argued, modernist texts are often preoccupied with consciousness and thus with showing how the mind is less stable and unified than was once thought; postmodernism is more interested in fictionality, that is, in revealing the condition of a text (and sometimes the self) as fictional, constructed, mediated, narrated (1984: 14). Whereas modernism challenged previous forms of narrative (such as realism) by offering an intensified and relocated realism focusing on the disunities of the subject, one postmodern strategy has been to reveal narrative's fictionality: at a certain point, developments "in" a plot can no longer be contained within any single *fabula*, thus revealing the artifice of the narration in effects ranging from the comic to the disturbing.

Disnarrations are "those passages in a narrative that consider what did not or does not take place" (Prince 1988: 1). Richardson notes a wry example near the end of Nabokov's *Lolita* when Humbert writes, "Then I pulled out my automatic – I mean, this is the kind of fool thing a reader might suppose I did. It never even occurred to me to do it" (2006b: 88). One glimpses the possibility of an alternative fictional reality; crucially, however, one never imagines that it *is* the narrative's reality. One never questions, in other words, that there is a single *fabula* governing the whole and that the disnarration is not actually part of it. While common in recent texts, disnarrations were wide-ranging in literature before modernism. The same may also be true of music.

A key moment in the narrative formed by the slow movement of Beethoven's "Hammerklavier" piano sonata, Robert Hatten has argued, modulates into G major and a passage articulated with hymn-like textures marking a religious or spiritual topic and thus "a vision of grace in the midst of tragic grief" (1994: 16). The vision might be read as a fantasy occurring in the experiencing consciousness of a persona undergoing the piece's travails;

it could also (not necessarily exclusively) be heard as a disnarration – a what-might-have-been, imagining the possibility of transcendence but not its actual attainment in this story. Either way, it permits the musical persona's apparent poise (what Hatten calls its "positively resigned acceptance") as the music slides back into tragedy (20).

An alternative glimpse of a utopia, and another potential case of musical disnarration, occurs at the end of Lutosławski's Symphony No. 3. Most of this symphony, composed for Georg Solti and the Chicago Symphony Orchestra, is a pathos-drenched, widescreen, Technicolor epic, complete with crowd scenes and rabble-rousing speeches, but undercut by an unremittingly bleak sense of Romantic Polish futility articulated by the thwarting of each near-overcoming. The main plot events revolve around the orchestra's struggle to forge a unified symphonic voice and perform a unison melodic utterance capable of propelling the music toward resolution. This teleological drive consistently fails to overcome musical forces seeking to shut down its efforts. Instead, the narrative seems set to end tragically, as Lutosławski pieces so often do – until, that is, a brief pause near the end of the piece, after which everything changes.

In place of tragic pathos, the music switches to an initially bathetic vision of an alternative reality, balancing diatonic allusions with post-tonal chromaticism and releasing long melodic lines harking back to Messiaen, Szymanowski, Mahler, Karłowicz, and beyond. A brief struggle to hang on to this new realm then occurs, as if to make the new state feel earned and thus believable, and a celebration of pentatonic fireworks seems set to usher in a joyous new age – before, suddenly, the dream collapses. A smear of dissonance dumps the music back where the symphony began: four authoritarian, hammer-blow Es, the polar opposite to the goal-state of fully chromatic yet lyrical melody targeted by the bulk of the plot and achieved in the penultimate vision of an alternative world. Parallels to contemporary Polish experience (Solidarity outlawed, martial law imposed) are there to be actualized, should one feel so inclined. The first Polish hearing of the piece occurred when a recording of the piece's premiere was played to an audience including Solidarity supporters in a church during martial law; perhaps the symphony's disnarration, in this charged context, sounded inspiring. Other Lutosławski endings of this period, however, also pop an unexpected bubble of optimism arising from a work otherwise framed as tragic struggle (e.g., *Chain 3*, 1986), as if to reveal the naïveté of such bubbles and/or to despair at their fictitiousness. A key to Lutosławski's modernism – indicating one potential gap between disnarrations since modernism and earlier ones – is a problematization of the likelihood of such visions even to be accepted as possible.

Nonetheless, a disnarration's "contradictions," Richardson argues, "can be contained epistemologically" (2006b: 88). A coherent and logically consistent narrative *fabula* remains unsullied by their inclusion. *Denarrations* are altogether more severe. Their destabilizations call the "reality" of a fiction into question. In a literary denarration, "the narrator denies significant aspects of his or her narrative that had earlier been presented as given"; for example, in a simple form, a narrative might read, "Yesterday it was raining. Yesterday it was not raining" (87). This is an arresting strategy of which Samuel Beckett was one of the masters. Richardson discusses a passage in *Molloy* where A and C meet in the country – only for the narrator later to suggest that A and C may have appeared in this place on different days and might also have been in different places entirely, not meeting at all. This obfuscates the *fabula* – one must either accept that one cannot know the true version of the fictional story or, alternatively, entertain the possibility of multiple truths. It is also an effect that is "composed-out" over the course of the novel: more sustained denarrations in *Molloy*, such as Moran's "denial of the opening lines of his narrative," are "implicit in this first textual undoing" (87). Such long-range denarrations, Richardson argues, take on "the features of entropy, and all creation, all difference, slid[ing] into the void" (93). The effect is not limited to avant-garde texts. One never really knows what happened, for instance, in Ian McEwan's *Atonement*, the discourse of which tells at least three different versions of a story, all contradictory; at the end of Yann Martel's *The Life of Pi*, the hitherto verified existence of Richard Parker, the Bengal tiger stranded with the boy on the boat, becomes unsettlingly enigmatic.

Could a musical narrative similarly relocate discontinuity, open-endedness, multiplicity, and ambiguity from the fragmentations of discourse to its story level? The shift of pitch focus from D and F to C and G at the end of Harrison Birtwistle's *Earth Dances* might lead one to doubt one's hearing of the structural cardinality of earlier events in the music focusing on D and F, in turn unraveling any musical plot one had hitherto been constructing in relation to that dyad. Arnold Whittall reads the shift as a "hero" expiring and "yielding place to something new," an interpretation requiring no denarration (1994: 153). Yet the possibility of hearing something more destabilizing (what if there never was a hero in the first place, no modernist pitch center that could not hold) might be considered in light of, say, the effects of the different versions of Eurydice's death in Birtwistle's *The Mask of Orpheus*. These vying narrative perspectives mirror the many versions of this myth (not least in Birtwistle's music); they may also remind one of the denarrational strategy of the "Four Postscripts by DRAMATIS PERSONAE" at the close of Iris Murdoch's *The Black Prince*, a novel published in 1973, the year Birtwistle began this opera – which is not to assert that Murdoch was an influence on Birtwistle. Rather, in the wake of the kind of metafictional games played by John Fowles in 1968's *The French Lieutenant's Woman*, such strategies were "in the air" of British culture.

The Black Prince's jarring codas take the form of responses (they read like equally pompous but differently annoyed peer reviews) that disagree with, and therefore undermine, each other and the already unreliable narration of the novel's anti-hero, Bradley Pearson. Murdoch's denarrations become narrative piranhas, reversing traditional readerly approaches (finding the "story," the fundamental structure, within the discourse) by stripping the flesh of every possible story off the discourse's skeleton. Part of the power of denarration, then, is to challenge the notion of a workable distinction between story and discourse – an idea with parallels in contemporary music theory and analysis, not least regarding modernist music.[7] Stories (like fundamental musical structures) are never real and do not exist outside of our acts of performance-telling, analysis-comprehension, or criticism-retelling; the fiction that they *might* be real, however, permits such activities to persist in many familiar forms. All one can posit after a denarration, however, is "a general, undifferentiated conglomerate of past events which may or may not have occurred, within an inchoate temporality that cannot be analytically reconstructed into any sustained order," as Richardson writes: "The work's discourse is determinate; its story is inherently indeterminable" (2006b: 94). One need not labor the point, but this suggests certain parallels between the experience of such texts and aspects of life in their various cultural communities during the twentieth and twenty-first centuries.

In a similar vein, *subjunctive narration* is Martin Fitzpatrick's coinage to identify "uncertain narrative, marked by an inherent unknowability . . . in which significant information is not epistemologically secure," and in which perceivers "cannot precisely determine the facts of the case": there are "things we as readers wish to know and cannot know," and subjunctive narratives "deliberately frustrate attempts to resolve that question" (2002: 244). The critical temptation, Fitzpatrick writes, is to resolve away "the epistemic lacunae" by recuperating it for a standard narrative model (the "indicative" narrative, say, familiar to both music and literary analysts, "in which facts are selected, interpreted, arranged, and presented, in narrative form," and it is the interpreter's job to know "the narrative's facts and their relation to each other" [244]). To do so, however, performs a disservice to many texts.

One of Fitzpatrick's examples is the status of the lost pet lemming, Ursula, in Thomas Pynchon's *Gravity's Rainbow*. Slothrop tags along with Ludwig, the boy who has apparently lost the lemming, but the narrator of the episode casts doubt on the existence of the lemming – and then does not tell the reader whether or not the lemming really exists in the *fabula*. This leads, in turn, to Fitzpatrick's key concern, which regards "point," an element of narrative he rates as being as crucial as story or discourse: "That the novel both poses so acutely the question of whether or not Ursula exists and so pointedly refuses to answer it, making Ursula's presence powerful and her status indeterminate, emphasizes that her significance is more pertinent than her factual status" (2002: 250). It is the "point" of a novel like *Gravity's Rainbow*, in other words, to invite the perceiver to consider the possibility that Ursula's significance, for instance, is her symbolic value: what she implies by neither being nor not being.

While worlds apart, in most respects, from *Gravity's Rainbow*, the ambiguities of tonal structure in Vaughan Williams's Symphony No. 6 may offer an example of a subjunctive musical narrative. The symphony does not close with a resolution of its first movement's harmonic destabilization, which challenges the tonic of E minor with keys ranging as far away as B♭ minor; it establishes a chilly equilibrium. When the piece ends, one feels it could rock back again to the ambiguous penultimate sonority, which leans in alternative tonal directions. The musical narrative withholds a satisfying sense of closure by evading the rhetorical or harmonic gestures needed to confirm whether the piece was truly "in" E minor (or any other key). There is no transcendence, no triumph, in the "extreme, anti-romantic bleakness of this Epilogue" (Whittall 1999: 67), and the sense of ambivalence when the symphony ends on E minor – but only just – feels as bereft of consolations as any other wasteland created in Britain in the wake of world war.

An alternative form of epistemological ambiguity is generated by *bifurcated narration*: texts within which, as Alan Soldofsky defines his concept, "a second, seemingly tangential narrative intrudes upon the first, generating a range of relationships between them" (2003: 312–13). One narrative can displace the other (or they may do so continuously); they may be linked, but the contiguity of their relationship may remain indeterminate; resemblances may be only metaphorical; one strand can disappear and then reappear at a certain point, making an initially latent link to other material suddenly manifest. Soldofsky's examples come from poems by Robinson Jeffers addressing "the modern world's chaos and terror" through structures exploring dialectical or dichotomous oppositions (2003: 313). Alternative examples from novels include the palindromic nest of narratives in David Mitchell's *Cloud Atlas* and the shifts between the opening chapters of different stories, and the chapters addressing "the reader's" attempts to read those openings, presented by Italo Calvino's *If on a Winter's Night a Traveler.*

Luciano Berio's *Rendering* can be heard as a bifurcating musical narrative. The piece has the misfortune (from the perspective of this essay) of an over-simplified description in Wikipedia's "Berio" entry: "*Rendering* (1989)," the online encyclopedia read at the time of writing, "took the few sketches Franz Schubert made for his *Symphony No. 10*, and completed them by adding music derived from other Schubert works." This might lead one to expect a composition akin to the performing editions of Mahler's Symphony No. 10. What one hears, however, is a constantly replayed slippage from "Schubert" to "Berio" and back again. As Giordano Montecchi (2005) states in CD sleeve notes quoted in the (more useful) Wikipedia entry on *Rendering* itself: "Schubert's fragments give rise to musical moments of vertiginous beauty which neverthe-less constantly founder in the emptiness of what was 'not done' – and Berio fills this emptiness with . . . an iridescent musical screed woven around the timbre of the celesta . . . separating the fragments and at the same time hold-ing them together."

It is more difficult to agree with the statement that, through this strat-egy, the last vestiges of the Schubert "reach the symphonic goal for which they were intended" (Montecchi 2005), which reads like the kind of attempt, noted by Fitzpatrick, to recuperate uncanny narration for more traditional interpretive models. *Rendering*'s continuous process of decentering highlights difference as much as a synthesis of the heterogeneous through a bifurcating musical discourse whose vying musical worlds may have something to say about the status of identity, truth, fiction, and reality in the postmodern world, but also say something about the place of beauty in contemporary music and its relationship to the past: both worlds become more wondrous through the uncanniness of their interwoven presentation.[8]

Considerations of narrative negation in music, I suggest, could inspire analytical investigations of multiplicity and ambiguity leading not to an "ex-clusive and closed hearing of ambiguous musical situations, but [to] an open and plural one" (Cross 2003: 3) in line with broader trajectories in current music theory. Furthermore, just as some of modern literature's favorite tricks have parallels in Laurence Sterne's *Tristram Shandy* (1759–66), correspondences between historically distinct musical repertoires may appear, leading to reflexive enrichments of our understanding of different repertoires. (Does the "Ode to Joy," for instance, begin with a bifurcation? Is Haydn's *Creation* non-narrative?[9])The critical narrative within which Richardson frames his spectrum of narrative negation certainly raises new questions about theorizing musical narrativity before modernism.

As his survey moves further away from standard models of plot-based narrative, Richardson investigates what he terms "'aesthetic' orderings": "motif-based, architectonic, numerological, or geometrical kinds of sequencing [which] are primarily formal designs that have little function other than that of satisfying a desire for symmetry" (2006a: 169). These include Proust's composing-out of the discovery of the "little phrase" of music by Vinteuil within *In Search of Lost Time*. At a certain point, Richardson suggests, "the theme [in the sense of an idea articulated by the text] does not merely accompany the narrative; instead, the narrative events are produced to accommodate the development of the motif" (170). His other examples of aesthetic ordering include the construction of the final fifteen chapters of Joyce's *Ulysses*, each of which "thematicize[s] a different organ of the human body" and foregrounds a particular art or science; "collage" compositions in which "key elements are recombined in a number of different arrangements or contexts and which constitute the nexus that connects the different units" via "a principle of coherence rather than progression *per se*, since after a certain amplitude is reached there is no inherent reason for the text to continue" (174), a view reminiscent of Webern's statement that the completion of the chromatic set heralds the logical ending of a post-tonal piece; or "serial constructs" (the term is from Dina Sherzer [1986]), as articulated in Robbe-Grillet's "The Secret Room," which is "shaped in the form of a temporal spiral," or Robert Coover's *Spanking the Maid*, "the obsessively re-enacted scene" of which "rises to a peak of physicality before rapidly subsiding" (174), forms of structural progression that bear similarities to the innovations of Debussy's *Jeux*, Boulezian spirals like *sur Incises*, and Ligeti's "The Devil's Staircase."

A subtext here – that "aesthetic" orderings in a novel are often metaphorical derivatives of musical structures – becomes manifest when Richardson expands on Proust's thematic variations:

> As the example from Proust suggests, the arrangement of a cluster of literary
> motifs may be modeled on or borrowed from standard musical progressions.
> For his entire novel Proust employed the structure of a Wagnerian opera;
> others have utilized the general structure of the sonata (Strindberg) or the
> symphony (Gide, Andrei Biely), the framework of jazz (Ralph Ellison, Toni
> Morrison), or the prescriptions of the classical Indian musical form, the *raga*
> (Amit Chaundri's 1993 *Afternoon Raag*). A trajectory provided by the fugue
> has at times proven irresistible, as evidenced by Thomas Mann's "Death in
> Venice" and the *fuga per canonemi* that orders the "Sirens" episode in *Ulysses*.
> (2006a: 171)

A difference between musical and literary narrative, however, is that these
"prescriptive" progressions were not introduced by modernist or postmodernist composers to problematize narrativity: they were central to music long
before modernism and during "the great era of narrative in music."

Michael Spitzer has identified the conventional repetitions and recapitu-
lations of certain musical forms as "the perennial Achilles heel of musical
narratology": "After the hero returns home with the reprise, is he then obliged
to begin his journey all over again?" Nor is Spitzer impressed by the "usual
escape hatch" – considering the recapitulation as "a scene of remembrance
of previous events, relegating the triumph to the coda"; he does, however,
speak of "the sonata form plot," as if hearing a sonata form as a version of an
archetypal musical plot (until one gets into the details at any rate) could be
less problematic (2004: 328). Spitzer's questioning is nonetheless pointed: in
musical narratives occurring within predetermined structural conditions like
those of sonata form, how is one to resolve the tension between "narrative"
and "aesthetic" principles?

As Richardson points out, even traditional modes of plot and emplotment "typically [work] in a kind of unacknowledged counterpoint with other
methods of progression" (2006a: 177). Many literary plots also develop their
own forms of repetition and recapitulation: for example, Frodo makes a journey to the village of Bree, where he is attacked by the evil Nazgûl; Frodo
makes a journey to Weathertop, where he is attacked by the evil Nazgûl;
other journeys and attacks follow; repeat signs aplenty there. And music,
more obviously than the novel, is an assemblage – sometimes its ordering is
narrative, sometimes musical. Another escape hatch is to co-opt the "aesthetic" principles (e.g., sonata form, the dynamics of tonal harmony) as plot
archetypes, as in Anthony Newcomb's (1984, 1987) or McClary's (2004) work
on plot paradigms and musical forms. Alternatively, one could accept the ten-

sion and, rather than seeking to resolve it, consider its critical implications. As part of such considerations, one might begin to entertain a strange thought: that some music was an experimental and self-reflexively problematizing form of narrative long before the modernist turn.

This is not only because of music's dueling forms of narrative and aesthetic progression, although these are a route by which one might project back into common-practice tonal repertoires the tensions between narrative and anti- or non-narrative structures to enrich one's critical strategies. Going further, though, musical narratives before modernism could be considered to move beyond what Richardson terms the Borgesian "forking paths" principle, as articulated by postmodern narratives offering different sequences of reading such as Ana Castillo's *The Mixquiahuala Letters,* choose your own adventure books, or hypertext narratives. In music, it is rarely the listener (unless one is wielding the skip or shuffle button) who chooses what happens next in terms of the order of events in a discourse. But just as, in the above examples, "the interpretation of the basic *fabula* will alter depending on which version [of the *sjuzhet*] is followed" (Richardson 2006a: 175), pieces of music are constantly encountered in different versions: every performance of a piece is a new *sjuzhet,* in which mediating interpreters – like a play's actors, directors, and designers – bear the potential substantially to alter the manner in which events are emploted, a *fabula* identified, a piece's "point" interpreted.

Even then, however, musical narrative can only go so far in individuating a plot's agents, actions, or events: in musical narratives, the reader must become one of the performers. Jean-Jacques Nattiez's famous argument against music's ability to tell a detailed story might thus be inverted to suggest why, both before and since modernism, music's innovative form of narrativity offers unique (and perhaps uniquely valuable) interpretive freedoms, not least through its exploration of the tension between the freedoms and restrictions of structure and interpretation: "Listening to *Till Eulenspiegel,* and with the help of the title, I can readily agree that it concerns the life and death of a character. I certainly hear that he moves, jumps, etc. But what exactly does he do? I don't know" (1990: 244). One may not know, and one is not explicitly told – but one can certainly *imagine.* The situation here is not so different, then, from many post-realist novels. As Ursula K. Le Guin writes regarding the Elizabethan world conjured up in *Orlando* by Virginia Woolf – or, rather, the world that Woolf's prose empowers the reader to conjure up ("an exotic world . . . dramatically alive," with a frozen Thames, "bonfires blazing on the ice") – a story is created in the interpreter's imagination not by spelling out every last detail, but through "specific descriptive details, not heaped up and not explained," yet "encouraging the reader's imagination to fill out the picture and see it luminous, complete" (Le Guin 2011: 3). Music has its own ways of nudging listeners in a certain narrative direction; some of them (e.g., embodiments of gesture) attain a level of specificity (perceived through the embodied cognitions of the listener) far outstripping the precision of literature's means for achieving similar effects.

Reconsidering earlier music through modernist or postmodernist repertoires and theories may therefore lead to new perspectives on problematic aspects of musical narrativity. Recent music's further problematization of narrative, and the extended powers of narration that it grants to the interpreter, also suggest interesting ways in which other objections to its discussion in post-tonal repertoires might be challenged.

NEGOTIATIONS

In a comment from the floor after the roundtable on narrative and music that closed the Sixth International Conference on Music since 1900 at Keele University, Björn Heile suggested (to paraphrase) that reading new music, indeed *any* music, as narrative robs it of its quintessential otherness; such a move renders music unproblematic and fit for consumption as just another narrative commodity. Another danger of narrative explanations, he suggested, was that narratives can fake the impression of having explained something, rhetorically inducing persuasion while masking the ways in which an account has been rationally deficient.[10] One might over-hastily answer those charges by counterclaiming that music's otherness as a narrative medium – its limited-aleatory narrativity, which invites the listener to decide who is jumping, why they are jumping, and so on – is what makes it so compelling, thus conceived, because musical narrativizations, taking place partially in the performative imagination of the perceiver, remain irreducibly particular and uncontainable.[11] Heile's thoughtful provocation, however, channeled a broader sense at the conference, and elsewhere in musicology and cultural studies, of the perils of the narrative turn, particularly when addressing recent texts. Thinking about how narrative approaches to music might play a useful role in tackling those problems is the cake that my conclusion now wishes to have and to eat.

Theodor Adorno asserted, regarding forms of nineteenth-century art like the realist novel, that such texts offer "the existing world a kind of solace" by positing a "well-rounded totality" that creates "the false impression that the world outside is such a well-rounded whole" too (1970: 2). He argued instead for an appreciation of art's "formal radicalism" as "social moment" (73) and that "art will live on only as long as it has the power to resist society" (321). Some conservative critics have taken such arguments as grist for the mill of their disavowals of modernism and other avant-garde movements, suggesting, as Georg Lukács (1957) did more elegantly than most, that social reality cedes, in modernist art, to moments structuring private worlds, detached from social reality. Musical narratives also enmesh listeners in performative interpretations fused with their own subjectivities. Yet the subjectivities informing those experiences of musical narrativity are historically and culturally situated, which in turn inflects their narrativizations. Where narrativity remains an active thread in music from modernism onward, this may suggest one limitation of arguments concerning music's social detachment.

Furthermore, just as modernist music ranging from Luigi Nono's *Il canto sospeso* and Hans Werner Henze's *Das Floß der Medusa* to Britten's *War Requiem* or even Jimi Hendrix's Woodstock performance of "The Star-Spangled Banner" professes – or, in the sway of formalist grand narratives arguing against the admission of such content, gauzily veils – a political intent, considerations of musical narrativity suggest other ways in which recent music might encourage thoughts beyond a withdrawal from the social. One approach to theorizing this idea goes back to Roland Barthes, writing about post-serial composition in "From Work to Text" (1971). For Barthes, "writerly" modernist novels (as opposed to "readerly" realist ones) permit readers freedoms and responsibilities denied to them by more conventional fiction (1982a: 142–48). Radical forms of narrative challenge interpreters, in Randall Stevenson's words, to "reconsider the nature of fiction and its relation to reality, and to reconstruct for themselves fictional worlds . . . transcribed in diverse styles and unusual structures" (1998: 220). Music, of course, is the writerly text *par excellence*, both before and since modernism. It is nonetheless striking that Barthes explained his author-resituating conception of textual meaning with reference, in part, to the developments of musical high modernism: "Today post-serial music has radically altered the role of the 'interpreter,' who is called on to be in some sort the co-author of the score, completing it rather than giving it 'expression.' The Text is very much a score of this new kind: it asks of the reader a practical collaboration" (1982b: 163). As Barthes went on to argue in *s/z* (1970), a development of his theories of narrative conceived alongside "The Death of the Author" (1968) and "From Work to Text," the writerly reader is "no longer a consumer, but the producer of the text" (1974: 4).

Written in the late 1960s and early 1970s, Barthes's thoughts on musical interpretation are most obviously relatable to (then recent) works involving degrees of aleatory – Boulez's *Piano Sonata No. 3*, say, or Stockhausen's *Klavierstuck XI* – in which key structuring decisions are made by the performer, realizing markedly individual and writerly (or composerly) interpretations of a musical text. Yet if one takes Barthes's purpose in mentioning such music as anything other than metaphorical, one might extend his ideas on interpretation to issues of musical meaning: a listener emploting within a musical narrative's matrix of restrictions and freedoms, for instance, is also a writerly interpreter. As argued above, music in a narrative mode has always been a writerly text. With post-tonal music's freeing of interpreters from earlier conventions of reading, however, and the provocations to interpret music as narrative arguably becoming stronger in some repertoires, musical narrativity's emancipation of the composerly listener intensifies. The developments in musical plotting addressed in the previous section of this essay, in turn, seem destined, perhaps even designed, to induce writerly acts of criticism.

Yet can one honestly declare such interpretive encounters to be empowering acts of resistance to this, that, or the other, or are they just passive, readerly consumptions of music in authorial disguise? Speaking of narrativity in music can feel close, at times, to an act of political incorrectness, and never more so than when dealing with post-tonal repertoires. This is not merely a matter of cutting against the razor-sharp lapels of modernist music's discourses of autonomy and formalism; after all, those blades have been dulled by recent revisionist scholarship (see, e.g., Wilson 2004). Jean-François Lyotard's *The Postmodern Condition* (1979), which famously inspired critiques of all but the most self-policingly circumspect micro-narratives, remains appropriately influential in musicology, encouraging narrative accounts of any kind to be viewed with appropriate skepticism about the proponent's theoretical, ideological, and even moral purposes; where grander structures need to be evoked, for instance, rhizomes are now trendier than plots. Furthermore, Lyotard's concerns have been rebooted, forcefully, by recent polemics such as the twenty-first-century dystopia of narratives charted by Christian Salmon in *Storytelling: Bewitching the Modern Mind* (2010). In this polemical project, Salmon pays close attention to narrative precisely because its uses are now so common and thus tempting to ignore.

Storytelling, Salmon argues, is enjoying a globalization-fueled golden age as the governmental, corporate, and media tool of choice for societal coercion and repression. Yet he rails against the fact that intellectual eyes have been averted from this process, not only by the seductive alternatives to narratological approaches offered by poststructuralist critical theory, but by the very promiscuity of narrative in everyday life. Long after the death of the author, anyone with a Facebook account is the narrator of his or her own commoditization. This type of narrative pervasiveness, Salmon suggests, has encouraged the concept's trivialization among the *cognoscenti*. Similarly, even within narratology, some scholars now question the wisdom of a "narrative turn" that saw the discipline sucking in, like an imperialistic vacuum cleaner, territories far beyond its traditional remit (Phelan and Rabinowitz 2006) – territories including the criticism and analysis of instrumental Western art music. Yet those averted intellectual eyes and ears have never been more keenly required. If the stories scholars tell about music from a narratological perspective need to be treated with due scholarly skepticism, the same must also be true of the storytelling accomplished by contemporary musicians.

The narrative Gandalf/Balrog is rampant, blurring boundaries between evidence and opinion. Salmon notes how legal proceedings, vaccination programs, presidential elections, humanity's response to global warming, and decisions on whether or not to go to war are now decided on the basis of which side can shape the most compelling narrative – or spin the environment within which those narratives will be perceived – as opposed to who can present the best evidence through scientific method, close argument, logical deduction, and so on – a point echoing one of Heile's claims about music and narrative. But contemporary cultural texts, including musical ones, are also part and parcel of these processes. One might therefore wish to consider, for example, the political roles of the narrative elements of recent works (and their promotion, critical receptions, etc.) by composers such as Krzysztof Penderecki and Steve Reich, both of whom have written pieces responding to 9/11. How do works like Penderecki's "Resurrection" Piano Concerto and Reich's WTC: 9/11 participate, in terms of their musical means and structures as much as their CD packaging and publicity, in the creation of environments encouraging political perspectives on charged issues like the War on Terror? Scholars should engage with at least some new music as a putatively narrative text, such as Penderecki's darkness-to-light structure – caricatured by one Polish critic as "Socrealistyczny Penderecki" (Chłopecki 2002) – in order to gauge the potential roles of its musical story; we must also test what lies beneath the ostensibly anti-narrative surfaces of some other pieces, as in Reich works exploring a traffic between minimalist techniques and more conventional forms of structuring – and sometimes packed with sampled "narrating voices" – better to chart a piece of music's participation in, or resistance to, broader narrative trends in its cultural and historical moment.

To offer a closing pair of examples from my own ongoing research in this area: Klein's introductory chapter quoted an analytical story I have told about Lutosławski's 1968 composition *Livre pour orchestre* (Reyland 2009). This piece (in Klein's retelling of my analysis) "begins as a non-narrative, with its breaks, non sequiturs, and intermezzi. Or perhaps the piece toggles between non-narrative and anti-narrative, navigating in the space between these two options. In any case, by the end of *Livre*, the anti-narrative forces have come together to make a neo-narrative with a trajectory and a climax to make any storyteller proud." The "book" of high modernism is rewritten, my analysis suggests, and the "Livre" becomes a symphony when unfinished arguments from its opening movement unexpectedly invade the finale, joining the dots of a (hitherto latent) longer-range musical plot and surging toward synthesis. To use Richardson's terminology, Lutosławski's piece denarrates what initially appeared to be both its story (actually an anti-story) *and* its mode of (anti-)storytelling in a moment of vertiginous narrative and ontological drama within which the return of the plot *is* the plot. This arresting strategy gives the idea of the narrative twist a late-modern wrench: what we thought we knew is not what we knew we thought.

A piece like *Livre*, however, also provides an example of a relatively recent musical narrative being created as part of a broader (and in Lutosławski's cultural context complexly veiled) political project, by demonstrating how a musical narrative can critique (or endorse) the notion of narrativity as part of a broader initiative. Lutosławski's piece encodes interlocking narratives of transformation from the level of thematic argument up to its ontological denarration; this has tempted me to speculate on the political subtexts of *Livre* and other Lutosławski pieces. Here was a composer working amidst the gray restraints of Communist Poland in the late 1960s; a composer who, two years later, completed a cello concerto that permitted its dedicatee, Mstislav Rostropovich, to make the (narrativizing) declaration that the brass's murderous assault on the soloist at the piece's climax represented "the Central Committee at full strength." The unabashed extra-musical sentiments of this reading inflamed Lutosławski, of course, although it may be useful to read his public remonstrations with Rostropovich as one of many nuanced bluffs in his public statements about music and the wider world.

The denarration in *Livre* overthrows a distinctly modish spin on conventions of structural governance. Mallarmé's writerly, mood-over-plot "Le Livre" model (an infinitely re-orderable album of self-contained fragments), admired by Barthes (1982b: 163) and musically adapted by Boulez and others, appears to have been one of Lutosławski's structural models when planning the piece. In its place, though, the denarration posits an organizational principle with an alternative pedigree, that is, the dialectical, teleological drive of a symphonic plot. This ties events together in a thread that surges toward, and in the end achieves, a thematic resolution to the piece's opening pitch-organizational enigma; in turn, the question of plot's possibility in Lutosławski's mode of modernism is answered. In terms of musical aesthetics, this has a polemical and reactionary air: Lutosławski, as his lectures of the period reveal, was in many respects a conservative with little time for, say, Boulez's and Stockhausen's innovative approaches to structural progression (the approaches that had so attracted Barthes). Less obviously, unless one knows about this stage in Poland's cultural history, Lutosławski's plot-driven pieces of the 1960s and after, by returning to musical narrative, reimagined a concept that had been sullied in Poland fifteen to twenty years earlier, when composers had been mandated with the state-endorsed, financed, and otherwise coerced articulation of Stalinist ideology through mediums including instrumental music.

The results of that process present beautiful examples of both the limits and the potential of musical narrative as a means of representing any one story. Stalin is reported to have said that seeking to impose Communism on Poland was as absurd as trying to saddle a cow. As transcripts from the Polish Ministry of Culture's "listening sessions" during *socrealizm* demonstrate (see Thomas 2005: 40–58), making the musical narrative of a socialist realist "Olympic" Symphony or *Concerto for Orchestra* represent, say, the forthcoming achievement of real and functioning Communism after a dramatic struggle out of the darkness of Western capitalism and the cult of the individual – and in a way that workers in the field might recognize and be suitably motivated by – was even harder than saddling a cow. The expressive potential of any music remains open to a plurality of divergent narrativizations and other forms of reading, and this is very much the point, I would argue, of music as a narrative medium: it is a form of narrative virtuality that only goes so far in outlining a plot and its resonances. This is always true of a narrative discourse; it is intensely true of musical narratives. The performerly and composerly listener/critic, more empowered by post-tonal music than by many other narrative media, must invent.

Seeking to be inventive, then, might one argue that pieces like *Livre* rehabilitated a form of musical narrativity – to cleanse it, post-*socrealizm*, and to inspire transformations of political consciousness in later (but still Communist) times – as the commune of the "Livre" is reconstructed to articulate an enlightening teleological action? Or to represent the power and possibility of change? Or to encourage the realization that "reality" may be different from what one is usually led to believe by those in power? That there might not, in fact, be only one reality? If so, Lutosławski's cultural work through musical narrative can be read in parallel, not only to broader currents in twentieth-century narrative art, but also to other compositional responses to Soviet cultural demands through the adaptation of modernist or postmodernist means – strategies that problematize, rather than entirely dispel, narrative structures, such as Arvo Pärt's substitute for Soviet propaganda narratives: "a spiritually inspired stasis to create an alternative to musical, historical, and cultural progress narratives" (Cizmic 2008: 64; see also Almén and Hatten in this volume).

A narrative approach is not the only, nor necessarily the best, way to interpret *Livre pour orchestre*: it is not the only productive way to engage *any* piece of music, and music's otherness always exceeds its profitably disruptive role on the occasions when pieces do invoke the possibility of reading through a narrative frame. Nonetheless, by examining some music through narrative-informed approaches, always in the wider context of contemporary scholarship's kaleidoscope of methodologies, one can access ideas that cannot be revealed in other ways and that therefore have the potential to make a unique contribution to criticism and scholarship, productive for creators, critics, performers, and audiences alike. As Fredric Jameson (2002) has argued, for example, a Marxist negative hermeneutic seeking to "unmask and to demonstrate the ways in which a cultural artifact fulfills a specific ideological mission" (281) could be "exercised *simultaneously* with a Marxist positive hermeneutic" seeking to decipher "the Utopian impulses of these same still ideological texts" (286). Narrative approaches along these lines should surely participate in evaluations of music's role in various golden ages of storytelling. In one historical moment and cultural context, for example, Lutosławski's *Concerto for Orchestra* looks set to prove that individual listeners, let alone social reality, remain stubbornly resistant to musical narratives; the Polish authorities, after socialist realism, moved elsewhere in their attempts to saddle captive minds. In the quest to understand another moment – the same piece's role in the twenty-first-century program of an American or a British symphony orchestra's subscription series, say, where it could function simultaneously as a decadent orchestral showcase and a reactionary musical narrative whose tragic-to-transcendent "expressive genre" (see Hatten 1991) helps listeners to shore up long-cherished aspects of false consciousness, such as their belief in the likelihood of overcoming personal adversity, or a sense of entitlement to the world's dwindling resources, having imagined that heroic overcoming somehow to have been their own achievement – it seems judicious to argue that the study of music and narrative still has a useful role to play.

NOTES

1. Kathryn Hughes, "The Other Avant Garde," *Guardian*, September 25, 2010, 6.

2. Providing encouragement for such connections, Piper and Benjamin Britten worked closely together when the painter provided set designs for some of the composer's operas.

3. Cone's notion of interlock is discussed in Cone (1962). Butler locates similar juxtapositions in Debussy and Schoenberg's music (1994: 11–12, 53).

4. Recent considerations of twentieth-century musical narratives and cinematic techniques include Leydon (2001) (on Debussy) and Burke (1999) (on Shostakovich).

5. For a discussion on this model of grief-work, see Stroebe and Schut (1999).

6. Important discussions of musical plot include McCreless (1988) and Maus (1988).

7. See Cross (2003); Fink (2001); and Whittall (1994, 1997).

8. See Cook (2006) for a discussion of uncanny juxtapositions in postmodern and other music.

9. In a paper presented at a Society for Music Analysis Study Day devoted to Haydn's *Creation*, Michael Spitzer (2007) called the three late oratorios "curiously non-narrative," proposing instead an analysis centered on notions of parataxis: additive, list-like constructions juxtaposing independent clauses.

10. I am grateful to Björn Heile for clarifying that my recollection of his statement is accurate (personal communication).

11. Discussion arising from this point, involving Lawrence Kramer and other panelists, suggested that it was not music that was the "other" but language itself. From a Lacanian point of view, the symbolic (language or any semiotic system) is already the "other" that confronts us. Narrativizing music cannot undo its otherness, because all systems of signification are already "othered" to begin with. However, that does not stop some critics (narratologically inclined or otherwise) from writing as if they had somehow undone music's otherness, brushing that fiction under the carpet with a flourish of critical narration.

WORKS CITED

Adorno, Theodor W. 1970. *Aesthetic Theory*. Edited by Gretel Adorno and Rolf Tiedemann, translated by C. Lenhardt. London: Routledge and Kegan Paul.

Almén, Byron. 2008. *A Theory of Musical Narrative*. Bloomington: Indiana University Press.

Barthes, Roland. 1974. *s/z*. Translated by Richard Miller. New York: Hill and Wang. First published in 1970.

———. 1982a. "The Death of the Author." In *Image, Music, Text*, translated by Stephen Heath, 142–48. London: Fontana. First published in 1968.

———. 1982b. "From Work to Text." In *Image, Music, Text*, translated by Stephen Heath, 155–64. London: Fontana. First published in 1971.

Botstein, Leon. 2001. "Modernism." In *The New Grove Dictionary of Music and Musicians*, 2nd ed., vol. 16, edited by Stanley Sadie and John Tyrrell, 868–75. London: Macmillan.

Burke, Richard. 1999. "Film, Narrative, and Shostakovich's Last Quartet." *Musical Quarterly* 83(3): 413–29.

Butler, Christopher. 1994. *Early Modernism: Literature, Music and Painting in Europe 1900–1916*. Oxford: Oxford University Press.

Chłopecki, Andrzej. 2002. "Socrealistyczny Penderecki." *Gazeta Wyborcza*, October 12–13.

Cizmic, Maria. 2008. "Transcending the Icon: Spirituality and Postmodernism in Arvo Pärt's *Tabula Rasa* and *Spiegel im Spiegel*." *Twentieth-Century Music* 5(1): 45–78.

Cone, Edward T. 1962. "Stravinsky: The Progress of a Method." *Perspectives of New Music* 1(1): 18–26.

———. 1974. *The Composer's Voice*. Berkeley: University of California Press.

———. 1982. "Schubert's Promissory Note: An Exercise in Musical Hermeneutics." *19th-Century Music* 5(3): 233–41.

Cook, Nicholas. 2006. "Uncanny Moments: Juxtapositions and the Collage Principle in Music." In *Approaches to Meaning in Music*, edited by Byron Almén and Edward Pearsall, 107–34. Bloomington: Indiana University Press.

Cross, Jonathan. 1998. *The Stravinsky Legacy*. Cambridge: Cambridge University Press.

———. 2003. "Editorial." *Music Analysis* 22(1–2): 1–5.

Fink, Robert. 2001. "Going Flat: Post-Hierarchical Music Theory and the Musical Surface." In *Rethinking Music*, edited by Nicholas Cook and Mark Everist, 102–37. Oxford: Oxford University Press.

Fitzpatrick, Martin. 2002. "Indeterminate Ursula and 'Seeing How It Must Have Looked,' or 'The Damned Lemming' and Subjunctive Narrative in Pynchon, Faulkner, O'Brien, and Morrison." *Narrative* 10(3): 244–61.

Harris, Alexandra. 2010. *Romantic Moderns: English Writers, Artists and the Imagination from Virginia Woolf to John Piper*. London: Thames and Hudson.

Hatten, Robert. 1991. "On Narrativity in Music: Expressive Genres and Levels of Discourse in Beethoven." *Indiana Theory Review* 12: 75–98.

———. 1994. *Musical Meaning in Beethoven: Markedness, Correlation, and Interpretation*. Bloomington: Indiana University Press.

Iser, Wolfgang. 1974. *The Implied Reader: Patterns of Communication from Bunyan to Beckett*. Baltimore: Johns Hopkins University Press.

Jameson, Fredric. 2002. *The Political Un-conscious: Narrative as a Socially Symbolic Act.* London: Routledge.

Klein, Michael. 2005. *Intertextuality in Western Art Music.* Bloomington: Indiana University Press.

Kramer, Jonathan D. 1978. "Moment Form in Twentieth-Century Music." *Musical Quarterly* 64(2): 177–94.

———. 1999. "The Nature and Origins of Musical Postmodernism." *Current Musicology* 66: 7–20.

Krauss, Rosalind E. 1986. *The Originality of the Avant-Garde and Other Modernist Myths.* Cambridge: MIT Press.

Le Guin, Ursula K. 2011. "Virginia Woolf (1882–1941)." In "Review," *Guardian*, May 14, 3.

Leydon, Rebecca. 2001. "Debussy's Late Style and the Devices of the Early Silent Cinema." *Music Theory Spectrum* 23(2): 217–41.

Lukács, Georg. 1996. "The Ideology of Modernism." In *Marxist Literary Theory: A Reader*, edited by Terry Eagleton and Drew Milne, 141–62. Oxford: Blackwell. First published in 1957.

Lyotard, Jean-François. 1984. *The Postmodern Condition: A Report on Knowledge.* Translated by Geoff Bennington and Brian Massumi. Manchester: Manchester University Press.

Maus, Fred E. 1988. "Music as Drama." *Music Theory Spectrum* 10: 56–73.

McClary, Susan. 2004. "The Impromptu That Trod on a Loaf: or How Music Tells Stories." In *Narrative Theory: Critical Concepts in Literary and Cultural Studies*, edited by Mieke Bal, 4: 269–86. London: Routledge.

McCreless, Patrick. 1988. "Roland Barthes's *s/z* from a Musical Point of View." *In Theory Only* 10(7): 1–29.

Montecchi, Giordano. 2005. Liner notes, translated by Karel Clapshaw, in *Berio: Orchestral Transcriptions* (Decca 476 2830).

Nattiez, Jean-Jacques. 1990. "Can One Speak of Narrativity in Music?" *Journal of the Royal Musical Association* 115: 240–57.

Newcomb, Anthony. 1984. "'Once More between Absolute and Program Music': Schumann's Second Symphony." *19th-Century Music* 7(3): 233–50.

———. 1987. "Schumann and Late Eighteenth-Century Narrative Strategies." *19th-Century Music* 11(2): 164–74.

Phelan, James, and Peter J. Rabinowitz. 2006. "Introduction: Tradition and Innovation in Contemporary Narrative Theory." In *A Companion to Narrative Theory*, edited by Phelan and Rabinowitz, 1–18. Oxford: Blackwell Publishing.

Prieto, Eric. 2002. *Listening In: Music, Mind, and the Modernist Narrative.* Lincoln: University of Nebraska Press.

Prince, Gerald. 1988. "The Disnarrated." *Style* 22: 1–8.

Reyland, Nicholas. 2007. "Lutosławski, 'Akcja,' and the Poetics of Musical Plot." *Music & Letters* 88(4): 604–31.

———. 2009. "*Livre* or Symphony? Lutosławski's *Livre pour orchestre* and the Enigma of Musical Narrativity." *Music Analysis* 27(2–3): 253–94.

Richardson, Brian. 2006a. "Beyond the Poetics of Plot: Alternative Forms of Narrative Progression and the Multiple Trajectories of *Ulysses*." In *A Companion to Narrative Theory*, edited by James Phelan and Peter J. Rabinowitz, 167–80. Oxford: Blackwell Publishing.

———. 2006b. *Unnatural Voices: Extreme Narration in Modern and Contemporary Fiction.* Columbus: Ohio State University Press.

Ricoeur, Paul. 1984. *Time and Narrative*, vol. 1, translated by Kathleen McLaughlin and David Pellauer. Chicago: University of Chicago Press.

Rothfarb, Lee. 2002. "Energetics." In *The Cambridge History of Western Music*

Theory, edited by Thomas Christensen, 927–55. Cambridge: Cambridge University Press.

Salmon, Christian. 2010. *Storytelling: Bewitching the Modern Mind.* London: Verso.

Sherzer, Dina. 1986. *Representation in Contemporary French Fiction.* Lincoln: University of Nebraska Press.

Soldofsky, Alan. 2003. "Bifurcated Narratives in the Poetry of Robinson Jeffers, C. K. Williams, and Denis Johnson." *Narrative* 11(3): 312–31.

Spitzer, Michael. 2004. *Metaphor and Musical Thought.* Chicago: University of Chicago Press.

———. 2007. "Three Acts of Haydn's *Creation:* Lateness, Parataxis, and the English Enlightenment." Paper presented at the Society for Music Analysis Spring Study Day, "Haydn's *Creation,"* Oxford University, February 10.

———. 2009. "Haydn's *Creation* as Late Style: Parataxis, Pastoral, and the Retreat from Humanism." *Journal of Musicological Research* 28(2–3): 223–48.

Stevenson, Randall. 1998. *Modernist Fiction: An Introduction.* Revised edition. Harlow: Longman.

Stroebe, Margaret, and Henk Schut. 1999. "The Dual Process Model of Coping with Bereavement: Rationale and Description." *Death Studies* 23: 197–224.

Taruskin, Richard. 2010. *The Oxford History of Music,* vol. 4, *Music in the Early Twentieth Century.* Oxford: Oxford University Press.

Thomas, Adrian. 2005. *Polish Music since Szymanowski.* Cambridge: Cambridge University Press.

Waugh, Patricia. 1984. *Metafiction.* London: Methuen.

White, Hayden. 1987. *The Content of the Form: Narrative Discourse and Historical Representation.* Baltimore: Johns Hopkins University Press.

Whittall, Arnold. 1994. "Birtwistle, Maxwell Davies and Modernist Analysis." *Music Analysis* 13(2–3): 139–59.

———. 1997. "Modernist Aesthetics, Modernist Music: Some Analytical Perspectives." In *Music Theory in Concept and Practice,* edited by James Baker, David Beach, and Jonathan Bernard, 157–80. Rochester: University of Rochester Press.

———. 1999. *Musical Composition in the Twentieth Century.* Oxford: Oxford University Press.

Wilson, Charles. 2004. "György Ligeti and the Rhetoric of Autonomy." *Twentieth-Century Music* 1(1): 5–28.

PART TWO

Theorizing Modern Musical Narrative

3

Narrative Engagement with Twentieth-Century Music: Possibilities and Limits

Byron Almén and Robert S. Hatten

Byron Almén and Robert S. Hatten

PART I. INTRODUCTION

Twentieth-century music offers an experimental laboratory within which the varying relationships between composition and signification can be evaluated. Whereas the viability, utility, and persuasiveness of narrativity as a perceptual and analytical paradigm applicable to eighteenth- and nineteenth-century Western art music has been well established by the last generation of scholars, its definition, parameters, and scope remain subject to debate. With the turn to modernism, however, even the most basic grounding of narrative in tonality and traditional temporality may appear to be undermined. Throughout the twentieth century, a bewildering variety of stylistic, aesthetic, and cultural approaches to temporal unfolding have had their impact on narrative strategies of interpretation. In this preliminary overview, we outline a range of relevant developments and provide three capsule analyses illustrating the robustness of a flexible approach to narrative interpretation based on Almén's (2008) adaptation of James Jakób Liszka's (1989) semiotic approach to narrative.

According to Liszka, the defining feature of narrative is *transvaluation* – a significant, temporalized change of state that affects the ranking of values in a given hierarchy (see part 3). As applied to musical works, transvaluation involves reversals that either upset or reaffirm the prevailing order, leading to a variety of outcomes (tragic, comic, romantic, ironic). Transvaluation, as the

fundamental condition for narrative, *may or may not* be enacted through the
staging of a higher-level narrative agency (as "teller") or of basic-level internal
and external agents (as "protagonist" and "antagonist").[1] If agency at either
level is engaged, the resulting *agential narrative* may draw upon a more specific
range of interpretive strategies beyond those required for *non-agential narratives*. Since agency is indeterminate even for some nineteenth-century musical works, grounding musical narrative in transvaluation ensures a broader
consideration of how narrative interpretation may be fruitful for post-1900
works – especially those that depart from traditional tonality or modes of
temporality.

Agential narratives are often buttressed by programmatic details, text,
or other devices that more precisely characterize the agents in question. One
might therefore begin by examining the extent to which certain works obscure, deform, or degrade narrative agency and/or its organization in a manner analogous to the experiments of modernist literature. These strategies are
not limited to music after 1900, but they increasingly occupy the foreground
rather than the periphery. We will explore some possibilities in part 2. The
distinction between agential and non-agential narratives is not, however, a
rigid one. Rather, we can imagine a continuum of narrative possibilities along
which agency becomes more or less pronounced. The same is true for the point
at which actorial strategies of transvaluation cede to those based solely on
non-actorial strategies of transvaluation. Agency can appear in less obvious
ways, either because the agents themselves are ambiguous or because they are
less denotatively specific. In György Ligeti's *Atmosphères* (1961), for instance,
one can discern a directed timbral and registral process that seems motivated,
even though traditional strategies for cueing agency (program, text, topical
reference, thematic or motivic integrity) are absent.[2] On the other hand, those
processes contain within themselves alternative modes of transvaluation from
those found in common-practice tonality.

At the boundary even of non-agential narratives are those works that
seek to erase or preclude narrative, whether by working against a listener's
expectations or by finding ways to discourage a listener from imposing a narrative reading. An example of the former is Philip Glass's opera *Einstein on
the Beach* (1976), where the generic expectation of a plot is denied and replaced
by symbolic references, abstract numerical and syllabic representations, and
a lyrical-circular approach to scene and temporality. An example of the latter
is the early minimalism of Steve Reich, which is expressly non-teleological
in its denial of goal or expectation; the absence of these qualities removes a

possibly essential feature of narrative patterning, precluding all but the most idiosyncratic interpretations. Likewise, the aleatoric works of John Cage by their very nature eschew all but accidental appearances of logical connectivity. Again the listener is constrained from most of the typical paths to narrative organization. With intention removed, we become aware instead of the human mind's potential for finding order in the apparently unordered or chaotic.

If we turn to *non-agential narratives* – those more general cases of narrative transvaluation where agency does not predominate but that are governed by changes in musical hierarchies interpreted as significant by the listener or analyst – other questions arise. Since narrative interpretation is dependent on a listener's interpretive standpoint, can any temporal medium like music ever be devoid of narrative? Put another way, how might a composer signal that his or her intention is to be non-narrative, even if narrative interpretation is unavoidable?

These questions open up interesting areas of inquiry, some of which we will pursue in the following two parts. But before we turn to our overview of possibilities, it may be helpful to distinguish narrative from other global modes of interpretation with respect to the traditions of interpretation associated with various genres prior to 1900. Vocal and/or dramatic genres such as opera, musical theater, oratorio, cantata, Requiem or Ordinary Mass, song cycle, tone poem, and programmatic symphony are readily associated with narrative organization through text and/or program. We would expect that the modernist experiments of Joyce, Proust, and their successors in literature would find echoes in these genres when appropriated by twentieth-century composers. But just as signification is possible in the absence of text or program, so might new types of narrative organization be possible in instrumental genres (symphony, sonata, string quartet, and the like) in which a premise is presented and worked out, creating discourse out of thematic, motivic, gestural, tonal, and/or harmonic events. Post-1900 compositional developments of these genres offer a rich source of investigation for discovering the limits and new potentialities of narrative.

An investigation must also take into account those distinctions among modes of representation that already existed prior to 1900. For example, the narrative mode is often juxtaposed with the *lyrical* (the primary mode of representation for songs and character pieces), which tends toward a spatial rather than a temporal signification: what is aimed at is a mood, reflection, or state of being rather than a significant temporal change.[3] Narrative can also be juxtaposed with a *ritual* mode, in which the performative enactment of an established sequence is foregrounded, or with *trance,* which attempts the transformation of ordinary consciousness onto another level, as if to convert the temporal into the eternal. These other modes of representation signify in their own right, yet they are not in themselves essentially narrative. They can become so, as when a lyric song ends with a surprising plot development or features the progressive evolution of a character. Our interpretation of twentieth-century narrative will encompass the lyrical, ritual, and trance modes when they appear in hybrid combinations with narrative. This is a vein that has been mined frequently since 1900.

As this brief introduction suggests, there are many points of approach for a study of narrativity in twentieth-century music. In this essay, we proceed by offering a modest survey of twentieth-century style history through the lens of narrativity, focusing on those styles in which narrativity, or its absence, becomes marked in some way. Part 2 presents a preliminary outline of the highly nuanced ways in which post-1900 musical styles have addressed issues such as agency and temporality, noting their consequences for narrative interpretation. Part 3 then returns to the concept of transvaluation, clarifying its fundamental role in creating narrative, even in the absence of agency or traditional forms of conflict. We then present three short analyses – of works by Penderecki, Messiaen, and Pärt – that address some of the issues raised in part 2 but with greater attention to specific pitch languages. Each of the analyses invokes a discursive strategy of *expansion* – a gradual approach to a point or points of climax. However, each work intersects in different ways with agency, tonality, gesture, program, and teleology.

PART 2. AN OUTLINE OF TWENTIETH-CENTURY TECHNIQUES AND AESTHETICS WITH IMPLICATIONS FOR NARRATIVE INTERPRETATION

Questions of narrativity offer a fresh perspective on the typically "progressive" categorizations of avant-garde techniques, styles, and aesthetics as attributed to twentieth-century musical works. One quickly discovers that even those styles that depart radically from traditional constructs such as tonality may not diverge so extremely from traditional narrative schemata (e.g., even an atonal work can project a tragic expressive genre or an ironic narrative). An example of this phenomenon can be found in Schoenberg's op. 19, no. 4 (Almén 2008: 183–86), a short piano piece featuring an atonal pitch language (apart from some fleeting tonal allusions) in combination with a clear progression of traditional topics. These topics (dance, recitative) are effective in part because they can be articulated through non-pitch parameters: meter, rhythmic motives, the contrast between metric clarity and instability, allusions to orchestral punctuations, and the like. Strikingly, Schoenberg can be argued to have employed these musical features in the service of an ironic narrative: "The unfamiliarity of the tonal language thus forms part of a larger narrative strategy of modern alienation and psychic disintegration. . . . The various *topoi* function like evanescent masks, tried on for effect, but discarded in self-loathing and disgust, and the atonal language merely serves to increase this sense of dislocation" (186). Conversely, those styles that appear more conservative tonally may nevertheless exemplify a more radical approach to narrative (e.g., a minimalist work may use familiar triads in non-teleological ways). For example, Brian Eno's ambient work "Ikebukoro" from *The Shutov Assembly* (1992) features a sixteen-minute unfolding of a D♭ major triad (with occasional foreign tones and coloristic sevenths) through electronically produced drones and bell-like sounds. As with the Schoenberg example, there are topical allusions: the piece's original function – part of a Japanese art installation – is evoked in the allusions to ritual bells, and there is also a striking effect that mimics the sound made by the wings of an enormous bird. Nevertheless, the tonal stasis of the work creates a lyrical or trance-like effect that denies teleology and, therefore, narrative.

In the following outline (see Table 3.1), we present several other intersections between narrativity and technique/style/aesthetic, addressing many of those twentieth-century innovations or experiments that have influenced our capacity to interpret narrative. These novel approaches (many of which were pioneered already in the nineteenth century) involve modes of temporality, tropes such as irony, and the treatment of subjectivity and agency, including specifically narrative agency. We also address two of the fundamental presuppositions of twentieth-century narrativity in music: its status as both an ideological construct and a listener's cognitive construct.

I. Temporality

Since music is a temporal art, it is not surprising that its narrativity is to some extent a temporal construct, and its special narrative effects are closely tied to its various plays with **temporality**, as implied by its own musical materials and *stylistically constrained sequences* (S, for short). In other words, these deformations depend crucially on our understanding of an underlying, *stylistically-*

TABLE 3.1. OUTLINE OF TWENTIETH-CENTURY TECHNIQUES AND AESTHETICS WITH IMPLICATIONS FOR NARRATIVE INTERPRETATION

I. TEMPORALITY

  A. Permutation of stylistically constrained sequences (S)

    1. Preservation of implied underlying S

    2. Obfuscation of implied underlying S

    3. Ellipsis: leaving out portions of S

  B. Montage effects (multiple, competing Ss)

    1. Disruption/interruption

    2. Stratification

      a. Spatial

      b. Actorial (see agential narratives)

    3. Psychological montage

    4. Surreal montage

  C. Dissolution of temporality (lack of clear S)

    1. Suspended time

    2. Cyclical time

    3. Symmetrical or mirrored time

    4. Moment time

    5. Trance time

    6. Numinous time

    7. Slow-motion time

    8. Foregrounding a parameter not associated with time

    9. Defaulting to gesture as local or global temporal reference

  D. Ignoring or rejecting temporality and stylistically constrained sequences

    1. Zero-degree time (absence of temporal situatedness)

    2. Intentional negation of time

II. TROPOLOGICAL NARRATIVES

III. AGENTIAL NARRATIVES

  A. Ambiguous subject

  B. Reordering of events involving a subject

  C. Displaced subject

  D. Other kinds of problematized subjectivity

  E. Narrative agency (as staged by the work)

IV. MYTH

  A. As supporting narrative interpretation

  B. As antithetical to narrative interpretation

V. IDEOLOGICAL AND COGNITIVE CONSTRUCTIONS

  A. Alternative ideologies

    1. Zero-degree narrative

    2. Anti-narrative

  B. Cognitive construction of narratives

informed temporality (T, for short).[4] For example, Bartók's adaptation of sonata form provides narrative expectations of stylistically constrained sequences of formal functions, even if the tonal relationships are new. Thus, in his String Quartet No. 6, a slow introduction is followed by a first theme group, and a transitional liquidation prepares the collectional shift to a second theme. What may confuse our sense of stylistically informed temporality is the extent to which Bartók introduces further development of a chromatic variant of the first theme into the second theme zone, prior to a return of the slow introduction that marks the beginning of the development section proper. But there are precedents in nineteenth-century sonatas (e.g., the first movement of Schubert's Piano Sonata in A Major, D. 959, which features extensive development of the first theme after the second theme has appeared and before a closing version of the second theme ends the exposition).

More extreme forms of this kind of **permutation** may involve the reordering of pitch and/or rhythmic/metric patterns in a given theme, as in Stravinsky, as well as the reordering of formal sections. If the S is at the level of the form, we may experience an effect corresponding to the distinction between story and discourse (cf. Chatman 1980; Genette 1980; Ricoeur 1984). Jonathan Kramer's "gestural time" is one example of such a reordering at the level of gestures whose implied function does not accord with their location but where their function strongly suggests an underlying S, as in his analysis of the first movement of Beethoven's String Quartet, op. 135 (1988: 150–61).

Some permutations **obfuscate** or destroy any sense of an underlying S (see, e.g., **moment time** below). The most common strategy is **ellipsis** (leaving out portions of an S), resulting in a series of episodes; this technique is found in narrative constructions from the earliest literary epics. A more abrupt episodic treatment involves ellipsis at the formal level, resulting in a series of discontinuous tableaux or episodes that may themselves be either open or closed and either elliptical or continuous. Examples include the disjointed episodes in Stravinsky's *Histoire du soldat* and the separate tableaux in Messiaen's *Saint François d'Assise*.

Musical **montage effects** – akin to the intercutting or layering of shots in a film – may include strategies of **disruption/interruption**, such as cutting off an S, either by silence or by means of a sudden, contrasting shift. Stravinsky pioneers this effect as a formal technique beginning with *Petrushka* and *The Rite of Spring*, but it can be found as a form of temporal compression in late nineteenth-century works such as Debussy's *Prélude à "L'Après-midi d'un faune"* (e.g., the juxtaposition of "dream" and "active" states in the compressed return). The collage-like and tropological potential of such concatenations of contrasting types has been explored for traditional and popular music by Nicholas Cook, who also invokes the montage effects crucial to Eisenstein's film aesthetic (2006: 130–32).[5] In support, he cites Roland Barthes's assignment of a third kind of meaning to such juxtapositions as found in montage (either simultaneous, in the frame, or successively, in a sequence of shots), which Barthes dubs "the obtuse meaning" (1977b: 55). Here, presumably unrelated objects or sequences become related in a form of meaning that is supplemental to more obvious textual or imagistic content. This is the level of the "filmic," and Cook proposes it as an essential, if non-verbal, form of musical understanding akin to Barthes's concept of the "grain" of the voice in his essay on singers (1977a). We discuss a related technique under the category of **tropological narratives** below.

Stratification – two (or more) simultaneous Ss (akin to Jonathan Kramer's "multiple time" [1988: 169]) – can be theorized in types indebted to Eero Tarasti's (1994) categories of spatiality and actoriality, which here intersect with his third category, that of temporality. **Spatial** suggests several ongoing activities (e.g., the competing performers against the background of the ongoing fair in the first tableau of Stravinsky's *Petrushka*); **actorial** implies two different characters (e.g., the Ballerina's and the Moor's themes played simultaneously in the second tableau of *Petrushka*); **psychological montage** articulates disruptions or overlaps in the stream of consciousness, either of the present or of memory/reminiscence. Consider, for example, Ravel's polytonal recall of dance motives near the end of his *Valses nobles et sentimentales*, or Ives's quotational collages – also enacting spatial and actorial roles – in works such as "Putnam's Camp" from *Three Places in New England*. **Surreal montage**, by contrast, suggests overlapping or confused dream states (possibly psychoanalytical in their inspiration, the prototypical example being Schoenberg's *Erwartung*; see also **agential narratives**) or altered forms of consciousness. These may combine with various strategies of **dissolution**.

Dissolution of temporality, leading to states of timelessness, may occur at various formal scales, creating effects such as **suspended time**, which places a foreground S under a fermata, as it were, or reduces it to a timeless background (e.g., the entrance of the celesta in the first movement of Bartók's *Music for Strings, Percussion, and Celesta*). Events, whether Ss or non-Ss, are recycled in **cyclical time**. Examples of the former range from Satie's endlessly repetitive *Vexations* (actually, 840) to Steve Reich's *Piano Phase*. Schoenberg's op. 19, no. 6 comes close to satisfying the latter (return of a non-S), with its cyclical return of a minimal S: two alternating, bell-like sonorities. Palindromes with temporal axes of symmetry (e.g., Webern's palindromes) create, in turn, **symmetrical or mirrored time.**

Each of the first three strategies of dissolution is utilized by Messiaen in his *Quatuor pour la fin du temps*. His "non-retrogradable rhythms" are rhythmic palindromes, his "modes of limited transposition" are symmetrical and thus already non-teleological to varying degrees, and his use of *talea* and *color*, techniques first found in the isometric motet (where pitch patterns and rhythmic patterns are intentionally non-congruent), all contribute to an effect of timelessness. Anthony Pople eloquently observes that the music for the piano and cello in the opening "Liturgie de cristal" simply "'is' without beginning or end – the same patterns [are] cycled and recycled with no apparent articulation in time. At the very least, it is as if, each time we listen to the *Quatuor*, for these three minutes or so we are eavesdropping on something everlasting" (1998: 18). Thus, a narrative impulse – possibly suggested by the clarinet's motivic development – can be understood to have been undermined for expressive reasons. Even the descriptive text appended to the movement cannot tip the balance toward narrativity in the music. As Pople summarizes, "The [descriptive] words outline events that happen in space and time – specifically, between three and four in the morning – whereas the music has little or no narrative quality. Indeed it cannot, for the presentation of the 'endless' music of the piano and cello requires such articulation to be withheld" (19).

Stockhausen, who pioneered the term **moment-form** (on which we base our category of **moment time**) considered the "overcoming of the concept of duration" to be the effect of works in which every moment is equally interesting and to be enjoyed as "something individual, independent, and centered in itself, capable of existing on its own" (1963: 199). These moments are non-teleological, in that they lack typical developmental or climactic trajectories (and thus, we may infer, they tend not to support narrative interpretations). Jonathan Kramer speculates about the importance of interpreting moment forms as *nonlinear*, even when the work appears to bring back earlier material:

> A return must *seem* arbitrary. Seeming arbitrariness pervades, for example, Stockhausen's *Kontakte*, Stravinsky's *Symphonies of Wind Instruments*, and Messiaen's *Chronochromie* (1960). Great artistry and compositional craft are needed to make purposefully ordered events seem random, even when they repeat earlier events. Coherence and continuity must be tucked away in the background (in both senses of the term), so that their force is felt only subliminally as a nonlinear phenomenon. One might also consider

in the category those less radical moments in more traditional trajectories when the condensation to a (lyrical) moment produces an effect by which awareness of time appears to cease. This could be considered as a shift from narrative to lyrical time. (1988: 208)

Trance time (Kramer's "vertical time") is a potentially emergent effect created by non-teleological repetitive or continuous structures that exceed a typical S (e.g., some early American minimalist music). In this music our sense of temporality is lost, since all events appear to be simultaneous – hence, for Kramer, vertical. (Interestingly, Stockhausen uses the image of verticality in his own description of moment forms.) Kramer offers an example of vertical time based on a composer's reported intentions, namely, Philip Glass's rationale (as quoted in Mertens 1983: 79) for his 1974 minimalist work *Music in Twelve Parts:*

> When it becomes apparent that nothing "happens" in the usual sense, but that, instead, the gradual accretion of musical material can and does serve as the basis of the listener's attention, then he can perhaps discover another mode of listening – one in which neither memory nor anticipation . . . [has] a place in sustaining the texture, quality, or reality of the musical experience. It is hoped that one would be able to perceive the music as a . . . pure medium "of sound." (1988: 376)

This, for Kramer, is "the timeless now of the extended present" (376), which he distinguishes from schizophrenic experiences of time in that the temporal continuum is not actually destroyed. Instead, we experience what Kramer calls "the time of timelessness" (378). In order for the work to have this effect, it must be relatively static in all its dimensions so as not to induce a teleological perception or interpretation (385). Thus, in comparison to moment time's varied and discontinuous moments, vertical time is best considered as a single, expanded moment (395).

Edward Pearsall emphasizes the importance of silence and non-discursive elements in anti-teleological works by composers such as Morton Feldman (2006: 53–57). He notes that "silence in *For Samuel Beckett* takes the form of a redundant, spellbinding texture created by repeating the same music over and over again" (54), but he also quotes Feldman's own characterization of silence in his music: "Silence is my substitute for counterpoint. It's nothing against something. The degrees of nothing against something. It's a real thing, it's a breathing thing" (Feldman 2000: 181, cited in Pearsall 2006: 54). In other words, the absence of goal-directed motion and the accumulation of silence must not be interpreted as mere negation in this music but as a positive form of organization with distinctive aesthetic properties.

The next four categories share aspects of the ones just enumerated, but they add a particular perspective or character of their own. **Numinous time** uses Ss that have, or assume, symbolic, religious, or spiritual resonance (e.g., the emergent effects of what might be called "spiritual minimalist music," as in works by Arvo Pärt and John Tavener). The often extra-musical significance afforded to a typically slow and relatively static or repetitive work may help induce a kind of meditative state akin to trance but focused on a particular spiritual oneness with creation or Creator. For example, in Tavener's *The Protecting Veil* (1987) for cello and string orchestra, a pedal drone, or *ison* (Tavener's own coinage, from a "sonic icon"), symbolizes eternity or the silence of God; its absence, then, symbolizes the void. Presumably, knowledge of this symbolism would affect the character of the timeless state one might attain when listening, even though this work has a more teleological, linear shaping and hence some degree of narrativity.

Extremely slow but otherwise unperturbed Ss that nearly exceed our capacity to recognize them as stylistic sequences form examples of **slow-motion time**. The background progression in the strings from Ives's *The Unanswered Question* may serve as a prototype for this category. The harmonic progression is present, and we are aware of it despite its glacial harmonic rhythm, but the effect is almost that of stasis. As in numinous time, Ives's programmatic cue (to hear the strings as representing the "Silence of the Druids – who Know, See, and Hear Nothing") may help induce the appropriate degree of timelessness. The work as a whole, however, has a clear narrative, involving the trumpet's question and the flute quartet's increasingly angry and parodistically mocking responses, even if "answer" and hence "ending" are conceptual categories that remain open in this work. The prototype of **foregrounding a parameter not associated with time**, or at least not *typically* temporally conceived, is found in Schoenberg's op. 16, no. 3, which features a non-temporal effect of slowly changing timbral color, supported by an imperceptible canon. Texture is another useful parameter to exploit in this way; passages of textural saturation or suffusion may suggest a timeless state of *plenitude* (Hatten 2004: 43–52), or "being" as opposed to "becoming," to borrow Tarasti's Greimasian modalities (1994).

Although Kramer develops a notion of "gestural time" as a species of "multiply directed time" (1988: 6), his categories are limited to the functions of initiating, continuing, and closing (compare Kofi Agawu's "beginning-middle-ending" paradigm [1991: 53–79]). By way of contrast, the history of a gestural

type, understood as a four-part rhetorical schema, is mapped by Patrick Mc-
Creless (2006) from its source in the nineteenth century (notably in works
by Beethoven, Chopin, and Liszt), where it is grounded in tonal syntax, to
twentieth-century compositions by Messiaen ("Le baiser de l'Enfant-Jésus"
from *Vingt regards sur l'Enfant-Jésus*), Boulez (the second movement of *douze
notations*), and, most tellingly, since no longer tied even to the tempered pitch
realm and hence primarily rhetorical, Mario Davidovsky's *Electronic Study
No. 1* (1960). The schema is a simple one and more effective because of its simplicity: a climb to an apex, a precipitous drop, a "crash," and a brief rebound.
Here, **defaulting to gesture as local or global temporal reference** can be
seen to support narrative, in that an originally local schema can expand to
the length of an entire movement or work.

Another option available to twentieth-century composers is **ignoring or
rejecting temporality and stylistically constrained sequences** altogether.
Thus, we might speak of **zero-degree time** when a composer does not *intend*
any Ss, and hence the composer's musical style or aesthetic is devoid of any
temporal situatedness. This may well be the case in some of the previously
listed approaches to temporality, such as moment time. One might also speak
of zero-degree narrativity when a composer does not intend even ostensibly
programmatic music to be understood narratively: "*Déserts* is one of Varèse's
few pieces with a programmatic conception, but it is not narrative. . . . [I]n rejecting the narrative approach Varèse said: 'There will be no action. There will
be no story. There will be only images. Purely luminous phenomena.'"[6] Many
of Cage's works present interesting cases with regard to narrativity. On the
one hand, he often foregrounds a theatrical element, which implies narrative
by association with drama: "A Cage piece, from the earliest happenings, was
a multi-sensorial event, sometimes a sumptuous challenge for the spectator, a
three-ring circus, sometimes just the opposite, a moment of imposed stillness,
a space for contemplation. Cage realized the importance of the visual to the
concert world, and his 'concerts' became theatrical events. He later said that
everything he did was theater" (Broyles 2004: 312). However, Broyles further
notes that "as Cage's career progressed, the traditional narrative receded into
the background in favor of sound and art" (314).

Negation of time occurs when a composer intentionally *negates* temporality, and the only temporality a listener will (inevitably) bring to the experience
of listening is that of everyday psychological time rather than any expectations
from the style (which in any case may not exist). Cage's aesthetic presents the
prototypical form of this kind of negation. As Michael Nyman notes:

It may seem that by laying out and filling empty spaces of time Cage was cutting music off from its supposed natural, organic roots – its sources of growth. But Cage was in effect *freeing* music – or, as he might have put it, freeing sounds of music. For he was advocating that music should no longer be conceived of as rational discourse, concerned with manipulating sounds into musical shapes or artifacts (motives, melodies, twelve-tone rows) as though they were parts of a discursive language of argument. . . . If music was to be a language at all, it would henceforward be a language of *statement*. (1999: 32–33)

The removal of intentionality for Cage may give sounds their freedom and presumably free the listener from any burden of implied interpretation, but Cage cannot avoid presupposing another kind of *intention* for the listener, who is (somewhat ironically, given Cage's attempted avoidance of such intentions) enjoined to hear freely at the level of sound and specifically *not* to impose dramatic, discursive, or narrative patterning to help provide meaning. Whether or not listeners choose, or are able, to hear Cage's music in that way remains an open question.

II. Tropological Narratives

If multiple narrative strands are juxtaposed in a way that emphasizes their similarity or difference, a troping akin to metaphor may create emergent meaning out of the connections among otherwise separate strands. Britten's *War Requiem* (1960) features three such strands: poetic reflections (lyrical and sometimes dramatic) on war that embody immediate experience, an "angelic" choir of boys commenting as from on high (quasi narrative), and a celebration of the Requiem Mass (ritual). Thus, a troping of representational modes (lyric, dramatic, narrative, and ritual) and their temporalities (from temporal enacting to atemporal reflection) will support the troping of expressed meanings. Narratives that involve tropes such as irony can also use traditional materials to produce radical narrative schemes (see Reichardt 2008 for Shostakovich's employment of this procedure). Such formal irony presupposes, however, the more traditional scheme(s) that are being undermined or even deconstructed. Thus, the narrative analyst is faced with unpacking a multi-level discourse, one in which the implied trajectories of the surface style are negated by the presumed ironies of the higher-level discourse.

Returning to Britten's *War Requiem*, the baritone and tenor setting of Wilfred Owen's poem "The Next War" exploits this notion of a multi-level discourse. The singers' personae are battle-hardened soldiers who have "walked quite friendly up to Death," "laughed with him," and called him their "old chum." Britten sets this text within a cheery, patriotic marching topos, with its quadruple-meter framework, dotted-rhythm motive, and evocations of a wind band ensemble with prominent snare drums. Examples of text painting contribute to the jaunty effect: Britten breaks out of the largely syllabic vocal texture with a jagged, stepwise melisma on the word "laughed," and the flutes imitate the wailing of artillery shells in the manner of a soaring countermelody. The ironic undermining of this narrative trajectory occurs in several ways. First, the song is embedded within a larger setting of the *Dies Irae* text from the Requiem Mass. Its appearance after verses pleading to God for salvation ("Rex tremendae majestatis") creates a semantic incongruity that suggests a tropological interpretation. Second, the contrast of texts is mirrored by the contrast of musical styles between the immediately preceding *Dies Irae* setting (somewhat ponderous, with sudden soprano outbursts) and that of the Owen poem. In that light, the cheeriness of the vocal duet seems excessive and forced. Finally, "The Next War" ends with a textual shift of discourse to a more objective and distanced level: "We laughed, knowing that better men would come, and greater wars; when each proud fighter brags he wars on Death – for Life; not men – for flags." Britten's setting becomes both more lyrical and more tentative at this point, as though in recognition of the hollowness of the singers' perspective. The jaunty march music resumes after this ironic peroration, but at a reduced dynamic level accompanied by a disintegrative ascent into a higher register.

III. Agential Narratives

In psychoanalytical narratives such as Schoenberg's *Erwartung* (1909, premiered in 1924), events unfold in such a way that the listener/observer is unsure of the status of events with respect to an internal agent, or, in the case of *Erwartung*, the drama's **ambiguous subject**.[7] **Reordering of events involving a subject**, in turn, can signify a significant difference between the way events involving an agent are ordered in relation to *story* (chronological order with respect to the constructed "world") and *discourse* (the ordering of events in the narrated "re-telling").[8] For example, Philip Glass's *Galileo Galilei* (2002) recounts events in the life of the scientist in reverse order.[9] In Glass's *Satyagraha* (1980), a narrative with a **displaced subject**, episodes from the life of Mohandas K. Gandhi are presented – also as tableaux – with a three-act scheme laid atop them, tying them to three figures important to Gandhi: Leo Tolstoy (a formative influence), Rabindranath Tagore (a contemporary), and Martin Luther King Jr. (a figure inspired by Gandhi). The agential separation of Gandhi and these three figures complicates the narrative trajectory of the work.[10]

Other narratives engage with alternative kinds of **problematized subjectivity**. Sarah Reichardt (2008) offers an engaging account of Shostakovich's String Quartets Nos. 6–9 in which she sensitively applies concepts drawn from Lacan (his psychoanalytical approach), Derrida (his notion of the supplement), and Bakhtin (his theory of the novel and its polyphonic, or dialogic, discourse). Her analyses demonstrate how Shostakovich manipulates sonata form or a cycle of movements to create unique narrative trajectories. Among her insights, she notes the way that a coda functions as a Derridean supplement (seventh quartet), how Shostakovich manipulates his own musical initials to "conjure" quotation of his more programmatic works and lead ultimately to the represented death of the composed subject (eighth quartet), and how unified subjectivity can fracture into a Bakhtinian multitude of voices (ninth quartet). One might observe that narrative can survive even the death or dissolution of the unitary subject voice, as long as that death is dramatized as a premise for the work. Further investigation of the relationship of agency to narrative will undoubtedly help us appreciate the variety of narratives and anti-narratives to be found in the last century's proliferation of musical styles.

Finally, corresponding to certain nineteenth-century practices, a composer may intentionally stage a higher-level **narrative agency**, with various possible effects on the listener. In literature, a narrator may be more or less transparent, depending on how much he or she comments upon or manipulates the story being told. Presumably, the less interference with the story, the less attention we are likely to pay to the artifice of the narrator as teller, and the more likely we are to experience the tale as enacted drama merely delivered through a narrative filter. But consider the effects of Stravinsky's narrators in works such as *Oedipus Rex*, where neutrality comes at the price of distance. Interestingly, such distancing effects may suggest the masks of an ancient Greek chorus and perhaps a more mythic mode.[11]

IV. Myth

Regarding **appropriations of myth to support narrative interpretation**, Victoria Adamenko's recent examination of the multiple intersections that obtain between myth and twentieth-century music proves enlightening. She identifies the basic structural ideas on which mythic thought has traditionally relied, such as opposition, symmetry, variability, and repetition. These structural ideas have always played important roles in the construction of musical forms. Nevertheless, in the twentieth century, these ideas gain a special role as their display is unmediated by the dominating force of long-established principles of organization, for example, tonality. The void created by the disappearance of tonality was inevitably filled with those prime elementary structuring methods first used in myths. (2007: xii)

Adamenko thus considers that the "basic structural ideas" that underlie myth – that reflect the "pattern-forming nature of the human mind" – come to the fore in the absence of more specific, complex, and traditional organizing principles like tonality. She also observes that twentieth-century composers have gone in different directions when appropriating mythic features consciously or unconsciously into their works, including the exploitation of binary oppositions, principles of symmetry, and the interplay of invariance and variability; a predilection for considering universals; interest in cosmogonic and eschatological narratives; and numerology, circular notation, and ritual evocations.

Some **appropriations of myth antithetical to narrative interpretation** emphasize a mythic timelessness – such as Messiaen's "Regard du père" from *Vingt regards sur l'Enfant-Jésus* or his "Louange à l'éternité de Jésus" from the *Quatour pour la fin du temps* – and present a temporal space that is largely anti-teleological. However, we strongly support the claim that myth can also continue to serve as a wellspring for narrative patterns post-1900, as will be demonstrated below, albeit at the opposite end of a continuum of compositional possibilities from the troping of myth as narrative antithesis. Indeed, among Northrop Frye's contributions to literary criticism was the recognition of the archetypal quality and mythic origin of four basic narrative motions – romance, tragedy, irony/satire, and comedy. Insofar as these narrative trajectories play a role in musical signification (see Almén 2008), they also partake of the mythic resonances associated with such trajectories – and such trajectories can be as applicable to the morphology, syntax, and semantics of twentieth-century musical styles as they are to music of the common-practice period.

V. Ideological and Cognitive Constructions

Given that a musical narrative's traditional invocation of agency, subjectivity, conflict, drama, order/progress, potential outcomes, and transformative potential may be too constraining for some composers, in the service of **al-**

ternative ideologies they may either unconsciously or intentionally reject various techniques that might imply narrative. A given musical aesthetic or ideology may thus fall into one of the two following categories. Pieces with **zero-degree narrative** are unwittingly devoid of the conditions for narrative interpretation; compare **zero-degree time** above. Even if a work is not zero degree with respect to ordered temporality, it may be zero degree with respect to narrativity (e.g., Varèse). **Anti-narrative** pieces consciously or intentionally undermine any tendency on the part of the listener to ascribe narrative; compare **intentional negation of time** above. We have seen this ideology with respect to Cage's aesthetic, and it may apply to some works of Varèse as well. An interesting interpretation of the music of Arvo Pärt (among others) is offered by Margarita Mazo, who notes not only the relevance of time as time-space but the absence of both linear *and* cyclic significance (1996: 394, cited by Cizmic 2008: 63). More relevant for our category of narrative as an ideological construct, Mazo attributes Pärt's radical simplification of style to his search for an alternative to Soviet cultural narratives. As Cizmic summarizes, "Pärt employs a spiritually inspired stasis to create an alternative to musical, historical, and cultural progress narratives" (2008: 64).

Narrative, to conclude, is ultimately a **cognitive construction**, which means that one may choose to interpret what might otherwise appear incoherent in terms of one or more of the above-mentioned deformations of more traditional narrative constructs. As with the deformations and secondary defaults of sonata theory (Hepokoski and Darcy 2006), this can be problematic for the theorist, since the preliminary mind-set of the listener – which is often "set" by exposure to the social contexts of performances, events, schools, manifestos, and the like – may be crucial in determining what narrative (or non-narrative) effects he or she will hear (or not hear) in the music. If a given composer claims his or her music to be "non-narrative," then a fair-minded listener might attempt not to impose narrative structuring where it was not intended. Conversely, a critic might dismiss a given composer's presumed naïveté with respect to cognition by pointing out obvious ways in which listeners cannot help but apply narrative schemata or be influenced by an implied *transvaluation*, a concept to which we now return.

PART 3. TRANSVALUATION

In *A Theory of Musical Narrative* (Almén 2008), narrative is defined as an act of *transvaluation*, a term employed by James Jakób Liszka in *The Semiotic of Myth* (1989). With respect to musical narrative, transvaluation involves tracking the perceived changes made to an existing hierarchy of values (a hierarchy typically, though not necessarily, established within some opening time span of the piece) from the particular interpretive perspective of one or more listeners or observers. The central features of narrative as applied to any medium or style, then, are (1) a focus on the change of the hierarchy of values (as established by the stylistic conventions of the piece in question, by the particular valences set up by the piece itself, and by the listeners' competence and interpretive predilections), (2) the fact that these changes involve pertinent features of the musical sign system itself, and (3) the irreducible role played by the listener/interpreter/analyst (as suggested by our last category in part 2).

Almén (2008) offers expansions of this definition that allow for diverse applications to works with various degrees and kinds of signifying mechanisms. For example, the tripartite analytical division into actorial (identifying the work's dramatis personae), actantial (identifying the functional behavior of these personae), and narrative (classifying the resultant transvaluative trajectory with respect to Northrop Frye's four narrative archetypes of romance, tragedy, irony, and comedy) components – also featured in Liszka (1989) – is best suited for works with actorial features, particularly the first two components. Reduced to the basic definition of narrative given above, however, it is clear that narrative patterns can be found in a larger subset of works than those that are more narrowly actorial in character. This is significant in light of many of the paradigmatic features of twentieth-century music noted in part 2, especially non-traditional temporalities, an ironic aesthetic stance, and the waning impact of tonality, agency, and undivided subjectivity.

It is important to understand the scope and nature of transvaluation when considering the narrative properties of a given work. For example, given the articulation of the four narrative archetypes in terms of two semiotic oppositions – order/transgression and victory/defeat – it would be easy to overstate the role of "crisis" or "conflict" in narrative. To be sure, conflict and crisis play an obvious part in many narratives, particularly strongly actorial ones. But Liszka's formulation is careful not to locate the narrative impulse in conflict pure and simple: it is the set of rules that articulate the initial hierarchy that are placed in crisis, not (or at least not necessarily) the actorial elements that may or may not help to flesh out this process.[12] Conflict between or among actorially invested musical entities is a *possible* by-product of certain narrative strategies, but it is by no means a *necessary* condition.

A tonal example of this principle can be found in the analysis of Chopin's G-Major Prelude in chapter 1 of Almén (2008); here, although there are motivic elements that are oppositional in terms of certain parametric features, particularly directionality, an informal explanation of the character of the narrative trajectory might be more aptly characterized as a gentle dialogue, a dance of possibilities, or a negotiated synthesis. The prelude thus enacts a transvaluation from an initial hierarchy of relatively distinct motivic elements in graceful dialogue with one in which those elements become relatively integrated in response to that dialogue. As we will observe below, narratives can place hierarchies in crisis even if the aesthetic character of that narrative might better be understood in terms of gentle interplay, an animated conversation, a ritualistic process, a display of wit, or even the emergence of some latent potential.

It is also important to note that in the semiotic opposition "order/transgression," the term *order* is employed in the sense of "hierarchy" or "ordering of values," *not* that of "stability" or "lacking chaotic features." Given that this term is typically applied first to the initial hierarchical configuration of a piece, it would be inappropriate and inaccurate to limit such configurations to those that are orderly or stable. Indeed, there are many pieces in which the initial "order" (hierarchy) is dysphoric, unstable, or problematic, motivating a transgression that addresses these instabilities or problems. In particular, most comic and ironic narrative archetypes would be untenable if the initial order was defined in terms of stability. Likewise, transgression need not be chaotic, destructive, or unstable – indeed, it is as likely to be configured as integrative or stable – but instead should be read as transgressive of some aspect of the work's initial configuration of values.

Returning to our discussion of twentieth-century music, a particularly interesting range of narrative investigation is found in the broad middle of a spectrum of signification. This middle region is bounded at one extreme by those pieces that are strongly actorial and contain clear agential profiles; such pieces could be approached using any number of traditional methods commonly applied to tonal music. Its other boundary is formed by those pieces that are explicitly anti-teleological and anti-narrative; such pieces contain narrative potential only to the degree that the listener imposes such an interpretation. Within the boundaries thus established, a wide variety of narrative strategies are possible.

Consider three brief examples, chosen both for their variety of pitch languages and signifying mechanisms and for a certain similarity of profile: all three pieces make use of a discursive strategy of *expansion*, that is, a gradual approach to a point or points of climax/resolution.[13]

1. *Krzysztof Penderecki*, Als Jakob erwachte *(1974) for orchestra and twelve ocarinas, also called* The Awakening of Jacob (Przebudzenie Jakuba) *or* Jacob's Dream

Als Jakob erwachte is a musical representation of the events related in Genesis 28:10–22. This passage relates a dream experienced by Jacob during a journey from Beersheba to Haran of a ladder reaching to heaven with angels "ascending and descending on it." Jacob heard the Lord speaking to him, renewing the covenant with him that had been made with his grandfather Abraham, promising to bless his future generations. The eponymous text appears in verse 16: "And Jacob awaked out of his sleep, and he said, 'Surely the Lord is in this place; and I knew it not.'" In answer to the dream, Jacob sanctified the spot to the Lord, placing a stone there and anointing it with oil.

The work was composed at a sort of aesthetic turning point in Penderecki's career, where the textural and timbral innovations – clusters, quarter-tone explorations, *glissandi*, wedges, the contrast of different orchestral groups, and the like – were often harnessed for narrative ends. A convincing narrative interpretation therefore emerges not from tonal features, which are largely eschewed, but from a combination of biblical allusion, text painting, basic conventional associations, and gestural trajectories of expansion, climax, and decline. The biblical reference supplies a narrative frame – a comic (in Frye's sense of the term) archetype concerned with the acquisition of knowledge through revelation: Jacob is visited by the divine and vouchsafed a vision of future glory. The piece thus combines a progressive non-tonal pitch language with a neo-Romantic gestural vocabulary and a clear significatory signpost established by the program. The absence of tonal principles is in no way an obstacle to interpretation.

Three large-scale dramatic phases can be discerned, apparently corresponding to aspects of the biblical tale. First there is a series of static clusters featuring contrasting instrumental groups that gradually increase in intensity and volume, a passage one might interpret as representing slumber or the dream-awareness of the presence of the divine. Second, *glissandi* and wedges begin to supplant the static clusters as the gestural expansion continues. This passage is clearly an example of text painting: the registral play evokes the ascent and descent of the ladder by the angels. Finally, the *glissandi* climax on a single pitch, after which the expansion gives way to a pulling back of intensity and volume, and the return of the opening clusters and isolated melodic intervals. This convergence on a single pitch has many possible gestural connotations that fit the narrative: one might suggest an epiphanic moment of waking awareness, or the enactment of the prophecy.

2. Olivier Messiaen, "La Résurrection du Christ," *from* Livre du Saint Sacrement (1984)

This tenth movement of Messiaen's last large-scale organ composition shares with the Penderecki example a reliance on an organizing textual reference, in this case the Resurrection, the central narrative moment of the Christian faith – indeed, the archetypal Divine Comedy. This movement also shares with the previous example a sense of expansion toward a climax. Unlike *Als Jakob erwachte*, however, there are no obvious examples of text painting, and the pitch language is at least partly informed by tonal principles, in combination with Messiaen's predilection for symmetrical modes and transpositions. In keeping with the trajectory of the Resurrection story, there is no decline following the expansion, which carries through to the end of the movement and the apotheosis point of narrative resolution.

The narrative trajectory of "La Résurrection" features four large gestural isotopies. The summary that follows sets aside detailed discussion of Messiaen's unique harmonic language to focus on the tonal analogues and the gestural tendencies of each passage.

1. Mm. 1–15: a series of three ascending progressions (mm. 1–3, 4–7, and 8–12) that combine local "dominant–tonic"-like pairings with a symmetrical ascending major-third sequence, reaching temporary plateaus that are more harmonically dense and static in their effect. The "dominant" and "tonic" harmonies, of course, are just analogues of these tonal phenomena, retaining the "root" motion and some other characteristic tones. A subsequent ascending progression breaks the pattern, removing the dominant–tonic effect but preserving the symmetrical ascent by major thirds, arriving on a sort of "arrival $^6_5$" F♯-major added-sixth triad – a typical strategy of Messiaen's for marking arrival points through the sudden appearance of an unusually unambiguous harmony. This arrival point is only partly confirmed, though, by a short descent to another added-sixth sonority that shares a common source in a single octatonic scale (Messiaen's Mode 2) but that loses the centric "tonic" pitch of F♯.

2. Mm. 17–20: a four-chord gesture is again cycled through an ascending sequential progression, but this time the sequential interval is a minor third, and the sequence breaks off before the fourth iteration, giving way to triadic harmonies initiated by the F♯-major "goal," which again is not allowed to conclude the passage.

3. Mm. 21–24: a further ascending passage, this time more gradual and increasing in textural density to arrive at . . .

4. Mm. 25–33: an extended analogue of a dominant pedal (C♯) that suddenly breaks free of its convolutions into a radiant F♯-major triad in root position – the first and only chord of its type in the piece – in the final measure.

In this movement, Messiaen uses familiar gestural and tonal implications – dominant–tonic motion, sequence, registral ascent, increase in textural density, and dominant pedal – to suggest the struggle to "overcome Death and the grave." In combination with Messiaen's relatively more complex harmonic language, the effect is of a victory hard-won, requiring multiple attempts and points of resistance or lack of progression. Again, it is the textual link that suggests the narrative trajectory, but tonal and gestural procedures contribute to the details of its unfolding.

3. Arvo Pärt, Spiegel im Spiegel (1978) for violin or cello and piano

In the previous two examples, the teleological quality of the musical material would be sufficient to suggest a narrative interpretation even in the absence of textual references to anchor those interpretations. At the same time, the role of tonal features in these examples is either attenuated (Messiaen) or nearly absent (Penderecki). With *Spiegel im Spiegel*, however, we find a piece with very strong tonal and pandiatonic features (F-major tonal center, hints of tonic/dominant/predominant functions, arpeggiations, major-mode scalar patterns, melodic cadential patterns) and an absence of narrative textual cues (the title, *Mirrors in Mirrors*, is more spatial than temporal in character). In none of these three examples is the textual reference pre-determinative of the work's narrative potential; rather, they might be described as suggestive, since in each case the narrative qualities of the music reinforce the presence or absence of such reference.

Spiegel im Spiegel unfolds according to a strict, additive process of growth and expansion. This process can be found in both the solo (violin or cello) and piano parts, but it is most clearly visible in the solo part. The first two solo phrases contain two-note pairs – first G–A, then B♭–A – that serve to initiate two patterns. First, each subsequent pair of phrases adds an additional pitch to the sequence that is a step away from the previous pitch while remaining part of the A-Phrygian scale collection (interpreted harmonically within the context of F major). Second, over the course of four phrases, the phrases alternate between (1) ascending toward the last pitch from below by step, (2) descending toward the last pitch from above by step, (3) descending away from the last pitch by step, and (4) ascending away from the last pitch by step. The process concludes when the phrase pairs each complete an octave before proceeding to the immutable cadence pitch A.

There is teleology of a sort in *Spiegel im Spiegel*: tensions arise and are resolved, goals are set up and reached. What is problematic about the teleological quality of this piece is the sense that the tensions, relaxations, strivings, and goals are ritualistically predetermined rather than suggestive of a human agency that is free to act in the moment. Put another way, the teleology of *Spiegel im Spiegel* seems to deny choice and therefore the possibility of narrative. If the end result is preordained by the process set up from the start, then there is no development that is responsive to events, no significant change, no *transvaluation*. Despite the illusion of motion and change, the effect is of a global topic – a kaleidoscope image or a mystical ritual – rather than of a narrative trajectory.

This piece might best be described as a *proto-narrative*. In such a circumstance, there is at least the potential that the pattern might be broken and a narrative trajectory achieved. If, for example, the final two phrases had been moved to the minor mode, we might speak of a significant change in the markedness and rank relations of the piece sufficient to mark it as narrative. In the absence of such change, we are left only with a romance narrative bereft of a transgressive transvaluation (the most likely interpretation in this instance) or an ironic narrative lacking any coherence.[14] It is not the lack of overt "conflict" that renders this narrative problematic – such qualities are surface phenomena – but rather the absence or near absence of transvaluation. This is not to say that a narrative mode of listening should be dispensed with in approaching this piece. On the contrary, one's interpretive reflection about this piece would constantly keep such a possibility in focus, leading to a productive tension between, on the one hand, a potential transvaluation constantly on the cusp of materializing and, on the other, the predetermined plan that undermines this potential. With reference to Mazo's cultural-historical insights (part 2, section V above), we note the cultural work performed by Pärt's resistance of narrativity, given that he worked for much of his career in a Soviet state where the political rhetoric was dominated by what we might call "narratives of social transvaluation." The intriguing possibility of a meta-narrative level, in which the potential for narrative itself undergoes transvaluation, may help illuminate other post-1900 compositional styles.

PART 4. CONCLUSION

The musical works discussed above have displayed the presence or absence of tonal features, the presence or absence of textual reference, and differences in teleological character, each of which may be considered as variables affecting the inference of a narrative trajectory. Comparisons are useful in establishing the role that each variable may play in enabling and supporting (or, conversely, in preventing or working against) narrative interpretations. The categories considered in part 2 of this chapter may serve as a further source for such variables. Comparisons might be made between one composer and another, between early and late works of the same composer, or between works in the same genre by different composers. Finally, as we have emphasized through-out this essay, the narrative impulse is such a potent human cognitive force for making sense of the world that it is inevitable listeners will attempt to engage narratively with post-1900 works, even when those works may appear to frustrate the effort. However, other means of perceiving coherence are also available as cognitive strategies. As Christopher Butler summarizes in refer-ring to the disruptions of formal continuity in Debussy's *Jeux* and Stravinsky's *Symphonies of Wind Instruments*: "Robbed of an internal narrative logic, the audience has to look for something else which is typical of modernism – an emotional coherence which can rationalize and put together apparently ran-dom associative fragments. And this move from causal narrative and logical argument to psychological association is one of the central developments of the period, supported by a radical, broadly Freudian reassessment of the na-ture of the person" (2004: 78–79). Nonetheless, as we have shown, narrative conceptions of music can be remarkably flexible and durable. Thus, even when narrativity appears most attenuated in post-1900 musical works, it offers a lens through which we can both assess and appreciate a composer's intentional or unintentional expressive effects, through various manipulations of listener ex-pectations with respect to a given sequence of events, and ultimately through the transvaluations that guarantee narrative coherence.

NOTES

1. For more on types of agency, see Hatten (2004, 2010).

2. See Drott (2001) for a discussion of agency in relation to the music of Ligeti.

3. There are other categories in which one might situate the lyric. One such category is the relationship between the singer or speaker and the listener, allowing for distinctions to be made between lyric, narrative, and dramatic works. Literary narratives feature a narration in which the listener is directly addressed. Dramas (and novels) feature a distinct separation between the singer/speaker and the listener, as though the action would proceed whether the listener was there or not. The lyric, by contrast, occupies a medial position between these extremes: the singer/speaker, though not speaking directly to the listener, speaks as though to be "overheard": an imagined audience is therefore presupposed.

4. For more on the issues of temporality in music, see the work of Lewis Rowell. Of special interest for twentieth-century musical trends is his list of recommended areas of study, which include "the digitizing of the world, which seems to have translated into a growing preference for discontinuity in music and the other arts," and "a return to a concept of time that can best be described as 'epic,' manifested in such things as flexible scripts, long performance durations, and a change in the nature of artistic apprehension – from a process of continuous sustained attention to a mode of attention in which listeners 'tune in' and 'tune out' periodically" (1996: 92).

5. The potential for temporal troping presented by music's cueing of "aspect," which often entails juxtapositions of events out of a presumed temporal "plot" sequence, is examined in Hatten (2006).

A twentieth-century work discussed there is Berg's Piano Sonata, op. 1, which begins with a phrase that has too final a tragic close, and thus, like a tragic Scottish ballad, "the dreadful outcome is already stated at the beginning and our interpretation of subsequent events is haunted by that knowledge" (66).

6. Varèse, "My Titles," unpublished notes, quoted in Mattis (1992: 192), cited in Broyles (2004: 304).

7. This work is also interesting insofar as it avoids the employment of material undergoing clear and unambiguous thematic return. With this important narrative device attenuated, the resources available to articulate changes in the discourse are similarly reduced.

8. Genette (1980) examines this relationship with respect to literary examples. An effective musical application can be found in Micznik (2001).

9. An analogous literary example is *Time's Arrow* (1991) by Martin Amis. Here the process is taken to an even greater extreme, since the protagonist himself experiences time passing in reverse.

10. This is further complicated by the fact that the tableaux are more precisely linked by thematic connection rather than historical sequence, even though it is possible to reconstruct a timeline of events from Gandhi's life stretching from 1893 to 1914. Organization by theme rather than event has the potential to deform a work's narrative, substituting a predominantly spatial orientation for a predominantly temporal one.

11. For more on the theme of masks in Stravinsky, see Carr (2002).

12. Confusing the latter for the former would lead to a "Spy vs. Spy" approach to narrative, where every opposition must be located in concrete entities. As

the Haydn analysis from Almén suggests, transvaluation need not be situated in this way: here the initial hierarchy invokes a particular understanding of formal procedures, which the work strategically undermines (2008: 169–74).

13. For more on discursive strategies, see Almén (2008: 187–221, 229).

14. Tragic and comic narratives are change-of-state narratives, since both require a definitive positive or negative shift of rank as the piece proceeds. By contrast, romantic and ironic narratives may, as it were, end up where they began with respect to the piece's internal hierarchical values.

WORKS CITED

Adamenko, Victoria. 2007. *Neo-mythologism in Music: From Scriabin and Schoenberg to Schnittke and Crumb.* Hillsdale: Pendragon Press.

Agawu, V. Kofi. 1991. *Playing with Signs: A Semiotic Interpretation of Classic Music.* Princeton: Princeton University Press.

Almén, Byron. 2008. *A Theory of Musical Narrative.* Bloomington: Indiana University Press.

Amis, Martin. 1991. *Time's Arrow, or The Nature of the Offense.* London: Jonathan Cape.

Barthes, Roland. 1977a. "The Grain of the Voice." In *Image, Music, Text,* translated by Stephen Heath, 179–89. London: Fontana.

———. 1977b. "The Third Meaning: Research Notes on Some Eisenstein Stills." In *Image, Music, Text,* translated by Stephen Heath, 52–68. London: Fontana.

Broyles, Michael. 2004. *Mavericks and Other Traditions in American Music.* New Haven: Yale University Press.

Butler, Christopher. 2004. "Innovation and the Avant-Garde, 1900–20." In *The Cambridge History of Twentieth-Century Music,* edited by Nicholas Cook and Anthony Pople, 69–89. Cambridge: Cambridge University Press.

Carr, Maureen A. 2002. *Multiple Masks: Neoclassicism in Stravinsky's Works on Greek Subjects.* Lincoln: University of Nebraska Press.

Chatman, Seymour. 1980. *Story and Discourse: Narrative Structure in Fiction and Film.* Ithaca: Cornell University Press.

Cizmic, Maria. 2008. "Transcending the Icon: Spirituality and Postmodernism in Arvo Pärt's *Tabula Rasa* and *Spiegel im Spiegel.*" *Twentieth-Century Music* 5(1): 45–78.

Cook, Nicholas. 2006. "Uncanny Moments: Juxtaposition and the Collage Principle in Music." In *Approaches to Meaning in Music,* edited by Byron Almén and Edward Pearsall, 107–34. Bloomington: Indiana University Press.

Drott, Eric. 2001. "Agency and Impersonality in the Music of György Ligeti." PhD diss., Yale University.

Feldman, Morton. 2000. "The Future of Local Music." In *Give My Regards to Eighth Street: Collected Writings of Morton Feldman,* edited by B. H. Freidman, 157–95. Cambridge: Exact Change. First published in 1984.

Genette, Gerard. 1980. *Narrative Discourse: An Essay in Method.* Translated by Jane E. Lewin. Ithaca: Cornell University Press.

Hatten, Robert S. 2004. *Interpreting Musical Gestures, Topics, and Tropes: Mozart, Beethoven, Schubert.* Bloomington: Indiana University Press.

———. 2006. "The Troping of Temporality in Music." In *Approaches to*

Meaning in Music, edited by Byron Almén and Edward Pearsall, 62–75. Bloomington: Indiana University Press.

———. 2010. "Musical Agency as Implied by Gesture and Emotion: Its Consequences for Listeners' Experiencing of Musical Emotion." In *Semiotics 2009: Proceedings of the Annual Meeting of the Semiotic Society of America*, edited by Karen Haworth and Leonard Sbrocchi, 162–69. New York: Legas Publishing.

Hepokoski, James, and Warren Darcy. 2006. *Elements of Sonata Theory: Norms, Types, and Deformations in the Late-Eighteenth-Century Sonata*. Oxford: Oxford University Press.

Kivy, Peter. 1980. *The Corded Shell*. Princeton: Princeton University Press.

Kramer, Jonathan D. 1988. *The Time of Music: New Meanings, New Temporalities, New Listening Strategies*. New York: Schirmer Books.

Liszka, James Jakób. 1989. *The Semiotic of Myth: A Critical Study of the Symbol*. Bloomington: Indiana University Press.

Mattis, Olivia. 1992. "Edgard Varèse and the Visual Arts." PhD diss., Stanford University.

Mazo, Margarita. 1996. "The Present and the Unpredictable Past: Music and Musical Life of St. Petersburg and Moscow since the 1960s." *International Journal of Musicology* 5: 371–400.

McCreless, Patrick. 2006. "Anatomy of a Gesture: From Davidovsky to Chopin and Back." In *Approaches to Meaning in Music*, edited by Byron Almén and Edward Pearsall, 11–40. Bloomington: Indiana University Press.

Mertens, Wim. 1983. *American Minimal Music*. Translated by J. Hautekiet. New York: Alexander Broude.

Micznik, Vera. 2001. "Music and Narrative Revisited: Degrees of Narrative in Beethoven and Mahler." *Journal of the Royal Musicological Association* 12(2): 193–249.

Nyman, Michael. 1999. *Experimental Music: Cage and Beyond*. Cambridge: Cambridge University Press. First published in 1974.

Pearsall, Edward. 2006. "Anti-teleological Art: Articulating Meaning through Silence." In *Approaches to Meaning in Music*, edited by Byron Almén and Edward Pearsall, 41–61. Bloomington: Indiana University Press.

Pople, Anthony. 1998. *Messiaen: Quatuor pour la fin du temps*. Cambridge: Cambridge University Press.

Reichardt, Sarah. 2008. *Composing the Modern Subject: Four String Quartets by Dmitri Shostakovich*. Aldershot: Ashgate.

Ricoeur, Paul. 1984. *Time and Narrative*, vol. 1. Translated by Kay McLaughlin and D. Pellauer. Chicago: University of Chicago Press.

Rowell, Lewis. 1996. "The Study of Time in Music: A Quarter-Century Perspective." *Indiana Theory Review* 17(2): 63–92.

Stockhausen, Karlheinz. 1963. "Moment-form: New Relations between Durations of Performance and Work and Moment." In *Texte zur elektronischen und instrumentalen Musik* 1, 189–210. Cologne: DuMont.

Tarasti, Eero. 1994. *A Theory of Musical Semiotics*. Bloomington: Indiana University Press.

4

Optional Extra? Contextualizing Narrative in the Critical Interpretation of Post-Tonal Composition

Arnold Whittall

The inner effect of music in all its greatness is undoubted, but cannot be resolved into thoughts. This is the mystery which undeniably lies in music.

FRIEDRICH SCHLEIERMACHER, *VORLESUNGEN ÜBER DIE ÄSTHETIK*, AS TRANSLATED IN ANDREW BOWIE, *MUSIC, PHILOSOPHY AND MODERNITY*

The ambivalent experience that one can both understand music in affective and other terms, and not be able to say in words exactly what it is that one understands, can be as much a source of pleasure as frustration, because there is always more to say and do in relation to music.

ANDREW BOWIE, *MUSIC, PHILOSOPHY AND MODERNITY*

CONTENT, CONTENTMENT, DISCONTENT

Fred Maus was surely right to conclude that "the exploration of instrumental music as narrative remains a tantalizing, confusing, problematic area of inquiry" (2001: 642). As Roger W. H. Savage has recently argued, "despite its obvious appeal, the temptation to ascribe a narrative content to linear progressions of musical events is doubly misleading... circumscribing music's exemplary possibilities through privileging narrative's anchorages in the field of our everyday actions" (2010: 105–106). Even musicologists who might be tempted to apply Maus's adjectives to all aspects of their discipline as they search endlessly and inadequately for the right words could eventually concede that introducing analogies with any other medium of expression places further layers of mystery between the sounding materials they start with and the verbal interpretations they end up with. Exploring the differences between instrumental music and verbal narratives might be seen as useful in helping to determine what a sonata or a symphony is, as opposed to a sonnet, a novel, or a stage play. But is the illumination more in the divergence than the intersection?

Just as the attempt to drive a wedge between two distinct and allegedly unrelated kinds of music – like tonal and atonal – can come to seem less convincing than a whole range of alternative designations – post-tonal, pantonal – that depend for their theoretical foundations and analytical validity on demonstrations of how some aspects of the old survive and thrive within the new, so descriptive categories from outside music refuse to be suppressed when music itself is under the spotlight. Not only do many instrumental compositions have descriptive or poetic titles that suggest some kind of parallel text to the musical one, but even compositions named after genres that have no equivalents in non-musical arts – sonata, toccata, variations – tend to have verbal instructions about expression and dynamic shading that can be interpreted in terms of degrees of cause and effect: because this passage is loud and violent, this next one will be softer and less aggressive. This hints at music as "patterned activity" (Maus 2001: 641). If, as theorists of literature have taught, to tell a story is to engage in such activity, then a non-texted musical composition might be shown to offer successions of topics or sound-pictures that activate their materials gesturally and expressively.

Most scholars specializing in post-tonal music, and mindful of the reservations of Maus and others, have been reluctant to move beyond the kind of exercise undertaken by Matthew McDonald (2004), whose exploration of "elements of narrative" in Charles Ives's *The Unanswered Question* requires awareness not only of Ives's own thinking as far as his very un-abstract title is concerned but also of Emerson's poem "The Sphinx." It is a long way from thinking of music-word relations in such work-specific contexts to a comprehensive embrace of narrative archetypes after the categories recently propounded by Byron Almén (2008) – a bold attempt to define differences between narrative and non-narrative music as well as to argue for a comprehensive convergence between four basic archetypes of literary narrative (comic, ironic, romantic, tragic) and various musical works.[1]

To consider the differences between such an initiative and other accounts of music that imply a blend of formal and expressive content (whether by way of rhetorical figures and topics or even broader historical-aesthetic categories like classical or modernist) is to be struck by the challenges that arise when such concepts are considered to involve anything more than the broadest of descriptive connotations from the tonal composer, as with Brahms's *Tragic Overture* or Sibelius's *Romance* for strings. It is one thing to claim that categories like comic and tragic can be as broadly relevant to post-tonal music (i.e., much of the more progressive music composed since 1900) as to tonal music: the assignment of these to specific narrative archetypes makes such transference a much more complex affair. It is therefore not surprising that historians and theorists of narrative have not, in general, taken naturally to the possibility that a musical work might (also) be relevant to their concerns.

One introduction to the subject puts it like this: "It is hard to look at the novel as if it were a kind of music, orchestrated simply for our enjoyment. It is in fact arguable that no narrative can achieve such a 'purely aesthetic' status – that all narratives, however playful, carry ideas and judgements with them" (Porter Abbott 2002: 62). One philosophical writer on music, Jerrold Levinson, would seem to concur, arguing forcefully that "the degree of analogy between literature or film on the one hand and music on the other is easily overstated. If one absorbedly tracks the evolution of a piece of music, if one registers its expressiveness throughout, if one intuitively senses what is happening and is about to happen at every point, then one basically understands the piece of music" (1997: 168). Yet even Levinson is soon conceding that "there is some appropriateness to viewing at least some nonrepresentational music as in a loose sense narrative," provided we accept that "a piece of music . . . is an irreducibly perceptual affair. What this means is that no conceptual condensation of its core-content is really possible, and no analytic distillation of its concrete form is central to its appreciation" (171). Levinson might therefore find himself going along with this recent musicological argument: "In the same way that the narration of a novel will range from the even and regular to the swift and elliptical, the varied pace of tonal change gains a degree of authority through the control it exerts on our sense of musical flow" (Butt 2010: 222). Importantly for the present subject, however, John Butt's confinement of that narrative analogy to unambiguously tonal music (Bach's *Passion* settings) indicates that it might not be easy to interpret post-tonal music in the same way – even if one subscribes to Butt's Ricoeur-based argument that "taking the novelistic analogy as a starting point, it is clear that most forms of music relate to narrative in the broadest way (that is, to a human sense of organization in time, rather than necessarily to the specific implications of a storyline) and to some sort of voice" (24).

Attempts to consider musical compositions in terms of narrative forms and processes will give short shrift to H. Porter Abbott's suggestion that musical works inherently have "a 'purely aesthetic' status," to the extent that "ideas" – and even "judgements" – are entirely absent from them. After all, Porter Abbott's argument that "most narratives of any complexity can be read as efforts to negotiate opposing psychological and cultural claims" (2002: 175) is just the kind of prescriptive generalization that musicologists devoted to the principle of a necessarily contextual hermeneutics would be likely to apply to their own subject matter. As Butt suggests, "it is difficult to avoid extra-musical readings of any music whatsoever since even a 'purely musical' reading will evoke ideals – such as unity, integrity or cohesion – which are among the moral or political values of a wider culture" (2010: 24). However, in a post-tonal context it may be less a matter of such "ideals" and have more to do with social and political states – fragmentation, stratification, the struggle to balance opposing tendencies while resisting chaos – which any "wider culture" ignores at its peril.

When the kind of compositions introduced below are considered, this distinction between tonal and post-tonal, classical and modernist, turns out to have fundamental implications for the application of theories of narrative. Even Almén's intricate three-stage model for an analysis culminating in the application of narrative archetypes risks implying that a decisive outcome of the essential contest between ordered and disorderly elements – a victory or a defeat – is required. This is more likely to be the case with common-practice, tonal compositions than with post-tonal, modernist ones – although, as the following narrative suggests, ideas about victory and defeat might continue to resonate relevantly even when decisive endings and resolutions are no longer present.

ARGUMENT BY ANALYSIS: THE CASE OF SCHOENBERG

Schoenberg's brief piano piece op. 19, no. 4 (1911), like the other five pieces in the collection from which it comes, is – as a miniature – hardly typical of its composer. But addressing the musical nature of its materials suggests to many commentators that it is fully representative of Schoenberg's post-tonal language, demonstrating that emancipation of the dissonance that led the composer away from diatonicism into extended tonality and on to suspended tonality, pantonality, and even – depending on your terminology – to atonality.[2] The preference for interpreting the piece's materials without reference to theoretical principles relating directly to the functions and materials of tonality reached its apogee in a pair of studies published in 2008, one offering "a set-theoretic perspective" and the other the use of "K-nets towards a transformational analysis" (see Forte 2008; Hascher 2008). Neither of these refers to the kind of alternative view of op. 19 that seeks to view transformation wholly in terms of tonal chords and key relations (see, in particular, Hicken 1984).

All these writers might have things to say about patterned activity as gestural choreography in another context, and especially if the composer had given the collection a title like *Dances and Laments* rather than Six Little Piano Pieces. But the cited texts proceed in the evident belief that such expressive factors do not affect the essential nature of the interpretive discourse they are providing. Their concern with Schoenberg's musical language does not require them to consider the possibility that what the materials and methods signify stylistically, as expression, might reflect what they signify technically, as structure. As Xavier Hascher summarizes the enterprise, "what is looked for in all circumstances, are reproducible models, forms of regularity and coherence. When, in addition, elegance comes into the picture, it is but a lucky encounter" (2008: 95). This suggests, appropriately, that while an analysis can acquire an aesthetic aura (and a classicizing or synthesizing one at that), it is not essential that it does so.

Byron Almén's use of op. 19, no. 4 to exemplify the "reproducible model" of the "ironic" narrative archetype shows a very different perspective (2008: 183–86). From the start, his perceptions are inherently comparative, and his observations are couched in such a way as to indicate his awareness of what – at the risk of a shorthand cliché – I will term the modernist multivalence of the music, which challenges forms of regularity and coherence rather than classically enforcing them. Of op. 19 as a whole Almén says that one of its "compelling features" is "the way in which the defamiliarization of pitch usage is reinforced by unusual gestures and narrative strategies," and his observation that "it would be overstating the case to say that gestures and associations borrowed from tonality do not appear in these pieces" leads to the central claim – suggestive of modernism, in my terms – that op. 19, no. 4 "both invokes and refuses to deliver on the implications of traditional gestures and topics" (184). Thus far the discourse remains within regions familiar from rhetorical analysis, but Almén then applies the definitive conceptual spin, as dictated by his categories, to his interpretation: "The result is an ironic narrative in which the initial hierarchy is almost overwhelmed by transgressive elements from the very beginning" (184). And not simply "ironic": the assigned category is that of "extreme tragic irony" in which "the initial hierarchy . . . is so weak as to be completely unable to withstand dissolution and breakdown" (186).

As Almén's analysis proceeds, it becomes clear that the effect of choosing one option from the available class of narrative archetypes is to heighten the autobiographical character of an individual hearing. The ascription of "extreme tragic irony" is therefore not a guarantee of approbation, and "transgression" appears to migrate from its immediate connotations of subverting hallowed yet exhausted structural models and expressive conventions (not by definition a bad thing?) to a judgment that the composer has failed to replace these features with viable alternatives. Almén proceeds to read a well-nigh tragic failure (not merely an ironic refusal) to counter the negative in the piece. Things are "out of focus and exaggerated," and the listener (i.e., Almén) feels that "the work has ended too soon" and that "the unfamiliarity of the tonal language . . . forms part of a larger narrative strategy of modern alienation and psychic disintegration. Schoenberg's continual shifting of the topical ground suggests an individual without direction or center or personality. The various *topoi* function like evanescent masks, tried on for effect, but discarded in self-loathing and disgust, and the atonal language merely serves to increase the sense of dislocation" (2008: 186).

Even if one disagrees with this critical judgment, as I do, that need not entail a rejection of narrative analysis by archetype as such. At the same time, however, the difficulties of establishing a definitive narratological category, for even the shortest post-tonal work, that all possible listeners could be expected sooner or later to endorse shows how distant from the musical materials categorized according to explicit theoretical principles that categorization will be. Almén's negative response to the Schoenberg seems to me like that of a listener trying to reconstruct a first hearing of this piece when it was new by someone knowing something of Schoenberg's recent personal life (the suicide of his wife's lover, the painter Richard Gerstl) and predisposed to map this fact onto the music: all is "alienation and . . . disintegration," with any forces that might make for cohesion – and even enjoyment – suppressed. Since I have consistently heard this music – marked *rasch aber leicht* (quickly but lightly) – as exuberantly witty, ebulliently engaged in a playful, boisterous spirit with its post-tonal discourse of dialogue between forcefulness and delicacy, and perhaps even consciously aimed to show that expressionism need not be all gloom and doom, this might bring it into the orbit of the comic narrative archetype, defined by Almén as "the successful overthrowing of the old order" and requiring that "a problematic initial hierarchy be transvalued in favor of transgressive elements" (2008: 74). But even that rather misses the point of the music's sharply pointed ambivalence: the ways its modernist tendency to suspend tonality requires the "old order" to remain in view not as something "problematic" but as a still relevant counter-pole. The outcome reinforces the ambivalence rather than resolving it.

WEBERN'S SENSE OF STRUCTURE

The possibility that op. 19, no. 4 (and op. 19 as a whole) differs from a common-practice tonal structure in not offering a decisive result to the playing out of the music's inherent tensions may lead those who consider their listening in retrospect to contemplate an interacting polyphony of continua: comic/tragic, integrative/disintegrative, or any number of alternatives. It leads me to a brief reconsideration of some of my own previous discussions of post-tonal compositions (and a consideration of one further piece). In writing about Webern's Variations for Orchestra, op. 30 (1940) under the title "Music-Discourse-Dialogue," I used Robert Hatten's definition of "discourse" (a "loose term describing the strategic or thematic/topical flow of ideas in a musical work") and Mikhail Bakhtin's definition of "dialogue" ("a process in which different modes of expression at once presuppose, question, and interpret each other") as starting points for a study of "possible parallels between verbal texts (with associated concepts acknowledged by the composer) and a musical work" (Whittall 1996: 268–69). Modes of speech that can also be modes of writing help bring the semantic complexity of the exercise into focus, with the flow of ideas between words and music being a sufficient connective to justify discussing the latter in terms of the former, even without a more formalized or explicit concept of musical narrative.

My concern to characterize Webern's Variations for Orchestra as a discourse involving dialogues of a different character, which do not so much tell a story about specific events in specific locations as evolve through gestural choreography over time, was prompted by Webern's own discussion of Goethe's concept of the metamorphosis of a "prime phenomenon" and the musical characterization of those metamorphoses in terms of motion within various continua – "lyric and dramatic, reflective and assertive, vulnerable and confident" (Whittall 1996: 272). The possibility of moving from such relatively general and abstract notions to more specific categories or topics led to the following observations:

> Given Webern's Goethean concern to associate the natural with the spiritual, it might seem attractive to propose [topical] categories that also serve to create a Beethovenian connection. After all, as Robert Hatten has observed, "in the works of Beethoven ... the pastoral involves the poetic conceit of feelings inspired by Nature ...": and Hatten's analysis of Beethoven's Sonata Op. 101/1 – "the mixing of tragic elements endows the pastoral with greater seriousness and the elevation of style in turn supports the interpretation of the pastoral as a poetic conceit for a spiritual state of innocence (or serenity) subject to the disturbances of tragic experience (or remembrance)" [(Hatten 1994: 92–96)] – might seem to offer a possible model for the expressive world of Webern's Op. 30. Yet, given the difficulty of translating Hatten's concretely defined topics of pastoral and tragic into Webern's twentieth-century post-tonal context, the enterprise must inevitably appear problematic. (297)

Nevertheless, my conclusion was that "op. 30 is a special work because we can sense, more clearly than elsewhere in Webern, the elements of a spiritual conflict between vulnerability (seeking serenity) and assertiveness (a tendency to violence) that outlines a profound dramatic tragedy. That is not to say that Webern was not, like Goethe, 'essentially optimistic,' but it is to suggest that the 'greater seriousness' which the tragic perspective creates for pastoral, as 'the pantheistic sense of God in nature,' confirms Webern's place in the great tradition stemming from Beethoven" (297).

Characterizing Webern's op. 30 as "a profound dramatic tragedy" suggests the prospect of alignment with the Almén categories. However, as Almén makes clear, there is a profound difference between identifying the presence of tragic topoi in music and showing that they "are ancillary to the structural core of the tragic narrative, the defeat of a transgression by an order-imposing hierarchy" (2008: 140). The singular specifics of this definition (whose relevance to Schubert's last piano sonata is debated in detail by Almén) are bound to clash with the core qualities of post-tonal modernism, whose progressions are so much less monolithic and whose conclusions are so much less decisive and more resistant to the forces of an "order-imposing hierarchy" (even that of the twelve-tone method) than this formula suggests.

For Webern the twelve-tone method offered a background of comprehensiveness and coherence – what follows the first six notes is "nothing other than this shape over and over again!!" (1967: 44) – which he understood as comparable to tonality (or at least to the monotonal system as formulated by Schoenberg, in which all possible keys occupied regions subordinate to the main key), yet whose generative network of invariants and variants (as shown in a matrix of series forms) is quite distinct from tonality's order-imposing hierarchy. It could never be plausibly claimed that the experience of post-tonal composition exactly mirrored that of tonal composition, and especially so if the latter is heard as the fulfillment of contrapuntal processes as explained by Schenker (i.e., as depending on a particular polarity between upper voices and a bass line and between dissonant and consonant intervals). Even plausible demonstrations of the presence of work-embracing hierarchies in post-tonal works are likely to underline the gulf between those compositions and their tonal equivalents. Any interpretive framework (like that of narrative archetypes) that overrides such polarities can only be a part of the interpretive network relevant to a post-tonal composition.

BOULEZ'S FEELING FOR FORM

The challenges to post-tonal analytical perspectives involving concepts of narrative become particularly intricate when elements of a text are involved that themselves challenge narrativity without completely rejecting it.[3] *Pli selon pli* (1957–62), Pierre Boulez's "portrait of Mallarmé," pictures the poet by way of music that sometimes sets words and sometimes does not. *Pli selon pli* might be said to tell the story of what happens to three of Mallarmé's sonnets when they are set and contextualized by Boulez. By 1962 Boulez had assembled a five-movement structure in which the sonnet settings (called "Improvisations") are framed by two large-scale orchestral movements, "Don" and "Tombeau," including only brief vocal contributions.

Boulez has always been a notably polemical writer, and his apparent contrariness was at its height in 1960, when, in the context of his (still unfinished) third piano sonata, he declared that "my present mode of thought derives from my reflection on literature rather than on music" (1986: 143). If he had Baudelaire's definition of modernism as "the transitory, the fugitive, the contingent, one half of art, of which the other half is the eternal and the immutable" in mind, he was no less excited by the challenge "of finding a musical equivalent, both poetic and formal, to Mallarmé's poetry," and by rising to this challenge to offer what might be termed a narrative of reproach to a cultural situation in which France had "completely lost its importance: there was no progress"

(Jameux 1991: 113).[4] In *Pli selon pli* one movement in particular, "Improvisation III" (which includes a setting of the sonnet "Á la nue accablante tu"), "evolves from a portrait of seductiveness by way of agitation and resistance to a state in which the seductive is masked by solemnity, the florid by the elemental, to match the degree of formal distillation from plenitude to essence" (Whittall 2004: 17).

My reading of "Improvisation III" was prompted by Roger Pearson's analysis of the original poem as a "siren song" that "both destroys everyday language and offers the prospect of poetic beauty." In Pearson's intricate but persuasive interpretation, the poetic text can be read not so much as obliquely telling a story about sirens and sailors, but as raising a series of questions about possible shipwrecks and the role of sirens in causing them. The suggestion that the sonnet embodies "the shipwreck of language" raises yet more possibilities. After all, a siren "is a means of signaling danger by sound, and this poem, by its own unique sign system, is signalling the dangers of univocal reading" (Pearson 1996: 226–27). My detailed narrative of how "Improvisation III" unfolds stemmed from these images (depicting sirens and being siren-like) and considered the possibility of the music moving ceaselessly and equivocally between the twin subjects, in terms of Boulez's declared aim of making "the sonnet *become* the music."[5] As with Webern's op. 30, a fundamental continuum between the extremes of aggressive assertion (the sirens' predatory seductiveness) and vulnerability (the sailors' need to resist) can be plotted, provided it is accepted that Boulez seems less concerned with an outcome, that is, the victory (or survival) of the sailors or the defeat of the sirens. The music is more focused on painting the persistent and fluctuating tension between sailors and sirens than on any resolution of that tension. The engagement with a world of things and substances that this suggests has parallels with Webern's interest in Goethe's ideas about the ways in which natural elements or objects – like plants – change as they wax and wane in time and space. This is the world in which post-tonal modernism itself waxes and wanes, hinting that its structures have stories in which human agents might be only of marginal concern – although, without human observation, those stories would pass by unnoticed and uncomprehended.

SUBSTANCE AND MEANING IN DILLON AND BIRTWISTLE

The issues involving the consideration of modernism as narrative and modernism as depiction or portraiture can be pursued in two challenging and impressive post-tonal compositions of recent years. In the case of James Dillon's *The Book of Elements* (1997–2002) for piano solo, one can chart a progression from title to material, searching both for clues to how the music's subject matter is characterized. The composer's own notes in the score explain that the five separate volumes of the "book" are associated with air, water, earth, fire, and the "void," respectively.[6] Rather like Webern and Boulez, Dillon might well have been creatively stimulated by the necessary distance between the "real" (as material) and the musical, and by the possibility of suggesting what happens to each of them as time passes.

A narrative for volume 1 of *The Book of Elements* can be proposed that indicates associations with "air" as the element within which sustained sounds (like bells) resonate: all eleven pieces embody activities that repeat, juxtapose, or superimpose oscillating patterns. Dillon's comment that "within the eleven brief, elliptical works that make up Volume 1 there are a number of symmetries, pairings and ratio crossings which are arranged to maintain unity within an epigrammatic and heterogeneous constellation of works" neatly – provocatively – balances connection against disconnection in classic modernist mode. The comment also suggests that the music is as much about the composer's response to the *idea* of the element as a "portrait in sound" as it is a characterization of the element itself. In one sense, therefore, the narrative trajectory might even be felt to represent the "victory" of substance over emptiness: the "defeat" of the void by meaningful activity. But the focus on such themes and topics creates an atmosphere in which repetition becomes plaintive, building what Dillon terms a "teasing melancholy." As in all authentically modernist art, associations with the tragic are never entirely excluded, even if they cannot invariably, or even frequently, be given the decisive archetypal trajectory favored by the Almén categories. A degree of doubt remains.

The element that features most prominently in the music and thought of Harrison Birtwistle is undoubtedly earth, and not only because of its obvious relevance to a title like *Earth Dances* but because of the degree to which solid objects and places – like Silbury Hill and the street layout of Lucca – serve as points of reference for particular kinds of musical structure and texture.[7] Such entities have a deceptive solidity, their internal juxtapositions and layerings masked but not to be forgotten by the chronicler of the composer's reactions in sound to their mechanics and dynamics. Like the other composers considered here, Birtwistle appears to be less interested in simple progressions from defeat to victory, conformity and transgression, and vice versa: he is more involved with uneasy interactions and the kinds of fluctuations along a continuum between polar opposites that happen when such tensions are projected across a span of time.

A solid object in and about time is the particular inspiration for Birtwistle's *Harrison's Clocks* for piano solo (1998). As a note in the score puts it, "the title of these five musical timepieces refers to the eighteenth-century clockmaker John Harrison whose struggle to develop the first reliable navigational chronometer is related in Dava Sobel's book *Longitude*." Birtwistle had actually composed a work called *Chronometer* in 1971–72, which inspired a striking description by Michael Hall that underlines the way the effect of the music migrates between the mechanical and the human:

> On Birtwistle's behalf, Peter Zinovieff made some hundred recordings of clocks of all descriptions, analysed them by computer and, on the composer's instructions, regenerated the chosen montage onto eight-track tape. Basically there are four types of material. The first consists of ticks laid against each other like strands of counterpoint, and underpinned by the ostinato of Big Ben. But no clockwork mechanism, no tick, is absolutely regular (at least to the perceiver) and when Birtwistle exaggerates the irregularities they become more and more like heartbeats. After a while, the throb of Big Ben turns into that other definition of pulse: the rhythmical contraction and expansion of an artery. The effect is like the throb in the ear heard in bed at night. (1984: 105–106)

Hall proceeds to describe the other musical elements – "textures which seem to derive from cogs and springs . . . the chime of one of the oldest clocks in the country, that of Wells Cathedral," and underlines "the surreal, the dreamlike quality of the piece" (105–106). Again, dreaming is what humans, not machines, do, and the sense of human unease, agitation, and elation when directly experiencing the passing of time and its marking is even more potent in *Harrison's Clocks* than in *Chronometer*. Like Boulez in works as different as the Piano Sonata No. 1 and *sur Incises*, Birtwistle makes much of the elemental contrast between genres one might categorize as recitative and toccata, the explicit rhythmic continuities of the latter offering rich opportunities for creating interactions between the relatively predictable or assertive and the relatively unpredictable or hesitant. The ways in which persistent ostinatos are varied and developed, for instance, can serve the interests of larger-scale pitch and rhythmic processes while challenging the potential for static stabilization that recourse to the genre of toccata could create.

The fifth and last of *Harrison's Clocks* is a fast and furious apotheosis of the dance that brilliantly conveys the anxious exuberance of a mechanism constantly threatening to move farther from system and closer to chaos but in the end doing neither and simply running down. This post-tonal archetype uses an edgily evolving flow of ideas to create a sense of that "teasing melancholy" so fundamental to post-tonal modernism, because what is most marked is usually the least stable. If it were argued that the degree of rhythmic invariance in no. 5 of *Harrison's Clocks* is sufficient to create an order-imposing hierarchy, then perhaps it could also be felt that the variations and the running-down contribute to a sense of transgression defeating, or gaining victory over, that hierarchy. The tension between what is regular and recurrent, in both pitch and rhythm, and what is not is palpable throughout, however, and the archetypal processes by which post-tonal music proceeds to closure make images of decisive victory or defeat seem beside the point, as if one is seeking to impose a definitive conclusion that both aesthetic aura and technical procedure resist. Whether such resistance also allows the perception of degrees of irony, comedy, tragedy, and even romance as the music unfolds is, undoubtedly, a matter of aural and intellectual taste.

The debate ("tantalizing, confusing, problematic") about the usefulness of topoi and/or narrative archetypes of the Almén variety within or alongside any other kind of analytical-critical narrative about a composition can also be continued indefinitely. Even those most skeptical about the capacity of post-tonal music to narrate, however, can begin to see the value of using narrative theory to contextualize analytical commentary – provided, of course, that one remembers Adorno's lapidary assertion that, "to the extent that music is like language, it is like notation in music history, a language sedimented from gestures" (2002: 139). As Roger Savage puts it, "the power of the language that words speak continues to invite us to think and to feel more. Conflicting and competing interpretations over music's social, political and cultural relevance all lead back to music's power to affect our understanding of ourselves and our world" (2010: 152). To end with a return to Andrew Bowie's sobering comment in my essay's second epigraph, "there is always more to say and do."

NOTES

1. Almén's theory of musical narrative builds on Frye (1957), Liszka (1989), and Tarasti (1994).

2. For an account of these issues of terminology, see Whittall (2008: 15–16, 18–19).

3. This section relates to Whittall (2004).

4. Jameux cites a conversation between Boulez and Jean-Louis de Rambures in *Réalités*, April 1965.

5. Boulez is cited without further reference in Bradshaw (1986: 186).

6. This section refers to Whittall (2007).

7. The relevant compositions are, respectively, *Silbury Air* (1977) for fifteen players, *Earth Dances* (1985–86) for orchestra, and *Endless Parade* (1986–87) for trumpet, vibraphone, and strings.

WORKS CITED

Adorno, Theodor W. 2002. "On the Contemporary Relationship of Philosophy and Music." In *Essays on Music,* edited by Richard Leppert, translated by Susan H. Gillespie, 135–61. Berkeley: University of California Press. First published in 1953.

Almén, Byron. 2008. *A Theory of Musical Narrative.* Bloomington: Indiana University Press.

Boulez, Pierre. 1986. "Sonate, que me veux-tu?" In *Orientations: Collected Writings,* edited by Jean-Jacques Nattiez, translated by Martin Cooper, 143–54. London: Faber and Faber. First published in 1960.

Bowie, Andrew. 2007. *Music, Philosophy and Modernity.* Cambridge: Cambridge University Press.

Bradshaw, Susan. 1986. "The Instrumental and Vocal Music." In *Pierre Boulez: A Symposium,* edited by William Glock, 127–229. London: Eulenberg.

Butt, John. 2010. *Bach's Dialogue with Modernity: Perspectives on the Passions.* Cambridge: Cambridge University Press.

Forte, Allen. 2008. "Schoenberg's Op. 19 No. 4: A Set-Theoretic Perspective." In *Proceedings of the Symposium around Set Theory,* edited by Moreno Andreatta, Jean-Michel Bardez, and John Rahn, 49–61. Paris: Éditions Delatour France–IRCAM–Centre Pompidou.

Frye, Northrop. 1957. *Anatomy of Criticism: Four Essays.* Princeton: Princeton University Press.

Hall, Michael. 1984. *Harrison Birtwistle.* London: Robson Books.

Hascher, Xavier. 2008. "Using K-nets towards a Transformational Analysis of Schoenberg's Op. 19, No. 4." In *Proceedings of the Symposium around Set Theory,* edited by Moreno Andreatta, Jean-Michel Bardez, and John Rahn, 63–96. Paris: Éditions Delatour France–IRCAM–Centre Pompidou.

Hatten, Robert S. 1994. *Musical Meaning in Beethoven: Markedness, Correlation, and Interpretation.* Bloomington: Indiana University Press.

Hicken, Kenneth L. 1984. *Aspects of Harmony in Schoenberg's Six Little Piano Pieces, Op. 19.* Winnipeg: Frye Publishing.

Jameux, Dominique. 1991. *Pierre Boulez.* Translated by Susan Bradshaw. London: Faber & Faber.

Levinson, Jerrold. 1997. *Music in the Moment.* Ithaca: Cornell University Press.

Liszka, James Jacób. 1989. *The Semiotic of Myth: A Critical Study of the Symbol.* Bloomington: Indiana University Press.

Maus, Fred E. 2001. "Narratology, Narrativity." In *The New Grove Dictionary of Music and Musicians,* 2nd ed., edited by Stanley Sadie and John Tyrrell, 641–43. London: Macmillan.

McDonald, Matthew. 2004. "Silent Narration? Elements of Narrative in Ives's *The Unanswered Question.*" *19th-Century Music* 27(3): 263–86.

Pearson, Roger. 1996. *Unfolding Mallarmé.* Oxford: Oxford University Press.

Porter Abbott, H. 2002. *The Cambridge Introduction to Narrative.* Cambridge: Cambridge University Press.

Savage, Roger W. H. 2010. *Hermeneutics and Music Criticism.* New York: Routledge.

Schleiermacher, Friedrich. 2007. *Vorlesungen über die Ästhetik.* Berlin: Reimer. First published in 1842.

Tarasti, Eero. 1994. *A Theory of Musical Semiotics.* Bloomington: Indiana University Press.

Webern, Anton. 1967. *Letters to Hildegard Jone and Josef Humplik.* Edited by Josef Polnauer, translated by Cornelius Cardew. Bryn Mawr: Presser.

Whittall, Arnold. 1996. "Music-Discourse-Dialogue: Webern's Variations, Op. 30." In *Webern Studies,* edited by Kathryn Bailey, 264–97. Cambridge: Cambridge University Press.

———. 2004. "'Unbounded Visions': Boulez, Mallarmé and Modern Classicism." *Twentieth-Century Music* 1(1): 1–17.

———. 2007. "The Elements of James Dillon." *Musical Times* 148 (1,899): 3–17.

———. 2008. *Cambridge Introduction to Serialism.* Cambridge: Cambridge University Press.

5

Archetypes of Initiation and Static Temporality in Contemporary Opera: Works of François-Bernard Mâche, Pascal Dusapin, and Gualtiero Dazzi

Márta Grabócz

THE INITIATION RITE AS A SUBSTITUTE FOR THE HERO MYTH IN LATE TWENTIETH-CENTURY OPERA

A number of important studies of twentieth-century theatrical and musical works have underlined the resurgence of ritual structures and journeys of initiation as the primary source of inspiration for a new theatrical and/or musical dramaturgy.[1] The publication of Tibor Tallián's analysis of Bartók's *Cantata Profana* (1930) in the early 1980s was a significant first step in this new development. The primary object of Tallián's work was to uncover instances of the analogy of the rite of passage. Tallián (1981) found that the *Cantata Profana* made use of ancient texts drawn from the Romanian *colindas*, which evoked the rite of passage of young people entering adolescence by uncovering the common mythical core shared by all the known religions and which aimed to provide faith, a belief in the possibility of a life centered around a vocation or a higher (spiritual) dimension. The use of traditional references served to uncover and transmit a new form of "transcendence" or a "life center" that could replace the religions that had disappeared. The *Cantata Profana* stages a passion, an itinerary to redemption. We learn how "the son of man" is transformed or transcended (transubstantiated) from a human state into something else: a God, a man – or animal – belonging to a higher dimension. We learn how the son of man will be transported from the daily sphere into the sacred sphere – the sphere of the species (Tallián 1981: 212).

Close readings of texts drawn from contemporary scenic works of music reveal the near systematic presence of mythological beings accompanied not by a dramaturgy or by a traditional narrative or dramatic-narrative structure, but by the juxtaposition or addition of repetitive states, similar phases, and reiterated stages. At the end of a series of recurrent events, the hoped-for or wished-for transubstantiation may or may not be achieved. The subjects and stories of these works revolve almost invariably around death, whether fictional or real. In this essay, I examine four works from this point of view:

1. *Temboctou*, an opera by François-Bernard Mâche (1982) and its modified 1995 version
2. *La melancholia*, an operatorio by Pascal Dusapin (1990–92)
3. *Medeamaterial*, an opera by Pascal Dusapin (1991–93)
4. *La rosa de Ariadna*, an opera by Gualtiero Dazzi (1995)

Before examining the common stylistic features shared by these works in spite of their different origins, I would like to return briefly to ideas developed by Carl Gustav Jung and his disciples concerning the process of maturation or individuation of man or, more precisely, the difference between the hero myth and the archetype of initiation.

Here is a preview of my main hypothesis: *while the subjects of operas written between the eighteenth century and the beginning of the twentieth century revolve exclusively around the significance and destiny of a hero (or heroine), twentieth-century opera (especially late twentieth-century opera) is centered primarily on the rite of initiation of a central character in the story.*

In a chapter on the figure of the hero in a collection of essays entitled *Man and His Symbols*, Joseph L. Henderson outlines the fundamental difference between the two journeys. At every stage of their life, human beings are confronted with a double and sometimes conflicting activity:

1. Individuals strive to discover and assert their individuality.
2. Yet the conscious Ego is forced constantly to return upon itself to re-establish its relation with the Self, with the totality of the psyche by way of maintaining a condition of psychic health. (1964: 101)[2]

The hero myth is thought to be the first stage in the differentiation of the psyche.

The individual undergoes a four-stage cycle: the Trickster cycle, the Hare cycle, the Red Horn cycle, and the Twins cycle, representing the efforts of the Ego to achieve a degree of relative autonomy in relation to an original "wholeness" (Henderson 1964: 103). For instance, during the Trickster cycle, we learn the following: "This figure, which at the outset assumes the form of an animal, passes from one mischievous exploit to another. But, as he does so, a change comes over him. At the end of his rogue's progress he is beginning to take on the physical likeness of a grown man" (104). The individual will be unable to integrate his adult surroundings if he fails to achieve a degree of relative autonomy (120). Writing of this "heroic system," Henderson observes: "Over and over again one hears a tale describing a hero's miraculous but humble birth, his early proof of superhuman strength, his rapid rise to prominence or power, his triumphant struggle with the forces of evil, his fallibility to the sin of pride (*hybris*), and his fall through betrayal or a 'heroic' sacrifice that ends in his death" (101). To avoid succumbing to the temptation of *hybris*, or excess, which creates an excessive degree of separation between the Ego and the Self, the myth of the Twins shows how "their own fear . . . forced them back into a harmonious Ego-Self relation" (123). To quote Henderson:

> In tribal societies it is the initiation rite that most effectively solves this problem. The ritual takes the novice back to the deepest level of original mother-child identity or Ego-Self identity, thus forcing him to experience a symbolic death. In other words, *his identity is temporarily dismembered or dissolved into the collective unconscious. From this state he is then ceremonially rescued by the rite of the new birth.* . . .
>
> The ritual, whether it is found in tribal groups or in more complex societies, invariably insists upon this rite of death and rebirth, which provides the novice with a "rite of passage" from one stage of life to the next, whether it is from early childhood or from early to late adolescence and from then to maturity.
>
> Initiatory events are not, of course, confined to the psychology of youth. Every new phase of development throughout an individual's life is accompanied by a repetition of the original conflict between the claims of the Self and the claims of the Ego. In fact, this conflict may be expressed more powerfully at the period of transition from early maturity to middle age (between 35 to 40 in our society) than at any other time in life. And the transition from middle age to old age creates again the need for affirmation of the difference between the Ego and the total psyche; the hero receives his last call to action in defense of Ego-consciousness against the approaching dissolution of life in death.

At these critical periods, the archetype of initiation is strongly activated
to provide a meaningful transition that offers something more spiritually
satisfying than the adolescent rites with their strong secular flavor. *The arche-*
typal patterns of initiation in this religious sense – known since ancient times as
"the mysteries" – are woven into the texture of all ecclesiastical rituals requiring a
special manner of worship at the time of birth, marriage, or death. (123, emphasis
added)

By way of bringing this line of thought to a close, I would like to quote
Henderson on the comparison he draws between two schemas, the heroic
and the ritual:

There is one striking difference between the hero myth and the initiation
rite. The typical hero figures exhaust their efforts in achieving the goal
of their ambitions; in short, they become successful even if immediately
afterward they are punished or killed for their *hybris.* In contrast to this, the
novice for initiation is called upon to give up willful ambition and all desire
and to submit to the ordeal. He must be willing to experience this trial
without hope of success. In fact, he must be prepared to die; and though the
token of his ordeal may be mild (a period of fasting, the knocking out of a
tooth, or tattooing) or agonizing (the infliction of the wounds of circumci-
sion, subincision, or other mutilations), the purpose remains the same: *to*
create the symbolic mood of death from which may spring the symbolic mood of
rebirth. (124, emphasis added)

If I have quoted Henderson on Jung's discussion of the hero myth and
the archetype of initiation at such length, it is because, since the middle of
the twentieth century, there has been a gradual return to an enumerative and
cyclical (not to say "static") structure in the great works of musical-dramatic
art as well as a return of the act of transubstantiation, of metamorphosis
through a voyage or journey.

Another recurrent theme is the defiance of death or of the void, from
György Ligeti's *Le grand macabre* (1977–78) to *Temboctou* by Mâche, or from
Proemio by Marco Stroppa and Adolpho Moricone (1991) to *Trois soeurs* by
Péter Eötvös (1998). Because of the recurrent use of the journey of initiation
(whether conscious or unconscious) in modern opera, there has emerged a
new form of musical and theatrical dramaturgy – an art built on stasis, enumeration, and variation. While the story of the hero recounts challenges,
intrigues, and events with a view to reaching an outcome or solution, the
journey of initiation abandons any quest for redemption from the very outset
by presenting merely the challenges, obstacles, and suffering that precede the

initiation rite, whether true or false, or the positive or negative transformation that results from the accumulation of experiences.

THE VIEWS OF COMPOSERS AND LIBRETTISTS/ WRITERS ON DRAMATURGY AND THE SUBJECT OF THE OPERAS UNDER ANALYSIS

1. Temboctou *by François-Bernard Mâche and Bernard Chartreux*

Writing of the ideas that led up to the composition of *Temboctou*, Bernard Chartreux, who wrote the libretto, comments:

> "Rester partir" ["une passion sous les tropiques" (a passion under the Tropics)]. . . . There is in this something of a facetious homage to the musical Passions, to the freedom . . . with which they recount a dramatic narrative – as in *La Passion selon saint Matthieu*, where it is presented, for instance, by his narrator – to a short scene of dialogue between "real" characters (Jesus and his disciples), followed by a commentary by the choir (etc.), the constant variation of their statements. . . . At the same time I was equally interested in the very idea of a journey as the archetype of all narratives. . . . Let us recall also that the secret thread of the journey of René Caillé (the hero of *Temboctou*) reflected the stages of a difficult and arduous journey under the tropics. (1982: 4–5)

Mâche adds: "René Caillé is a living contradiction. . . . A fake Arab, a fake scholar, in 1827 he became the first discoverer of a fake glory. Whether it swallows him up or consents to spit him out dying toward Europe, Africa constitutes a 'non-place,' a utopia for the small peasant in the era of Romanticism. René Caillé merely pursued the archaic image of a maternal and dangerous Africa" (1995).

2. La melancholia *by Pascal Dusapin*

In the subject of *La melancholia* (1992), Dusapin's object was to realize or represent "an exemplary space . . . a place of exchange between the roots of man and the cosmological structures":

> What interested me in the *Melancholia* was not to write an apology of the madman or of the man who sits upon his rock, but rather to construe the gradual ascent of this reality (i.e., melancholy) through the movements of

thought up until the seventeenth century. The result is a highly complex system of intelligence . . . in which the relations connecting man to the world and the universe are almost formalized.

By contrast, modern man is only connected to technology; his sole concern is to master instruments, in music and elsewhere. . . .

If I chose not to go beyond the seventeenth century in the textual material which I used, it is because it was during this period that melancholy was . . . [acknowledged] as the sole network of superhuman and cosmogonic powers. . . .

The primary interest of this philosophy of art and thought is that it is not centered upon the ego: the egomaniac network that first erupted in the nineteenth century and continued into the twentieth century has yet to be put in place, and the one elaborating thought is not driven by an individual impulse. . . .

In the twentieth century, human questioning concerning the cosmos was driven by an ideology of rarity. After having been (elected) "mad," the artist became rare, caught in the grips of an illness worse than all the illnesses he had ever had to face: egomania, the conviction that his individual being is more important than anything governing the space in which he lives.

The text of the interview accompanying the performance of *Medeamaterial* and *La melancholia* in Brussels includes a "manifest" against the cult of the Ego and an apology for "cosmic questioning" (or for a "total psyche," in Jung's words), "this vaster, richer entity (preserved and perpetuated in ancient and symbolic representations), the entity that provides the strength which the Ego lacks."[3]

3. La rosa de Ariadna *by Gualtiero Dazzi and Francisco Serrano*

The use of the figure of the Minotaur in *La rosa de Ariadna* by Dazzi and Serrano is suggestive of a desire for the same level of complexity since the age of reason and the era of the French *Lumières*. Serrano writes:

The Minotaur is the condensed reality of a double symbol; a monster yet also a prince: the son of the queen. . . . He represents not merely the brute and untameable power of the instinct, which continues nonetheless to exist, but also something more: a being with a dual essence. His roar sings the praise of the terrestrial world. . . .

In the light of this interpretation [of Greek myths], we are, all of us, both Theseus and the Minotaur. Yet according to Nietzsche, who studied the myth in depth, Theseus rejected life by killing the bull, thereby reducing life to mere reflexive forms. *It is the triumph of reason, of the man of order submit-*

*ted to the gods, over the will and vitality of instincts. According to the myth, far
from seducing Ariadne, Theseus abandons her on the island of Naxos.*

  *By this account La rosa de Ariadna is the love story of Ariadne, the symbol
of the soul, and the bull-god, representing the vital and fertilizing forces of nature.
This is perhaps why we might say, with Umberto Eco, that among the many
intrigues invented by men, the history of the labyrinth is "a condensed form
of the future." (1995: 10–11, emphasis added)*

For Dazzi, the subject of the work reflects the "failed meeting between
Ariadne and the Minotaur": "Even if the text follows a 'dramatic thread,' it
never yields to the stereotypes of the conventional libretto. It never really
assumes a direct theatricality, in such a way that the composer had to create
'small internal dramaturgies'" (Serrano 1995: 9).

The common textual feature of all these plays is *repetition in the descrip-
tion of the same state of soul* throughout a true or imaginary journey and articulated solely by variations. The texts of *La melancholia, Medeamaterial,
Temboctou,* and *La rosa de Ariadna* are marked by a single state of soul, a
central atmosphere that undergoes only very minor changes along the way.
In *La melancholia,* this is expressed in the description of the characteristics of
Saturn, a planet that influences one of the four humors of the human body.
Medeamaterial "functions like a great 'lamento' in which Medea advances dramatically in pain," as Pascal Dusapin explains. *Temboctou* stages the repetition
of an increasingly trying quest, while *La rosa* includes a lamentation of the fate
of the Minotaur, a monster living in utter solitude and somewhat softened
by his meeting with Ariadne. All these texts are based on an anti-discursive,
anti-linear, and anti-teleological logic and tradition.

STASIS IN TWENTIETH-CENTURY MUSIC

The representation of the journey of initiation – and of a non-directional,
non-heroic, and unambitious journey – has significant implications for musical performance. All these works are founded on a compositional art based
on musical stasis. Since Cage, Stravinsky, and Messiaen, we have known that
the representation of an Indivisible Whole, devoid of duality (Cage), of ontological time as opposed to psychological time (Stravinsky), and of the desire to present "the theological rainbow" (Messiaen) tend to create a kind of
"zero" time, a circular or cyclic time juxtaposing or superimposing stasis and
directionality. For other composers, time becomes space (see, in particular,
Ligeti's *Atmosphères, Lontano, Lux Aeterna,* etc.), or an instant is magnified

or enlarged (see Stockhausen's *Momente, Kontakte*). The dramaturgy of stasis thus becomes a challenge for twentieth-century music.

It was via the archetype of initiation that stasis entered the realm of musical theater and opera. A number of musicologists and composers have sought to provide descriptions of the different expressions of stasis in music, such as the different manifestations of stasis at various points throughout the history of music analyzed in the work of Jonathan Kramer. Daniel Charles describes several categories of stasis: repetition, drone, ondular movement, verticalization, "zero" time, and so on. Lewis Rowell (1987) presents two broad categories of stasis: the aesthetic categories, and their technical performance, such as *ostinati*, process music, dense musical textures (Xenakis, Ligeti), random ordering (Stockhausen), transcendental particularism (Varèse), aural collage, and found objects that prevent the linear construction of the listening process. Though he does not mention the term *stasis* as such, Costin Miereanu (1995) describes different morphological categories and musical aspectualities of stasis:

1. The zenithal category ("invariant" aspectuality = identical repetition, petrification, congelation)
2. The meteoric category ("punctual" aspectuality = action of starting, triggering: form of rocket, or shattering, piercing, folding, etc.)
3. The enveloping category ("floating" aspectuality = undulating/undulated sound action)

Miereanu (1995) has identified and labeled other techniques, including:

1. Blow-up, slow-motion deconstruction (= extension, enlargement of certain areas and details)
2. Pyrotechnics, from spatiality to temporality (= polyphony-heterophony of candles; star topography)
3. Polylogues, interference, and stratification (= continuum, broken thread, etc.)

These new terms describe in a metaphoric way stasis realized by repetition, by isolated actions, by effects evoking space and water, by continuums, and by imitation of fire sounds.

MUSICAL EXPRESSIONS OF STASIS

In the four operas discussed, stasis is often achieved via a narrative thread, a drone, or an entangled polyphonic structure in the instrumental scores. Stasis may also be expressed through repeated motifs in the solo score or even via sustained chords in the choir or orchestral scores. These observations will be illustrated by a number of musical extracts drawn from the works discussed above.

1. From *La rosa de Ariadna,* I refer to the scene that precedes the arrival of Ariadne. The listener initially hears a thread of sound (an audible drone), then a part of the Minotaur's sinuous monologue (in which the lyrics refer to "terre blafarde, sable indigent; illusions d'un palais déserté" [pale earth, indigent sand; illusions of a deserted palace]), then the entry of the choir: "La nuit avance et revient sur ses pas. Le temps n'existe plus" (The night advances and retraces its steps. Time no longer exists) (Examples 5.1a and 5.1b).[4]

2. From *Temboctou* I select the extract representing a stage of this specific journey: the fourth scene entitled "Les travaux des champs" (Work in the fields), "La caravane s'arrête auprès d'un joli ruisseau" (The caravan stops beside a pretty stream). Here stasis is achieved through polyrhythmics based on the hiccup technique or through the superimposition of ten or so tempi and their various divisions, thus producing a random effect in the gradual filling up of the sound space. The gradual accumulations and superimpositions create a musical representation of the storm breaking (Examples 5.2a and 5.2b).

3. From the first part of *La melancholia* ("Unius de quattuor" [one of the four humors]), I quote examples of *juxtaposition* and *superimposition,* respectively, as representations of stasis.

a. Juxtapositions

(1) The declamation of the English horn solo and tenor with the lyrics: "Ces hommes reçoivent des rayons de lumière morcelés et mutilés" (These men receive divided and mutilated rays of light) (Example 5.3a, mm. 26–34).[5]

(2) This is followed and completed by the monotonous choral recitative reinforced by the clarinets and bassoons from m. 35 with the lyrics: "A l'instar des prophètes, ils se mettent à 'parler' naturellement des choses divines" (Like the prophets, they begin to "speak" naturally of divine things).[6] The music illustrates the word "speak" through onomatopoeia by describing the sound chaos of Babel.

(3) In mm. 35–40, a sustained chord in the other instruments accompanies the hectic polyphonic texture of the first and second violins (Example 5.3b).

b. Superimpositions

(1) Further on (mm. 42–50), the contralto solo develops the idea of "l'effet nuisible d'une grande tristesse" (the harmful effect of a great sadness).[7]

EXAMPLE 5.1A. Dazzi, *La rosa de Ariadna,* page 50.
Reprinted with the kind permission of the composer.

She is accompanied by the sustained cluster of the choir and the polyphonic
texture of the chords. After a rich passage for the choir and the ensemble,
which remains generally static, the contralto begins a long lament in a quasi-
Oriental style. Her speech about "le chagrin sans désastre" (sorrow without
disaster) (Hildegard von Bingen) is marked by a static and ethereal aura produced by the choir, the brass, and the strings. The contralto melody revolves

EXAMPLE 5.1B. Dazzi, *La rosa de Ariadna,* page 51.
Reprinted with the kind permission of the composer.

around a central formula, evoking the image of stasis par excellence (Examples 5.3c and 5.3d).

4 and 5. *Medeamaterial* includes two diametrically opposed instances of stasis: the stasis of the melismatic laments of Medea and the stasis of the "energico meccanico" – "agitato," or static – of the representation of Jason. The two styles suggest a sense of cold and/or a very intense feeling of estrangement or distanciation.

EXAMPLE 5.2A. Mâche, *Temboctou*, page 70.
Reprinted with the kind permission of the composer.

EXAMPLE 5.2B. Mâche, *Temboctou*, page 71.
Reprinted with the kind permission of the composer.

EXAMPLE 5.3A. Dusapin, *La melancholia*, mm. 30–35.
© Éditions Salabert/Universal Music Publishing Classical – with kind permission.

EXAMPLE 5.3B. Dusapin, *La melancholia*, mm. 36–41.
© Éditions Salabert/Universal Music Publishing Classical — with kind permission.

EXAMPLE 5.3C. Dusapin, *La melancholia*, mm. 42–47.
© Éditions Salabert/Universal Music Publishing Classical – with kind permission.

EXAMPLE 5.3D. Dusapin, *La melancholia*, mm. 48–54.
© Éditions Salabert/Universal Music Publishing Classical – with kind permission.

EXAMPLE 5.4. Dusapin, *Medeamaterial*, mm. 1–10.
© *Éditions Salabert/Universal Music Publishing Classical – with kind permission.*

The original stasis and initial distance in the voice of Medea is produced by the two pivot notes (D and F) around which Medea's questioning concerning the role of Creon's daughter – her rival – tends to revolve and gravitate (see Amblard and Dusapin 2002) (Example 5.4). In the first part, the effect of alienation is produced by the drone and by the "Morse" signals of the organ (Example 5.5).

6. The musical image of Jason's entry is produced by an *ostinato*, a "mechanical" music; the permutation of the rhythmic motifs evoke walking or violent dancing. The timbre is also very metallic and cold: keyboard with continuo produced by plucked chords (lute, theorbo *ad libitum*) and by the strings playing either *ponticello* or *pizzicato* (Example 5.6).

In addition to stasis, the second fundamental effect of the archetype of initiation is *the new role of affects*. Lamentation and mourning are omnipresent. Aside from lamentation, funeral chants, and moribund recitals, as affects, there are only images of nature, of the universe and collectivity, or of the

EXAMPLE 5.5. Dusapin, *Medeamaterial*, mm. 34–40.
© *Éditions Salabert/Universal Music Publishing Classical—with kind permission.*

nocturnal palace, the image of a flower, of terror, of fright, the images of the imaginary *Dies Irae* (*La melancholia*, act 2, "Il quarto loco"), the image of the creation of the world (*La melancholia*, act 3), images of the Africa of fantasies and mirages, of giant women, of the visitation of death, of specters and of visions, or of light, monstrosity, that is, the images of life, of the collective unconscious, of cosmogony (see *Temboctou*).

7. Lastly, I present the penultimate image of *La melancholia*—a musical image of a kind of creation of the world out of chaos. The lyrics that accompany the image are "Aux révolutions de ce cercle septenaire des vertus spirituelles, par l'énergie divine est créé un certain office des planets—alors rendu souverain—par lequel ce monde est éclairé" (From the revolutions of this septenary circle of spiritual virtues, by divine energy a certain office of planets—thus becoming sovereign—is created through which this world is enlightened).[8] The production of this musical image as a culminating or climactic point is produced by the following technical devices: swirling instrumental and vocal *tutti* in continuous rotation with *fortissimo* dynamics (mm. 396–445). The culminating point of the image of creation is accompanied by the following lyrics: "La plus haute planète et les surpassant toutes, est

EXAMPLE 5.6. Dusapin, *Medeamaterial*, mm. 124–31.
© *Éditions Salabert/Universal Music Publishing Classical—with kind permission.*

celle que les hommes appellent 'Saturne'" (The highest planet, the planet
that surpasses all, is the planet that men call "Saturn") (m. 420).[9] The Greek
lyrics, quoted from Hesiod's *Theogony*, 729, add: "C'est là que les titans sont
cachés dans l'ombre brumeuse" (It is there that the titans hide in the obscure
shadows) (Example 5.7).

EXAMPLE 5.7. Dusapin, *La Melancholia*, mm. 419–24.
© Éditions Salabert/Universal Music Publishing Classical — with kind permission.

To conclude, I would like briefly to recall some of the historical categorizations of the musical forms elaborated by the great German, Czech, and Austrian musicologists such as Herman Erpf, Ernst Bloch, Karl Wörner, and Vladimir Karbusicky, who single out three (or five) broad categories of archetypal forms (*Urformen*) in the history of music:

1. The primitive historical forms, such as the various "enumerative" forms (*Reihenform*)
2. The "equilibrium" or palindromic forms (*Gleichgewichtsform*)
3. The "evolutive" forms, in continuous development or evolution (*Entfaltungsform*)

According to Karbusicky (1990: 195–96), the historically most ancient or primitive forms – the "enumerative" forms – are subdivided into three categories:

a. Infinite production or simple enumeration (abcdef, etc.)
b. Eternal return, that is, cyclical forms, rondo forms (abacada, etc.)
c. The additive and tectonic process, which uses only one material (e.g., the fugue: a a' a'' a''', etc.)

According to Karbusicky's theory, the two remaining archetypal forms (see numbers 2 and 3 above) emerged at a later stage of historical development: the "equilibrium" form appeared in the eighteenth century, while the form of "dramaturgy in four acts," or "evolutive" form, emerged in the nineteenth century.

The current return to the most ancient kind of structure – a form using enumeration, repetition, and addition – raises a crucial issue for the process of listening to and analyzing contemporary works of opera (and, sometimes, for listening to contemporary instrumental works). Are we seeing the end of (a period of) history, or are we witnessing instead a new beginning?

NOTES

All translations in this essay are by the author.

1. See Schechner (1988) on performance theory; see also Charles (1984, 1986, 1987, 1989, 1998, 2001) on the aesthetics of performance and the poetics of the multiple and its relationship to transcendentalism; and see Mâche (1991, 1998, 2001) on the resurgence of the sacred and the role of myths.

2. "The Self . . . is different from the Ego. The Self is our psychic totality, constituted by consciousness and the infinite ocean of the soul upon which it floats"

(Henderson 1964: 128, quoting Jung, *L'homme à la découverte de son âme [Modern Man in Search of a Soul]*).

3. Translated from an interview with Pascal Dusapin, "Le don du mail noir," *Art et culture* (Brussels), March 1992, 2–3.

4. The lyrics are in Spanish: "La noche avanza y vuelve a retroceder como une pulsación." See pages 50–51 of the score. The score includes a French translation, which is used in this essay.

5. The quote is from Galenus: "Videlicet morbo melancholico laborantes, irradiationes recipiunt, verum particulatas et destruantas" (We can see that these men who suffer from melancholia receive divided and mutilated rays of light); see the texts quoted on pages iv–v of the score (introduction) and also on pages 30–67 for the described excerpt.

6. The quote is from Galenus: "Quapropter ad instar prophetarum de rebus divinalibus naturaliter loqui incipiunt. Sed loqueam."

7. Johannes Thrithemius: "Die groesse oder vile ainer Melancholischen traurigkait ist krefftiger une schadt auch mer dann alle Teüflische wurchung, dann woelichen der boess gaist uberwindt er mit aigner traurigkeit des menschen" (A great or entire melancholic sadness is more harmful than any diabolic influence, because the one that the malevolent Spirit oppresses, he oppresses with the sadness of man). See page iv of the score.

8. The quote is from Saint Ambrose, *Epistolae ad Horatianum:* "Atque orbem operatonis divinae vigore praestantem, septenarium quoddam ministerium planetarum creatum advertimus, quo hic mundus illuminatur." See page v of the score.

9. The quote is from Chaucer, *The Canterbury Tales:* "The heveste and aboven alle Stant that planete which men calle Saturnus." See page v of the score.

WORKS CITED

Amblard, Jacques, and Pascal Dusapin. 2002. *L'intonation ou le secret.* Paris: Ed. Musica Falsa.

Charles, Daniel. 1984. *Musik und Vergessen.* Berlin: Merve Verlag.

———. 1986. "Semiotics of Musical Time." In *The Semiotic Web*, edited by Thomas A. Sebeok and Jean Umiker-Sebeok, 468–76. Bloomington: Indiana University Press.

———. 1987. "Son et temps." *Semiotica* 66(1–3): 171–79.

———. 1989. *Zeitspielräume, Performance-Musik-Aesthetik.* Berlin: Merve Verlag.

———. 1998. *Musiques nomads.* Paris: Éditions Kimé.

———. 2001. *La fiction de la postmodernité selon l'esprit de la musique.* Paris: Presses universitaires de France.

Chartreux, Bernard. 1982. *Rester partir.* Collection "Théâtrales." Paris: Edilig.

Henderson, Joseph L. 1964. "Ancient Myths and Modern Man." In *Man and His Symbols*, edited by Carl G. Jung, 95–156. New York: Random House.

Karbusicky, Vladimir. 1990. *Kosmos, Mensch, Musik.* Hamburg: Verlag Dr. R. Kramer.

Kramer, Jonathan. 1989. *The Time of Music.* New York: Schirmer.

Mâche, François-Bernard. 1991. *Musique, mythe, nature ou les dauphins d'Arion.* Paris: Klincksieck.

———. 1995. Biographical note in program for *Opéra de Massy.*

———. 1998. *Entre l'observatoire et l'atelier.* Paris: Éditions Kimé.

———. 2001. *Musique au singulier.* Paris: Éditions Odile Jacob.

Miereanu, Costin. 1995. "Vers une nouvelle microstructure." In *Fuite et conquête du champ musical,* 149–70. Paris: Meridiens Klincksieck.

Rowell, Lewis. 1987. "Stasis in Music." *Semiotica* 66(1–3): 181–95.

Schechner, Richard. 1988. *Performance Theory,* rev. and expanded ed. New York: Routledge.

Serrano, Francisco. 1995. "A propos de La Rosa de Ariadna." In the libretto and text of *La rosa de Ariadna* for performance at Festival Musica, Strasbourg.

Tallián, Tibor. 1981. "Die Cantata profana: Ein Mythos des Übergangs." *Studia Musicologica Academiae Scientiarium Hungaricae* 23(1–4): 135–200. Abridged German version of Tallián (1983).

———. 1983. *Cantata profana: Az átmenet mitosza (Cantata Profana: The myth of passage).* Budapest: Magvetö.

6

Agency, Determinism, Focal Time Frames, and Processive Minimalist Music

Joshua Banks Mailman

In his 2004 essay "Continuous Time and Interrupted Time: Two-Timing in the Temporal Arts," Peter Kivy argues that differences between how we experience time in music versus literature become apparent not from their continuities but from their interruptions. We tolerate interruptions in reading, whereas we do not tolerate them in musical listening. The reason, Kivy argues, is one of attitude toward what is being experienced: fictional stories have built-in contingency (a sequence of events determined as the story unfolds). Music, by contrast, is experienced as deterministic (a sequence of events determined in advance). Kivy argues that the differences arise partly because a person is often rehearing music, prompting determined expectations of what lies ahead; whereas with a work of literature, it is more likely a person is reading it for the first time. Kivy's distinction is partly based on varying experiential habits and is thus not an absolute but a matter of degree.

Nevertheless, note that this determinism is not just a matter of genre conventions or expectations, which can be manipulated. Anything that can be manipulated is *not* determined, so it must be explained differently, as I will do. Note also that this determinism is not just the quasi determinism of some events seeming to *cause* subsequent ones – a phenomenon prevalent in both literature and music – but rather the sense that the total sequence of events is determined in advance. It cannot be, however, that music is experienced generally as totally deterministic, for this would make musical narrative impossible. Putting it differently: insofar as music is experienced as deterministic (in the sense of composed in advance), this is something musical narrativists ignore, suppress, or work around. Musical narrativity implicitly rejects the deterministic view. For instance, as Pasler writes, "musical narrative must . . . start with something which is incomplete and enticing so that the listener is interested in its future possibilities" (1989: 241). Lurking behind musical narrative is a simple premise: that which is inevitable is hardly worth mentioning in a narrative unless – and I'll return to these caveats – it is caused by or causes something else that is not inevitable. Our narrative point of view about music seems to clash with the deterministic one asserted by Kivy.

Edward T. Cone (1977) explains how there can still be suspense in a rehearsal (rereading) of a musical work just as there can be with a detective story. Yet this does not quite address how twentieth- and twenty-first-century technologies have drastically expanded the tendency to *re*hear music, such that Kivy's distinction seems to have more purchase than ever before. In the wake of a revolution in listening habits and compositional practices developed in the twentieth century, our musical narrative point of view cannot be taken for granted. This revolution arises partly from the advent of mechanical reproduction of sound. Arved Ashby (2010), inspired by Jacques Attali (1985), writes that composed music is a reliving, or experiencing, of an unreduced duration of time from the past, which has already "occurred" (lapsed). The listening experience is a "copy" of a previously elapsed duration of time. Thus, recorded music especially is distinctly temporal, compared to other forms of escapism, such as literature.

Since agency (volition, choice) seems the most distinctive trait that partitions time (past from future), music's temporality problematizes agency. An original lapsing of time is partly contingent on agency, but the reliving of it cannot be contingent in any way if it is a copy. A duration of time copied from the past brings with it a paradox: on the one hand, a copy implies that every opportunity for choice (exercise of agency) in the original is duplicated with an opportunity for choice in the copy; on the other hand, a copy implies that exactly the same set of events in the original are necessarily duplicated in the copy: the two implications are mutually exclusive.

Yet, narrative interpretation of music may play a crucial role in negotiating this paradox because it promotes the fact that even when aware of how the compositional process determines the course of a piece of music, we nevertheless can experience its events as if they are being decided as we go.

That is narrative's natural mode. By contrast, Kivy argues that with repeated hearings our focus moves toward anticipating what we know will happen next, which pushes the deterministic view into the foreground. But the paradox I just mentioned illustrates how this is not the case because the sense of agency apparent from an original duration of time is just as much part of that duration when copied as the events that occur in it. Thus, as long as the events in the original duration do not seem predetermined in the first place, they will not seem predetermined in the copy of that duration. This is one reason why narrative experience survives among the repeatable experiences of musical works afforded by the unprecedented modes of music's mechanical reproduction in the twenty-first century.

The situation for musical narrative is more difficult when the events of the "original" duration seemed predetermined in the first place, as with music whose compositional *modus operandi* is strongly deterministic, arising from the same technologies that brought about changes of listening habits. With such music, narrative arises less obviously, so it provides an ideal context for exploring issues of narrativity. Specifically, the late twentieth-century surge of compositional approaches based on automated processes poses a significant challenge to musical narrativity because it hinders the listener from assigning agency to individual events within the unfolding of a musical work. Thus, approaches to narrative in twentieth-century music may differ significantly from those for common-practice repertoire.

Whether such music is narrative is not inherent but emerges from the interaction of the listener as interpreter (Almén 2003; Reyland 2007, 2009). Every narrative analysis depends on a critical meta-language that arises from outside the sounds of the piece (Pearsall and Almén 2006). For Beethoven the critical meta-language derives intertextually from normative practices of the surrounding repertoire; for less normative music, such as that of the twentieth century, a narrative cannot rely on an intertextually fueled conventional meta-language and therefore must develop in a suitably particularized *ad hoc* fashion, which I demonstrate below, as I have with other repertoires (Mailman 2009, 2010a, 2010b).

The remainder of this essay considers the narrativity of processive minimalist music both as an instance of modernist developments in twentieth-century music and as an instance of the broader musical landscape to which the concept of narrativity applies. First, I distinguish between teleology and determinism, explaining how each relates to conventions of narrative and musical style. Then, I present *diachronic decision trees* as schematic models of narrative, which, in terms of agency, distinguish between narrative in more conventional music and in twentieth-century processive music. From this I develop the concept of *narrative framing functions* and apply it to Alvin Lucier's minimalist composition *Crossings* (1984). The last section suggests an inter-opus narrative interpretation of processive minimalist music as follows: contrary to dystopic visions of the oppressive role of computing machines, processively deterministic music exemplifies the empowerment of humans as creative agents, able to evoke new narrative contexts through the use of technology.

TELEOLOGY, CONVENTION, AND DETERMINISM

I mean *determinism* in the philosophical sense of *free will vs. determinism*. *Determinism* is beyond the control of *free will*. *Free will* is manifested as *agency*, which is present in inverse proportion to determinism. By *determinism* I do not mean the generic expectation of reaching a goal or being foiled from reaching it, but rather I mean something more severe and absolute. Destiny, by contrast, is narratively interesting insofar as it is less absolute than determinism. Destiny might or might not be fulfilled, which is why we care about it. Destiny may mean determinism or teleology, but the latter plays more of a role in narrative. Consider that destiny without agency is neither tragedy nor triumph; each requires agency for its narrative interest. This means that destiny in the strict sense of determinism seldom plays a role in narrative. Yet destiny in the sense of a goal, a teleology, often plays a role in narrative. What is sometimes called "destiny" in discourse about narrative is actually teleology. Teleology is not determinism. In fact, narrative involves at least some sort of indeterminacy to create suspense.[1] Suspense in a narrative is made possible by the combination of teleology and indeterminism in the form of agency.

In a narrative, various aspects of stylistic convention and normative practice serve either deterministically or teleologically. In musical narrative, it is the stylistic conventions and normative practices that are *at play* in a particular situation that serve teleologically, earning significant discursive attention. By contrast, those conventions and practices that serve deterministically in a particular narrative are the less alluring regulative features of stylistic decorum (such as tonal and contrapuntal practices) that do their job backstage and thus go unmentioned.

Sonata form is a good example of how stylistic convention and normative practice can serve teleologically. The restoration of originally off-tonic thematic material to the tonic key serves as a deterministic feature in a sonata form, but it is more interesting narratively to treat it as a teleological feature, which is what is usually done, so that a sonata movement gains dramatic charge. Charles Rosen (1980) promoted this narrative-dramatic characterization of sonata form, which finds its more recent incarnation in the theory of James Hepokoski and Warren Darcy, who assert that "the broad trajectory of the sonata may be understood as an act of tonic-realization" (2006: 232). My point is that you cannot have it both ways; tonic attainment cannot be considered an act with narrative charge and at the same time be considered determined; to have narrative charge, it must have the possibility of being otherwise; it must be a goal whose fulfillment is within reach through the power of agency but that is not assured in advance.

Usually, the tonal-oriented narrative of a sonata is one of triumph, but it can be otherwise. An example, which parallels and amplifies one of the great mythic-tragic agential blunders, is what Stravinsky called the "nearly sonata Allegro" of the pas de deux in his ballet *Orpheus.* The moment is during Orpheus and Eurydice's attempted journey to the surface, which begins as a sonata-allegro form. During this, an abrupt silence commences when "Orpheus tears the bandage from his eyes and Eurydice falls dead"; the silence leaves the sonata form hanging in the dominant rather than returning to the tonic.[2] Of course, whether or not Eurydice's second death is destiny (fate) depends on how one interprets the legend, but its tragedy requires the possibility that the goal might have been achieved if only Orpheus had kept his nerve. Stravinsky's musico-dramatic strategy depends on the teleological (not deterministic) interpretation of sonata form, where the goal of the transgressive protagonist is mapped to the goal of tonic-realization. An inverse situation can obtain when convention represents the will of established order rather than that of the transgressive protagonist, who bears a conflicting teleology. Here tragedy emerges from the failure to surmount convention, as shown in Robert Hatten's (1994) analysis of the tragic expressive genre of the slow movement of Beethoven's "Hammerklavier" Sonata. Its tragedy requires that the convention in question is not determined but could be surmounted through the power of agency. In this case, the protagonist's agency strives heavenward, away from convention's gravitational pull, only to be dragged back down into willing surrender. Again in this situation, convention acts teleologically (as the will of the established order) rather than deterministically. Such teleological uses of musical convention can act in both tragic and triumphal trajectories within a narrative. In the next section, I provide a schematic way to model tragic failure and triumphal fulfillment as different trajectories within a partially deterministic context.

A SCHEMATIC MODEL ADDRESSING ISSUES OF NARRATIVITY
FOR ALL MUSIC INCLUDING THAT SINCE 1900

What might help narrativists navigate the waters of post-conventional music since 1900 is a schematic model of how narrative operates in conventional and unconventional contexts. These include the more deterministic musics of the twentieth century, such as processive minimalism and algorithmic composition, and less deterministic free-atonal and improvised music. In addition, the model addresses more conventional situations in music as well as the contexts of the real world in which most written narratives occur. Conventionally, narrative depends on some notion of contingency (what might or might not happen). The appropriate model, then, is based on Bergson's (1889) theory of time, whereby "free action" occurs in the time that passes, which can be represented as a "fork in the road" or, as I depict it, a *diachronic decision tree.*

The decision tree model for musical narrative is shown in Example 6.1.[3] It also models the physical and social actions of everyday life, such that musical narratives compatible with the model correlate to narratives of everyday life, that is, to the real world. In the real world, a descriptive stream (a *Dimension of Freedom,* the vertical axis in the diagram) might be what door to open, whom to invite to dinner, what joke to tell, and so on. In music, it might be harmony, voicing, key, texture, topic, phrase type, and so on. The nodes in the tree are decision points, representing a state (on the vertical axis) at a point in time (from left to right) at which a choice can be made, leading to branches extending to other nodes.[4] Each slanted line between nodes is a short-term deterministic process. The background represents what cannot happen in the musical work; at any point in time, all states that do not have nodes are states that cannot occur at that time. Thus the background represents all those matters of the musical work we regard as precluded once the piece begins. (An eighteenth-century piano sonata in C major cannot end on an F♯ chord played by a trombone choir, just as Juliet cannot send Romeo an instant text message; these actions are precluded by stylistic context.) This off-limits area indirectly determines what is possible in the narrative: it is the *deterministic context* of the work.[5]

A narrative may reference multiple agents. The narrative perspective depicted in the diachronic decision tree model collapses onto one plane the decision points of all the agents (each of which has its own subset of deci-

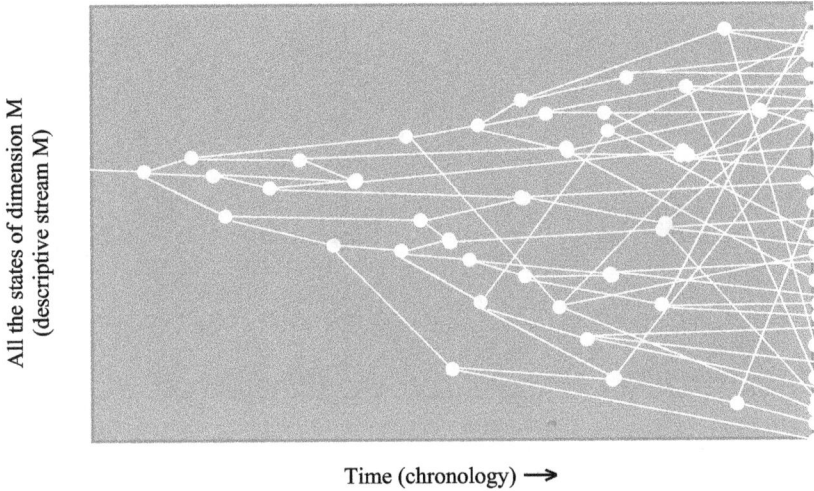

EXAMPLE 6.1. Diachronic decision tree representation of narrativity.

sion points). Likewise, each state is global, encompassing the sub-states of all agents (and non-agential entities).

In the *diachronic decision tree* model, *cause* is expressed by the fact that each branching decision partly determines the future by setting out what options are open; it *causes* the next set of possibilities by precluding some events from happening. The idea of *plotting* – "a sense of direction, a sense of laying out a certain path which the reader can follow" (Meelberg 2006: 147) – is represented literally by the paths that can be traversed diachronically on the tree.

Annotations on the model depict various teleologies, and from these we determine the archetypical narrative trajectories of triumph (comedy and romance) and defeat (tragedy and irony/satire). In a victorious trajectory, the outcome is the goal state of the protagonist; in a trajectory of defeat, the outcome differs from the protagonist's goal and is not even within the range of acceptable outcomes for the protagonist, who is worse off than at the beginning of the narrative. Example 6.2 depicts narrative trajectories of victory and defeat on diachronic decision trees. Example 6.2a shows the outcome as the protagonist's goal state. Various scenarios can trigger such a trajectory, but in this example notice from the brackets along the right margin that the range of states acceptable to the protagonist and those acceptable to the antagonist can overlap. What distinguishes comedy from romance is whether the protagonist is the transgressor or the representative of the established order. Either way, a

a

Example of a Trajectory of *Victory*

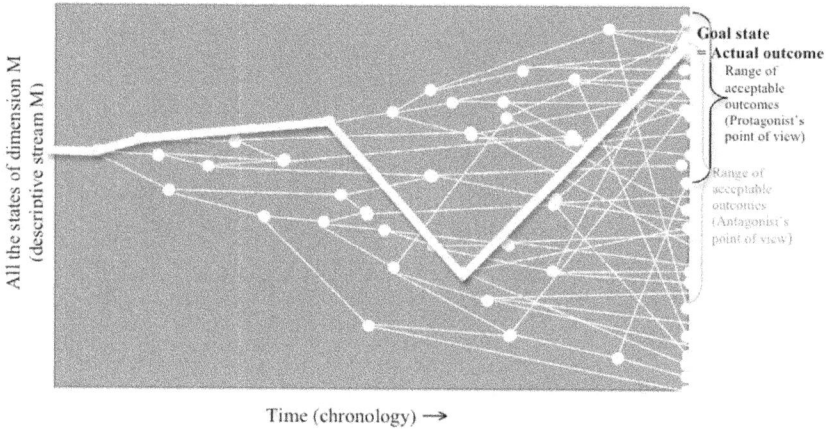

All the states of dimension M (descriptive stream M)

Goal state = Actual outcome

Range of acceptable outcomes (Protagonist's point of view)

Range of acceptable outcomes (Antagonist's point of view)

Time (chronology) →

Comedy, if protagonist = **transgressor**

Romance, if protagonist = **established order**

b

Example of a Trajectory of *Defeat*

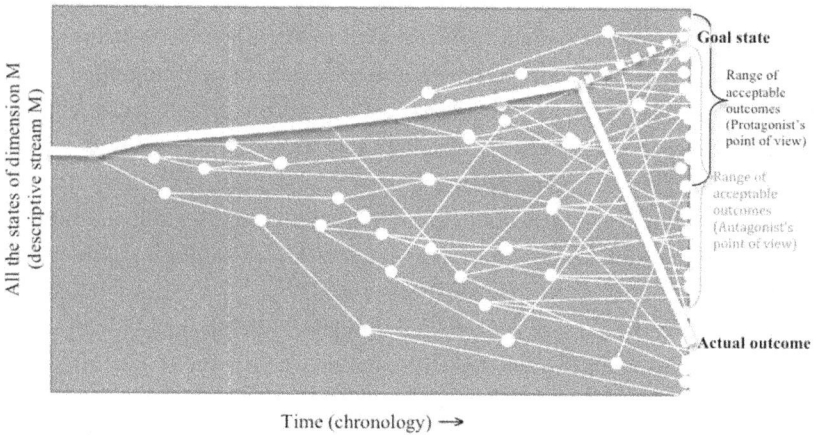

All the states of dimension M (descriptive stream M)

Goal state

Range of acceptable outcomes (Protagonist's point of view)

Range of acceptable outcomes (Antagonist's point of view)

Actual outcome

Time (chronology) →

Tragedy, if protagonist = **transgressor**

Irony/Satire, if protagonist = **established order**

EXAMPLE 6.2. Diachronic decision trees showing narrative trajectories, which reflect goal states, actual outcomes, and acceptable ranges.

narrative of victory can begin with a state that is acceptable to the antagonist but not the protagonist and end in a state that is satisfactory to all.[6] Trajectories of defeat work in a quite different way, which illustrates the distinction between teleology and determinism. As Example 6.2b shows, the outcome can differ dramatically from the goal state. Tragedies, for instance, often begin in a state that is marginally acceptable to both the antagonist and protagonist, whose ambition drives toward a higher goal state; the goal-directed decisions (actions) of the protagonist lead instead to an outcome that is unfortunately not even within the range of acceptable states, neither for the protagonist nor even the antagonist. It remains to be seen to what extent these tendencies, which occur in literature, also occur in musical narrative, or whether music could even articulate them.

A case of seeming correspondence between literature (Goethe's *Wilhelm Meister*) and music (Beethoven's "Hammerklavier," movt. 3) is what Hatten shows as the *expressive genre* of "tragic-to-transcendent" through abnegation (a transcendent inner state achieved by spiritual acceptance of a tragic situation) (1994: 1–28, 281–86). In two ways the proposed model could account for this expressive genre. One possibility is that it is a tragic narrative trajectory in which, during the course of the narrative, the range of acceptable states is expanded to include the once tragic outcome, even though it was not previously acceptable. Alternatively, the outcome, though not the original goal, falls within the original range of acceptable states, in which case the ultimate spiritual acceptance is toward the *status quo*, which the protagonist fails to exceed.

FOCAL TIME FRAMES AND
NARRATIVE FRAMING FUNCTIONS

Although agency is important to narrative, the assertions of agency most important to a narrative need not occur within the time frame that the narrative focuses on. Consider biblical narratives like that of Noah's ark. The assertions of agency within its focal time frame (God's decision to cleanse the world and Noah obeying God's edict to build the ark) subordinate themselves to future assertions of agency occurring in the post-flood world. Such biblical stories serve as *prefacing narratives,* stories focusing on time frames that precede the assertions of agency that fuel their narrative power. Several instances of modernist literature focus on time frames after death, among them Nabokov's novella *The Eye* (1930), Sartre's play *No Exit* (1944), Carter's opera *What Next?* (1997), and, with a time frame following the protagonist's probable murder of her lover, Schoenberg's monodrama *Erwartung* (1909). All these are *consequential narratives*, in that their time frames follow the assertions of agency that fuel their narrative power.

The role of prevalent iterative processes in common-practice music suggests what narrative function similar processes evoke in other repertoires, such as those after 1900. Often they serve a prefacing or consequential function. The introductions to Beethoven's Ninth Symphony, Wagner's *Rheingold*, and Ferruccio Busoni's *Doktor Faustus* project their dynamic forms processively as gradual surges of collective energy. In the Prelude to *Das Rheingold*, the inevitable process of the flowing river (depicted as a gradual increase in pitch range, rate of repetition, number of *ostinato* layers, orchestral thickness, and proportion of upward motion) prefaces Wagner's entire *Ring* tetralogy, full of momentous decisions leading to both triumphant and ultimately tragic outcomes. Its narrative traction increases from the connections between its main motive, the nature motif, and that of *Erda* (mother earth), the Rainbow (which ends the opera), and the Norns (who weave time). As Darcy puts it, the processive *Rheingold* Prelude "serves as a metaphor for the creation of the world and depicts the gradual evolution of impersonal natural forces into human consciousness" (1993: 86).

When such *CollectiveEnergy* fluctuates in a monotonically increasing trajectory, it parallels the "rising crescendo pattern typical of *Gagaku* compositions, which proceed from slow to fast, by the *Jo-ha-kyu* principle – a cumulative increase in music and martial arts; rising speed, volume and inflection. . . . [S]teadily [rising] *CollectiveEnergy* has a rhetorical effect that builds interest in what is to follow (a symphony, an opera, or just an inevitable climax)" (Mailman 2010b: 501). In music, the progress of iterative processes seems inevitable (deterministic) such that they effectively lead to, from, or between junctures of volition, points at which choices are made, agency asserted. The deterministic nature of the processes contrasts with the freedom before or after them.

What can serve as preface can also serve as consequence. The title of Beethoven's Piano Sonata op. 81a, "Das Lebewohl" (The farewell), evokes narrative. Like the introductions and preludes just discussed, the coda of Beethoven's sonata (movt. 1) forges dynamic form by applying an iterative process to repetition. Its horn call motive ($\hat{3}$–$\hat{2}$–$\hat{1}$ over $\hat{1}$–$\hat{5}$–$\hat{3}$) in the upper voices echoes slightly later in the lower voices. As Example 6.3 shows, the following process begins at m. 197. At first (mm. 197–213) the lower voice echo is offset from the upper voice by four measures, then (mm. 223–29) by two measures, then (mm. 227–38) by one measure, then (mm. 239–41) by half a measure. The

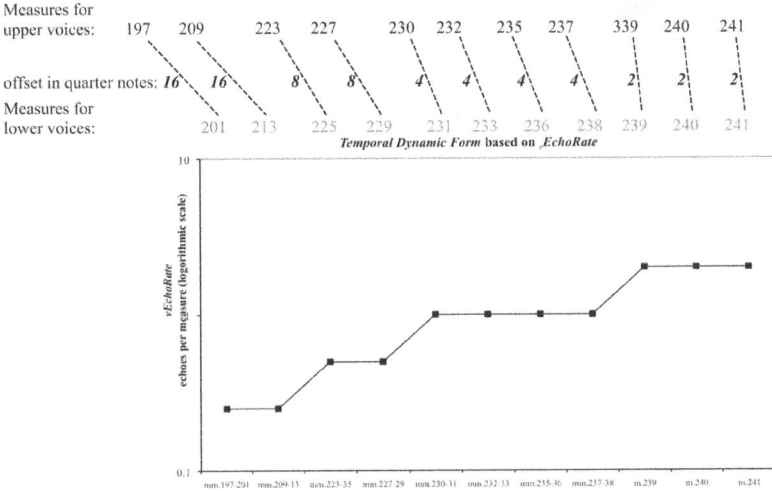

EXAMPLE 6.3. Beethoven's "Lebewohl" horn call motive in upper versus lower voices in the coda of op. 81a, movt. 1.

EchoRate serves as the primary vessel of form for the coda, which is heard as an iterative process of acceleration. The notion of *EchoRate* casts allusions to issues of motion and position in physical space, especially when suggesting a portable outdoor instrument such as a horn, and especially in a narrative context that suggests departure. The steadily surging *EchoRate* of the horn

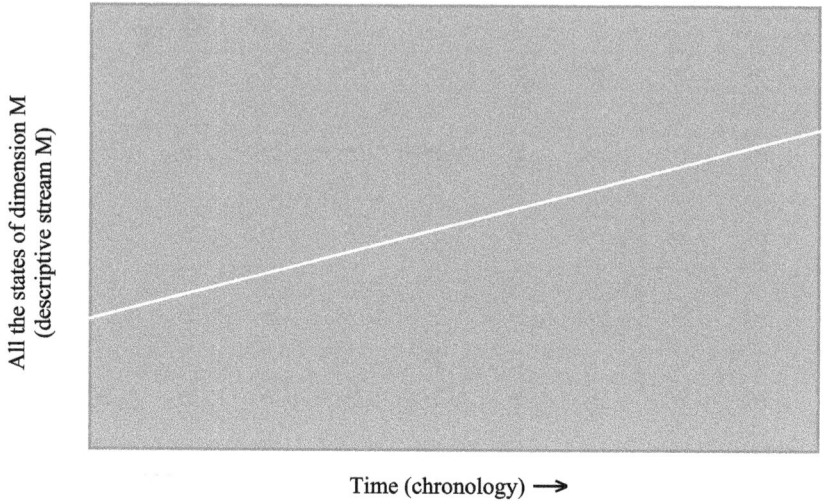

EXAMPLE 6.4. Diachronic decision tree representation of a hypothetical minimalist process piece.

call motive suggests the acceleration of a departing horse or carriage. Whatever decisions there were about leaving during the sonata movement are over by the time we reach the coda; departure is now inevitable but follows as a consequence of earlier decisions, before the time frame of the coda. The accelerating *EchoRate* of the farewell horn call in the coda evokes the inevitability that follows as a consequence of prior decisions from (or before) the main part of the movement.

It might be argued that such narrative allusion, from the time frame of a deterministic process backward or forward to a decision-filled time frame, requires that the two time frames be literally connected within the same work. Actually, there *is* no such requirement, if you consider, for instance, Reger's half-hour long *Symphonic Prologue to a Tragedy*, op. 108 (1908), a work unconnected to any specific tragical narrative, though its narrative function is quite clear from its title.[7] Granted, Reger's work is not processive like the preludes and codas just discussed. But the point is that a narrative serving a prefacing or consequential function need not include junctures of volition within its own time frame because it can draw its agential fuel from literal or imagined events leading to or from it. Such temporal elasticity of agency is a distinctive innovation of twentieth-century music and literature, such as the cited works of Sartre, Nabokov, Carter, Schoenberg, and Reger.

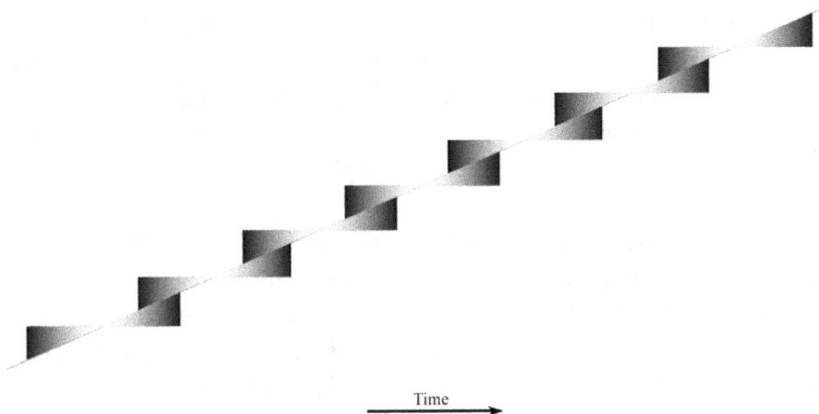

Time

EXAMPLE 6.5. Visualization of a representative fragment of Lucier's *Crossings* (1984).

Where authorship cannot be assigned to events within the time frame of the piece of music, junctures of volition have to be located outside, before its process starts (or after it ends). Example 6.4 shows a corresponding diachronic decision tree; the states in the descriptive stream could be degrees of offset distortion (heard in Reich's music) or the pitch of a pure sine wave oscillator (heard in Lucier's). There are no nodes in the graph because within its time frame there are no junctures at which an event is volitional. Once the process starts, every event is determined. Positing junctures of volition outside a work's time frame is an imaginative act of the listener-interpreter based on the facts of the music and facets external to it, as occurs – albeit differently – when narratives of Beethoven or Chopin evoke theories of topoi, *Formenlehre*, phrasing, or chord grammar, for instance.

LUCIER'S *CROSSINGS* (1984): A VENETIAN BLINDS NARRATIVE

The long-range form of Alvin Lucier's *Crossings* (1984) is especially clear; it arises processively, in this case from a *glissando* of a pure sine tone that slowly (over sixteen minutes) ascends from infrasonic to ultrasonic. A discrete process combines with this *glissando*, creating a series of short-range continuous processes. A divided orchestra alternates in playing the consecutive pitches of a rising chromatic scale that interacts with the *glissando*. One ensemble initiates and sustains a pitch just higher than that of the *glissando* such that their mutual dissonance creates beats; as the *glissando* rises, the speed of the beats slows; when it reaches a unison with the instruments, the beats momentarily cease; as the *glissando* ascends above the pitch of the instruments, the beats gradually accelerate. Eventually, the other ensemble enters and sustains a pitch a semitone higher, starting this short-range process again (the first ensemble stops its pitch before the *glissando* reaches the pitch of the second ensemble).

A representative fragment of Lucier's *Crossings* appears in Example 6.5, a diagram that encapsulates its dynamic form arising through its processes. The diagonal line depicts the sine wave *glissando*. The horizontal lines depict the sustained pitches of the orchestra. The darkness of the shading corresponds to the speed of beats; the shading fades as each horizontal line approaches the rising diagonal and then darkens as the rising diagonal surpasses it. This fading-then-darkening process represents the short-range processes of decreasing-then-increasing beat speed that is repeated over and over while the *glissando* slowly rises to create the long-range form of the work. Thus a narration is depicted visually.

The transformational long-range process of Lucier's *Crossings* might appear to be a vehicle for narrative *transvaluation*, James Liszka's (1989) concept of a cultural hierarchy that shifts over time, cited by Byron Almén (2008) as a basis for reading narrative archetypes. For instance, *Crossings* could be like the triumph of the anthropomorphized "little engine that could." Yet, to gain narrative traction, transvaluation would require agential action denied by the extreme processive nature of Lucier's *Crossings*. Its engine is pure machine, without will.

At first hearing, *Crossings* evokes the revving of an airplane engine or perhaps something foreboding: ominous sirens or a nuclear explosion in slow motion. On their own, these are not narratives, and they reflect neither the short-range nor long-range formal trajectory of the work. Rather, the short-range and long-range aural effects suggest deterministic natural processes, perhaps as experienced slowly over time by a person able to make choices, or exercise volition, either prior to or after the process. In other words, as is the case for all processive minimalist music, the unfolding of each process is narratively restrictive; it suggests a deterministic process exclusive of human agency. For the sake of narrative, then, such agency is most plausibly relegated to points outside (before or after) the duration of the musical processes.

The combination of continuous (*glissando*) and discrete (chromatic scale) processes experienced both as one long-range process and as a series of short-range processes (beat acceleration and deceleration) is difficult to identify in our perceptual experience, and still less obviously relatable to human affairs we'd find narratively interesting. Yet an appropriate scenario does come to mind: the morning sunrise as experienced through venetian blinds. Imagine our protagonist in bed with a headboard beneath an east-facing window. As the sun rises, a ray of its light peeks through the lowest pair of blinds, sweeping vertically across the protagonist's eyes. As it sweeps, the direct light on the eyes gets clearer and then less clear, as the sun's light passes increasingly and then decreasingly through the space between the pair of blinds. This process repeats over and over again as the sun rises, pushing its light through the gaps of successively higher pairs of blinds. Gradually, too, the overall ambient light of the room increases.

This is a narrative account, but not of the processes in isolation, for which there is a persuasive causal account, one that is entirely synoptic (non-narrative): the earth rotates such that the sun appears to rise when viewed from the earth's surface, and the venetian blinds systematically filter the sun's light as it appears to rise. The rising-sun-seen-through-venetian-blinds processes are analogs to the psychoacoustic processes of Lucier's piece, which also have a syntoptic causal account: the sine wave oscillator is programmed in advance to keep rising automatically. By contrast, the narrative account promotes the point of view of an agential observer experiencing deterministic processes as they elapse in time. The rising-sun-seen-through-venetian-blinds analogy suggests a context whereby junctures of volition may relate to deterministic processes of nature as observed by an agent.

Therein lies the narrative interest. It emerges from the interaction between deterministic processes and the undetermined choices we make before, after, or in the midst of them – think of Faust dreading the toll of midnight. We may imagine our protagonist in bed being awakened slowly by the rays of the sun through the venetian blinds on the morning of his execution, his last experience of a sunrise, after having made some inconvenient choices in the past. Or, more optimistically, it is the morning of an Olympic figure-skating competition or chess championship match. While listening to Lucier's *Crossings*, we imagine our protagonist gradually waking, then lying in bed, anticipating the events of the big day, the decisions to be confronted, the crucial choices to be made; this imagined context occurs while we experience the musical processes signaling, through the inevitable elapsing of a natural process, the ever approaching events – all of which is rich with narrative potential because the possibility of choice, the exercise of volition, carries such narrative resonance. Although deterministic process music lacks narrative interest when considered purely in isolation, through its role as preface to, consequence of, or transition between junctures of volition, it is infused with narrative interest similar to that of the deterministic processes in everyday life. Though it is more particularized and *ad hoc*, as appropriate to the idiosyncratic nature of much post-conventional music since 1900, the discourse that creates such infusion is no more invasive than that which relies on an intertextual apparatus of terminologies and categories appropriate for Western art music of the common practice.

TECHNOLOGY, AGENCY, AND OUR RELATION
TO MACHINES AND NARRATIVE

It is tempting to read the extreme determinism of some minimalist processive music as a sign or expression of a fatalistic view of humans as machines controlled by larger forces. This comes with the tendency in some humanistic discourse to see machines as dehumanizing or anti-human. Zaide Smith's (2010) reactionary review of the film *The Social Network* in the *New York Review of Books* is a recent example that exaggerates the legitimate anxieties expressed by twentieth-century dystopic fiction, such as Aldous Huxley's *Brave New World*, George Orwell's *1984*, and Arthur C. Clark's *2001: A Space Odyssey*. I hope it is possible to mind the warnings of such dystopic fiction while acknowledging the fact that computing machines are not solely the vehicles of corporate or government exploitation or control over people; nor do they necessarily reflect conformity or fatalistic defeat of humans to larger evolutionary forces.

The dystopic interpretation of processive music unnecessarily de-narrativizes the listening experience of such works. Moreover, it fails to exploit the opportunities for the new kinds of narrative experiences that such music offers. Above, I discussed how processes in music often depict narratively significant natural forces or physical processes (such as the flow of a river or the motion of a horse and carriage), which lead to, follow from, or transition between one or more junctures of volition. For this reason, the initiation of a process is a significant exercise of agency. The creation of a process is even more significant. The use of artificial means (such as music) to depict natural processes in a narrative is an assertion of creative will, and the means by which it is achieved may be a triumph of human ingenuity taming natural materials and forces.[8] The creation of such processes can take on a life of its own, independent of any specific narrative. And here is where the real ontological adventurousness begins. Now the composer ventures beyond the kinds of processes nature creates on its own and forges new processes that may allude to familiar natural processes in quite unfamiliar ways, thus accessing narrative possibilities unavailable before. These may reveal new aspects of human perception of, and interaction with, nature. In this way, certain uses of technology (such as minimalist and algorithmic processive musical composition) help people assert an Enlightenment idea that humans are separate from nature and masters of their own destiny. Thus technology serves as a vehicle for the expressive ontological adventurousness of much modernist (and postmodernist) music, an adventurousness that compensates for the processive determinism of some of this repertoire. In addition to the intra-opus narrative function of deterministic processes (evoking possible junctures of volition situated just outside their time frames), they also have an inter-opus narrative function, which is that they emerge as an artifact of the ontological adventurousness afforded by technology, which in turn enriches the evocative potential of intra-opus narratives.

CONCLUSION

Narratives of processive minimalist music are feasible because deterministic processes play significant roles in verbal narratives and overtly narrative musical works by preceding, following, or connecting assertions of agency. The crucial difference is that since processive minimalist compositions often lack junctures of volition within their time frames and also lack stylistic conventions, the narrative interpretation of these works requires more ad hoc imaginative play, which cannot rely on stable symbolism (or semiosis) the way more conventional music can. It is hoped that such ad hoc imaginative play may enrich the narrative interpretative possibilities of more conventional music as well as enhance the aesthetic appreciation of processive minimalist music by infusing new narrative possibilities into the listening experience.

NOTES

1. Narrative involves suspense even in its bare essence. If, as Hayden White (1980) declares, narrative translates knowing into telling, then at any given point before the end of a narrative, some of what is known has not yet been told: in this way narrative is inherently suspenseful.

2. As Maureen Carr explains: "Stravinsky's tireless efforts to find the most suitable way of creating the musical setting for the 'pas de deux' show the care with which he was crystallizing his linear style for this scene. His own interpretation of Sonata-Allegro form evolved from the musical materials he chose and his effort to unite the musical argument with the story line. He had to allow for the death of Eurydice. As Orpheus and Eurydice began their journey there was no hint of the imminent dangers that would surface" (2002: 264).

3. The vertical axis corresponds to different states in this dimension; no ordering or ranking is implied. This hypothetical decision tree shows only *one* dimension of freedom to be explored in a narrative, which may jump between multiple descriptive streams, describing physical actions, social actions, and so on. Each descriptive stream corresponds to a *Dimension of Freedom* of an agent, represented by its own decision tree.

4. Narratives assume such a decision tree (rather, a set of such trees, each corresponding to a descriptive stream exploited in the narrative) in that the tree models the sense of agency (freedom to act) to which we are drawn.

5. It is impossible to articulate this fully, since it includes everything we think of as the conventions of form, rhythm, harmony, counterpoint, and so

on, whose theorizing continues. Nevertheless, every narrativist of common-practice repertoire has some idea of what the conventions are and are not; knowing these conventions is a basic conceit of narrative practice.

6. There are exceptions, such as in the quasi-heroic *Magic Flute,* where the antagonist, the Queen of the Night, is banished.

7. Reger's stand-alone tragic prologue was not an isolated instance in turn-of-the-century Germany, as it follows Max Schillings's *Symphonic Prologue to King Oedipus,* op. 11 (1900). We could interpret Messiaen's *Quartet for the End of Time* (1941) as a consequential narrative, occurring in a post-agential time frame; it happens to be full of deterministic processes such as isorhythm, although they are static, reflecting the title of the work.

8. This idea relates to an *extended mind thesis* articulated by George Theiner: "We engineer workspaces so that frequent tasks can be completed more rapidly and reliably" (2011: 20). This allows composers, for instance, to experiment in more daring ways. As Roger Reynolds explains: "Speed is not just a matter of convenience. It is the difference between guesswork – I'll try this and hope I'm right – and interactive work in which constant adjustments are possible as one seeks a particular result" (quoted in Mailman 2004).

WORKS CITED

Almén, Byron. 2003. "Narrative Archetypes: A Critique, Theory, and Method of Narrative Analysis." *Journal of Music Theory* 47(1): 1–39.

———. 2008. *A Theory of Musical Narrative.* Bloomington: Indiana University Press.

Ashby, Arved. 2010. *Absolute Music, Mechanical Reproduction.* Berkeley: University of California Press.

Attali, Jacques. 1985. *Noise: The Political Economy of Music.* Translated by Brian Massumi. Minneapolis: University of Minnesota Press.

Bergson, Henri. 1889. *Essai sur les données immédiates de la conscience.* Published as *Time and Free Will* (1910). London: Sonnenschein.

Carr, Maureen. 2002. *Multiple Masks: Neoclassicism in Stravinsky's Works on Greek Subjects.* Lincoln: University of Nebraska Press.

Cone, Edward T. 1977. "Three Ways of Reading a Detective Story – or a Brahms Intermezzo." *Georgia Review* 31: 554–74.

Darcy, Warren. 1993. *Wagner's "Das Rheingold."* Oxford: Clarendon Press.

Hatten, Robert S. 1994. *Musical Meaning in Beethoven: Markedness, Correlation, and Interpretation.* Bloomington: Indiana University Press.

Hepokoski, James, and Warren Darcy. 2006. *Elements of Sonata Theory: Norms, Types, and Deformations in the Late-Eighteenth-Century Sonata.* Oxford: Oxford University Press.

Kivy, Peter. 2004. "Continuous Time and Interrupted Time: Two-Timing in the Temporal Arts." *Musicae Scientiae,* Discussion Forum 3: 141–55.

Liszka, James. 1989. *The Semiotic of Myth: A Critical Study of the Symbol.* Bloomington: Indiana University Press.

Mailman, Joshua. 2004. "Humans and Machines Make Sweet Music." *Rochester City Newspaper,* May 26.

———. 2009. "An Imagined Drama of Competitive Opposition in Carter's *Scrivo in Vento,* with Notes on Narrative, Symmetry, Quantitative Flux and Heraclitus." *Music Analysis* 28(2–3): 373–422.

———. 2010a. "Emergent Flux Projecting Form in Ruth Crawford Seeger's Quartet (1931)." Paper presented at the Conference of the Society of Music Theory, Indianapolis.

———. 2010b. "Temporal Dynamic Form in Music: Atonal, Tonal, and Other." PhD diss., University of Rochester.

Meelberg, Vincent. 2006. *New Sounds, New Stories: Narrativity in Contemporary Music.* Amsterdam: Leiden University Press.

Pasler, Jann. 1989. "Narrative and Narrativity in Music." In *Time and Mind: Interdisciplinary Issues. The Study of Time* vol. 6, edited by J. T. Fraser, 232–57. Madison: International Universities Press.

Pearsall, Edward, and Byron Almén. 2006. "The Divining Rod on Imagination, Interpretation, and Analysis." In *Approaches to Meaning in Music,* edited by Edward Pearsall and Byron Almén, 1–10. Bloomington: Indiana University Press.

Reyland, Nicholas. 2007. "Lutosławski, 'Akcja,' and the Poetics of Musical Plot." *Music and Letters* 88(4): 604–31.

———. 2009. "Listening for the Plot: Towards a Reader-Response Theory of Musical Narrativity." Paper presented at a seminar during the Directions in Musical Research series at the Institute of Musical Research, London.

Rosen, Charles. 1980. *Sonata Forms.* New York: Norton.

Smith, Zaide. 2010. "Generation Why?" *New York Review of Books,* November 25.

Theiner, George. 2011. *Res cogitans extensa: A Philosophical Defense of the Extended Mind Thesis.* Berlin: Peter Lang.

White, Hayden. 1980. "The Value of Narrativity in the Representation of Reality." *Critical Inquiry* 7(1): 5–27.

7

Musical Prose and Musical Narrativity in the *Fin de Siècle*

Elisheva Rigbi

❧

One of the few uncontested truths in narrative scholarship is that the modernist prose fiction of the early twentieth century manifests a greatly increased disparity between story and discourse, effected in part by manipulations of the representation of temporality: on the one hand, fragmentation and discontinuity, and on the other hand, the interpenetration of traditionally dichotomous disparates such as subjective and objective, past and present. It is further agreed that both result in a weakening of the linear, directional quality so central to traditional notions of narrative. All this is commonly associated with a general rise in the cultural prestige of Subjectivity, concomitant with the disillusionment with the "Dream of Reason" and its attendant values.

In this chapter, I will show a similarly increased disparity between story and discourse in the music of the period effected through similar means. I shall demonstrate this mainly through musical prose: a phenomenon of rhythm, melody, and form for which the period was noted and that has been paradigmatically associated with Arnold Schoenberg and Max Reger. I will argue that the disparity between story and discourse in music of the *fin de siècle* enhances its narrativity even though its directional qualities are weakened by musical prose, since it is precisely the discontinuities of musical prose that correlate with a greater reliance on extra-opus reference, congeneric as well as extra-generic. I shall then explore the broader implications of all this for the temporal structure of music, an essential component of musical narrativity. Finally, I shall situate this decline in directionality and continuity in the greater context of *fin de siècle* culture, showing that the decline in directionality was not restricted to *fin de siècle* music and literature but is manifest throughout contemporary culture, in the sciences – human as well as natural – and in philosophy.[1]

One should add that, given that directionality in Western art music has most often been attributed to tonality and that *fin de siècle* musical prose is found in both tonal and non-tonal contexts, this approach will provide a further example of why narrativity in music should not be equated solely with tonality, even though in many cases it is informed by it.

THE CHANGING MEANING OF "MUSICAL PROSE"

The simplest, most traditional definition of musical prose is as that which is not musical poetry. Since the distinction between poetry and prose has customarily depended heavily on matters of prosody, including meter, in its basic sense "musical prose" denotes free musical diction, that is, the irregular, ambiguous, indistinct, or absent parsing of the temporal flow of music. Since such parsing occurs in music on various orders of temporal magnitude and involves all musical determinants, "musical prose" could, in principle, be generalized to apply to all of them. Here, however, I'll follow prevalent usage and concentrate on aspects of melody – rhythm, motivic and thematic characteristics, and form – and their implications.

The most intuitive aspect of *fin de siècle* musical prose concerns rhythm on all structural levels and orders of magnitude. The extreme rhythmic density and complexity of the music of Debussy, Scriabin, Richard Strauss, Franz Schreker, and early Schoenberg, to name a few, is well known. The huge variety of rhythmic values and subdivisions, the proliferation of accents, agogic "stretchings" (e.g., in Mahler) and syncopation on all orders of magnitude, and the frequent changes of tempo obscured all sense of beat, let alone its metric regularity. In addition, the fuzzier the harmony became (as a result of chromaticism or of increased harmonic density, as in Reger), the lesser the resistance of harmonic rhythm to the rhythmic entropy on other levels, while the growing tendency to polyphony (because of weaker tonal cohesion or of "historicism") multiplied all the above, further exacerbating the rhythmic indeterminacy. Likewise well known are the abundant metric changes and polymeters – notated or otherwise – in the *fin de siècle* oeuvres of Stravinsky, Schoenberg, Schreker, Debussy, Ferruccio Busoni, Alexander Zemlinsky, and many others.

However, in its most common *fin de siècle* usage, "musical prose" concerned irregular phrase length on the musical surface, usually expressed as the avoidance and often outspoken negation of periodic phrase structure, the latter a favorite punching bag of progressively minded musicians of the day. This is how Alban Berg used the term in his famous essay for the 1924 Schoenberg *Festschrift*. In this sense, musical prose was nothing new in the *fin de siècle*. Not only was pre-Classical music rife with musical prose, but, as Hermann Danuser (1975) has shown in his seminal study, the practice of musical prose as the conscious avoidance of periodic phrase structure starts in the early nineteenth century with Weber, Berlioz, Schumann, and (later) Wagner, often supported with rhetoric based on vocabulary borrowed from contemporary discourse on literary prose but notably avoiding the actual expression "musical prose" (see also Dahlhaus 1988b). As shown by Carl Dahlhaus and Danuser, the reason for this omission was the same that, a few years earlier, had induced the early Romantics to validate literary prose by claiming it to be the highest form of poetry, concealed behind an irregular and ostensibly mundane verbal surface, and extolling its "hidden symmetries" and even a latent "ordered periodic structure," namely, the negative connotation of the prosaic.[2] Musical prose, as un-poetic by definition, was not only disordered and chaotic but also unspiritual and incapable of attaining the Sublime, that Romantic version of the Divine that had been associated with poetry for millennia (at least until the emergence of the System of the Arts in the eighteenth century). To paraphrase Goethe, prose was an ungodly *Tohuwabohu*. In describing his own times as the "Prosaic Era," Goethe used this Hebrew term taken from the second verse of the book of Genesis, where it denotes the state of formlessness and void that prevailed before the first day of Creation, that is, a state of things ungraced by Divine Will.[3] The only times before the *fin de siècle* that "musical prose" or its derivatives were used, they were used pejoratively.

It was only ca. 1900 that the expression "musical prose" was rehabilitated, so that in 1911, Max Hehemann, Reger's biographer, could take pride in his own times as "our era of musical prose" (1911: 10). Closer to our own time, the discourse of the later twentieth-century modernist avant-garde has tended to conflate the notion of musical prose with that of developing variation, usually presenting musical prose as the outcome thereof. The foundational text here is, of course, Schoenberg's "Brahms the Progressive" of 1947 (1984). This conflation masks an epistemological contradiction between the two notions: developing variation, as the derivation of everything from a single *Grundgestalt*, expresses the traditional Enlightenment values of unity, cohesion, and ultimate closure (represented and epitomized in music as organicism). Musical prose, by contrast, in constantly producing something new through refraining from repetition, parallelisms, or similarity—and in which, to quote Schoenberg, each and every phrase is singular like "a maxim, a proverb, an aphorism" and likewise has the "full pregnancy of meaning" (1984: 415)—represents the opposite values of irreducible plurality and instability that may apply to any level of structure. Thus, for example, on a sub-thematic level, great variety and plurality of elements hinders their integration into larger articulations. On a thematic or formal level, musical prose denotes irreducible thematic plurality, so that if we understand form as something comprehensive, thematic material ceases to be a determinant of form, or, alternatively, form becomes a much looser conceptual manifold. The first example to come to mind here is Mahler, despite the presence of textbook periods in his works. Not only is the technique of "constant variants" (Adorno 1992) an expression of the musical-prose aesthetic of plurality, but even more so are the extreme contrasts of mood, expression, style, dynamic level, instrumental color and register, and the close proximity of melodic materials that seem to lack all interface and interrupt each other brutally or confront each other simultaneously in the texture with no hope of resolution. Extreme contrast is but an intensification of plurality through increased density. Mahler's preference for non-imitative counterpoint, leaving aside the presence of *stretti* and *fugati* in his music, is not the result of technical shortcomings (as suggested by some of his contemporary detractors) but an aesthetic choice manifest in his music from quite an early stage. The same goes for the disintegrated, "centrifugal" orchestration. The cadenza for flute, horn, and cellos (with basses) at the close of his Symphony No. 9, first movement, cited by Adorno as an expression of irresolvable dialectical antithesis (1992: 157), is one example of many in that symphony of the disintegration of texture itself because of the growing chasm of multidimensional disparity separating its constituents.

On the highest level of magnitude, musical prose is manifest in the stylistic pluralism (hybridity) of so much *fin de siècle* music, which prevents the integration of the multiple stylistic areas in a piece into a unified whole. Besides the obvious example of Mahler, Busoni's practice of quotation, interpolation, embedding, and other forms of recomposition as well as his ideal of "Young Classicism" (1979b: 20) offer examples of this hybridity. The *fin de siècle* proclivity for stylistic pluralism takes on added significance, since it was precisely at this time that style came to be viewed (by Guido Adler) as "the highest ideal unity" and was institutionalized into the new science of *Musikwissenschaft* as the core of its fundamental methodology (1919: 110; see also "Situating Musical Prose" below). Therefore, especially with the weakening of tonal support for form, musical prose deprives music of one of its major traditional points of reference – abandoning it, so to speak, to endless flux. As Dahlhaus claimed, musical prose is the melodic and rhythmic analogue of the emancipation of the dissonance rather than a case of a "melodic and motivic logic" that ostensibly emerged as a substitute for tonal logic (1988b: 105).[4]

Against all this, it is noteworthy that during the *fin de siècle*, unlike in later twentieth-century modernist discourse, musical prose was regarded as the *polar opposite* of developing variation for the very same aesthetic reason. That is how Webern understood it in his article in the 1912 Schoenberg *Festschrift*. Musical prose was also universally identified with flux, ambiguity, obscurity, immeasurability, elusiveness, instability, and irrationality – all qualities traditionally associated with the Subjective and now unanimously recognized by contemporaries as distinctive of the music of the times and as representing an anti-rational, anti-Enlightenment spirit. Thus, for example, Hugo Riemann describes the music of his day in 1894: "A motley such as there has never been, a multitude of crossing and conflicting aspirations, a war between principles that are most decisively contradictory" ("Wohin steuern wir?" [1894], in Riemann 1900: 42). Similarly, Rudolf Louis begins the first chapter of his *Die deutsche Musik der Gegenwart* (1909) by noting that, "as in other domains, in music, too, the present is most monstrously multifarious in its forms and full of contradictions" (1909: 12), and Walter Niemann writes of "stylistic chaos" and "great ambiguity" in his widely read *Die Musik der Gegenwart und der letzteren Vergangenheit* (1913: 153, 189–90).

A few years later, Ernst Kurth writes of "a fracturing in a thousand different directions . . . the most extremely different stylistic moments, working on each other in no order whatsoever" (1917: xi), and Hans Mersmann of "a period full of chaos and contradiction" (1923: 8). Finally, Guido Adler, founding father of modern academic musicology, ascribed to the finale of his good friend Mahler's Sixth Symphony "an architectural style of the Tower of Babel" (1982: 56) and summarized the situation in his influential *Handbuch der Musikgeschichte* as follows: "We are witnessing a confusion and conflict of styles, music is as if gripped in a whirlpool. . . . [It] must soon arrive at the point of crisis . . . as in a rising fever" (1930: 998). Evidently, many agreed on the description of the music, regardless of whether they approved of it or not.

Making the connection between musical prose and flux, Hehemann called the art of his "era of musical prose" the "art of transitions," writing of

Reger: "Musical prose is his means for the art of subtle transitions and inter-mediate values, through which he has proven himself to be a true son of our times" (1911: 13). This brings to mind the "art of constant transition" exalted a few years later by Kurth in his *Grundlagen des linearen Kontrapunkts* (1917). In view of the traditional German distinction between prose as *ungebundene Rede* (unbound speech) and poetry as *gebundene Rede* (bound speech), Kurth's unqualified preference for the "unbound" melodic style of Bach, which he op-poses to the Classical melodic-periodic style (explicitly identified as "bound"), makes his best-selling book a manifesto of musical prose, representing the final stage of its aesthetic validation.

Hehemann identifies musical prose as "freely shaped recitative-like melody" (1911: 13), recalling, of course, Schoenberg's *Das obbligate Rezitativ*, the last of the Orchestral Pieces, op. 16, which is a-thematic, asymmetrical, and non-repetitive like its twin opus, *Erwartung*, op. 17, so frequently cited as the paradigm of musical prose, notwithstanding the presence of some rarified sub-motivic and fixed-pitch connections. More importantly, the two pieces, together with op. 11, no. 3, were understood in their day as lacking any thematic or motivic development and presented as the opposite of developing variation – for example, by Webern (1912). While it is true that, during the *fin de siècle*, Schoenberg explored compositionally both of these ostensibly op-posing possibilities – musical prose and developing variation – it is significant that, aesthetically, he posited in those days as highest desideratum a state of radical musical prose: a chaotic, a-thematic, and a-motivic state. Thus he wrote in 1909, the year of both op. 16 and *Erwartung*, in a famous letter to Busoni:

> I strive for complete liberation from all forms
> from all symbols
> of cohesion and
> of logic.
>   Thus:
> *away with "motivic working out."* (cited in Auner 2003: 70)

MUSICAL PROSE AND MUSICAL REFERENCE

Projecting from the *fin de siècle* view of musical prose as radical melodic plural-ism, if one were to construct an Ideal Type of musical prose, one would arrive at a series of musical incommensurables. Indeed, as Schoenberg wrote, in such a state there can be no coherence, no logic. Neither can there be any structure,

process, development, and direction, nor any meaning. Of course, fragmentation does not occur in *fin de siècle* music to such an extreme degree of totality,
but it does occur there to a markedly increased extent. As demonstrated
above, this was widely remarked upon and recognized by contemporaries
as the most distinctive feature of the music, whether they called it "musical
prose" or not, and whether they liked it or not.

In view of this, one might be inclined to conclude that musical prose
reduces the prospects for musical narrativity to almost nil. However, the opposite is the case. The greater the plurality (as indeterminacy or as fragmentation), the lesser the intra-opus, "syntactic" support for musical meaning, and
the more listeners must resort to external frames of reference in order to make
sense of the music, let alone make it meaningful. In other words, if musical
prose as the fractured musical given is musical discourse, then listeners must
construct some kind of musical story in order to make any sense of it. To
the question, What is musical story? the answer here is that musical story is
anything that helps one make that sense, musical or otherwise – namely, associations, intertexts, topoi, or simply generic or stylistic logic.

It is significant, therefore, that the connection between musical prose
and associations was explicitly made by *fin de siècle* writers. Schoenberg, for
example, in "Brahms the Progressive," describes musical prose as intended
for the "educated listener who, in a single act of thinking includes with every concept all *associations* pertaining to the complex" (1984: 414, emphasis
added). In the same essay he also describes musical prose as an *abbreviation*,
since the great associative freight turns each of its singular and pregnant
constituent ideas into a "whole complex" that says "in a *condensed* form what,
in the preceding epochs, had at first to be said several times with slight variations before it could be elaborated" (1984: 408, emphasis added). The notion of abbreviation had already been used by Schoenberg during the *fin
de siècle* in a section of his *Harmonielehre* (1911) devoted to "abbreviations of
set patterns through omission of intermediate steps" that present only the
"premises" and the "conclusions" while omitting the reasoning that connects
them, on the assumption that it is self-evident to the educated listener (1978:
359). A little earlier in the book, Schoenberg remarks that one need not spell
out in composing the derivation or theoretical justification of exceptional
or singular events (here: alterations), since, "unlike a snail with its shell, a
composition does not have to drag around with it forever, wherever it goes,
a *motivic etymology*, an exact legal proof of its right to exist" (1978: 354–55,
emphasis added). More significant is that Schoenberg calls such abbrevia-

tions "clichés" (1978: 359). In other words, the less unified the musical text, the more listeners must turn to external frames of reference, and then the only way they can do so is by increasingly relying on cues that are easily recognized and identified with the meaning-providing frame, or, in other words, on clichés or topical gestures. A similar argument has been made by Vera Micznik (2001) concerning Mahler. However, she is not always clear as to the precise relation between thematic pluralism and narrativity.[5] In fact, what Schoenberg describes in *Harmonielehre* is a *necessary connection* between musical prose and external reference – stylistic, generic, or topical. Granted, Schoenberg refers here primarily to harmonic frames of reference, but the ideational, semantic, and cognitive connection that he later makes between musical prose and associations supports applying it to other musical aspects, especially in view of the compositional connection that he made between the two terms in those years.

Here again the paradigmatic example is *Erwartung,* so radical in its musical prose and yet so saturated with associative meanings. The work has been described as the closest to a-thematicism and as being in a constant state of flux wherein every motif is transformed before it has had the chance to consolidate an identity and acquire meaning (Neighbour 2010). But this refers only to internal meaning and cannot account fully for the work's intelligibility and richness of meaning, as it ignores the wealth of external *musical* associations informing the piece. It is doubtful, for instance, that one can follow *Erwartung* musically without reference to tonal associations, if only in the form of the centers created *inter alia* through triadic emphases or "clearings" within more complex sonorities, which, in turn, are heard as "clearings" only in relation to an associative tonal frame.[6] Likewise doubtful is the idea that one could process the continuous melodic *Fortspinnung* of *Erwartung* without reference to those typical Romantic gestures – the stepwise-descending, long-short figures that join together the faint trace of a resolving dissonance (which never really resolves here) with the essence of Romantic agony, both referring back to the *pianto* figure. Similarly dependent on a web of *musical* associations are the extended melodic surges followed by a short and very partial release, described by Paul Bekker as "bearing the unmistakeable stamp of Wagnerian diction," and which refer us to the latter's tonal implications, conspicuous even though they are consistently unrealized (1924: 279). Moreover, Bekker describes the music of *Erwartung* as the *abbreviatur* (abbreviation) of traditional forms just as poetically, dramatically, and ideationally the work is, for him, the "reflex" of events that do not occur in it and the sublimate of the entire

Romantic tradition (1924: 281). Bekker regards the piece and musical prose in general predominantly from the perspective of associative meaning – musical and beyond.

Much more explicit are the stylistic and generic clichés encountered in much *fin de siècle* music that create a real correlation between musical prose and the preponderant stylistic pluralism mentioned above. It is not only that stylistic pluralism inevitably results in musical prose but also that radical musical prose leads to a multi-stylistic reading of the music. Thus, for example, the extreme topical and stylistic disjunction between thematic materials in the first movement of Mahler's Sixth Symphony is foregrounded by its morphological and syntactic discontinuity no less than it informs it. It is likewise possible that at least some of the quotations, paraphrases, and other seemingly specific intertextual references whose sources have perplexed Mahler's analysts are but those analysts' projections, prompted by their frustrated attempts to arrive at coherence and cohesion by syntactic means.

When musical prose occurs on a more minute scale, fragmentation is such that the themes or motifs have no chance to establish a concrete individuality, encouraging one to hear them more as references to familiar genres or styles. A prime example is Debussy's *Jeux*. Listening to the piece, one cannot avoid a feeling that the short thematic fragments emerging from the dense motivic web are somewhat anonymous. One recognizes their styles long before one recognizes them in and of themselves. Thus, for example, one instantly recognizes an "Oriental" melody at reh. **17** (bassoon and flute), **19** (oboe and English horn), **39** (clarinet), and around **40** (flute, then horn), but it takes more hearings to recognize that the first two occurrences are of the same motif, while the last two are of another one. Similarly, one recalls a Romantic melody at **50** (solo violin and cellos) or a waltz (strings, mainly from **28+4** to **34**; alternating with other gestures) long before one can recall any specific melody or motif. In other words, one interprets the fragmented thematic materials as stylistic gestures rather than specific identities and thus musical prose as stylistic pluralism.

Another type of cliché involved with *fin de siècle* musical prose is thematic or formal gestures. Thus, for example, the *cantabile* clarinet melody that opens the first movement of Reger's Clarinet Quintet, op. 146, is typically theme-like in its placement, its eight-measure periodic structure, and its conspicuity against the materials and texture of the strings. However, it receives absolutely no development in the movement, returning only once, unchanged, in the recapitulation (m. 168). Unsurprisingly, this melody became a subject of debate concerning whether or not it is the first theme of the movement (see Kühn 1973; Dorfmüller 1966). Similarly, in the slow introduction to Schreker's *Kammersymphonie* (1916), a two-measure descending chromatic figure played in octaves by the first and second violins (soloists, m. 3 through the first beat of m. 5), stands out not only against the rest of the airy, shimmering texture but also against its own continuation (mm. 5–6) by virtue of its high register and relatively long rhythmic values, thereby giving an appearance of a theme in itself and, furthermore, of a reference to the Tristan prelude. However, in contrast to the other thematically functioning elements in the work, whose constant variability leads one to perceive them more as global qualities such as character, style, and mood, this "theme" is hardly developed in the symphony, resurfacing in exact repetition only to usher in the Adagio section (**12**), which doubles as second theme cum slow movement and in the "subdominant," but in very similar orchestration in the parallel place in the "recapitulation" (which doubles as the last movement of a four-movement symphonic cycle). It recurs once more, toward the trio analogue in the scherzo (at **29**+5), doubled by all four violin parts and both viola parts, then to be repeated on its dominant by cellos, basses, and horn. Here it appears in a much thicker texture, but, as in its other occurrences, it is stated in its entirety and cannot be said to receive any development that can be called thematic, because any such development is submerged in the dense proliferation of constantly varied chromatic figures and minute figurations that constitute the main substance of the symphony (e.g., **1**-4 [flute] or **30** [violas and clarinet]; in both cases the motif developed is the end of the "theme").[7]

    In other words, the thematic salience of an element (as part of its musical processing) now depends *not* on its syntactic functioning (i.e., on being developed), as in common-practice notions of form, but rather on the *lack thereof* (i.e., on its singularity). It is correlatively increasingly supported by non-syntactic (i.e., extra-opus) reference, which may be intertextual, as in the Tristan association in the Schreker or more general (i.e., to stylistic and generic conventions). Since in the Reger and Schreker examples cited, these conventions have to do with the differentiation between thematic and developmental sections obliterated by both musical prose and developing variation, an effective interface of the two is created, notwithstanding their aesthetic disparity. Other thematic gestures (clichés) are, for example, Reger's periodic antecedents that are conspicuously *not* followed by their consequents (e.g., op. 118, first movement, mm. 13–17) and the lengthy series of *Zweitaktgruppen* in the first movement of Mahler's Fourth Symphony (exposition) that avoid precisely those parallelisms that would enable periodic closure, creating what Bekker termed a "malicious parody on Biedermeier" (1921: 150–55).

In all the examples cited above, the fragmentation of musical discourse effected by musical prose directs listeners away from the syntactic toward the semantic, that is, away from the text and toward its multiple contexts – both musical and extra-musical – that they must construct in order to endow the discourse with meaning and that therefore function as its "stories." This increased interpretive activity highlights the disparity between musical story and discourse in *fin de siècle* music that had been more masked in earlier repertoires, foregrounding the dual temporal structure that is essential to narrative.

TEMPORAL IMPLICATIONS

Having established the correlation between musical prose and the increased disparity between musical discourse and musical story, let us now explore its implications for the temporal structure of music – which is a major aspect of its narrativity. Musical prose as abbreviation represents a divergence between discourse and story time as concerns duration (in Genette's sense). Whereas in verbal narratives such disparity through abbreviation is a common traditional feature, in music it constitutes a reversal of common practice. In common-practice musical narrative processing, the story (that which constitutes the fundamental logic or structure) is usually represented fully within the discourse (or expected to be so by the pertinent theories), while the discourse, if one adopts Schenkerian terms, is furthermore a *prolongation* of the story. Musical prose, as we've seen, is, in contrast, the *abbreviation* of the story, which is hence *not* represented in the discourse.[8]

Musical prose represents a divergence between story and discourse time not only concerning duration but also as regards order (in Genette's sense), if achrony (i.e., indeterminate or indeterminable order of events) is considered as a category of temporal order. In paradigmatic modernist literary narrative discourse, one refers the events – both external and internal – to their "correct" linear order in the story. The story is thus always more linear and directional than the discourse, on the assumption that courses of action and reaction in "the real world" are always directionally ordered. In musical prose, in contrast, the reverse may be the case, since the constructed musical storyworlds are not necessarily ordered in themselves, linearly or at all. They are, if anything, less ordered the more radical the musical prose, since, as I've shown elsewhere, the greater the fragmentation and (correlatively) the density, the more one tends to perceive the musical storyworlds as homogeneous global qualities, that is, as *less articulated and ordered* (see Rigbi-Shafrir 2002: chap. 6). Furthermore, it is not certain that the multiple musical storyworlds evoked by musical prose can be joined together to a continuous story line, directional or not (beyond, perhaps, a self-referential meta-narrative story about change of musical idiom and the kind of processing that it entails).[9] Finally, the only vestige of unilinearity in such a radical situation of musical prose would be in the discourse rather than in the story by virtue of coinciding with "real" narrating time. However, the constant need to construct musical storyworlds in order to establish even the basic articulations (characters, events) of the discourse, let alone trace their connections, detracts from the experience of this linearity. If directional sequence is, indeed, essential to narrative, and if narrative is a fundamental form of cognition, then the less things "add up" musically, the more incentive there is to construct broader semiotic circles, extending beyond the musical text. As narrative analysis of common practice music has amply shown, such broader circles of meaning can be and indeed are inscribed in music that is upheld as the model of *musical* continuity, coherence, and unity. However, the fractured utterances of musical prose and their multiple musical storyworlds make such narrative readings – musical and beyond – absolutely *sine qua non*.

SITUATING MUSICAL PROSE

In its *fin de siècle* sense, then, musical prose represents irreducible plurality that, in itself, involves increased reference to extra-textual domains, which, in turn, function as story to the musical given as discourse. This results in an unprecedented and greatly foregrounded disparity between musical discourse and story, paralleling the one manifest in early modernist prose fiction yet differing in some of its temporal attributes. In turn, it becomes clear that the aesthetic of musical prose is the antithesis of organicism. The musical work is no longer a cohesive and self-sufficient organic entity unified by its own "inner law" but a permeable "open work" (in Eco's sense) penetrated to its core by multiple contexts. In fact, it has no core of its own, only as the nexus of these multiple contexts.

If the organic – that great idea of the late eighteenth and nineteenth centuries – as subject only to its "inner law" and as "its own cause" thereby attained objective status and represented the Enlightenment values of objectivity and rationality upon which the entire Western project of knowledge had been constituted, at least since the scientific revolution, then the aesthetic of musical prose, as its negative image, signifies the demise of those values throughout Western culture ca. 1900, in those great upheavals I have described elsewhere as the "breakdown of the Rational Paradigm" (Rigbi-Shafrir 2002). Briefly, this Rational Paradigm (and the entire Western tradition that had exemplified it) was constituted on an absolute division between subject and object, implying the category of substance and a referential concept of knowledge that conceived of truth as full subjective compliance with its object, construed as *given* and absolute ("standing in its own right"). Consequently, truth, too, was conceived as absolute, unchanging, universal, and one. Even after Kant, this remained the implied epistemological model. *Fin de siècle* thought replaced this "copy theory" with a new concept of knowledge as creation – as a completely *free* and *incessant* creative process whereby both objects and subjects come into being through their articulation or "objectification" from an indeterminate continuum of "life" (Wilhelm Dilthey's *Lebensphilosophie*, etc.) or "pure experience" (William James's "radical empiricism"), which is the totality prior to all distinction, including that between subject and object.

In the new mind-made, man-made world of the *fin de siècle*, nothing was given: there were no self-sufficient objects, only objectifications determined and re-determined by their mutual context alone. Although the notion of an inextricable subjective element in all knowledge had been a recurrent theme of skepticism since antiquity, it had never become mainstream before the *fin de siècle*, the bulk of the Western tradition having been devoted precisely to combating doubt and promoting objective certainty. Besides, when skeptics throughout the ages doubted the attainability of objective knowledge, they inevitably participated in the mainstream image (though not necessarily the assumption) of objectivity "unto itself" and knowledge as its faithful, albeit unattainable, representation. In contrast, *fin de siècle* thinkers largely abandoned both image and assumption of substance and objective knowledge but, rather than lament this, saw in the new creative form of knowledge a source of stimulation, meaning, and increased dignity. Even the few who did retain a notion of metaphysical substance (e.g., Bergson) joined the others in a reversal of its attributes, describing it now as fluid, continuous, changeable, and resistant to reason and regarding unchanging certainty and universal validity, coherence, and unity as the most "artificial," hence farthest removed from "reality." The most extreme expression of the changed concept of knowledge is, perhaps, the Pragmatism of William James, which symmetrized the concept of truth so that it was now measured against the subject rather than the object, as before.

This new *Weltanschauung* of the *fin de siècle* inevitably entailed a decline in directional features (Rigbi-Shafrir 2002: chaps. 1–3). A constitutive trait of traditional Western structures of knowledge had been a certain constant asymmetry, or directionality, that was inherent in the irreversible priority of object to subject, of the world to knowledge-about-the-world upon which they were constituted. The symmetrization of the subject-object dichotomy in the new *Weltanschauung* removed the grounds for these directional tendencies, and the result is manifest throughout contemporary Western culture in the wholesale abandonment of the causal, teleological, genetic, evolutionary, and "historical" explanations preferred in the nineteenth century as *exclusive* hallmarks and guarantors of objectivity (precisely *because* of their directional form) and their replacement by non-directional, structural, functional, holistic, and circular forms of knowledge, which now acquired canonic status. The "crisis of historicism" (in its multiple senses), for example, so much talked about in the early 1900s, was a crisis of directional notions resulting from their very directionality, since it became evident that the premises of unilinear temporal directionality and of the historical essence of human reality were incompatible with the requirements of scientific objectivity in the human sciences. Among the correlates of the crisis of historicism one might mention the "emancipation" of *Verstehen* – locus of the hermeneutic circle and previously regarded as a non-scientific (albeit necessary) auxiliary to inductive and deductive methods and causal knowledge or the emergence to dominance of structural and descriptive linguistics (in place of nineteenth-century historical philology) and of sociology (in place of parts of the historical discipline that had been the nineteenth-century paradigm of humanistic knowledge). Similar transformations in psychology are evident in the emergence of holistic psychologies, the most famous of which is Gestalt theory, alongside the directional stimulus-response structures of the academically more established experimental psychology.[10] Finally, in the arts, the crisis of objectivism was manifest not only in the widespread abandonment of mimesis, in artistic practice as well as in art theory (e.g., Russian formalism), but also in that weakening of directionality for which early modernist fictional narrative is so famous. And, yes, also in musical prose.

Here, one might ponder the fact that it was precisely at this moment that the organicist aesthetic of absolute music reached a zenith of cultural prestige as music (viewed from the absolute perspective) became a paradigm for all other modes of symbolization, including language. Aspiring now to "the condition of music," all of them attempted an autonomistic or systematic (in the case of language) approach while downplaying aspects of objective reference or historical development. Moreover, at the same time, much music-theoretical and aesthetic discourse radicalized organicism (e.g., Schenker, Schoenberg, and, a bit later, August Halm), which was furthermore institutionalized into the new discipline of *Musikwissenschaft* by Adler through the method of "style criticism." What should one make of this striking incongruity? Answering that would be beyond the scope of this essay. Let it suffice to say that during the *fin de siècle*, as a constituting period of modern musicology, there flourished many varieties of discourse about music. Alongside the radicalized organicist theories of Adler, Schoenberg, Schenker, and Halm, who (with the exception of Schoenberg) objected strongly to the pluralist music of the *fin de siècle*, there were alternative approaches that upheld the inherent plurality, changeability, and inevitable connectedness of the musical work as an "objectification of Life" (to use Dilthey's term) and enthusiastically supported the new pluralist music of the day. I have mentioned Busoni, with his aesthetic of the unlimited variability of the musical work and ideal of the stylistically pluralist "Young Classicism," which bears unmistakable affinity to the philosopher Ernst Bloch's contemporary notion of "nonsynchronicity."[11] Also mentioned was Ernst Kurth, whose oeuvre at least starting from *Grundlagen des linearen Kontrapunkts* is a comprehensive project of outspoken musical *Lebensphilosophie*, with all its holistic and circular implications. In this connection, one should also mention Janáček's harmonic theories, culminating in his *Theory of Harmony* (1912), which based harmonic progressions on a "chaotic moment" of chordal interpenetration and portrayed the musical process in general as a holistic one wherein clearly defined and relatively stable entities emerge from an obscure, fused totality identified as a source of beauty, character, and expression. The affinity to *fin de siècle Lebensphilosophie* is further highlighted when Janáček identifies the "chaotic moment" with the "fullness of Life."[12] Finally, I have mentioned Paul Bekker, who was not only highly sensitive to the connection between musical prose and extra-textual reference but who, in 1916, called for replacing the organicist notion of form as sound image with a notion of what he called "sociological form" that comprehends both sound image and the surrounding world(s) (1916: 17–32).[13] With the exception of Janáček (as theorist), all of them were highly influential in their day, which raises questions of reception history: why were their approaches not institutionalized into academe? Why (and when) did their influence wane? These questions, too, exceed the scope of the present essay. However, I hope to have succeeded in showing the direct correlation between musical prose, as exemplifying the new *fin de siècle* aesthetic of plurality, and an increased disparity between musical story and discourse; that this disparity, in foregrounding external reference and thus highlighting the dual temporality that is a hallmark of narrative, serves to intensify the narrativity of much *fin de siècle* music even as its directionality is undermined by musical prose; and that all this occurs irrespective of questions of (a)tonality, so that one can regard musical prose and cognate phenomena as a major vehicle for the continuing narrativity of music after the demise of tonality.

NOTES

All translations in this essay are by the author.

1. By *fin de siècle* I refer to the period roughly between 1890 and 1920, a time that has usually been viewed as transitional in music history but that I have described elsewhere as a music-historical period in its own right that participates fully in contemporary culture and signifies the beginnings of postmodernism at the very height of modernism (Rigbi-Shafrir 2002).

2. Quotations from Friedrich Schlegel and Schelling, respectively, in Danuser (1975: 17–32).

3. Quoted from Goethe's essay *Geistesepochen* (1817) in Danuser (1975: 18).

4. See also Dahlhaus's essay "Emancipation of the Dissonance" (1988a). However, Dahlhaus's analogy rests on Schoenberg's rejection of ornament, expressed in harmonic theory in the notion of inessential "non-harmonic tones."

5. While Micznik (2001) is very persuasive on the semantic richness of Mahler's multiple themes, elsewhere she regards the "multitude of thematic building blocks" as a substitute for weakened tonal syntax (instead of its analogue), coupling it with developing variation as a source of a new syntax in a way incompatible with the *fin de siècle* attitude.

6. Schoenberg himself notes *Erwartung*'s reliance on "older forms," so that one should not regard it as a stage in the abrogation of tradition – as in the avant-garde narrative of progress that has informed the historiography of *fin de siècle* music until quite recently (1978: 418–19). In a more general vein, he states that "in [the composer's] subconscious lies a wealth of old knowledge, which he will resurrect whether he wants to or not" (1978: 416).

7. Micznik (2001) describes the themes of the first movement of Mahler's Ninth Symphony similarly, referring to them as "refrains" and "incantations." In contrast to Mahler, however, Schreker's theme doesn't participate in the developmental processes in the symphony, bearing no affinity to the rest of its motivic substance.

8. In this context, one should mention the extensive use of ellipsis (the most extreme form of abbreviation of discourse vs. story) in the harmonic thought and practice of Reger. "Unexpected

progressions" where "any chord can follow any chord" are explained only by "intermediate harmonies" constructed mentally by the listeners in a process of reinterpretation (*Umdeutung*) and whose quantity sometimes exceeds that of the actually notated and sounding chords, thereby multiplying the density or "speed" (Genette) of the musical discourse, which is often extremely dense to begin with (Grabner 1920: 7). Reger draws on Riemann's harmonic theories as well as on his aesthetic notions of active and selective hearing, subverting them through application *ad absurdum*. See also Reger's own *Beiträge zur Modulationslehre* (1922), although it makes use only of diatonic *Umdeutungen*.

9. While this question requires further investigation, it is already clear that the pluralistic harmonic idiom used by Busoni, for example, in his *Sonatina Seconda* (1912) involves harmonic vocabularies/story lines that contradict each other.

10. On other early twentieth-century holistic psychological theories, see Ringer (1969: 374–84) and Ash (1998: 307–22). The acknowledged background of most was the "analytical and interpretive psychology" proposed by Dilthey in his *Ideen zur beschreibende und zergliedernde Psychologie* (1894) as the foundation of the human sciences. Later, it was subsumed by his notion of *Weltanschauung*.

11. Bloch's notion of *Ungleichzeitigkeit* has been variously translated into English as "nonsynchronicity," "nonsynchronism," "nonsimultaneity," and "noncontemporaneity" (see Durst 2004: 29n5). Developed during World War I in *The Spirit of Utopia* (1918), the concept was used at first mainly in a social sense to indicate the presence in any given period of cultural elements of differing historical provenance. However, Bloch's later exploration of montage and other "disruptive and interpolative techniques" in expressionism and surrealism as an ideal of modern art supports its usage in an intra-opus sense (see Durst 2004: 1–32).

12. See Beckerman (1994). By 1912 Janáček had replaced the expression "chaotic moment" with that of the "twine" that ties together different chords through interpenetration.

13. The influence of Bekker, for many years the music critic of the *Frankfurter Zeitung*, on Adorno is evident, though not always noted.

WORKS CITED

Adler, Guido. 1982. "Gustav Mahler." In *Gustav Mahler and Guido Adler: Records of a Friendship*, edited by Edward R. Reilly, 13–73. Cambridge: Cambridge University Press. First published in 1916.

———. 1919. *Methode der Musikgeschichte*. Leipzig: Breitkopf und Härtel.

———, ed. 1930. *Handbuch der Musikgeschichte*. Berlin-Wilmersdorf: Heinrich Keller.

Adorno, Theodor Wiesengrund. 1992. *Mahler: A Musical Physiognomy*. Translated by Edmund Jephcott. Chicago: University of Chicago Press.

Ash, Mitchell G. 1998. *Gestalt Psychology in German Culture 1890–1967: Holism and the Quest for Certainty*. Cambridge: Cambridge University Press.

Auner, Joseph, ed. 2003. *A Schoenberg Reader: Documents of a Life*. New Haven: Yale University Press.

Beckerman, Michael. 1994. *Janáček as Theorist*. Studies in Czech Music no. 3. Stuyvesant: Pendragon Press.

Bekker, Paul. 1916. *Das deutsche Musikleben.* Berlin: Schuster und Loeffler.

———. 1921. *Gustav Mahlers Sinfonien.* Berlin: Schuster und Loeffler.

———. 1924. "Schönberg: *Erwartung.*" In *Arnold Schönberg zum fünfzigsten Geburtstage, 13 September 1924 (Musikblätter des Anbruch VI/Sonderheft),* 275–82.

Berg, Alban. 1924. "Warum ist Schönbergs Musik so schwer verständlich?" In *Arnold Schönberg zum fünfzigsten Geburtstage, 13 September 1924. (Musikblätter des Anbruch VI/Sonderheft),* 329–41.

Bloch, Ernst. 2000. *The Spirit of Utopia.* Translated by Anthony A. Nassar from the 2nd German edition (1923). First published in 1918.

Busoni, Ferruccio. 1979a. "The Essence and Oneness of Music." In *The Essence of Music,* translated by Rosamond Ley, 1–16. Westport: Hyperion Press. First published in 1921.

———. 1979b. "Young Classicism." In *The Essence of Music,* translated by Rosamond Ley, 19–23. Westport: Hyperion Press. First published in 1920.

Dahlhaus, Carl. 1988a. "Emancipation of the Dissonance." In *Schoenberg and the New Music,* translated by Derrick Puffett and Alfred Clayton, 120–27. Cambridge: Cambridge University Press.

———. 1988b. "Musical Prose." In *Schoenberg and the New Music,* translated by Derrick Puffett and Alfred Clayton, 105–19. Cambridge: Cambridge University Press.

Danuser, Hermann. 1975. *Musikalische Prosa.* Regensburg: Gustav Bosse.

Dorfmüller, Kurt. 1966. "Regers Klarinettenquintett op. 146." In *Max Reger zum 50. Todestag am 11. Mai 1966,* edited by Ottmar Schreiber and Gerd Sievers, 191–203. Bonn: Ferd. Dummler Verlag.

Durst, David C. 2004. *Weimar Modernism: Philosophy, Politics and Culture in Germany, 1918–1933.* Lanham: Lexington Books.

Grabner, Hermann. 1920. *Regers Harmonik.* Munich: Otto Halbreiter Musikverlag.

Hehemann, Max. 1911. *Max Reger: Eine Studie über moderne Musik.* Munich: R. Piper.

Kühn, Hellmut. 1973. "Sang und Gegensang: Zu Regers Klarinettenquintett opus 146." *Neue Zeitschrift für Musik* 134: 141–43.

Kurth, Ernst. 1917. *Grundlagen des linearen Kontrapunkts: Bachs melodische Polyphonie.* Bern: Max Drechsel.

Louis, Rudolf. 1909. *Die deutsche Musik der Gegenwart.* Munich: Georg Müller.

Mersmann, Hans. 1923. *Musik der Gegenwart.* Berlin: Julius Bard.

Micznik, Vera. 2001. "Music and Narrative Revisited: Degrees of Narrativity in Beethoven and Mahler." *Journal of the Royal Musical Association* 126(2): 193–249.

Neighbour, Oliver. 2010. "Schoenberg." In *Grove Music Online.* Accessed 9 November 2010.

Niemann, Walter. 1913. *Die Musik der Gegenwart und der letzteren Vergangenheit bis zu den Romantikern, Klassizisten, und Neudeutschen.* Berlin: Schuster und Loeffler.

Reger, Max. 1922. *Beiträge zur Modulationslehre.* 22nd ed. Leipzig: C. F. Kahnt. First published in 1904.

Riemann, Hugo. 1900. *Präludien und Studien II.* Leipzig: Hermann Seemann Nachfolger.

Rigbi-Shafrir, Elisheva. 2002. "The Modern in Music 1890–1920 against the 'Crisis of Historicism' and the Breakdown of the Rational Paradigm: A Critical Analysis of a Style." PhD diss., Hebrew University of Jerusalem (in Hebrew with English summary and table of contents).

Ringer, Fritz. 1969. *The Decline of the German Mandarins: The German Academic Community, 1890–1933*. Cambridge: Harvard University Press.

Schoenberg, Arnold. 1978. *Theory of Harmony*. Translated by Roy Carter from the 3rd ed. (1922). Berkeley: University of California Press. First published in 1911.

———. 1984. "Brahms the Progressive." In *Style & Idea*, edited by Leonard Stein, 398–441. London: Faber and Faber. First published in 1947.

Webern, Anton. 1912. "Schönbergs Musik." In *Arnold Schönberg* (no editor listed), 41–47. Munich: R. Piper.

8

Narrative Nostalgia: Modern Art Music off the Rails

Lawrence Kramer

Narrative has had a strange fate in the past century and a quarter. Thanks to the proliferation of narrative media, from mass-market print to Kindle, from cinema and broadcasting to the Internet, more narratives have been unleashed on the world than in all of previous history. Many more. When Roland Barthes declared in 1966 that "the narratives of the world are numberless," he did not know the half of it (1988: 79). Yet it is widely understood that modernity essentially rendered narrative obsolete. As Walter Benjamin (1969) said, not liking it at all, modernity brought storytelling to an end. Most of the great modernist artworks, in all media, seem premised on the bankruptcy of narrative. The stories keep coming, but the life has gone out of them, except perhaps when they reflect on the premises and often the impossibility of their own telling. How these trends might be reconciled is a good question.

The particular concern of this volume is, of course, what happened to narrative or narrativity in music since 1900. It should be acknowledged at the outset that the topic is impossibly broad; no account of it can hope to do more than characterize a prevailing tendency or two among many counterflows and tributaries. The difficulty is compounded by the need to distinguish between the instance or genre of narrative, on the one hand, and narrativity, their condition of possibility, on the other, and again between the era of modernity and modernism, its exemplary aesthetic disposition.[1] Music implicates itself differently with each of these terms, which, however, being music and therefore protean, it loves to swirl together.

My own particular concern is with modern art music; I will leave it to others to address the other kinds of music that proliferated in the modern era even more broadly than narrative did. The default assumption seems to be that a narrative impetus was built into eighteenth- and nineteenth-century art music on both formal and tonal grounds and that on the same grounds it either was largely banished in the twentieth century or became problematic and required various modes of recuperation, recovery, or reinvention. The result might seem to be a classic unicorn hunt: we don't know how to find our quarry, and if we found it anyway we might also find that it doesn't exist. But the situation – the story, if you will – is more complex than that, and the question it poses deals less with technical means than with expressive and cognitive ends.

For it did not take the twentieth century to render narrative as such problematic; one might even suggest that skepticism about narrative has long been part of its very definition. The key question about narrative in music (or, for that matter, in culture) since 1900 is not whether it has been subject to skepticism, mutation, or deconstruction but what distinctive forms of these vicissitudes it has assumed and why.

To help prepare an answer, I propose to linger a little on two emblematic works of literary modernism, in part because they offer some real clarity on the issue, in part because the expressive and cognitive ends I spoke of cut across media in multiple directions, and in part because I maintain that narrative is fundamentally the art of recounting, of putting stories into words, and that once disengaged from that context, even as metaphor, the concept of narrative becomes at best a poor fiction of coherence. Narrative is grounded in a demand or desire to *tell* something, and it cannot be budged from that ground. As I have suggested elsewhere, music typically addresses narrative from a certain distance by adopting a variety of supplemental, performative, and critical relations to narrative forms. Music assumes narrativity by hosting features of narrative that migrate among media, not by fabricating second-hand modes of a recounting it cannot plausibly perform (Kramer 1995). For a few moments, then, let's stick with words.

The first of my emblematic texts is Kafka's story "In the Penal Colony." Its narrative, in one dimension a narrative about narrative, centers on a writing machine – of sorts. The machine writes on the bodies of convicted criminals. It inscribes on them an inverted statement of their crimes: whatever command a criminal has disobeyed is incised on him, with flourishes, front and back, recto and verso. The machine does this in such an exquisitely calibrated way that just as the criminal dies of the wounds inflicted by the needle-pens that write on him he achieves, or so the story goes, a moment of perfect epiphany, the word made flesh. In this way, the writing machine puts its subject, who comes to read himself as a text, in the classical position of narrative closure: the end of the story, prefiguring the end of life, reveals the meaning of the whole. But this custom, the narrator tells us, is dying out, and when the last of its officials puts himself in the criminal's position he has so often forced upon others, the writing machine goes haywire, scribbling the man's body all over with nonsense and, in the place of an epiphany, driving a spike through his skull. The machine of modernity has worn out the authority of narrative form it originated to serve; modern narrative tells only the story of its own collapse.

My second text is less violent but still disconcerting. At the end of Joyce's *Ulysses*, the long day's Odyssey of Leopold Bloom ends with his slipping into the marriage bed, where Bloom's Penelope, Molly, lies half asleep. But whereas the original Odysseus triumphantly reclaims his wife and his bed, and reclaims his wife precisely by telling the story of his bed, Bloom remains a kind of failed suitor, like the suitors of Penelope whom Odysseus has killed. Bloom is Ulysses inverted. Accordingly, he places his head at Molly's feet and ends, quite literally, by kissing the ass of the wife who has cuckolded him. When a consummation parallel to that of Odysseus and Penelope does nonetheless occur on the last page of the novel, it belongs only to the memory of something irretrievably lost. More precisely, it belongs to, and occurs as, the running down or running out of text as Molly falls asleep; the novel ends by spinning out the fiction of a beginning as a kind of bedtime story.

From these two texts I would like to extract two theses. The first, from Kafka, is that modernity does not make narrative disappear but instead renders it inoperable, a machine that cannot be fixed. There are plenty of narratives in modernity; the question about them is not their presence or absence but their status. And their most typical status is the topic of the second thesis, from Joyce. It is that modern narrative becomes less a mode of presentation than an object of presentation and that this object is above all a lost one, an impossible object, knowable only in and by its withdrawal. In this role, narrative may become the object of either nostalgia or of dismissal, but what it cannot become is fully, unreflectively present. In other words, modern narrative becomes a version of Lacan's *objet petit a*, the locus of a desire that at best must accept its endless deferral in lieu of fulfillment. Narrative becomes a phantasmal form, never quite what it seems to be, whether with or without the entanglements of desire, with or without the envelope of nostalgia. With

them, narrative is a receding ideal; without them, it is rejected matter. Narrative under modernity thus becomes the broken lens through which whatever
succeeds or survives it is perceived.

In music no less than in fiction. From roughly the mid-eighteenth to the
turn of the twentieth century, roughly, again, from Bach to Mahler, both of
whom are equivocal examples, music tends to assume a certain narrativity as
inherent to its movement in time. The narrativity thus assumed is relatively,
even largely, free of irony. It is like a Kantian category, a perceptual grid that
produces knowledge and does so in going without saying. Music in the twentieth century tends to break down this narrative regime, which, however, never
disappears entirely. The narrative impetus tends to become ironic, and the
ironic detachment shades into objectification. Narrative, instead of disappearing, reappears: appears differently. Confronted with the narrative as object,
the narrative object, we have to decide whether to treat it as a souvenir or as
mere bric-a-brac, whether to save it or throw it out.

This interplay, which is sometimes a loss of distinction, between detachment and nostalgia is famously evident in the last number of Schoenberg's
Pierrot lunaire. The text explicitly calls up – and calls *to* – narrative nostalgia,
which it claims to enjoy in the act of wishing for it:

> O alter Duft aus Märchenzeit,
> Berauschest wieder meine Sinne . . .
>
> Ein glückhaft Wünschen macht mich froh
> Nach Freuden die ich lang verachtet
> [O old perfume from the days of fairy tales,
> Again you intoxicate my senses . . .
>
> I'm cheered by a happy wish
> For joys I long disdained.]

With each iteration of the refrain, "O alter Duft aus Märchenzeit," the piano
calls up (calls to?) a tonal sound across the music's atonal space: twice to an
E-major chord under "-zeit," and then to a group of parallel chords (the last
one augmented) under "Duft." The tonal calls bespeak an indeterminate irony,
voiced in the conclusion as "aus Märchenzeit" sounds "atonally" with a dying
fall over and beyond an E pedal, the faintest vestige of the earlier chords. In
the acoustic world of *Pierrot,* it is perfect triads that are dissonant.

But tonality as such has nothing to say about narrative; it is simply available as a narrative medium. Besides, the twentieth century was full of tonal
(if not of common-practice) music. Hence an even better example, because

its idiom is still rich in tonal memories that it continues to enjoy, is Debussy's *Jeux*. Debussy composed this "Danced Poem" as a ballet score for Nijinsky and Diaghilev in 1912–13; for many years it was the stepchild among Debussy's orchestral works because of its unprecedented lack of continuity. Pierre Boulez said of it that *Jeux* "marked the arrival of a kind of musical form, which, renewing itself from moment to moment, implies a similarly instantaneous mode of perception. . . . The general organization of the work is as changeable instant by instant as it is homogenous in development" (1968: 353). The piece consists of a string of discrete episodes, each marked with its own melodic signature, that conspicuously lack either additive or linear relationships among themselves. They are also highly changeable within themselves. The only thing that holds them together – and we will come back shortly to this "only thing" – is the reversed recurrence of the opening at the close. Even that minimal continuity was an afterthought. Given the prevailing lack of connectedness, it approaches self-parody. As Debussy's contemporary Émile Vuillermoz noted, the music "changes speed and nuance every two measures; it abandons a figure, a timbre, a gesture, in order to go headlong in another direction" (quoted in Berman 1980: 226). And as Laurence Berman observed, "Vuillermoz [was] speaking almost literally. . . . The score contains upwards of sixty tempo markings, distributed over about eighteen minutes of playing time" (226).

Such a "form" or "organization" – the terms are vestiges of the very mentality that the music abandons – entails the withholding or suspension of narrative, which depends on significant repetition. The associated ballet scenario performs the same lack. Arbitrarily started and stopped by the bounce of a tennis ball, the action consists of the repeating curbing of action. A man and two women dance the "games" of seduction, risking but always averting the formation of a love triangle, which would at once impose a plot. At the climax the three dance together with mounting ecstasy and engage in a triple kiss, but their consummation is interrupted by that bouncing ball. This is a ballet in which, though actions occur, nothing happens.

The same may be said for the music, but in order to say it properly, we need to digress a moment. In the early 1980s *Jeux* was the object of revealing close studies by Berman (1980) and Jann Pasler (1982). These studies were particularly concerned with establishing the underlying formal integrity of the work, variously called its "coherence" or "continuity" or "essential order and clarity," despite the authors' acknowledgment that, as Pasler put it, "*Jeux* lies at the crossroads of a change in aesthetic values from the need for continuity to the desire to create discontinuity" (1982: 75).[2] In the scholarly world of the early 1980s, that desire could not be allowed to stand. Understanding music depended on the "need" for organizing principles expressible in technical terms. Demonstrating coherence, continuity, essential order, and the like was simply what one did; it was the instituted language of understanding, even if the understanding itself pointed another way – for Pasler to the ballet scenario, for Berman to the music's expressive content. Like Boulez, therefore, both writers located the coherence of *Jeux* in its temporal organization, which, unlike Boulez, they cast along narrative lines. Pasler found "the key to the form" in a consistent pulse overlaid with a symmetrical pattern of contrasting meters. Berman found order and clarity in the emulation of ritual time, merging at the climax, the triple kiss, with "a classical dialectical action" integrating polarized elements of tempo and motive.

But a classical dialectical action requires a classical dialectical context of growth and mutual influence, which is precisely what *Jeux* refuses to supply, and metrical symmetry in the context of melodic and formal asymmetry may be a hollow sign, a barely apprehensible residue, of the continuity whose absence it is supposed to remedy. Times have changed, and we no longer need to overlook such considerations. We may, of course, still look for occult coherence if we want to, but we no longer *have* to. We are not obliged to "reconcile" continuity and discontinuity or to interpret change as the temporal form of resemblance. We are free to take this music in terms that preserve its self-presentation. We can say of *Jeux* without embarrassment that it lacks coherence, that it unfolds by averting or evading continuity, and that in doing so it forms both an alternative to narrative order and clarity and a travesty of it. The music draws its faux-circular form around a questionably mimetic action that unfolds in real time. The occasional traces of melodic or timbral recurrence serve primarily to affirm the minimal phenomenological continuity of time passing, an external counterpart to a Bergsonian or Husserlian version of internal time consciousness (see Bergson 2002; Husserl 1964).

This minimum, however, is still felt to be necessary, as it would no longer be fifty years later in, for example, Karlheinz Stockhausen's *Momente* (1962–69). Stockhausen's thirty "moments," their sequence changing from performance to performance, take the discontinuities of *Jeux* to the *n*th degree with the aim of embodying "the eternity that does not begin at the end of time but is attainable in every moment" (Stockhausen 1963: 199). In *Momente* time loses its consistency. In *Jeux* the consistency of time replaces the consistency of narrative, which is why Boulez speaks of homogeneity as well as instantaneity in the work and goes on to remark on how difficult it is for the conductor to "preserve that fundamental unity while . . . casting into relief all the ceaselessly occurring incidents" (Boulez 1968: 354). Debussy himself said much the same thing when expressing displeasure at the first concert performance: "It seems to me that the diverse episodes lacked homogeneity. The tie that connects them is subtle, but it exists nonetheless?"[3]

The subtlety of that tie consists in its lack of any discernible character; it is not something that appears but the medium of appearance. Its realization in *Jeux* as the pure temporal flux of duration consummates a tendency that Debussy's contemporaries, Henri Bergson among them, had long heard in his music. As Pasler notes, "In a 1910 interview, Bergson called Debussy's music 'a music of *durée*,' and confessed that he had an 'intuitive predilection' for it, while Debussy's friend Louis Laloy claimed that there are 'secret correspondences' linking Debussy and Bergson. . . . For both the composer and the philosopher, time is a free-flowing medium that depends for its perception on what is filling it, . . . [an idea that] led both Debussy and Bergson to focus on qualitative instead of quantitative change" (1982: 74). The justness of these observations highlights the problem with the institutional demand to show coherence, continuity, or essential order in such music, especially in a limit-work like *Jeux*. The quality of the music as *durée* depends precisely on the absence of the kinds of continuity sought (or invented, or installed) by the protocols of such a demonstration.

In its checkered, fluctuating, episodic movement, *Jeux* produces what in classic Aristotelian terms would be precisely an anti-narrative process. For Aristotle the elements of plot are supposed to be unified by probability or necessity; episodic plots are defined by the absence of either, and in that sense they are not really plots at all. In more contemporaneous terms, the music of *Jeux* unfolds in a manner reminiscent of the exotic travelogue panoramas familiar from the Parisian trade expositions of the later nineteenth century, but with a twist: there is no destination, only an end. A similar description applies loosely to Ravel's nearly contemporary song "Asie," which sails along from one episode to another following the vagaries of its travelogue-text, much as visitors to the *Maréorama* at the 1900 Exposition followed the panoramic depiction of a sea voyage from Paris to Constantinople accompanied by phonograph music that "took on the color of the country at which the ship [was] calling" (quoted in Williams 1991: 210).

An even closer model is the type of free-floating fantasy associated with dreams, hypnosis, and suggestion. French psychology in the later nineteenth century, under the rubric *psychologie nouvelle,* took these phenomena as the basis of a theory of mind that, as Alfred Fouillée put it in 1891, "wrested from us the illusion of a bounded, impenetrable, and autonomous ego" (quoted in Silverman 1989: 90). The mind was more a by-product of fantasy than a receptacle for clear and distinct perceptions; its volatile stream of impressions was meandering rather than linear, guided by unconscious impulse more than by rational interest.

This "atmosphere of psychic life" – the phrase is Fouillée's – pervaded the material world, which in turn furnished a model for new forms of both fine and decorative art equally pervaded by the vagaries of suggestion and association. *Psychologie nouvelle* and *art nouveau* are linked by more than chance phraseology. For Emile Gallé, a decorative artist, modern art objects should be both the product and the image of quasi-hypnotic trance: "The painter of the walls that surround me . . . must transfigure wood into bouquets, rugs into prairies, wallcoverings into ether, where, completely captive, I inhale" (quoted in Silverman 1989: 239). Both the mind and the rooms that mirror it become what Deborah Solomon has called "chambers of suggestibility" – fluid, prolific, and, in this context most significantly of all, the very Other of narrativity and narratability. Likewise for Georg Simmel, commenting on the work exhibited by Rodin at the Paris Exposition of 1900, "What characterizes the modern age is the tendency to live and interpret the world according to the reactions of our inner life, the dissolution of solid content in the fluidity of the perfectly insubstantial soul, whose only forms can be forms of movement" (quoted in Silverman 1989: 314). This fluid movement is neither headed toward a goal nor guided by probability or necessity: rather the reverse. It anticipates the emergence of what Gilles Deleuze (2005) called the "time-image" characteristic of cinema and therefore of modern visual culture: a condition of indiscernibility between the real and the imaginary, past and present, the observed and the fantasized, the sequential and the static.

Jeux dissolves the solid content of musical narrativity in the same way as the mind of *nouvelle psychologie* dissolves the material world and the art of *art nouveau* dissolves shapes and spaces into whorls and tangles. The immediate result in the music is to emphasize the singularity and fleetingness of the orchestral sonorities. As each episode fades into the next, they form what one might later have called a signifying chain of the kind described by Lacan in a now-classic image: "rings of a necklace that is a ring in another necklace made of rings" (1977: 153). As each potential kernel of narrative disappears to be replaced by another in this chain of chains, one hears narrativity continually looming and dissolving away. The theater of this fantasy, however, its chamber of suggestibility, is the one thread of narrativity that *Jeux* will not relinquish, the large meta-narrative frame imposed by movement in a circle – in the music, by the truncated return of the vague opening chords; in the ballet scenario, by the returning tennis ball.

This double return, however, is not really circular in the usual sense; it is arbitrary, anti-organic, a curtailment rather than a denouement. Unlike the modes of repetition that prepare and consummate narrative closure, this one marks a contingency that the ballet program and the music alike designate as random or at least unknowably contingent. The characters have no identities; the tennis balls come from nowhere; the ballet's eroticism has no source but dance itself; the music consists in its own continual evaporation. And there needs to be nothing more, for there is no narrative energy here to bind; the signifying chain of episodes simply stops, and stops at the very point where closure might have emerged. But the music expresses no regret at this, rather, the opposite; it seems to take an ironic pleasure in it. The irony, though not the pleasure, links this music rather oddly with Thomas Hardy and Benjamin Britten, as will soon appear.

The source of both the irony and the pleasure is a narrative that persists in the scenario of *Jeux* by appearing there as an object, not a process. This object, however, is not given but withheld, withdrawn, and the form of its withdrawal is, so to speak, its retirement from its office. It is not a mere absence but, as I suggested earlier, a lost presence, something that persists while – persists *by* – remaining out of reach. The irony and the pleasure afforded by this untold tale are like those one might find in an object of daily life, once useful, now obsolete, once functional, now ornamental. Such things grown useless may carry a melancholy charge, and in much modern music they do just that; Debussy himself might be said to mourn the loss of narrativity in a work like the piano prelude "Des pas sur la neige" with its frozen, repetitive motion that has neither aim nor direction but cannot stop its automaton-like persistence. But *Jeux* willingly empties itself of aim and direction in order to fill itself with pure contingency, equally content if what it brings is conjunction or disjunction between one episode and another. The music is a practical demonstration, without the rhetoric of shipwreck, of the principle enunciated in Mallarmé's iconic anti-narrative title: a throw of the dice will never abolish chance.

The premise of *Jeux* is the emptiness of narrative movement, and the process of *Jeux* – of its *jeux*, its games – is the emptying of narrative movement. For that reason, *Jeux* is also an illustration of the principle that musical narrativity is hermeneutically complex but often analytically simple, sometimes even analytically indifferent. It literally does not matter how one analyzes the episodes, as both Pasler and Berman do in some detail, or if one analyzes the episodes at all, even if, in doing so, one "discovers" occult relations linking part to part and parts to whole. None of this rises to the level of narrativity, which may support or even invite analysis but does not, and must not, depend on it. Musical narrativity can dispense with structural elaboration. What it cannot dispense with is the presentation of a narratable action, an event about which one can, in principle, build a story.

By making the requirement of the narratable action evident by its lack – a tellingly symbolist gesture – *Jeux* provides us with a few more theses to pursue. In withholding the narratable action, just what does it withhold? Not narrative voicing: the circular form provides that, albeit emptily. Not narrative mimesis: the program or ballet scenario supplies that, albeit senselessly. What is withheld is a singular pivot, a turning, a *peripeteia*, as measured by contingent, non-generic, non-programmed, non-scheduled change. Such a change, a classic requirement, present in Aristotle's *Poetics*, must be clear and on the surface, impossible to miss. Prominent musical examples would include the frenzied outburst on the *Muss es sein* motive that interrupts the finale of Beethoven's F-Major Quartet, op. 135, the shattering *fortissimo* breakthrough in the slow movement of Mahler's Fourth Symphony, the serene ascent of the Bach chorale "O Ewigkeit, Du Donnerwort" in the second movement of Berg's Violin Concerto, and so on. Nothing subtle or occult about any of them.

This mode of turning rises to narrativity when it allies itself with active cultural tropes and the preexisting narratives that articulate them. Narrativity is always metaphorical in the sense that it is always transferable from one realization, one manifest statement or event, to another. Each turn is singular, but each is also exemplary in its singularity. This combination of turning and iterability is what constitutes narrativity in music and perhaps elsewhere: not some structural type or formula, not tonality, and certainly not mere coherent sequence. The coherent sequences of the world may not be numberless, but they are numerous: discursive, additive, lyric, sequential, logical, topical, ritual, and many more. Furthermore, the criteria of turning and iterability imply that narrativity is primarily an object of description; in a sense, no narrative is told until it has been told back. Narrative is thus as much the product of the verbal dexterity, the tropes, and the style that go into describing it as it is of the musical or fictional events that attract the description.

What, then, can we tell *Jeux* about its own narrativity, such as it is?

Jeux addresses itself to narratable action not by evasion but by withdrawal. The process operates throughout as one episode sidesteps into another; it becomes conclusive when the action of the final episode approaches narrativity only in order to withdraw it. This withdrawal is the force of the triple kiss. Regardless of whether one hears this moment as dialectical or quasi-organic or simply as a prolonged intensification, the kiss arises as a *peripeteia* that might have been, the moment that, in a narratable world, would have changed everything but that here simply cancels everything. Or rather, simply yields without protest, perhaps with pleasure, to cancellation by the chance return of that tennis ball and the reversed opening.

This cancellation is already immanent in the triple kiss itself, which takes the musical form of a long slow echo, an acoustic dissolve. The music erupts in a Wagnerian *fortissimo* along with a broadening of tempo and a change of meter. But the big moment lasts for exactly one measure and a beat, then begins to mimic itself in a long *decrescendo*, most of it *pianissimo*, that takes ten measures more to fade into the subsequent frame. The fadeout also incorporates slowed-down reminiscences of a motive heard near the beginning of the piece, but there is nothing dialectical about these reminiscences, which show the motive changing shape, losing definition, crumbling away. The triple kiss thus gives the absence of *peripeteia* a positive form, precisely the form of the narrative object. Or rather two narrative objects, since the ensuing return of the opening is also a mere vestige of narrativity, a frame structure that is a denial of itself, a chiasmatic X, the frame turned inside out.

Berman understands this concluding collapse as a sign of modernist irony: "The climax of 'Jeux,' with its brief aftermath, . . . tells us that the act of joyous consummation, like the artist's truth, is achieved only with considerable effort . . . [and] that, after all the effort, the experience passes, almost as if it had been a dream" (1980: 237). The point is well taken, as is Berman's suggestion that *Jeux* forms a detached, quasi-ritualistic return to the scene of Debussy and Mallarmé's *Afternoon of a Faun*. But the rupture of the consummating moment may actually be a productive, even an affirmative event. It permits the narrative object to emerge as such and to engage with the hopes or fantasies it invites rather than to present itself as an illusion that invites only credulousness or regret. The sensory presentation becomes, for a moment, the materialization of an absence. The same logic extends to the subsequent frame, which with its reversed reprise of the opening marks the point at which all narrativity has departed. Hence the closing measures implode into pinpricks of sound in empty space, flecks and shimmers that disappear in an instant.

In modern works, the narrative object typically takes the form of a phantasm: either a denatured form of the pivot, the narratable action, or an incorporated fragment of the kind of music that would once have, and once did, find its meaning through a narratable action. The music for the triple kiss in *Jeux* is just such a phantasmal pivot; another is the climax to the opening movement of Bartók's *Music for Strings, Percussion, and Celesta*. The movement is a slow fugue that begins on a bare A, gathers to its climax on a *fortissimo* E♭, and then unwinds with the fugue subject in inversion. But the symmetry falters; the unwinding becomes an unraveling, like the end of *Jeux*. As how could it not? For the pivot, the unharmonized tritone, is a null point, a non-event, minimally holding the place of the narratable action that once could have either produced a fully symmetrical reversal or motivated the collapse of one. Bartók's fugue enacts the withdrawal of story into mechanism.

For an example of the incorporated fragment we can scroll forward to Frederic Rzewski's piano piece "Cadenza con o senza Beethoven," composed in 2003. This cadenza, deliberately misnamed, since it stands entirely by itself, is based on Beethoven's Fourth Piano Concerto. But the cadenza overtly quotes the concerto only twice, near the close, where there briefly surfaces a fragment of a theme and a chromatic phrase from the most often played of Beethoven's own cadenzas for the concerto. Bartók's movement contains an element of nostalgia, even of mourning, given the starkness of the music and its twisting, semitone-dominated fugue subject; the Rzewski piece resolutely shuns nostalgia as it turns the celebrated lyricism of Beethoven's concerto into a source of noisy exuberance. But to say as much is slightly too simple, for the Bartók cannot escape the nostalgia embedded willy-nilly in its fugal form, and the detachment of the Rzewski cannot resist the faint touch of Beethovenian lyricism amid its own tumult.

The intricate interplay between nostalgia and detachment in the narrative object, narrative in retreat and in retrieval, is now our topic. To explore it fully, we need to turn from instrumental to vocal music, where the intervention of text complicates the issue of narrative. Britten's song cycle *Winter Words*, for tenor and piano to texts by Thomas Hardy, provides a resonant test case, in part because Hardy's texts themselves constitute a critique of narrativity. They also constitute a critique of modernity, for Hardy, whom we usually think of as a Victorian, wrote these poems in the 1920s, having outlived the modernist Debussy by a decade. Britten's settings depend on elements of both nostalgia and detachment without belonging stably to either mode.

The process begins with the selection and arrangement of texts. The poetry of *Winter Words* consists of four anecdotes surrounded by a double frame. The anecdotes, numbers 3 through 6 of the cycle, all involve stories that come to the wrong end or to no end at all. These poems all travesty the inherited norm, which, in the manner of balladry, absorbs narrative into the reiterative design of the lyric; in each of these poems, the absorption is a nullification. In "The Little Old Table," for example, the "creak" of the "little wood thing" tells a tale that the speaker once misunderstood and that his successor as the owner of the table will not even recognize as a "history." In "Proud Songsters," birdsong at dusk inspires the speaker to construct a narrative in reverse, the end of which is the symbolic return of the singing birds to the primordial matter from which they came, "nor nightingales, / Nor thrushes, / But only particles of grain, / And earth, and air, and rain."

The poems of the inner frame, numbers 2 and 6, deal with abortive railway journeys. The symbolism is double: on the one hand, the trains embody the presence of modernity with its mechanization of both space and time; on the other, they embody the primary rhythm of journeying as such, which is also the primary rhythm of narrative, the classic Aristotelian movement from beginning to middle to end. Both poems trace the nullification of that movement under the conditions of modern life: one describes an actual journey with no known end; the second, an imaginary journey with no means to begin. The first of the pair, "Midnight on the Great Western," addresses the default of narrative explicitly and right away, observing of its "journeying boy" that he is "Bewrapt past knowing to what he was going, / Or whence he came." The companion poem, "At the Railway Station, Upway," embodies the default of narrative in the ironic "twanging" of a violin that cannot quite manage to become music.

The poems of the outer frame articulate the same nullification in the vast, typically Hardyesque frame of cosmic time. Number 1, "At Day-Close in November," begins the cycle with an ending. In the autumn dusk, the aged speaker sees the falling leaves of beech trees he had planted in his youth. But the leaves refuse to tell even the familiar story of youth and age; they float past "like specks in the eye," leaving the purblind speaker to construe this loss of narrative as a, as the, universal condition: "The children who ramble through here / Conceive that there never has been / A time when no tall trees grew, / That none will in time be seen." The poem anticipates the reverse narrative of "Proud Songsters" and identifies an empty beginning with an equally empty end, thus emptying the middle that is the substance of narrative and the stuff of narrative time. This emptying out reaches its own empty end in the final poem, "Before Life and After," which ends the cycle with a beginning – in this case, the beginning of all things in "nescience," the nonconsciousness of nonexistence, for which the speaker longs. The narrative impulse finds its consummation in a naked allegiance to the death drive that Peter Brooks, following Freud, found in the desire for an ending to every story but that narrative must continually resist if the right end is to be found. But the narrator's longing for nullity is only the other side of his longing for the consolations of narrative that are continuously being stripped from him. Narrative appears in these poems not as a form or a genre or a mode but as an object, or, more exactly, a fragmented array of objects, that are the more desirable as they are the more lost or unobtainable. Britten's grouping of these poems brings out, as in performing music one might bring out an instrumental voice, the repositioning of narrative as an object, albeit an imaginary object, the object of narrative nostalgia.

Britten does not so much set the poems of *Winter Words* as he sets their nullification and objectification of narrative, their regret and desire for narrative. Although the songs do to some extent interpret or represent the poems, they do so primarily as part of an interpretation or representation of the poems' mode of utterance. Instead of telling a story, the music – and this is what marks it as modern – seeks to inhabit a world in which storytelling has become a chimera.

This effort is at its most strenuous in the railway songs, which will be my focus here. Both songs conflate their character's inability to "live and interpret" life in narrative terms with the music's inability to sustain a narrative line. The technique by which the music mimics or accompanies narrative – what I have elsewhere called its narratography – becomes the means by which narrativity recedes into the distance and becomes an objectified absence.

"Midnight on the Great Western" is framed by a slow chordal passage for piano alone that repeatedly fades to *pianissimo* at the beginning, does so again at the start of each verse, and returns at that dead level, marked "from afar," at the end. Like its counterpart in Schubert's "Am Meer," to which it palpably alludes, this frame is expressively remote from the body of the song, which thus assumes an uncertain status from the outset. Like the journeying boy, the song knows neither where it comes from nor where it is going – and neither do we. What we do know is that the piano is trying to match the voice as a storyteller by mimicking the sound and motion of the train, a texture it

the jour - - - - 3 - neying_____ boy,

EXAMPLE 8.1. Britten, "Midnight on the Great Western,"
melisma on the "journeying boy" (mm. 11–15, voice only).

maintains throughout the first half of the song, the AA of an AAB bar form.
Thereafter the texture gets, well, derailed, as a slow episode interrupts the
piston-like movement after only two measures. The episode is set off – in-
ternally framed – by transpositions of the original framing passage, and its
isolation envelops both the boy and the speaker who apostrophizes him. The
suspension of motion coincides with the moment in both the text and the
voice when the nullity of the boy's supposed journey becomes most pressing:

> What past can be yours, O journeying boy
> Towards a world unknown,
> Who calmly, as if incurious quite
> On all at stake, can undertake
> This plunge alone?

The frame, it seems, has also lost its way and fallen into the song proper,
blocking both past and future. When the chugging of the train resumes in
the piano, its "deliberate motion" (thus Britten's marking) has no more force;
it is not going anywhere.

The voice, meanwhile, has even more serious problems. Its possession of
the text assures it of at least a minimal narrative identity, but that very text
forces it into repeatedly asking questions for which there is no answer, no context, no story. The voice enunciates the text in the manner of a recitative, with
one note per syllable in narrow compass – except, that is, when it encounters
the phrase "journeying boy," which four times provokes a long florid melisma.
The melismas arrest the narrative and replace it with its classic antagonist,
lyric, but a lyric that is itself strangely dislocated, self-estranged. Each of the
four melismas articulates an extended dominant, and each goes awry as it
ends. The first and longest, a dominant of C minor, breaks off as its third
degree sours from B to B♭ (Example 8.1); the second is a strophic repetition
of the first; the third, a dominant of B♭, sours its own third from A to A♭ and
overlaps the bewildered slow episode; and the last, back on the dominant of
C minor, "resolves" onto the E of C major, anticipating an E/E♭ antagonism

EXAMPLE 8.2. Britten, "Midnight on the Great Western,"
return of melisma at end of first strophe.

that will bedevil the close of the song. After each melisma, the voice picks up
the recitative-like narrative thread only to find that the melismas have a ripple
effect; they return, on the very phrases meant to mark narrative closure, as
each section of the song concludes (Example 8.2).

The melismas on "journeying boy" draw out the irony in the phrase they
set. The boy on the train is not journeying; he is wandering, caught in an aim-
less movement that is also a suspension of movement and that "bewraps" him
in futility. But the irony is compound; it turns on itself as well as on the boy
and the song. For the melismas are lyrical not only in genre but also in expression. They are songful as the rest of the song is not; they mark not only the
absence of narrative but also the longing for it. They hold the place of narrative as a lost object; they become the ghost or trace of what they exclude. This
spectral incorporation of the lost solidity of narrative echoes with the added
irony of the closing melismas – spectral afterthoughts in their own right. Each
sets a word that is the object of a negation but sets it with deliberate, almost
malicious beauty: "whence" when the boy knows not whence he came; "living"
as a lamp's "sad beams," not the boy's "listless form and face," seems a "living
thing"; and "are" in the closing phrase "but are not of," referring to a "region of
sin" that, so the music insists, in contradiction, the boy is *of* indeed.

"At the Railway Station, Upway," divides the journeying boy into contrary personae, a boy with a violin and a handcuffed convict who wait for the
train together as a constable looks on, an ambiguous smile on his face. The boy
offers to console the convict by playing his violin; the convict responds with a
mocking song, "'This life so free / Is the thing for me'"; and the constable, "as
if unconscious of what he had heard," just keeps smiling, his silence, perhaps,
the true narrative voice of the poem and perhaps of the song, no less.

The song is the pivotal number in the cycle. It not only forms the frater-
nal twin of "Midnight on the Great Western" but also acts as a moment of
deferral in the cycle's drift toward the embrace of nescience, which begins in
the preceding song, number 6, "Proud Songsters," and culminates in the con-

EXAMPLE 8.3. Britten, "At the Railway Station, Upway,"
opening (mm. 1–3) imitation of mistuned violin.

cluding song, number 8, "Before Life and After." The boy in "At the Railway
Station" seeks to hold nescience back with the music of his violin; the song
takes up his effort and gives it narratographic form, but only to make the surrender to nescience inevitable, as the effort fails on both levels.

Both the vocal and piano parts of this song break down into discrete elements that are not so much articulated as jumbled together; as in "Midnight
on the Great Western," the form that the song adopts to tell a story becomes
the first sign that there is neither a story to be told nor a way to tell one. The
vocal part is divided among the boy, the convict, and the narrator, with the
smiling constable silent; the different voices are distinguished from each other
in the classic manner, by distinct melodic profiles and registral tendencies.
The narrator's part is recitative-like, as it was in "Midnight"; the convict's is
singsong; the boy's is folk-like. It is worth noting in passing that the boy's two
statements are set to the same music, echoing the strophic repetition in the
first half of "Midnight" and, as in the earlier song, marking the point from
which disintegration inevitably sets in. The piano part consists of imitations
of double-stops and arpeggios on the boy's violin; a rapid staccato flutter that
follows the characters' statements like a mocking echo; and patches of long
single notes divided by twittering grace notes, a texture that suggests a continuo line with the figured bass stripped out.

The associations among these elements are disordered both chronologically and expressively until after the convict sings, as if their coordination,
in the end, were as much a mockery as his song. The song begins with the
piano, as violin, trying to play arpeggios and fifths on the instrument's open
strings, only to find them going in and out of tune (Example 8.3). Before the
boy, who tells us he has no money, even offers to play his instrument, "and a
nice one, 'tis," the song informs us that it is only a cheap fiddle. The boy's two

EXAMPLE 8.4. Britten, "At the Railway Station, Upway," ending.

statements, arching along a natural A-minor scale, are themselves out of tune with the recitative line in the piano, which sustains the contradictory notes of C♯ and E♭. The fiddle begins to "twang" before it is said to, and only the "grimful glee" of the convict's song brings it into tune in a monotonous, mindless C major – a single arpeggio repeated eleven times as the convict's song fades from its initial defiant *fortissimo*.

　　The song ends as the boy continues playing, reprising the arpeggios and chords of the opening measures: another frame, another empty circle, no less so here than in *Jeux*. For nothing has happened, no journey has been made: the boy has never attained to the primary musical narrativity of melody; he has barely managed to play in tune, and that only briefly; he repeats his futile gestures an indefinite number of times before the train comes in, and comes in from an unknown point of origin en route to an unknown destination; and the convict indeed lives "a life so free" – free, that is, of any possible story, for his journey does not trace a narrative, having neither beginning nor, but for the twang of the violin, middle; it is all end. The man is handcuffed in more ways than one. And the song? That handcuffs itself; it ends with the piano rising into the high treble, fading into the distance, with an echo of the boy's A-minor voice (Example 8.4). But the echo, like the violin figuration, is full of wrong notes. It may be the last vestige of narrative desire, a slim trace of the narrative object, but it is all in tatters. From the point of view of the cycle, only the absolute closure of nescience can restore, by obliterating, the arc of narrative.

To conclude, I will try to take my own composition, "Ecstasis: Prelude and Variations for Piano," as a route to a larger perspective. Of late I have been trying to pursue in music some of the questions that attract me in musical scholarship. "Ecstasis" is an example: composed in 2007, it represents an effort to find a form for continuous change that is neither narrative nor additive but that is nonetheless wholly perspicuous: a form capable of treating the narrative object as the narrative object treats narrative itself, at a remove that is also an embrace, but here without nostalgia.

The easiest way to introduce the piece is to adapt the program note from the score. *Ecstasis*, the Greek word from which the English "ecstasy" derives, literally means "to be moved out of place." It refers to a passage beyond the given, a movement outside the place of one's known or familiar self. In *Being and Time*, Martin Heidegger proposes that the most "authentic" form of *ecstasis* is a rapture, a being carried away, that we do not simply yield to but actively resolve on (1962: 387–88). We step away from stasis onto a plane of continuous dynamism. We become ourselves by leaving ourselves behind, yet without forgetting that who (and what) we become is a transformation of all we have been before.

The movements identified as Prelude and Variations deal, respectively, with the allure of *stasis* and the allure of *ec-stasis*. The Prelude is both static and cyclical; its slow revolutions present a single extended melody without alteration but from different points of view, a kind of cantus firmus but in the "wrong" voice. The Variations seek an "ecstatic" dynamism that proliferates at many levels. The variations take flight from two musical ideas, a theme and a chord progression stated at the outset, but it is not just these ideas that are varied; so are the expressive episodes formed from the variation process, and so are the larger sections formed from the episodes in turn. The work as a whole reaches its "ecstatic" conclusion when the highest-order variation has happened three times – when varied variation has been varied, a process clearly marked by reprises of the initial theme and chord progression. This formal pattern, however, is not the "point" of the music but merely the medium in which the risks, rewards, forces, and feelings of *ecstasis* can best proliferate.[4]

To this I will add only that each of the two movements includes an encounter with narrative desire. In the third segment of the Prelude, intrusive chords try to disrupt the cyclical pattern, to break it into telling a story. The effort fails, leaving the chords with nothing to show for it but their own sheer incongruity, which is to say their non-narratability. The chords themselves are caught up in a cycle they refuse to acknowledge; their content changes, but their type remains rigid in a fourfold series. The Prelude acknowledges the narrative object only by shutting it out. The Variations are more hospitable; finding a place for the narrative object is part of their purpose. To that end, they open themselves to the incorporation of a phantom slow movement: three discontinuous segments in decelerating tempos set within the crystalline structure of the primary fast movement in three continuous segments of accelerating tempos. The narrative object, at least as I hear it, thus finds its place not as a source of either irony or nostalgia but simply as a participant in a process that it cannot, and does not wish to, govern.

And perhaps it is fair to surmise that this participant role is the underlying model or ideal, the second act or afterlife of narrative, even where irony and nostalgia are forcefully present, as they are, respectively, in *Jeux* and *Winter Words*. Heidegger has something to say about this under the rubric of what he calls repetition, retrieval, or reprise, with a play on "fetching-back," the etymological meaning of the common German word *Wiederholung*:

> When one has, by *Wiederholung*, handed down to oneself a possibility that
> has been [before], the Dasein that has been there [formerly] is not disclosed
> [merely] in order to be actualized all over again. . . . Rather [*vielmehr*] the
> repetition *replies* [*erwidert*] to the possibility of that existence that has
> [already] been there. But at the same time the reply to that possibility, in
> resoluteness, as made in the blink of an eye [*als augenblickliche*], is the *contra-
> diction* [*Widerruf*] of that which in the present is working itself out as "past."
> (1962: 437–38, my translation)[5]

The simultaneity of continuation and cancellation resembles the Hegelian *Aufhebung*, which, however, is itself submitted to a *Wiederholung* in Heidegger's formulation. Heidegger's repetition as retrieval permits no synthesis of terms, as the verbal counterpoint between *wider* in *erwidern* and *Widerruf* and between the *wider* of these terms and the *Wieder* of *Wiederholung* seems meant to demonstrate.

Ideally speaking, any performance of a classical score, that is, of a notated work taken as the object of realization and interpretation, is a *Wiederholung* in Heidegger's sense. So there is a way in which the relation of twentieth-century classical music to narrative is neither epochal nor exceptional. But if we take the music thus "retrieved" as itself a retrieval of or reply to what has already been, its relation to narrative changes and does become epochal and, therefore, in historical terms exceptional, even if the exception quickly becomes the new rule. Like its counterparts in other high-art media, twentieth-century classical music retrieves narrative, replies to narrative, by incorporating rather than exemplifying it. The music invites the listener not to identify with narrative but to regard it, desire it, distance it, appropriate it, deny it, and so on: in some way to receive it rather than belong to it. Narrative persists in this music by becoming a semblance, something between an artifice and an artifact. Its possibility no longer takes the form of the power to mend what Paul Ricoeur calls "the discordance of time" with "the concordance of the tale" (2007: 102); rather (*vielmehr*), narrative arises as the retreat from modernity of that very power, expressed in the reciprocation/revocation that retrieves narrative as the object of irony or fantasy, observation or pursuit.

The repetition of Heidegger's *Wiederholung* brings what has passed or been cast away back, not to a point of origin but to a point of reorigination. It is decidedly unlike the "binding" repetition that Peter Brooks took as a precondition for narrative closure and therefore for narrative itself. Rather (again *vielmehr*), this repetition continually insists on the incompletion of every story; it fetches back (*wiederholt*) narrative openness at every possible turn toward narrative closure. Perhaps it would be more accurate here to speak of *re-iteration*, the hyphenated form pointing up the redundancy obscured in the standard spelling of the English word. The modernist mode of telling re-iterates narrative: replies to it, retrieves it, reprises and revises it. Re-iterated narrative thrives on its own obsolescence. Perhaps it does so in part because re-iteration loops back onto itself in narrative form: re-iteration is narrative re-iterated. And narrative re-iterated is the fate of narrative in twentieth-century music.

TEXTS BY THOMAS HARDY FROM *WINTER WORDS*

"AT THE RAILWAY STATION, UPWAY"

"There is not much that I can do,
For I've no money that's quite my own!"
Spoke up the pitying child –
A little boy with a violin
At the station before the train came in, –
"But I can play my fiddle to you,
And a nice one 'tis, and good in tone!"

The man in the handcuffs smiled;
The constable looked, and he smiled, too,
As the fiddle began to twang;
And the man in the handcuffs suddenly sang

With grimful glee:
"This life so free
Is the thing for me!"
And the constable smiled, and said no word,
As if unconscious of what he heard;
And so they went on till the train came in –
The convict, and boy with the violin.

"MIDNIGHT ON THE GREAT WESTERN"
In the third-class seat sat the journeying boy,
And the roof-lamp's oily flame
Played down on his listless form and face,
Bewrapt past knowing to what he was going,
Or whence he came.

In the band of his hat the journeying boy
Had a ticket stuck; and a string
Around his neck bore the key of his box,
That twinkled gleams of the lamp's sad beams
Like a living thing.

What past can be yours, O journeying boy
Towards a world unknown,
Who calmly, as if incurious quite
On all at stake, can undertake
This plunge alone?

Knows your soul a sphere, O journeying boy,
Our rude realms far above,
Whence with spacious vision you mark and mete
This region of sin that you find you in,
But are not of?

NOTES

1. On the difference, see my "Musical Narratology: A Theoretical Outline" (1995). Unlike those working in the tradition of A. J. Greimas, I resist the definition of narrativity as the organizing principle of all discourse, in part because my conception of narrativity is more specific and in part because I think the organizing principle of all discourse is a chimera;

there is no such thing. See Greimas and Courtés (1982).

2. "Coherence" and "continuity" are from Pasler (1982: 75); "essential order and clarity" are from Berman (1980: 226).

3. "Il m'a semblé que les divers épisodes manquaient d'homogénéité. Le lien qui les relie est subtil, mais il existe pourtant?" (quoted in Pasler 1982: 69n21).

4. A freely downloadable PDF of the score is available from the online library of the American Music Center.

5. *Erwidert* also carries the senses of "returns," "answers," and "pays back."

WORKS CITED

Barthes, Roland. 1988. "Introduction to the Structural Analysis of Narrative." In *Image, Music, Text*, translated by Stephen Heath, 79–124. New York: Macmillan.

Benjamin, Walter. 1969. "The Storyteller." In *Illuminations*, edited by Hannah Arendt, translated by Harry Zohn, 83–110. New York: Schocken.

Bergson, Henri. 2002. *The Creative Mind: An Introduction to Metaphysics*. Translated by Mabelle Andison. New York: Kensington.

Berman, Laurence. 1980. "'Prelude to the Afternoon of a Faun' and 'Jeux': Debussy's Summer Rites." *19th-Century Music* 3(3): 225–38.

Boulez, Pierre. 1968. *Notes of an Apprenticeship*. Translated by Herbert Weinstock. New York: Knopf.

Brooks, Peter. 1992. "Freud's Masterplot: A Model for Narrative." In *Reading for the Plot: Design and Intention in Narrative*, 90–112. Cambridge: Harvard University Press.

Deleuze, Gilles. 2005. *Cinema 2: The Time-Image*. Translated by Hugh Tomlinson. New York: Continuum.

Greimas, A. J., and J. Courtés, eds. 1982. *Semiotics and Language: An Analytical Dictionary*. Bloomington: Indiana University Press.

Heidegger, Martin. 1962. *Being and Time*. Translated by John Macquarrie and Edward Robinson. Oxford: Blackwell.

Husserl, Edmund. 1964. *The Phenomenology of Internal Time-Consciousness*. Edited by Martin Heidegger, translated by Calvin O. Schrag. Dordrecht: M. Nijhoff.

Kramer, Lawrence. 1995. "Musical Narratology: A Theoretical Outline." In *Classical Music and Postmodern Knowledge*, 98–121. Berkeley: University of California Press.

Lacan, Jacques. 1977. "The Agency of the Letter in the Unconscious or Reason since Freud." In *Écrits: A Selection*, translated by Alan Sheridan, 146–78. New York: Norton.

Pasler, Jann. 1982. "'Jeux': Playing with Time and Form." *19th-Century Music* 6(1): 60–75.

Ricoeur, Paul. 2007. "The Poetics of Language and Myth." In *Debates in Continental Philosophy: Conversations with Contemporary Thinkers*, edited by Richard Kearney, 33–52. New York: Fordham University Press.

Silverman, Deborah. 1989. *Art Nouveau in Fin-de-Siècle France*. Berkeley: University of California Press.

Stockhausen, Karlheinz. 1963. "Momentform: Neue Beziehungen zwischen Aufführungsdauer, Werkdauer und Moment." In *Texte zur Musik*, 1: 189–210. Cologne: DuMont Schauberg.

Williams, Rosalind. 1991. "The Dream World of Mass Consumption." In *Rethinking Popular Culture*, edited by Chandra Mukerji and Michael Schudson, 198–238. Berkeley: University of California Press.

PART THREE

Interpreting Modern Musical Narrative

9

Agency Effects in the Instrumental Drama of Musgrave and Birtwistle

Philip Rupprecht

❦

Accounts of narrative in instrumental music frequently invoke a concept of *agency*: when listeners can imagine human actors within musical textures, the sounding actions of performers assume a motivated quality and generate plot sequences analogous to those in literature or drama. Anthropomorphic agents are more or less closely identified with specific musical actions, yet the concept is also diffuse and mutable. Consistent agents in Classical-period chamber works are the exception, not the rule, in that the local source of an action within a polyphonic texture may shift rapidly throughout pieces. Only in concertos does the soloist often play a fixed role as a determinate instrument-agent. The concept of agent, as elaborated by both Edward T. Cone and Fred Maus, may encompass shared themes or motives rather than the contributions of any particular instrument.[1] The musical agent, broadly conceived, is a type of narrative actor, a surface manifestation of a more basic narrative role, the syntagmatic function A. J. Greimas terms *actant*.[2] In 1960s instrumental works by Thea Musgrave and Harrison Birtwistle, though, musical agents are far more fixed and consistent than in Classical-Romantic-era scores. These agents are crisply defined and sustain identities over long single-movement forms. This chapter will explore distinctive agency effects – specifically, formations of instrument-agent and player-agent common to works of instrumental drama by British composers in the 1960s, a genre with ties to Mauricio Kagel's "instrumental theater," on the one hand, and texted music theater, on the other.

While it would be absurd to claim national exclusivity in the realm of musical genres, the term *instrumental drama* here denotes a cluster of works close enough in spirit and technique to form a recognizable subgenre flourishing in British art music.[3] To begin with, discussion will be framed historically by sketching some features of the European avant-garde scene of the mid-twentieth century in order to situate the British works within their proper context. With closer readings of Musgrave's Chamber Concerto No. 2 (1966) and Birtwistle's *Verses for Ensembles* (1968), I will explore some theoretical dimensions of musical agency more directly. Specifically, the dramatic form of Musgrave's piece suggests the centrality of a concept of *instrument-agent*, where a given instrumental strand of the texture (here, the viola) assumes a fixed proto-dramatic role in the work's unfolding. A comparable fixity of role animates Birtwistle's score, too, but here the physical mobility of performers onstage also foregrounds their status as *player-agents*, actors whose performance is defined apart from identification with any single instrument. To conclude, I invoke models of agency borrowed from the sociologist Erving Goffman, models in which the familiar interpersonal exchanges of social life are understood as performances. When presentation of a self is understood as a type of role playing according to fixed rules of conduct, it is possible to glimpse analogies between our experience of agency in musical works and in the wider world of social encounter.

ON THE SCENE: MUSICAL PERFORMANCE
AS THEATER CA. 1960

What Mauricio Kagel in 1960 referred to as the "theatricalization" of instrumental performance is hardly unique to works by the British avant-garde. While the precise form of drama enacted varies widely, an overall turn to a more scenic emphasis – stressing the act of performance itself – brings with it a sense of player agency distinct from the usual discourse of chamber music. Kagel's notion of "instrumental theater" covers works by Berio, Ligeti, Dieter Schnebel, and Kagel himself, some of which incorporate spoken words; the genre borders equally on the theatrics of Cage's silent piece, 4'33", or Ligeti's wordless 1961 lecture.[4] By the early 1960s, the idea of an "agile music theater" assumed performers conversant with mime, singing, movement, and instrumental playing (Domenico Guaccero, cited in Borio 1993: 139). The more outré performances at the 1963 Palermo Festival were reported by British critics merely as "dotty experiments."[5] Yet, as Cornelius Cardew observed, "'music theatre' or 'music that is not music' was the subject of a great deal of discussion" (Cardew 1963: 886).[6] The works by Musgrave and Birtwistle stake out more circumscribed territory. On a formal level, their scores take on connotations of defined ritual or dramatic actions, including mythic archetypes, while evading programmatic storytelling. Central to the British repertoire of wordless instrumental drama is an idea of the instrumentalist as bona fide character or role player.

Musgrave has spoken often of her interest in "almost a theatrical element which uses the players like *dramatis personae*" (1973: 790). Discussing her Clarinet Concerto (1968), in which a peripatetic soloist moves onstage between various sections of the orchestra, she notes "'dramatic-abstract' ideas: that is, dramatic in presentation but abstract because there is no programme or 'story'" (Musgrave 2010; see also Musgrave 1983: 28). The focus on a soloist as protagonist is equally clear in comments by Birtwistle, whose dramatic approach is announced in work titles with mythic resonances. *Linoi* (1968) refers to Greek myths of Linus, a brother of Orpheus murdered with a lyre by Apollo or Herakles. Such events are enacted in the piece, but the composer has fashioned a drama operating at more than one symbolic level: "*Linoi* is really about trying to find melody, which is never quite achieved and expressed in the clarinet as a sort of frustration; it starts screaming. He keeps making these attempts, three beginnings, and just as it's going to happen . . . well, it's a death you see" (Birtwistle 2001: 14). Birtwistle personifies the clarinetist ("it . . . he"), identifies him eponymously with Linus, and ascribes emotional-psychological motives to wordless melodic actions; the work as a whole traces the plot sequence of the myth, articulated in specific timbres and gestures. The piano, plucked and struck inside the instrument, acts (in Stephen Pruslin's view) "first as harp, then as weapon of destruction, finally as lamenting gong" (1998: 8).

Birtwistle's interest in ancient myth is equally clear in *Tragoedia* (1965), a work "concerned with the ritual and formal aspects of Greek tragedy rather than with the content of any specific play" (1967). Again, instruments assume abstract roles – Birtwistle treats the cello and horn as (in his words) "odd men out" within the string quartet and wind quintet, and the two ensembles are mediated by a third individual, the harp. Richard Rodney Bennett's sextet *Commedia I* (1972) takes a comparable approach, defining instruments as *commedia dell'arte* characters – the flute, Columbine; the bass clarinet, Pantaloon – their role playing set off schematically as a sequence of solos and duos. In all of these works, instruments and their players behave in a highly individuated manner. Evocation of dramatic personages defines a distinctive genre: with *Tragoedia*, Birtwistle intended to "bridge the gap between 'absolute music' and theatre music. It contains a specific drama, but this drama is purely musical" (1967).

Neither Birtwistle nor Musgrave has ever been drawn to the rigorous theoretical reflection favored by European avant-gardists, and yet it seems clear that British composers – comparatively reticent about conceptual matters – were attuned to concepts of instrumental theater so vigorously debated at Darmstadt during the 1960s (see Kovács 1997; Rupprecht 2008). Of course, proto-dramatic descriptions of instrumental music did not originate with postwar modernists. Heinrich Koch's famous reference to the eighteenth-century concerto as a "passionate dialogue" between soloist and orchestra is strikingly anthropomorphic: "He expresses his feelings to the orchestra, and it signals him through short interspersed phrases sometimes approval, sometimes acceptance" (Koch 1969, 3: 332, translation from Koch 1983: 209). Koch emphasizes an interplay between those onstage, only incidentally witnessed by an audience – a situation he compares to Greek tragedy, "where the actor expressed his feelings not towards the pit, but to the chorus" (3: 332; 1983: 209). The analogy between a musical performance and spoken stage drama is taken up again in Kagel's influential statements on instrumental theater in the early 1960s.

For Kagel, musical performances closely resemble those of conventional stage drama in three respects – the use of a podium, physical movement on-stage, and the role of individual interpreters in creating the performance (1963: 285–99; 1997). He goes on to illustrate a heightening of motivated agency in discussing his own work *Sonant* (1960/. . . .). The score of one movement, "Fin II," is comprised entirely of printed verbal instructions to each of the five players on how to imitate one another in various precisely timed actions contributing to the ensemble performance. One percussionist is told to imitate the other, then "resume your own role of independent musician" by silently laying down sticks, then return to imitation, "but only of his gestures and not of his sounds." The other percussionist is asked, while playing, to speculate philosophically: "Now is the time to wonder whether the joy of drumming arises only from the need of beating a rhythm or also from that of taking part somehow in a general gesticulation."[7] *Sonant* spells out the operational details of a given gesture and also a player's mental attitude to the instrument employed and to fellow players. In other works of the period – *Sur scène* (1960) and *Heterophonie* (1961) – Kagel abstracts the physical motions of conventional music making in order to defamiliarize them.

Control of actions, as Dieter Schnebel observed at the time, extends the avant-garde concern with parametric thought: "The composer controls not only the relationships of pitches, sounds and noises, but also the linkage of the actions in which they are embedded. . . . [H]e composes relationships and actions" (1972: 288, my translation). Compositional emphasis shifts from sounding results to the prescription of actions, a development with links to Cage's music of the early 1950s.[8]

Action, in the manual operational sense, is the privileged term in Kagel's instrumental theater. The outer drama of his *Match* (1964) is of "markedly 'sporting' character" (Kagel [ca. 1967]) as two cellists at either end of a stage compete under the watchful eyes of an umpire-like percussionist, center stage. The metaphoric transfer is underlined when "players" call specific shots (each cellist shouts *Olé*; the percussionist blows a whistle). The inner action here is intrinsically kinetic, a drama of string-playing techniques and endless varieties of sound – action is as much the unfolding of distinctive bodily exertions as the achievement of specific acoustic results (see Heile 2006: 47–48). British composer Bernard Rands in *Actions for Six* (1963) notates proportionally spaced events that are coordinated throughout by physical signs from each player, an approach with links to Kagel and especially to Rands's teacher, Berio.[9]

Cage's influence is cited again in Kagel's "theater" essay, specifically for his concentration on unforeseen performance results and his ability to provoke audiences into a lively interplay with performers onstage. The American composer's impact on the seriously playful European avant-garde is often noted; Kagel's casual reference to a *British* source for instrumental drama, though, might give historians of the European avant-garde pause. Kagel notes the "transformation of vacuum cleaners . . . into musical instruments" in a 1956 concert of comedy works organized by Gerard Hoffnung – a reference to Malcolm Arnold's *Grand, Grand Overture*, with the Amadeus Quartet as *concertante* cleaning crew. He goes on to compare Arnold's spoof specifically to Cage's *Concert* for piano and orchestra: each piece, Kagel observes, provokes lively audience reactions (1963: 289).[10] The instrumental drama idea had by the late 1950s gained an international profile.

An Anglo-European nexus for the 1960s genre of instrumental drama does not stop with Kagel's appreciation of Hoffnung's amalgam of "conventional celebration and solemnity" (1963: 289). One performer in the Paris premiere of Kagel's *Sonant* (February 1, 1961) was Cardew, who by the mid-1960s represented the closest British link to the theatrical and post-Cagean wing of the Continental avant-garde (292). Cardew's purely verbal score, *The Tiger's Mind* (1967), is overtly theatrical: six players memorize a loosely mythic text – "The tiger fights the mind that loves the circle . . ." – then improvise "actions and situations" involving six named characters (Cardew 1967). By 1968, when Cardew helped present the first London performance of Kagel's *Sur scène*, a British music theater movement was in full swing.[11] It is amid this lively avant-garde turn to music as theater that we can situate the flourishing, in Britain, of a distinctive genre of instrumental drama.

DRAMATIC-ABSTRACT FORM: MUSGRAVE'S
CHAMBER CONCERTO NO. 2

The treatment of instrumentalists as characteristic personages appears central to the genre of instrumental drama emerging in the 1960s. Where the musical agency effects of Classical-period chamber music are, as Maus says, "indeterminate" in textural presentation – themes and motives migrate between instruments fluidly – a very different dramatic scenario is typical in Thea Musgrave's music. In Musgrave, particular types of musical material are consistently assigned to a single instrument throughout a work's formal progress. In her Chamber Concerto No. 2, the viola always personifies "Rollo," a character named in the score and in program notes. Rollo's simple tuneful music contrasts vividly with the more chromatic idiom favored by the concerto's main quintet (flute, clarinet, violin, cello, piano). Since the musical role here is tied to a single instrumental timbre, I will speak of an instrument-agent within the texture (or of "viola-Rollo"). This form of musical-dramatic individuation lies beyond the norms of conventional concerto discourse, where agent definition can blur (if solo and *tutti* share material) or simply fade, if either soloist or orchestra loses particularity within a shared argument (see Kerman 1999). An instrument-agent, though, is defined by consistent attributes of timbre and musical behavior and will usually involve the actions of one physical performer.[12]

Musgrave's idea of dramatic-abstract form is bound up with a composerly concern with form itself. Musgrave once described her creative process in terms of an initial vivid flash, giving a work's "dramatic formal shape" *in toto* (1969: 153). In the case of Chamber Concerto No. 2, that shape is far from traditional, and the work's overall plot sequence assumes that listeners will recognize a named instrument-agent, Rollo, personified by the viola. Talk of form here also encompasses questions of rhythm and notation. Mus-

grave – like most progressive composers in the early 1960s – was moving away
from note-against-note rhythmic activity within ensemble works toward an
interplay of actions coordinated differently than in traditional polyphonic
textures. *Ad libitum* or *ostinato*-based passages, cueing of entrances between
parts, un-metered phrases (notated without bar lines), the coordination of
simultaneous independent tempi – all such features of Musgrave's music of
this period closely parallel developments in the work of figures as diverse as
Stockhausen, Lutosławski, Carter, and Foss.[13] Closer to home, Musgrave
was surely aware of Mátyás Seiber's experiments with limited performance
freedoms (see Keller 1960) and the freer ensemble interplay of Britten's *Curlew
River* (1964). Her most direct model, though, was American.

The chamber concerto's subtitle, "in homage to Charles Ives," is a belated
result of Musgrave's discovery of Ives's music in 1953 at Dartington (where
William Glock gave a talk on the composer's music), an encounter that deep-
ened when she heard John Kirkpatrick speak at Tanglewood in 1958 (see
Musgrave 1983: 25–26). Musgrave found in Ives's Quartet No. 2 a vivid display
of instrumental personalities (Carter's contemporaneous interest in instrumental "scenarios" also suggests Ives's influence).[14] In the violin-piano duo *Colloquy* (1960), she adopted an overtly dialogical form generated by contrasting
instrumental agents, providing movement titles (Disagreement, Digressions,
Development, Agreement) that resemble those of Ives's quartet.[15] In her Trio
for Flute, Oboe, and Piano, also from 1960, Musgrave developed a strongly
rhetorical mode of speech by loosening rhythmic strictures, juxtaposing met-
ricated passages with more freely aligned and much-ornamented segments,
marked *quasi improvisando*. Such passages heighten a listener's sense of instruments as proto-dramatic roles speaking individually in a present-tense drama.
The definition of instruments as agents in Musgrave's music is tied, then, to
a specific technical innovation – controlled freedom of rhythmic utterance.
The marked spontaneity of improvisation, "real" or composer-notated, further
deepens effects of agency.[16]

Musgrave's Rollo character, in both name and attributes, is taken over
directly from Ives's imaginary embodiment of the Victorian Conservative.
Quoting Ives, she calls Rollo "'one of those white-livered weaklings,' unable
to stand any dissonance" (see the footnote to the passage marked "Rollo's 1st
appearance," reh. **24**). The phrase is the first of several verbal notes Musgrave
prints in the score itself. As in Kagel, the performer's ability to convey specific
actions entails adopting a precise mental attitude; projecting agency within
the texture requires a sense of character and role. Musgrave's score verbally

EXAMPLE 9.1. Musgrave, Chamber Concerto No. 2 (1966),
Rollo's first appearance (score notated in C).

flags Rollo's "appearance," and her note functions like the thumbnail character descriptions printed in dramatic scripts. Like Kagel, she gives a player very precise indications as to the demeanor of viola-Rollo at a given moment. Rollo must "enter unobtrusively," and his first phrase should sound "nonchalant" – a fairly specific indication covering mental state and its public, social display (Example 9.1). Events in Ives's quartet offer a clear model: there, Rollo is played (in every sense) by Violin 2. He interrupts Ives's Arguments movement twice with snatches of unaccompanied "burlesque cadenza," headed *Andante Emasculata*, briefly coaxing his colleagues into a cloyingly tonal *Largo sweetota* before being gruffly cut off by a chromatic *Allegro con fisto* from the full quartet.[17] These are Rollo's only direct appearances, but Ives's texture elsewhere maintains a conspicuous individuality among the four instruments.

In printed notes and interviews, Musgrave has glossed the concerto's plot as a sequence of interactions between viola-Rollo and his colleagues. The gist of the drama is "the idea that Rollo keeps interrupting a rather sophisticated argument by the other players; he seizes on some tiny aspect of what they are playing and by a quite different association of ideas turns it, Ives-like, into a well known folk- or hymn-tune"; she speaks of Rollo as a "disruptive element" but also of the other players interrupting *him* (Musgrave 1973: 790; 2001: 8). Elsewhere, Musgrave describes Rollo's interruptions as being prompted by what he *hears*. The concerto's drama is vividly auditory: "Rollo, the viola," as

Musgrave explains, hears motives within the piece "with very different ears, so he turns this motive into a sort of traditional tune, which is 'The Keel Row'"; two further familiar tunes follow: "He hears a minor third which comes out of 'Swanee,' and then he plays 'All things bright and beautiful,' because of an interval" (1983: 27). Rollo's hearing resembles those isolated moments in opera when a character's singing is heard *as song* by others onstage (see Abbate 1991: 119–23). The concerto dramatizes motivic interplay as a process of social interaction prompted by the players' listening. The interruptive aspect of musical entrances depends on the discursive shift of boldly displayed quotation – the simple tunes, introduced by a highly individuated player-agent, don't fit, and they belong to Rollo. Single-handedly, he upstages his colleagues' activities.

Rollo's presence as character in the concerto is defined by instrument-agent rather than by a dedicated player – the violist is Rollo, but the same player serves at other times as the unnamed violinist.[18] Rollo's identity is a function of the tunes he quotes and of his instrumental voice, not his location onstage or the physical player realizing his music. By their very incongruity, Rollo's tunes establish his isolation from the piece at large and his essentially anti-heroic role in the work's plot.

Each of Rollo's three appearances is rich in dramatic implications and dialogic interplay with the group. His first appearance, playing "The Keel Row," creates harmonic polarity between his plain diatonic melody and the quintet's dense chromatic responses. The verbal commentary Musgrave prints in the score ("Why don't they join in? Let's try again") spells out viola-Rollo's attitude to the situation, much as a cartoonist might give a comic-strip character thought bubbles. This first interruption clashes with the music's metric framework; Rollo's "2nd appearance" (so announced in the score at **31+6**), playing "Swanee," aligns rhythmically with the other players' running-note scherzo, and this time they cannot ignore his musical presence. Individuals within the quintet pick up the new tune's signature rocking third ("*Swanee Ri-*ver"), above all the cellist, who seizes on it as germ for a declamatory solo. This suddenly emerging cello agency sounds highly dramatic, set against the piece's prior focus on ensemble utterance. The quintet's norm is a busy, collaborative discourse in which individual utterances are fragments of a *moto-perpetuo Fortspinnung* (Example 9.2). Against this brilliant but slightly anonymous-sounding backdrop, Rollo's enticement of the cello into a "Swanee"-inspired solo is a real coup. The thematic event could be parsed in purely structural terms, but a dramatic hearing recognizes the impact of

EXAMPLE 9.2. Musgrave, Chamber Concerto No. 2,
minimal agent definition in the quintet music.

Rollo's arrival. Viola-Rollo's well-defined presence as instrument-agent asserts a form-defining force.

Understanding of the concerto's overall formal shape goes hand in hand with tracing its agency strategy. The wild climax when quintet members "obsessively repeat fragments from all of Rollo's themes" (Musgrave 2001: 8) achieves its formal and expressive point by heightened activity in various parameters (Example 9.3). Sheer textural density is crucial here, but the underlying transformation, again, is one of musical agency: ensemble members become soloists. Quintet members, in their independent mimicry of Rollo, achieve a rhythmic and gestural independence lacking in the coordinated ensemble utterance.

Musical agency, including that of instrument-agents, works along a continuum defined according to attributes, actions, and behavior patterns. If viola-Rollo is a stable instrument-agent throughout the concerto, he is also intrepid in attempting to join a quintet discourse he is musically distant from. The more temporary agency achieved by the violin, flute, and clarinet at the climax projects character in sounding gesture, albeit in a more derivative and less rounded way. Rollo's colleagues, at the climax, build an anarchic ensemble of isolated phrases culled from earlier quintet music, together with fragments of Rollo's tunes. Since Rollo himself is absent at the climax, the score's motivic exchange is entirely a one-way affair: they copy him, but he never plays their music.[19] Various dramatic interpretations of this climactic scene present themselves to the listener: that Rollo has distracted his colleagues from seri-

EXAMPLE 9.3. Musgrave, Chamber Concerto No. 2,
"The others no longer interrupt, but . . . obsessively repeat
fragments from all of Rollo's themes" (Musgrave 2001: 8).

ous to frivolous matters; that he has bewitched or hypnotized them; more benignly, that he has won them over, liberating them as solo instrument-agents. The music's expressive detail invites a subtle dramatic narrative, grounded in anthropomorphic interpretations of thematic performances by instrument-agents: Rollo, having blundered into a scene he is unprepared for, persuades his initially standoffish company to indulge in musical behaviors that are for them unfamiliar, even bizarre and clownish .

Each instrument at the climax responds to Rollo in a distinctive tone of voice: the violin at one point plays "Swanee" in artificial harmonics. The flute's response is more playful, by turns bird-like or excitable, all trills and nursery-rhyme tunefulness (Example 9.3). The clarinet part is marked *Tempo di Rollo*, an inscription encapsulating the centrality of the category of instrument-agent – embodied in a named character and habitual musical role – to the entire drama.

The drama of agency is also, implicitly, one of social hierarchy, if read semantically for signs of status or class. The folk song "Keel Row," Stephen Foster's "Swanee," and the Victorian children's hymn "All Things Bright and Beautiful" are musical emblems of Anglo-American oral and vernacular traditions. Their simple diatonicism stands in maximum relief against the octatonic harmonies of Musgrave's music for the full quintet. The four-square comes up against the self-evidently modern. Musically, Rollo's quotations gesture toward the milieu of village church, classroom, or private parlor, referents socially and historically distant from the elite secular realm of the recital hall. The quintet's "rather sophisticated" music excludes Rollo initially; his alterity and his unlikely triumph lend rich allegorical resonances to the music's dramatic plot.

Latent semantic trappings, like the concerto's intertextual borrowing of Ives's Rollo character, are ultimately secondary to a manifest formal drama. Musgrave's personification of an outsider figure is grounded in a relatively abstract drama centered on an interplay between wordless instrument-agents. Transformations of character and tone represent the concerto's main formal and dramatic development, forged in an idiom supple enough to catch minute shadings of mood. The resulting drama remains abstract; like most untexted art music, it lacks real-world referents. But the personalities who animate the drama – distinctive instrument-agents and at least one highly individual "character" – emerge with unusual expressive precision.

ACTION AS SOCIAL RITUAL: BIRTWISTLE'S
VERSES FOR ENSEMBLES

Physical onstage motions by the performers become significant to a drama of agency in a number of late-1960s scores. Musgrave's Clarinet Concerto and Boulez's *Domaines* are cases in point, but it is in Birtwistle's *Verses for Ensembles* (1968) that such choreography plays a particularly elaborate role in the definition of musical agents. Here, the players' numerous movements around the stage are rigorously scripted throughout the piece's half-hour span in a choreography diagrammed in the score. Birtwistle's thirteen performers subdivide into three main ensembles: a quintet of brass, a quintet of winds, and three percussionists. Wind and percussion players move stage location as a group at various points, shifting in the process between instruments of contrasting pitch and timbre. Among the brass, the two trumpets act as twins, moving up- or downstage; the horn player also moves, and – typically for Birtwistle – plays a major *concertante* role in the proceedings. Only the two trombones remain seated throughout. During the central phase of the score, all five winds take solos on their high instruments (bassoon, clarinet, oboe, E♭ clarinet, piccolo). Each soloist moves for the solo to Desk A, stage left in Birtwistle's plan (Example 9.4).[20] Birtwistle glosses the score's spatial dimen-

seating arrangement

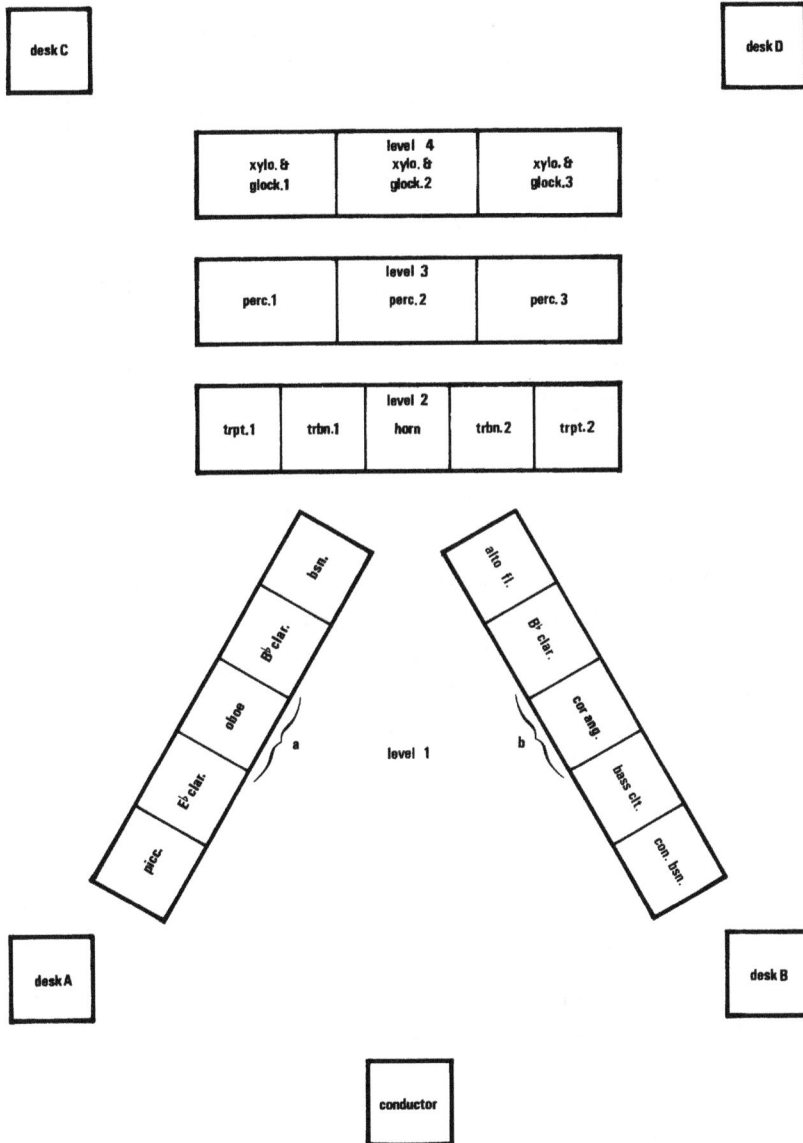

EXAMPLE 9.4. Birtwistle, *Verses for Ensembles* (1968), seating arrangement chart.
*Birtwistle VERSES FOR ENSEMBLES. © 1972 Universal Edition (London)
Ltd., London/UE 15331. © Renewed. All rights reserved. Used by permission of
European American Music Distributors LLC, U.S. and Canadian agent for
Universal Edition (London) Ltd., London.*

sion as "different kinds of music attached to different ensembles, who play them in a sort of 'territory'; it's a territorial piece, and it's completely logical that they play where they play" (1997: 12). Mention of territory already has a sociological ring to it, evoking the idea of co-presence in face-to-face human interactions – a point I will return to later on. Meanwhile, it seems productive to consider *Verses* with these social behaviors in mind as an intricate drama of ritualized encounter – a patterned sequence of actions conducted by performers with varying degrees of agency. At one level, the score projects actions of great formality, especially where material is performed by an ensemble; but *Verses for Ensembles* is equally rich in solo utterances, and it is the individuated forms of agency they project in relation to the larger social groups that command dramatic attention.

A lack of bridge passages gives Birtwistle's piece, in his own words, a "hard-edged" discourse – *Verses* foregrounds abrupt dialogic shifts between unblended ensembles (Birtwistle 1997: 12).[21] This is an obvious contrast to the lyrical continuity of Musgrave's dramas, and the more broken musical flow in Birtwistle promotes a different scenario of musical agency. Birtwistle's later statement that "I regard instruments as actors, and I'm intrigued by their role playing" (quoted in Adlington 1999: 38) references the performer's identity with a role. But the comment also admits *distance* from that role – analogous to the distance felt in dramas performed in masks. *Verses* defines agents who enact a kind of ceremonial, a drama operating first and foremost at archetypal symbolic levels. This drama of agency defines and enacts distances between player, instrument, and role.

A closer look at how the players move onstage sheds light on their status as agents. The events of the first few minutes trace a sequence of actions effected by players moving about the stage and also shifting between instruments, following the score's precisely located visual cues.

A Ro Brass with Horn solo; Percussion; High Winds (*left*)
  R3 Percussion; *Trumpets move to front stage*
  R4 Trumpet signals, with Brass unison counter line; *Winds move left to right*

B R6 Low Winds (*right*); *Trumpets return to seats*

All players are musically active in the opening, and even before anyone makes a physical move, listeners experience lively interplay between brass, untuned percussion, and wind groupings, the latter in their stage-left/shrill-timbred form. From the outset, the horn assumes a dominant role, leading the brass

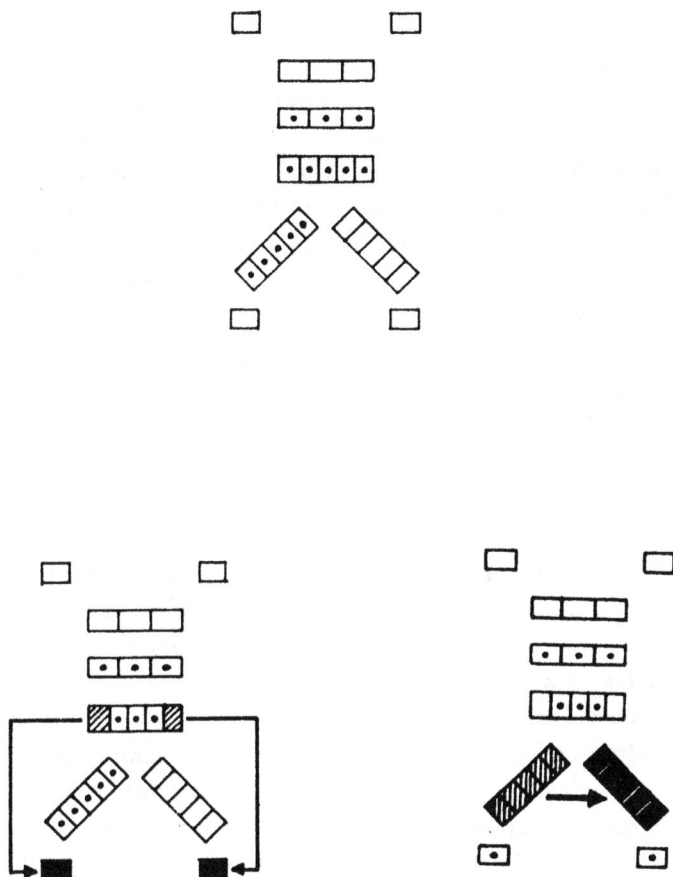

EXAMPLE 9.5. *Verses for Ensembles*, initial seating and visual cues for first two stage maneuvers (at reh. 3 and reh. 4).
Birtwistle VERSES FOR ENSEMBLES. © *1972 Universal Edition (London) Ltd., London/ UE 15331. © Renewed. All rights reserved. Used by permission of European American Music Distributors LLC, U.S. and Canadian agent for Universal Edition (London) Ltd., London.*

with a tumbling solo phrase. The percussion quickly establish a subsidiary dramatic role, mediating between wind and brass ensembles or supporting their separate utterances. The first extended ensemble (reh. 3) is the moment at which Birtwistle first calls for a stage movement, in this case bringing the two trumpeters to front of stage: one left, one right (see Example 9.5 for the visual cue). These trumpeters, unlike the horn, are not individuals but twins, shadowing one another in an organum-like doubling of gesture.

But it is the physical fact of their movement to the front of the stage – and their heightening of a crackling cross talk between stage left and right – that contributes to their status as paired instrument-agents. The trumpets are *of* the brass ensemble but momentarily stand apart, a separation the staging clarifies. Their music interacts with that of their home ensemble (whose forceful counter-line is the first unison of *Verses* and thus the first sonic union of instruments within an ensemble), but in presenting a fanfare-like scenic event, they do dramaturgic work, heralding the first real change of thematic-harmonic direction.

Throughout *Verses*, stage motions highlight musical shifts, a doubling of perceptual channels that reinforces the sense of unfolding ritual. The trumpet signal heralds the first *group* maneuver, that of winds left to right, who play from the new location in low-pitched timbres. Stage movement and change of musical topic coincide, and as this new, much softer material begins (labeled B in the summary above), the trumpets return to sit with their brass colleagues.

With its choreography, *Verses* effects a clear separation of player-agent from instrument-agent. The woodwinds as a mobile group are player-agents, defined by their visible left-to-right maneuver. But the same move, and Birtwistle's delineation of a change of musical topic, also defines *instrument*-agents in a timbral and territorial way – the obvious fact that high winds play on the left, low winds on the right. Birtwistle's dual definition of agency opens up conceptual and physical distance between performers and roles, players and instruments. A player-agent who moves around without changing instruments dispenses with the contrast among instruments; conversely, if *Verses* had used separate performers for high and low wind quintets, a display of player-agents would be lost along with stage movements. The choreography intermingles two ways in which dramatic agency presents itself to a witnessing audience. The interplay of the choreographic and the sonic makes for a sequence of proto-dramatic entrances: each new sounding event is prefigured by a physical preparation, and so the drama carries an inbuilt suspense.

Verses does not lack for conventional harmonic-thematic argument, but the import of specific pitches is at times reduced, notably in the wind mobiles (of which B, reh. **6** in the score, is the first). Such passages notate only rhythm with fixity; players choose among local pitch successions, and precise harmonic results vary. In the later brass *ritornello* phrase that punctuates woodwind solos (first heard at reh. **33**), players choose dynamic level, timbre (five possible mute types), and phrasing (*legato, staccato,* or mixed), maximizing the distinctiveness of the sounding result, one view of a cubist musical object.

About the *ritornello*, Birtwistle comments: "Every time it recurs it's slightly different, so that you never get the complete picture" (1997: 14). Definition of musical agents here has as much to do with scenic, timbral, and gestural traits as returning motivic or melodic units. Performer choice admits great variety of sonic detail throughout *Verses;* the one thing that is always fixed throughout is the choreography of stage movements.

The central sequence of five woodwind solos (reh. **34–52**) might be called reinterpretations of one another, since they are grounded in a shared horn solo and percussion accompaniment (see Beard 2000: 139). In spite of the evident structural similarities of the solos (e.g., each is forty beats long), the overriding impression they make is of separate dramaturgic appearances, each one a highly individualized instrument-agent, each playing a manifestly unique role. A hearing of *Verses* attuned to its variety of solo agents supports an allegorical understanding of its latent semantic dimension. The main ensembles, for instance, might be deemed a type of musical community, and their various interactions, including those of their individual members, a display of social hierarchy. As in all ritual, individual gestures are intrinsically meaningful in a nonverbal channel; as in drama, roles are assumed by actors whose agency and individuality are prominent.

Considering the display of agents in *Verses for Ensembles,* critics have occasionally hinted at the nature of the musical roles. Michael Nyman compares the horn's "magisterial" role to that of other master-of-ceremonies figures in Birtwistle, notably Choregos in *Punch and Judy* and Father Christmas in *Down by the Greenwood Side* (1969: 48; 1971: 121). Michael Hall senses an internalized conflict of "self-assertion" and "the equally strong pull of the group," and he notes the ecclesiastical trappings of the winds sitting in two rows, like choir stalls (1984: 52). The display of agents is clearest in the solo episodes for obvious scenic reasons: each solo agent walks to Desk A, plays continuously without interruption, then returns to sit down. The common setting for each appearance is the adjunct role of the solo horn, stage right, and supporting percussion accompaniment. The choreography on its own terms shows the audience player-agents; but once in position, *instrument*-agents come to the fore, since Birtwistle is at pains to create a highly diverse group of musical personalities. Audiences witness a distance between theatricalized players and the roles they take on.

As evidence of the range of personalities among instruments, consider the contrasting attributes of the opening solo for bassoon and of the piccolo solo closing the sequence:

EXAMPLE 9.6. *Verses for Ensembles,* bassoon and piccolo as soloists (score notated in C).
Birtwistle *VERSES FOR ENSEMBLES.* © 1972 Universal Edition (London) Ltd.,
London/UE 15331. © Renewed. All rights reserved. Used by permission of European
American Music Distributors LLC, U.S. and Canadian agent for Universal Edition
(London) Ltd., London.

bassoon (reh. **34–36**)	piccolo (reh. **50–52**)
trills	rapidly repeating single-note attacks
angular melody contours	ascending-scale figures
short gestures (3–5 pitches)	longer gestures (9–14 pitches)
harmonics	flutter-tongued

EXAMPLE 9.6. *(continued).*

These musical character traits are not entirely discrete – both instruments play angular lines – but the list captures what is typical. Contrasts of distinctive traits build on each instrument's technical possibilities, supplementing the very basic timbral-pitch opposition of baritone bassoon and shrill piccolo, but beyond this, it is clear that the score defines agents of strikingly varied disposition (Example 9.6). Taking the implicitly anthropomorphic charge in all claims for agency at face value, the hermeneutical listener will easily ascribe motivation or interactional traits in each case: the bassoon is ruminative, unsettled, short-winded, and concludes in a restrained way. The piccolo, on the other hand, is voluble and exuberant, racing around in confident ascending lines, saving his or her most animated playing for the second half of the solo, and ending by reiterating opening points in a literal repeat. (The personality contrasts also further the cumulative formal argument of the solo sequence, which begins tentatively and builds to a peak of excitement.)

Solo instrumental personalities also define themselves by interaction with the horn. The horn's basic instrument-agency is defined by fixed musical behaviors, a returning pitch sequence, and the forty-beat rhythmic cycle. The horn, in a sense, leads each soloist through a single, unvarying pathway five times. In each solo, there are three phrases, with marked pauses after fifteen, nine, and finally sixteen beats. With the uneasy bassoon, the horn is coaxing, patient, or phlegmatic; with the garrulous piccolo – something of a show-off – the horn takes a more declamatory line, competing for attention in the conversation. As usual, various semantic interpretations are possible – that the horn works to assert and maintain a social prominence and autonomy; or that he/she is seeking to control a disruptive subordinate.

AGENCY AS PRESENTATION OF SELF:
AN EVERYDAY PERSPECTIVE FROM GOFFMAN

Recalling Birtwistle's earlier remark on *Verses for Ensembles* as a "territorial piece," I return in closing to the sociological perspective on face-to-face human interaction alluded to earlier. It may be worth taking seriously a metaphorical view of the behavior of musical agents, defined either as an instrument-agent (Musgrave's viola-Rollo) or else by a foregrounding of the player as agent, an effect achieved by onstage choreography (Birtwistle's peripatetic performers, moving between instruments and locations). We are accustomed to thinking of musical agents in anthropomorphic terms – as individual people or characters rather than diffuse forces.[22] What, then, might we glean from a sociology of everyday human encounter, in particular from an analysis that interprets social interactions as quasi-dramatic performances? How far might one push analogies between music's agency effects and what Erving Goffman termed "the presentation of self"?

What Goffman wrote in the mid-1960s about social encounters is apt to the interplay of agents already explored in Musgrave and Birtwistle: "A brief time span is involved, a limited extension in space, and a restriction to those events that must go on to completion once they have begun. There is a close meshing with the ritual properties of persons and the egocentric forms of territoriality" (1967: 1). Goffman's conceptual field spans the formality of ritual and the more volatile impromptu behavior of individuals who in social settings express selfhood in ways both conscious and inadvertent.[23] His sociology construes selfhood with minimal psychological background, stripped back to rituals of role playing. He speaks of a double definition of self, both as "an image pieced together from the expressive implications of the full flow of events in an undertaking" and as a "kind of player in a ritual game," one who copes diplomatically or otherwise with the situation at hand (31). Social interactants pursue a *line*, a pattern of verbal and nonverbal acts, and attempt to maintain an image of self (keeping *face*), delineated precisely by social attributes. A sense of respect is sought by both participants (interruptions avoided, attentiveness); politeness rituals abound (greetings and farewells); social activity falls into units defined by paired interchange. "Ritual equilibrium" is maintained while perpetuating an idea of place in a social order. Such models of the social self, highly patterned as they are – relatively free of semantic specifics – map with surprising directness onto music's wordless rhetoric.[24]

The presentation of self in Musgrave's Chamber Concerto No. 2 is tied to the consistency of viola-Rollo's performance as instrument-agent. From a Goffmanesque perspective, one might add that it is significant that Rollo's own "sincerity" is never in doubt – the music lacks signs that his behavior is a put-on, and the image of self he projects before other quintet members is consistent. None of his three folkish tunes fits the reality of the main quintet, but, ultimately, the piece's dramatic progression reflects Rollo's ability to impose his own definition of the situation on others present. Reading the concerto earlier, I proposed that Rollo's appearances, in their musical allusions, trace an implicit narrative of class hierarchy. At a more local level, though, an account of instrument-agents as social interactants need not invoke semantic specifics. It is enough, for example, to hear the structure of a given strip of activity in terms of the give-and-take of everyday social encounter. Viola-Rollo's first appearance, in that case, takes the familiar form of an awkward snub: the expressive front Rollo so cautiously presents is pointedly ignored, the conduct the viola-agent enacts rejected out of hand. At the broadest level of plot, the piece traces Rollo's efforts to belong, a story with patent social dimensions.

Goffman's anatomy of the invisible rules of social encounter suggests many parallels to the agency effects on display in Birtwistle's *Verses for En-*

sembles. Here, the presence of strongly defined instrument-agents with consistent musical identities is supplemented by the work's emphasis on physical, mobile player-agents. Again, one listens in metaphorical but precise ways to the performances in *Verses* as redolent of the play of roles in social encounter. The schematic nature of the exchanges between various ensembles (high or low woodwinds, brass, percussion) and soloists, the lack of any shared material, the focus on patterned, cyclical routines – all of these contribute to a ritualized effect. The inherent formality of requiring instrumentalists to move to a specific point in space before they begin to play heightens a sense of individuals – both instrument-agents and player-agents – performing actions according to a governing set of rules for public encounter.

Given Birtwistle's emphasis on player-agents as mobile performers of specific roles, one might consider the score's eponymous ensembles less as traditional choric-textural groupings of like-timbred instruments than as proto-social collectives, cooperating in the performance of a specific action and the dramatized display of that action. Such a grouping, in Goffman's terms, is a *team*, a set of individuals who "co-operate in staging a single routine" (1959: 79). Birtwistle's treatment of the three percussion players is a case in point. While they acquire a group identity as player-agents by their physical movement between pitched and non-pitched instruments, their team role is always far less dramatically central than that of the groups or soloists they mediate between. But to reduce the conduct of such personalized agents only to a conventional textural-functional label ("accompanist," say) is to give short shrift to Birtwistle's clear interest in their presence as stage performers of a wordless secret theater. The horn, meanwhile, does not belong to any team. His (or her) function is that of a director of the overall performance, a prominent instrument-agent, and (since he or she is mobile) a player-agent, one invested with considerable ceremonial power (on director functions, see Goffman 1959: 97–100). That sounding role is reinforced physically in Birtwistle's score, where the horn sits center stage, directly facing the conductor.

If Classical-period chamber-musical discourse conveys an agency that is, as Maus says, "indeterminate" in its diffusion among shifting instrumental textures, the agents in the 1960s instrumental dramas of Musgrave and Birtwistle offer a very different model. In both composers' scores, the experience of a witnessing or listening audience is bound to center on agents of remarkably fixed identity. Musgrave's delineation of Rollo is accomplished by projecting his identity as an instrument-agent with musical behaviors that are, in context, eccentric. Birtwistle, too, devises instrument-agents of recognizable personality, but the agency of *Verses* is also *over*-determined, since the physical agency of the player is scenically apparent apart from the instrument he or she animates. These player-agents might appear closer than conventional instrumental performers to theatrical actors, yet it is important to realize that they remain bound within the musical world of Birtwistle's piece. Their identity as agents remains a part of the virtual world of the artwork, for their movements are themselves part of the score's fixed gestural sequence. Such virtual agents, however undeniably physical and kinetic, remain distant from the actual agents familiar in other types of performance – the pianist performing a Beethoven sonata, for example.[25] Agency effects, ubiquitous in so many musics, occupy almost too broad a field of possibility to be captured by any finite conceptual scheme. Still, in seeking to acknowledge the interplay of instrument and player – in mapping the mysterious space between performer and role – we get closer to that combined spirit of playfulness and formality so characteristic of art music in the 1960s.

NOTES

1. On inconsistency of agent definition in orchestral and chamber music textures, see Cone (1974) and Maus (1997: 120–23). On overt polarization between concerto soloist and orchestra, see Kerman (1999).

2. Greimas replaces a traditional idea of characters (dramatis personae) in narrative with a distinction between "*actants,* having to do with narrative syntax, and *actors,* which are recognizable in the particular discourses in which they are manifested. . . . [I]f an actant (A_j) can be manifested in discourse by several actors (a_1, a_2, a_3), the converse is possible, just one actor (a_j) being able to constitute a syncretism of several actants (A_1, A_2, A_3)" (1987: 106–107). Greimas's scheme echoes both Propp's (1968) account of narrative in folklore and Souriau's (1950) division between figures and six underlying functions in stage dramas.

3. Richard Rodney Bennett, in *Commedia I* (1972), explores comparable instrumental-drama concepts. Gordon Crosse's 1970s concertante works – for example, *Ariadne* and *Wildboy* – are highly gestural but lack the sense of personal agency apparent in the works of Musgrave and Birtwistle to be discussed here.

4. See Kagel (1963: 285). On European exemplars of the genre, see Sacher (1985) and Kovács (1996). Kovács dates the earliest version of Kagel's essay to a 1960 radio talk. On Ligeti's Alpbach lecture, see Toop (1999: 80).

5. "The Funny Side of Music at Palermo," *Times* (London), October 12, 1963, 12; see also Peter Heyworth, "Right at the End of the Road," *Observer* (London), October 13, 1963, 26; and Smith Brindle (1959).

6. On multimedia theorizing in the Palermo-based journal *Collage* after 1963, see Borio (1993: 118–27).

7. Kagel, *Sonant* (1960/. . . .), "Fin II," English-language instructions, percussion

I and II parts (Peters Edition 5972, 1964). Kagel cites the instructions directly (1963: 298). A close study of *Sonant* appears in Sacher (1985: 149–93).

8. Schnebel, in his 1966 Darmstadt lecture, "Sichtbare Musik," refers specifically to Cage's *Water Music* and other works (1972: 320).

9. The work was premiered at Darmstadt in 1963, the year of Berio's *Instrument und Funktion* course.

10. The garbled French translation of Kagel's lecture renders Hoffnung's concert as an English festival of *musique de l'espérance*. The recording of the Arnold is reissued on *Hoffnung's Music Festivals*, EMI CMS 763302-2.

11. Focus Opera Group presented Cardew's *Schooltime Compositions* alongside the Kagel in March 1968; Cardew was the translator of the English score of Kagel's *Sur scène* (published by Henri Litolff in 1965). Cardew's contacts with Kagel go unmentioned in Nyman's influential 1972 *Experimental Music*, a study emphasizing an "Anglo-American experimental tradition" rather than European influences (1999: xvii). For an overview of the music theater genre post-1960, see Adlington (2005).

12. Exceptions include music for piano duet or percussion duo, where a team might perform as one instrument-agent. Distinctions between the sounding timbre of an instrument-agent and its physical source in performer activity will be most vivid in live performance, less evident in recordings, where listeners track timbres and gestures without visual information.

13. Musgrave recalls encountering Foss's ideas on controlled ensemble improvisation during her 1958 residency at Tanglewood (1983: 19). Lutosławski's notational practices in scores such as *Jeux vénitiens* (1961) became known to

British composers particularly after his 1963 visit to Dartington summer school. Musgrave recalls "long conversations" with Lutosławski, specifically on notation (28).

14. On the resemblance between Ives's Rollo and the Violin 2 personality in Carter's String Quartet No. 2, see Schiff (1998: 73).

15. Musgrave's *Colloquy* titles, noted in a *Times* review of the premiere (July 12, 1960), were dropped in the published score.

16. Even in a Beethoven quartet, Maus argues, for a listener "it is as though the future of the agent is open – as though what he will do next is not already determined" (1997: 121). Such arguments might locate musical sequences closer to a dramatic than a literary model of narrative; for helpful consideration of "narrative universals" as realized in specific media, see Almén (2008: 13–14).

17. The published score (New York, 1954) prints Ives's markings but omits penciled comments visible in the manuscript, including the name "Rollo Finck," alluding to a conservative New York critic, Henry Finck.

18. The quintet includes other doublings for flute (on piccolo and alto flute) and clarinet (bass clarinet), but these timbral shifts are not linked to agent-defining activities such as Rollo's tune quotations.

19. The nearest Rollo comes to performing *with* his colleagues as equals comes in his brief "Swanee-third" comments on the cello's expansive first solo at reh. **35**.

20. Birtwistle's score does not specify whether soloists at Desks A–D stand or sit. For his **17** solo, the horn player is told to "remain standing" after moving back from Desk A. In many performances, all solos are delivered standing, as in a jazz big band.

21. A fellowship student at Princeton in 1966, Birtwistle may well have been familiar with Edward T. Cone's well-known analysis of interlock in Stravinsky's music (see Adlington 1999: 134).

22. Eero Tarasti speaks of musical agency broadly in terms of *actors*, a category "represented by all those features that render abstract musical structures as anthropomorphic" (1994: 106). Actoriality, in Tarasti's analyses, often encompasses the activity of traditional themes and motives.

23. Goffman distinguishes between the expression a social actor gives (often verbally) and the unintentional signs he or she "gives off" in social settings by posture and demeanor (1959: 2–5).

24. On ritual in social interaction, see Goffman's essay "On Face-Work" (in Goffman 1967).

25. On virtual and actual agents in music, and the vicissitudes of a listener's emotional responses, see Hatten (2010). My thanks to Robert Hatten for helpful discussion of this question.

WORKS CITED

Abbate, Carolyn. 1991. *Unsung Voices: Opera and Musical Narrative in the Nineteenth Century*. Princeton: Princeton University Press.

Adlington, Robert. 1999. *The Music of Harrison Birtwistle*. Cambridge: Cambridge University Press.

———. 2005. "Music Theatre since the 1960s." In *The Cambridge Companion to Twentieth-Century Opera*, edited by Mervyn Cooke, 225–43. Cambridge: Cambridge University Press.

Almén, Byron. 2008. *A Theory of Musical Narrative*. Bloomington: Indiana University Press.

Beard, David. 2000. "An Analysis and Sketch Study of the Early Instrumental Music of Sir Harrison Birtwistle (c. 1957–77)." PhD diss., Oxford University.

Birtwistle, Harrison. 1967. "Tragoedia." Liner note to recording *Crosse, Wood, Birtwistle*. Argo ZRG 759.

———. 1997. "Territorial Rites 2" (interview with Ross Lorraine). *Musical Times* 138 (November): 12–16.

———. 2001. Interview with Colin Anderson. In notes to recording *Refrains and Choruses*. Deux-Elles, CD DXL 1019.

Borio, Gianmario. 1993. *Musikalische Avantgarde um 1960: Entwurf einer Theorie der informellen Musik*. Laaber: Laaber-Verlag.

Borio, Gianmario, and Hermann Danuser, eds. 1997. *Im Zenit der Moderne: Die internationalen Ferienkurse für neue Musik Darmstadt, 1946–1966*. 4 vols. Freiburg: Rombach.

Cardew, Cornelius. 1963. "Palermo." *Musical Times* 104 (December): 886.

———. 1967. "Sextet: The Tiger's Mind." *Musical Times* 108 (June): 527–30.

Cone, Edward T. 1974. *The Composer's Voice*. Berkeley: University of California Press.

Goffman, Erving. 1959. *The Presentation of Self in Everyday Life*. Garden City: Doubleday Anchor Books.

———. 1967. *Interaction Ritual: Essays on Face-to-Face Behavior*. Garden City: Anchor Books.

Greimas, Algirdas Julien. 1987. "Actants, Actors, and Figures." In *On Meaning: Selected Writings in Semiotic Theory*, 106–20. Minneapolis: University of Minnesota Press. First published 1973.

Hall, Michael. 1984. *Harrison Birtwistle*. London: Robson Books.

Hatten, Robert S. 2010. "Musical Agency as Implied by Gesture and Emotion: Its Consequences for Listeners' Experiencing of Musical Emotion." In *Semiotics 2009: Proceedings of the Annual Meeting of the Semiotic Society of America,* edited by Karen Haworth and Leonard Sbrocchi, 162–69. New York: Legas Publishing.

Heile, Björn. 2006. *The Music of Mauricio Kagel.* Aldershot: Ashgate.

Kagel, Mauricio. 1963. "Le théâtre instrumental." Translated by Antoine Goléa. In *La musique et ses problèmes contemporaines 1953–1963,* edited by Jean-Louis Barrault et al., 285–99. Paris: René Julliard.

———. [ca. 1967]. "Match for Three Players." Liner note to recording *Mauricio Kagel: Match für 3 Spieler; Musik für Renaissance-Instrumente.* Deutsche Grammophon 137 006.

———. 1997. "Neuer Raum – Neue Musik: Gedanken zum Instrumentalen Theater." Reprinted in *Im Zenit der Moderne: Die internationalen Ferienkurse für Neue Musik Darmstadt, 1946–1966,* edited by Gianmario Borio and Hermann Danuser, 3: 245–53. Freiburg: Rombach. First published 1966.

Keller, Hans. 1960. "Improvisation." *Listener* (June 30): 1153.

Kerman, Joseph. 1999. *Concerto Conversations.* Cambridge: Harvard University Press.

Koch, Heinrich Christoph. 1969. *Versuch einer Anleitung zur Composition.* Munich: Olms. First published 1793.

———. 1983. *Introductory Essay on Composition.* Translated by Nancy Kovaleff Baker. New Haven: Yale University Press.

Kovács, Inge. 1996. "Instrumentales Theater." In *Von Kranichstein zur Gegenwart: 50 Jahre Darmstädter Ferienkurse,* edited by Rudolf Stephan et al., 333–39. Stuttgart: DACO Verlag.

———. 1997. "Musik und Szene." In *Im Zenit der Moderne: Die internationalen Ferienkurse für neue Musik Darmstadt, 1946–1966,* edited by Gianmario Borio and Hermann Danuser, 2: 311–32. Freiburg: Rombach.

Maus, Fred Everett. 1997. "Music as Drama." In *Music and Meaning,* edited by Jenefer Robinson, 105–30. Ithaca: Cornell University Press. First published 1988.

Musgrave, Thea. 1969. "Starting Points." *Listener* (January 30): 153.

———. 1973. "A New Viola Concerto." *Musical Times* 114 (August): 790–91.

———. 1983. Interview in Oral History American Music project, tape 122. New Haven: Yale School of Music, typescript.

———. 2001. Liner note to recording *Pierrot Dreaming.* Clarinet Classics, CC0038.

———. 2010. Program note to Concerto for Clarinet. www.chesternovello.com (accessed June 2010).

Nyman, Michael. 1969. "First Performances: Two New Works by Birtwistle." *Tempo* 88 (Spring): 47–50.

———. 1971. "Harrison Birtwistle." *London Magazine* 11(4): 118–22.

———. 1999. *Experimental Music: Cage and Beyond.* 2nd ed. Cambridge: Cambridge University Press. First published 1974.

Propp, Vladimir. 1968. *Morphology of the Folktale.* 2nd ed. Translated by Laurence Scott. Austin: University of Texas Press.

Pruslin, Stephen. 1998. Note for recording *Hymnos.* Clarinet Classics, CC 0019.

Rupprecht, Philip. 2008. "'Something Slightly Indecent': British Composers, the European Avant-garde, and

National Stereotypes in the 1950s." *Musical Quarterly* 91: 275–326.

Sacher, Reinhard Josef. 1985. *Musik als Theater*. Regensburg: Bosse.

Schiff, David. 1998. *The Music of Elliott Carter*. 2nd ed. Ithaca: Cornell University Press.

Schnebel, Dieter. 1972. *Denkbare Musik: Schriften 1952–1972*. Edited by Hans Rudolf Zeller. Cologne: M. DuMont Schauberg.

Smith Brindle, Reginald. 1959. "Reports from Abroad: Venice Festival." *Musical Times* 100 (December): 677.

Souriau, Étienne. 1950. *Les deux cent mille situations dramatiques*. Paris: Flammarion.

Tarasti, Eero. 1994. *A Theory of Musical Semiotics*. Bloomington: Indiana University Press.

Toop, Richard. 1999. *György Ligeti*. London: Phaidon.

10

Narrativities in the Music
of Thomas Adès: The Piano
Quintet and *Brahms*

Emma Gallon

INTRODUCTION

The music of Thomas Adès is by turns captivating, scintillating, dramatic, and enigmatic, its vocabulary poised teasingly between the traditionally familiar and the ruggedly contemporary. The intricate ways in which disparate musical and extra-musical threads entwine in Adès's works belie the deceptively attractive musical surface. Along with the journalistic acclaim that Adès's music has received, most of the scholarship surrounding his works to date has focused on the semantic richness of his music (see Whittall 2003; Fox 2004; Venn 2006), while only one article interrogates its structural intricacy in any great depth (Roeder 2006).[1] This essay argues that a narrative approach is particularly able to draw together both the expressive resonance and structural detail of Adès's music in order to understand better its interpretive potential, a key consideration as part of wider contemporary trends, given Adès's international reputation as a leading composer.

The prevalent tendency to narrativize experienced events, so natural an impulse that "to raise the question of the nature of narrative is to invite reflection on the very nature of culture and, possibly, even on the nature of humanity itself" (White 1980: 5), arguably makes narrative one of the most pertinent metaphors for music in relation to human experience. In addition, as narrativity can operate independently of any other readily audible or ideological organizing system, the classic example of which is tonality, this approach to analysis appears to be a highly valid method for interpreting twentieth- and twenty-first-century music, which often presents challenges to such systems. This essay initially outlines the particular narrative stance to be taken, necessary, as the enlivened interest in this mode of analysis has allowed the term *narrative* to encompass wide-ranging and eclectic clusters of methodologies. More specifically, it considers the possibility of *narrativities*, in which elements of narrativity can be discerned on multiple levels of a text. It can be argued that some music prompts such a pluralistic technique of interpretation more than others, as Jonathan Kramer (1981) suggests of postmodern music and, more relevantly here, John Roeder (2006) claims of Adès's works. This study will go on to show the potential of reconceiving Adès's music in terms of narrativities, as, rather than sweeping over the individual layers of his multifaceted compositional style, this approach takes them into account and provides a fitting tool with which to disentangle the structural and signifying strands that contribute to the music's complex expressive effects. My particular focus will be on the Piano Quintet (2000) and *Brahms* (2001).

THEORIZING NARRATIVITIES

The most comprehensive analytical study of Adès's music to date, carried out by Roeder, attempts to show in detail the multiple temporalities that Adès's music encourages the listener to perceive through the superimposition of different lines of pitch and metric continuity. After Christopher Hasty's (1986) meditation on succession and continuity in twentieth-century music, Roeder defines continuity as "an association between two percepts, formed when the second realizes a mental projection that was made as part of the first" (2006: 122).[2] Roeder's extensive analytical examples of metric and pitch(-class)-interval continuity in Adès's works show "how they are made to co-operate so as to articulate and direct the temporal flow" in multiple cohesive streams (2006: 122). In addition, these "fundamental concepts of continuity" (122) provide the means to ground some of Kramer's temporal metaphors, including "narrative," though critical exploration of this term is avoided. Through a more rigorous theorization of narrativity and narrativities it will be possible to scrutinize the role of the streams of continuity and other characteristic traits of Adès's music, not only in terms of structure but also in terms of expressive meaning, an equally significant aspect of its impact that Roeder neglects. These narrativities potentially could be bound to one another intrinsically, contributing to an overall narrative meaning, or they might suggest conflicting narrative interpretations, as they unfold at different rates, vie for prominence, or appear utterly incongruous.

The advantage of this pluralistic approach is that it does not attempt to impose any false unity on the interpretive breadth of the numerous and occasionally ambiguous ways in which it is possible to hear music, particularly of the twentieth century onward, as addressed throughout this volume, yet it draws them fruitfully together under "narrative." Indeed, Nicholas Reyland suggests that an approach based on narrativities "might . . . provide a more realistic account of how music is encountered, emplotted and narrativized by perceivers responding not to the signs of one particular system of signification within a piece but rather to a pick and mix of concatenized signs from across the different levels and interacting codes of a musical narrative" (2005: 314). As Reyland suggests, listener and music are complicit in the recognition of these narrative strands as the listener responds to a multiplicity of interpretive cues inherent to a piece of music. Nevertheless, Reyland's listener chooses only one narrative path from a number of potential narratives that the material presents. By contrast, I argue that some music (including many of Adès's works) encourages the listener to perceive and retain multiple narrative processes together, as interpretive cues for separate narrativities coexist simultaneously, the identity and narrative function of which will now be considered.

This essay proposes a medium-independent definition of narrative that will enable narrative analysis of music without necessarily resorting to frequently superficial literary analogies. The working definition of narrative will be *a sequence of events related, represented, or mediated by an agent.* This definition is primarily derived from those put forward by Mieke Bal – "a text in which an agent relates ('tells') a story in a particular medium" (1997: 5) – and Vera Micznik – "a 'representation' or 'recounting' of at least two real or fictional events or situations in a time sequence by at least one – actual or implied – narrator" (2001: 194). Many definitions agree on the inclusion of what is narrated as well as the act of narration, or what I will term *organization* and *agency*, whose reciprocal relationship establishes the minimal condition for narrativity, as narrative content cannot exist without the narrative act and vice versa.[3]

A focus on the qualities or properties of narrative formed by organizational and agential interaction, or its narrativity, will replace any urge to declare that a given piece by Adès is or is not a narrative to be grasped as a whole by the listener, which runs the risk of labeling for its own sake. Thus, the multiple interpretive strands within Adès's music will be conceived as *narrativities* rather than *narratives*. Granted, it could be argued that these are merely individual strands within a work's complex (singular) narrativity. However, the use of the plural narrativities is preferable as an analytical tool in the context of Adès's music, whose more plausible responses (such as Roeder's) consider its multiplicity. The consistency with which the listener is persuaded to hold multiple layers of musical information at any one time ensures that to conceptualize these as narrativities is stylistically appropriate. It also loosens the restrictions of analytical prose in order to give a greater impression of the multifarious roles and operations of the lively exchanges and ambiguities endemic to the musical discourse, rather than homogenizing the separate strata under *narrativity*.

The musical cues that can trigger a narrative interpretation must function organizationally or agentially. The collective existence of and perceived interactions between the two on more than one level are necessary to an understanding of the work's narrativities. The organizational cues within a piece of music constitute the narrative content of its layers. As narrative meaning is cumulative – temporally bound and dependent on the memory of what has gone before – the analysis of organizational criteria focuses on how the piece is structured through time, which involves the changing and developing values and relationships between events. This particular approach is approximately equivalent to Eero Tarasti's (1994) analysis of the development of temporal attributes (rhythm, meter, memory, and expectation), spatial attributes (harmony, tonality, register, and range), and actorial attributes (themes and motifs) as part of a narrative trajectory. Agency, although defined more broadly than "narrator" here, is specifically bound to the act of narration. It is the agency (explicit or implicit) behind the text that converts it into meaningful signs within a particular context, thus framing organized sequences of events as narrativity. Though an elusive concept, a text's agency can be observed, for example, in the context or code in which we interpret the piece, as a "voice" or commentary that emerges through musical gaps and patterns, and through inter-musical and extra-musical references, not forgetting that multiple agents can operate from one or more of these sources.[4]

The various ways in which both types of musical cues interact to assume narrative function can be categorized broadly into two narrative processes that demonstrate the interrelation of the two aspects. First, the agential cues prompt the hearing of musical organization as "told" events; second, the organizational cues indicate the temporalization of agential criteria as emergent from the unfolding structural processes in music. These processes can be cued by any number of musical gestures or procedures (often simultaneously in Adès's music) within the discursive contexts of a given work; furthermore, they are shaped by interpretive paradigms such as the listener's memories and expectations or associated extra-musical dimensions. Examples of the resulting intricate networks of narrativities in the Piano Quintet and *Brahms* reconcile these abstract narrative processes with specific musical operations, as the analyses demonstrate how the structural and expressive mechanisms of Adès's pieces function idiosyncratically as narrative layers within the musical text, eliciting an interpretive richness of understanding his music. The analytical strategy that follows will isolate each layer of narrativity in turn within both works in order to clarify the varying degrees of their presence, their constituent musical cues, and the details of their operation, after which the summative effects of their simultaneous coexistence will be considered.

CASE STUDIES: PIANO QUINTET AND *BRAHMS*

The Piano Quintet and *Brahms* are linked by Adès's preoccupation with the music of Brahms. The quintet is set in Brahms's favored sonata form and situates within a twenty-first-century context a similar desire for metric ambiguity present in Brahms's own Piano Quintet in F Minor. The piece *Brahms* superimposes allusions to the composer from the smallest harmonic tic to full-scale quotations from specific works. The way that the music of Brahms is invoked will inform the narrative readings of the pieces, since this overt collision between the past and the present has expressive significance for both works as well as implications for their structural features. In other words, it conditions the relationship between each piece's organizational and agential features on at least one of their narrative levels. Nevertheless, aside from this interpretive common ground, the two pieces effectively exhibit contrasting means by which Adès's music engages a narrative mode of interpretation.

Time's Arrow in the Piano Quintet

The Piano Quintet, commissioned for Adès and the Arditti Quartet, is characterized vibrantly by rhythmic and metric complexity, including frequent

EXAMPLE 10.1. Adès, Piano Quintet, opening of first subject.
© *Copyright 2007 by Faber Music Ltd., London. Reproduced by
kind permission of the publishers.*

changes of time signature, the simultaneous use of different meters, uncon-
ventional time signatures (such as $\frac{3}{5}$ and $\frac{2}{7}$), and the multiple temporalities that
conflicting streams of pitch and metric continuity can evoke. The piece opens
with one such example of pitch continuity. The first three arpeggiated chords
on the solo first violin are a play on traditional horn fifths, providing tonal
ambiguity but constructed entirely logically in terms of pitch continuity. The
expected conventional progression (I in C major to follow the initial I–V) is
replaced by a consistent pitch pattern (Example 10.1). In repeating the +2 +3
+4 interval spacings between the notes of each line of the first two chords,
the third chord realizes the pitch changes that they project. This introductory gesture demonstrates in microcosm both the tension between setting up
and thwarting customary expectations and the hidden (less readily audible)
continuity that belies much of the musical material in the Piano Quintet.

As well as the pitch continuity that punctuates this first subject (despite
its harmonically discontinuous avoidance of traditional resolution), the distinctive sonic character of alternation between fragments of both whole-tone
scales forming the melody ensures the coherence of this line in its second and
third statements on the piano and remaining strings, respectively, against conflicting accompaniments. For example, at reh. 1, the piano's statement of the
first subject is more rhythmically unstable than the violin's statement because
of a succession of irregularly related beat durations performed in meters of $\frac{3}{5}$,
$\frac{5}{8}$, $\frac{4}{5}$, and $\frac{2}{4}$. Nevertheless, the piano's statement coheres against a series of eighth
notes in $\frac{4}{4}$ in the violin (Example 10.2), as its distinct whole-tone pitch patterns
and internal metric structures cooperate to complicate the perception of the
accompaniment's uniformity. The patterns of continuity that supplement the
music's polymetric framework, suggesting different rates of motion, continually frustrate the listener's expectations, as they are left fumbling for metric

EXAMPLE 10.2. Adès, Piano Quintet, rhythmically consistent eighth notes (reh. 1).
© *Copyright 2007 by Faber Music Ltd., London. Reproduced by kind permission of the publishers.*

accents that are anticipated but rarely occur. The music does not permit the listener to hear the regular patterns and directional impulses within each layer without the other lines impeding their attempt. This phenomenon characterizes the majority of the musical processes of the first and second subjects throughout the piece.

A method such as Roeder's might consider such patterns of continuity as sufficient to ground narrative metaphor in themselves. I would argue, conversely, that their characteristics, in the form discussed above, are merely organizational cues for the first layer of narrativity to be considered here: as internal musical mechanisms, the conflicting lines are only able to supply the narrative substance and not the narrative act or the agency that emerges from the gaps between the lines when the listener takes into account the piece's discursive contexts, primarily in this case, in relation to the sonata-form tradition.

In light of such an unusual rhythmic and metric design, requiring virtuosic playing reminiscent of a Ferneyhough score, Adès's setting of the quintet in sonata form, a powerful emblem of the Classical-Romantic tradition, was something of a surprise, as evident from the gasp of disbelief from the audience at the German premiere when the performers turned back to the start of the piece to repeat the exposition in full (Fox 2004: 48). In more traditional sonata-form movements, there is a hermeneutic tradition to hear one or both subjects as musical protagonists moving through different spatio-temporal states and acting upon each other and their environments. This interpretive possibility seems less obvious in the Piano Quintet, if indeed it is possible at all. The background musical events have such an effect on the behavior of themes and how we perceive them that we feel less like the themes themselves are agents and more like an external agent is acting upon them, threatening their stability at every moment. I propose that this agent is *time*, the effect of which we can perceive on the level of thematic organization, cued by the non-congruence of the multiple streams of continuity within a polymetric framework. In the quintet, meter fails to fulfill its traditional function as a vessel for the music, providing a fixed pulse that is nuanced by rhythm. Instead, meter becomes a "volatile force" that acts upon the subjects, shaping the way in which we perceive their characters, drives, and directionality as they are superimposed (Service 2000). Time thus collaborates with sonata form as a rhetorically charged agential cue, the perceived historical anachronism of which, within a post-tonal context, reinforces the smaller-scale metric disruptions on an organizational level by way of this large-scale temporal displacement to form one of the piece's strands of narrativity. Yet sonata form is also used organizationally, as time's agency operates concurrently on a formal level, providing a simultaneous layer of narrativity that conflicts with the temporal one. Conventionally, the particular narrative archetype that sonata form unfolds, consisting of goals, tension, release, suspense, and climax, forms its own dramatic action: its narrative structure is its signification.[5] Despite the mutual complication of the superimposed meters, patterns, and lines that might conceal a sonata-form schematic, an increasing appearance of recognizable formal indicators begins to support the role of sonata form as an organizational tool, with its associated teleological drive. Once sonata form has been cued by the repeated exposition after **12**, it is possible to discern first and second subjects, transition, development, and the like. True to the nature of the piece, however, the subject presentations are complicated; initially in the exposition, for example, after the second subject's triple presentation, it is repeated once more in A major with functional harmony, an unexpected deviation from the piece's non-tonal norm that might have been placed within the more adventurous, fluid development. Additionally, while the development conventionally cultivates the first subject's and, particularly, the second subject's characteristics, a two-note motif on C and E♭, thematically inconsequential in the exposition, is developed unexpectedly into a dramatic theme of its own at **15**, rivaling the subject material in its climactic importance. Nevertheless, the listener is encouraged to perceive the unidirectional goal orientation of this narrativity, even while its very presence is impugned by the simultaneous existence of incompatible postmodern temporalities. As Roeder states of the peculiarity of postmodern time, its multiple temporalities stand "in implicit opposition to the putatively coherent temporality of other musics" (2006: 121), attributes made explicit in the Piano Quintet through the forced coexistence of the two.

The implications of maintaining the pushes and pulls between the two narrativities for both the music and the listener are brought to the fore in the recapitulation shortly after **19**. In the program note to the quintet, Tom Service (2000) describes the recapitulation as a "gigantic accelerando which speeds up to four times the original speed, and generates enormous, seemingly unstoppable momentum. The effect is of a dramatic and temporal compression: it is as if the whole work were squeezed into this musical black hole." Although the recapitulation is under half as long as the exposition without the repeat, it does not omit any great quantity of music, but, in combination with the *accelerando*, makes economical use of the exposition material. For example, the three presentations of the first subject that were initially heard in turn are layered upon each other at the start of the recapitulation.

As a result, the awareness of time that prevails in the recapitulation represents the culmination of the convoluted temporal nature of the whole piece. However, time operates as a duplicitous agent in the end; although the listener's formal expectations are far from thwarted, as the goal of the piece's underlying teleological drive is achieved, the brevity of the recapitulation merely emphasizes the *function* of the section as recapitulation over and above the musical content that was favored in the exposition and the development. At that moment the piece adheres too closely to a sonata-form model before time swiftly pulls the recapitulatory rug from underneath us, and we are denied the conclusive stability of a satisfactory return of familiar content. The recapitulation's fulfillment of a function in lieu of a euphoric re-accomplishment of the opening material thus provides an unsettling commentary that exploits the listener's capacity to retain potentially contradictory interpretations, as it stresses at once the musical viability and the historical-temporal ambivalence of a sonata-form piece in the twenty-first century. The intricate web of narrativities weaved from temporal manipulation of the music, formal restructuring, and the simultaneous response to and frustration of the listener's memories and expectations allows our interpretation of the piece to transform as it progresses. The piece is situated somewhere between a creative reimagination of sonata form and an anachronistic commentary, while the listener is forced continually to reread and reinterpret its implications because of its conflicting (yet intrinsically bound) narrative levels. Time manipulates not only the thematic subjects of the piece but also the listener's interpretive processes. In fact, time gets the last laugh with a tongue-in-cheek V–I cadential gesture in C, "resolving" the unfulfilled horn fifths of the opening measure.

The Ghost of Brahms

Allusions to the music of Brahms are vividly brought to the fore in the commentary surrounding Adès's *Brahms*, which is hardly surprising, given the piece's title and program. Composed for Alfred Brendel's seventieth birthday, *Brahms* is a captivating setting of Brendel's poem "Brahms II" in its original German about the visits of the piano-playing, cigar-smoking ghost of Brahms to a house at night. While the Piano Quintet engages resiliently with its past formal model, *Brahms* is described explicitly as an "anti-homage" to the composer that explores the limitations of his material. As an additional point of curiosity, Adès has stated that "Brahms is unable to allow his ideas and material to breathe within his structures: as if he deliberately disables his instinct" (Service 2001). Thus, *Brahms* traces the concern with the relationship between contemporary music and the musical tradition differently when considered against the quintet, although the pieces explore the same broad theme. Additionally, in contrast to the absolute music of the Piano Quintet, the text in *Brahms* has implications for a narrative interpretation of the work, which results from the interweaving of musical and textual narrativities. The following discussion of *Brahms* will move flexibly between the poem and the music to demonstrate variously their interaction, interdependence, and independence within this mode of interpretation.

The ways in which the ghost of Brahms is summoned in both the poem and the music form part of the piece's pervasive Gothic effect, though I will argue that the work is an example of the Gothic with a comic turn, after Avril Horner and Sue Zlosnik's (2005) comprehensive study of this typically modernist literary and artistic mode. By virtue of its incongruous collision of the potentially terrifying and the absurd, the comic Gothic is already based on compound narrativities. The separate Gothic and comic narrative strands, cued as such by contrasting discursive strategies, will be unraveled and considered in turn in order to show the mechanisms beneath their intricate entwining, which contribute to the work's expressive effect and the uneasy relationship between the past and present that it addresses.

After a short musical introduction based primarily on harmonic and falling melodic thirds (more of which later), the first four lines of the poem immediately evoke some common Gothic motifs, such as the night, the haunted house, and the prowling ghost of a long-dead Romantic figure:

When at dead of night the ghost appears	Wenn nachts das Gespenst erscheint
and starts prowling round the piano	und sich ums Klavier herumtreibt
then we know	dann wissen wir
Brahms has arrived	Brahms ist gekommen
(*Brahms*, lines 1–4/mm. 9–26)	

The "stylized theatricality of the Gothic" (Horner and Zlosnik 2005: 166) exploited here is paralleled by similar musical clichés that evoke this atmosphere: the dark, low-register *tremolo* in the bass beginning at m. 10 and the trembling quality of the strings' alternating notes and ghostly rising wisp of the flute line in mm. 24–26, which complement the vocal line's half-whispered *con terrore*, "Brahms ist gekommen" (line 4). The dramatic diminished-seventh chord on C♯–E–G–B♭ over an added F in m. 26, which Service (2001) observes is a reorchestration of a similarly sudden attack in the introduction of Brahms's First Piano Concerto, confirms without doubt the presence of Brahms. These motifs, marking the poem and the music, act as organizational "nodal points," to use Edward Venn's term (2006: 105), which allow reciprocal interpretation of the information between the two media, both determined by and contributing to the Gothic association's agential role in the translation of the motifs into meaningful signs. The simultaneous arrival of Brahms's ghost in the music and the text at m. 26, which represents the culmination of the sinister undertones of this opening section, establishes that, on this interpretive level at least, one layer of narrativity is unfolded between the two media at an identical rate, hereby referred to as the "musico-poetic narrativity."

Nevertheless, this coherent Gothic plot is offset by the comic turn, perhaps the chief contributor to the distinctive character of the piece. The initial reference to the supernatural in the first four lines of the poem and the potential fear they evoke are immediately subverted by the following:

It wouldn't be quite so bad	Das wäre weiter nicht schlimm
if his cigar smell	wenn nicht dieser Zigarrengeruch
didn't stink out the music room	das Musikzimmer tagelang
for days on end	verpesten würde
(*Brahms*, lines 5–7/mm. 28–44)	

This comic turn in the poem continues as the household reacts with mild frustration to the peculiar idiosyncrasies that Brahms flaunts. Even the children later hear his piano playing as a nuisance ("Not Brahms again" [line 11]) rather than reacting to the ghost as one might expect, with a mixture of awe and dread. The placement of the revered past master in such absurd circumstances at once exploits and undermines the Gothic Romanticism hinted at in the beginning of the poem.

This same comic turn begins much sooner and more gradually in the music than in the poem. As a result, the stretched-out, musical-comic turn is characterized by interpretive dynamism and narrativization, in contrast to the somewhat static description that the poem maintains. Thus I will address this specifically musical layer of narrativity with the extra-musical associations of the poetic comic merely contributing agentially to the humorous impression. This "music-only narrativity" emerges from a divergent interaction of contrasting organizational and agential features, unfolding simultaneously against the musico-poetic narrativity, particularly highlighted by the rare moment of disjunction between the media.

Adès has explained that *Brahms* is a "piece about the logic of Brahms's music and not about the beauty and warmth," a statement that Fox later refines in commenting that Adès explores "the patterns within which that logic manifests itself" (2004: 47), having abandoned Brahms's logic proper with regard to functional tonality. The eight-measure introduction contains all the musical material derived from such patterns that will be developed throughout, the first four measures of which appear in Example 10.3.

Perhaps the most clearly identifiable allusion to Brahms is the sequential chains of thirds that open the work, the first four notes of which (B–G–E–C) are a reworking of the opening notes of Brahms's Fourth Symphony, which remain omnipresent throughout Adès's piece in one form or another. However, it immediately becomes clear that Brahms could never have written this piece, as the chains of thirds continue throughout the piece to the point of obsession, exploring the registral extremes of the orchestra and frequently causing pervasive and uncanny false relations. While it is not possible to fault the pattern's internal logic, Adès "deliberately disables his instinct," as the thirds continue to repeat beyond the point at which the listener is able to respond seriously to them (Service 2001). Perhaps the following explanatory analogy will be useful within this context. Lewis Carroll has noticed "the curious phenomenon . . . that if you repeat a word a great many times in succession, however suggestive it may have been when you began, you will end by divesting it of every shred

EXAMPLE 10.3. Adès, *Brahms,* vocal repetition against vertical thirds (mm. 1–4, dynamics omitted).
Music © Copyright 2009 by Faber Music Ltd., London. Text © 1996 by Alfred Brendel. Reproduced by kind permission of the publishers.

of meaning, and almost wondering you could ever have meant anything by it" (Lecercle 1994: 23). Thus, what began both as an allusion to Brahms's Fourth Symphony and as a comment on his characteristic elaboration of melodic and harmonic thirds ultimately replicates the poem's comic turn, as it becomes absurd through idiosyncratic repetition in much the same way as the fictional ghost's nightly wanderings.

The music-only narrativity, comprised of the patterns of thirds alluding agentially to Brahms, serves to embroider the fictional tale of Brahms's ghost, as the listener is encouraged to perceive it as a critique of Brahms from a contemporary musical perspective, which counteracts the rather playful resurrection of the composer's ghost. Although, as Venn (2008) argues, to spot the allusions to Brahms's music is a listening strategy cued by the piece's surrounding discourse (the title, the program, and, particularly, the program note), in effect making *Brahms* itself ghost-like as a simulation devoid of its own content, paradoxically, the incessant repetition of a Brahmsian character-istic merely reinforces the "Adèsness" of the music. Most of the piece bolsters this interpretation as it interweaves allusions to several pieces by Brahms and the topical spaces they imply, such as the lively *capriccio* or the lullaby; the more that Brahms's pieces are inventively layered, the more Adès's musical language materializes in the invention.

In the final third of the piece, from m. 81 onward, movement by tone begins to predominate in the vocal melody, culminating in a sequential pas-sage that sets the word "Brahms" compulsively until it degenerates into an eccentric written-out *accelerando*, arguably a verbal equivalent to the obsessive chains of thirds throughout the piece (Example 10.4). The orchestration and harmonic style of the passage begin, at least, with characteristically Romantic gestures, in particular, the sensuous parallel thirds that accompany the bari-tone on the woodwind and horns, which continue even as the melody's octave displacement of every other note in mm. 91–92 mirrors the absurdity of the ghost's uncanny repetitions of his own name.

This passage represents the interpretive crux of the music-only narrativity in relation to the piece's engagement with the past musical tradition. Horner and Zlosnik argue of the connection between the comic Gothic and historical temporality that "if Gothic is seen as a critique *of* modernity, the comic turn indicates a deconstructionist turn inherent *within* it" (2005: 166). In other words, Gothic Romanticism in the literature and the arts of the twentieth century onward often laments the loss of coherence of the modern subject, while the comic tendency to parody its theatricality provides an all-too-rare celebration of our current modernity. At the endlessly repeating melodic sequences at mm. 86–99 we realize that we are in danger of becoming like the children in the poem, who cover their ears and cry "not Brahms again," and that it is in fact Brahms who has lost his coherent subjectivity, needing to reassert his presence and identity in "a plaintive tenor" (line 19) in both the music and the poem. The comic turn in the Gothic has made this inversion explicit: we are not prompted to mourn the loss of Romanticism, with its familiar tonality and yearning sequences; rather, we are playfully invited to

EXAMPLE 10.4. Adès, *Brahms,* vocal repetition against vertical thirds
(mm. 86–94, dynamics omitted).
*Music © Copyright 2009 by Faber Music Ltd., London. Text © 1996
by Alfred Brendel. Reproduced by kind permission of the publishers.*

consider an anxiety of influence from the perspective of Brahms, who might
consider his music forgotten in Adès's twenty-first-century manifestation
of its characteristics. In expanding what remains implicit in the poem, the
music-only narrativity as critique of Brahms supplements and eventually su-
persedes the musico-poetic story, although the former is cued to be perceived
and interpreted as such by the latter through invocations of Brahms and the
device of the comic turn, which connect both narrativities.[6] Ultimately, this

tendency toward parody and the comic is subsumed into a piece of music that is appealing in its own right and on its own terms: the limits of Brahms's material are effectively worked into a "compelling dramatic miniature" that appears, above all, to privilege the possibilities created by the coexistence of the past and the present (Service 2001).

CONCLUSION

Thus, we see that Adès's music engages a narrative mode of interpretation in contrasting ways, as the different rates and layers of simultaneously unfolding signification, or narrativities, characteristic of much of Adès's repertoire (whether based on continuity patterns or not) are typically manifested in distinct ways between works. In terms of the relationship between present music and past tradition that both pieces examined here overtly address, *Brahms*, although styled as an anti-homage, seems the more benevolent of the two, as the piece's narrative layers *cooperate* to offer an innovative and imaginative treatment of Brahms's stylistic traits. The Piano Quintet causes perhaps greater interpretive disorientation as a result of the much messier relationships between the tangled structural narrativities posited by the contradictory roles of time as agent. The sonata-form signposts introduced on a formal, large-scale temporal level *conflict* with the smaller-scale musical temporalities that attempt to deny a sense of teleological direction. Yet in the end, this increasingly familiarizing device ironically *deceives* the music and listener alike, as the content of the recapitulation vehemently repudiates its function.

In sum, it is specifically the acknowledgment of and relationships between the narrativities that variously cooperate, conflict, deceive, and the like, that contribute to the divergent expressive interpretations of the Piano Quintet and *Brahms* in this particular reading, although both pieces are concerned with the same subject. In teasing out the separate organizational and agential cues and the multiple levels on which they interact, it is possible to scrutinize in more detail the musical operations that form the multifaceted signifying impact of Adès's works and the simultaneous ambiguities that the listener is obliged to hold. In the limited space available, it has not been possible to indulge in as much analytical detail as Roeder's article, which would offer more nuanced interpretations of the music. Nevertheless, in couching the above in narrative terminology and conceptualizing the musical mechanisms as narrative processes, this analysis has been able to consider structure and expression mutually and in equal proportions for a more rounded interpretation of Adès's music, in which the semantic dimension is as vital as its structural idiolect, though the two have misleadingly remained separate in Adès scholarship for the most part. The existence of multiple narrativities in Adès's music supports the hypothesis that it is representative of contemporary trends while it enjoys considerable worldwide success, as the plurality of the numerous stories, the invocations and denials of ideologies, and the richnesses, tensions, and ironies in response to the past characterize the bodies of musical works that have brought us into the twenty-first century.

NOTES

This research was made possible with funding from the Arts and Humanities Research Council as part of a larger project in which this article is included. All musical examples © 2000 and 2001 by Faber Music Ltd. Reproduced by kind permission of the publishers.

1. Roeder (2009) has also written an article more recently on *Arcadiana*, but the focus is on transformational theory, using Adès's music as an example, as opposed to increasing the understanding of structural processes in the string quartet.

2. Roeder's definition of continuity also shows similarities with Jonathan Kramer's notion of linearity, which he equates with the perception of "cause and effect, progress, and goal orientation" (1981: 539).

3. The terms *organization* and *agency* are not simply synonymous with *story* and *discourse*. It is not within the remit of this essay to access the story level or the chronological events as separate from

their representation in narrative, since it will approach narrative from an interpretive, as opposed to *poietic*, stance. Thus, this conception of organization, as well as agency, is inseparable from discourse, as the listener always receives the narrative content in its mediated form.

4. Works by Carolyn Abbate (1991), Lawrence Kramer (1990), and, in particular, Robert Hatten (2004) have been particularly influential in this conception of agency.

5. Such musical attributes lead Hepokoski and Darcy to state that "the sonata invites interpretation as a musically narrative genre" (2006: 251), and this narrative intent is present throughout their analyses.

6. I use the term *supplement* in the sense that Lawrence Kramer (after Derrida) uses it, in that the supplement not only remedies a lack but also replaces the whole that has had its wholeness put into question by the very necessity of a supplement (1995: 111).

WORKS CITED

Abbate, Carolyn. 1991. *Unsung Voices: Opera and Musical Narrative in the Nineteenth Century*. Princeton: Princeton University Press.

Bal, Mieke. 1997. *Narratology: Introduction to the Theory of Narrative*. Translated by Christine van Boheemen. Toronto: University of Toronto Press.

Fox, Christopher. 2004. "Tempestuous Times: The Recent Music of Thomas Adès." *Musical Times* 145: 41–56.

Hasty, Christopher. 1986. "On the Problem of Succession and Continuity in Twentieth-Century Music." *Music Theory Spectrum* 8: 58–74.

Hatten, Robert. 2004. *Interpreting Musical Gestures, Topics and Tropes: Mozart, Beethoven and Schubert.* Bloomington: Indiana University Press.

Hepokoski, James, and Warren Darcy. 2006. *Elements of Sonata Theory: Norms, Types and Deformations in the Late Eighteenth-Century Sonata.* New York: Oxford University Press.

Horner, Avril, and Sue Zlosnik. 2005. *Gothic and the Comic Turn.* Basingstoke: Palgrave Macmillan.

Kramer, Jonathan. 1981. "New Temporalities in Music." *Critical Inquiry* 7(3): 539–56.

Kramer, Lawrence. 1990. *Music as Cultural Practice, 1800–1900.* Berkeley: University of California Press.

———. 1995. *Classical Music and Postmodern Knowledge.* Berkeley: University of California Press.

Lecercle, Jean-Jacques. 1994. *Philosophy of Nonsense: The Intuitions of Victorian Nonsense Literature.* London: Routledge.

Micznik, Vera. 2001. "Music and Narrative Revisited: Degrees of Narrativity in Beethoven and Mahler." *Journal of the Royal Musical Association* 126(2): 193–249.

Reyland, Nicholas. 2005. "'Akcja' and Narrativity in the Music of Witold Lutosławski." PhD diss., Cardiff University.

Roeder, John. 2006. "Co-operating Continuities in the Music of Thomas Adès." *Music Analysis* 25(1): 121–54.

———. 2009. "A Transformational Space Structuring the Counterpoint in Adès's 'Auf dem Wasser zu singen.'" *Music Theory Online* 15(1).

Rosen, Charles. 1988. *Sonata Forms.* Rev. ed. New York: Norton.

Service, Tom. 2000. Program note to Adès, Piano Quintet, op. 20. London: Faber Music.

———. 2001. Program note to Adès, *Brahms,* op. 21. London: Faber Music.

Tarasti, Eero. 1994. *A Theory of Musical Semiotics.* Bloomington: Indiana University Press.

Venn, Edward. 2006. "Asylum Gained? Aspects of Meaning in Thomas Adès's *Asyla.*" *Music Analysis* 25(1): 89–120.

———. 2008. "Smoke and Mirrors: Thomas Adès's *Brahms.*" Paper presented at the CarMAC conference, Cardiff University.

White, Hayden. 1980. "The Value of Narrativity in the Representation of Reality." *Critical Inquiry* 7(1): 5–27.

Whittall, Arnold. 2003. "James Dillon, Thomas Adès, and the Pleasures of Allusion." In *Aspects of British Music of the 1990s,* edited by Peter O'Hagan, 3–27. Aldershot: Ashgate.

II

Britten's *Serenade* and the Politico-Moral Crises of the Wartime Conjuncture: Hermeneutic and Narrative Notes on the "Nocturne"

Sumanth Gopinath

The *Serenade* for tenor, horn, and strings, op. 31 (1943) numbers among Benjamin Britten's best-known compositions. A polished jewel in the composer's variegated *oeuvre*, it is surprising that Britten initially regarded it as "not important stuff, but quite pleasant" (cited in Carpenter 1992: 184). Yet, part of what distinguishes the *Serenade* has precisely to do with its "light" character; for all of its moments of darkness, it retains an overall unseriousness that rendered the work especially palatable to traumatized wartime (British) audiences. In the hermeneutic investigation that follows, I'll consider various meanings of the cycle by examining its broad thematic and narrative contours before focusing on the "Nocturne" movement. The latter contains hidden intimations of military violence as viewed through the lens of the sexual-political ideologies harbored by Britten and others within the artistic subcultures to which he uneasily belonged. In doing so, the *Serenade* reemerges as weighted more heavily toward matters of consequence, both personal and political, while also deflecting attention from them through the use of framing devices.

THE *SERENADE* AS MORAL AND NATIONAL ALLEGORY

Given the *Serenade*'s artistic and popular successes – critical acclaim and recording sales marked its breakthrough status for the composer (Kildea 2002:

227–29, 231) – commentary on it has been extensive. Although most writers read the work relatively literally – as a series of settings about dusk and night-time in accordance with its original title, "Nocturnes" (Mitchell 1989: 22–24) – and identify copious instances of text painting or musical topics, a few have attempted more hermeneutic interpretations. At least two tendencies can be identified. The first might be termed "moral" and extends back to the *Serenade*'s dedicatee, Edward Sackville-West, who noted in 1944: "The subject is Night and its prestigia: the lengthening shadow, the distant bugle at sunset, the Baroque panoply of the starry sky, the heavy angels of sleep; but also the cloak of evil – the worm in the heart of the rose, the sense of sin in the heart of man" (cited in White 1954: 43). Humphrey Carpenter has noted that Sackville-West's reading of the work "is probably close to Britten's own" (1992: 186), given that the former helped the composer select the texts. Although this "moral" interpretation did not specify a source of moral crisis, Carpenter does so himself, arguing that Britten's homosexuality and pedophilia were the "causes [of] such agonies of conscience in the *Serenade*" (187).

The second interpretive tendency is, in contrast, national. The earliest impetus for such readings was Britten's choice of English texts spanning five centuries, as opposed to texts of single authors in Italian (*Seven Sonnets of Michelangelo*, op. 22, 1940) or French (Rimbaud, in *Les illuminations*, op. 18, 1939) (see Carpenter 1992: 166–69; White 1954: 42–43; Mitchell 1952: 46–47; Hollander 1981: 131). Arnold Whittall insightfully discusses the "individuality of [Britten's] Englishness in the *Serenade*" (1993: 372), which avoids the place-focused impersonality of the English pastoral tradition (Vaughan Williams, Delius, etc.) even as it evokes the latter through its pastoral character and first-movement title. Whittall draws out some important strands of the national/military interpretation, including Britten's pacifism and ambivalent attitudes toward nationalism and the connection between the *Serenade* and *Peter Grimes*. These two strands are interlinked: the composer's operatic masterpiece is set on the east coast of England and based on the poetry of George Crabbe, of whom E. M. Forster noted, "To talk about Crabbe is to talk about England" (cited in Carpenter 1992: 155).

The wartime elements of the *Serenade*, however, cannot be confined to the "Englishness" of its poetic texts. Also important within critical discourse on the piece is the association of the horn with militarism in the cycle's second song, "Nocturne." Based on Tennyson's famous poem "The splendour falls on castle walls," Britten's song features imitation bugle calls played on the horn. Following the confusion between the horn and bugle in the poem itself

("Blow, bugle, blow, set the wild echoes flying / Blow, bugle; answer, echoes, dying, dying, dying" and "The horns of Elfland faintly blowing!"), the horn in "Nocturne" evokes the military topic, which several commentators have identified as drawing a link between it and Britten's later *War Requiem* (1962), which uses the horn in a similar capacity (Palmer 1984: 317n15; Evans 1979: 91; Watkins 2003: 426; Monelle 2006: 110).

Others make claims about the *Serenade* that resonate with one or both interpretive tendencies, but few have synthesized or reconciled these perspectives (Barringer 2011 comes closest). One solution would be to expand Philip Brett's insights that the composer's "outlaw status as a homosexual [and] his conscientious objection . . . were inextricably intertwined, not only in him as an individual, but also in British culture" (2006: 177) and that Britten adopted a "left-wing, pacifist, agnostic and queer . . . identity niche in which to lodge his particular personal concerns, though few of his friends believed that he was ever entirely comfortable with it" (Brett 2001: sec. 2). We might note that the narrative that unfolds over the course of the *Serenade* maps onto a number of different scenarios. The narrative content of the work is framed by the horn solos of the "Prologue" and "Epilogue" as an evocation or dream of a distant past, then begins in earnest with the twilight pastoralism of the "Pastoral" and fairy-tale naïveté of the "Nocturne" before giving way to deep moral anxiety in the "Elegy" and purgatorial terror in the "Dirge." Having reached the dysphoric peak of the cycle, the hunting song, "Hymn," acts as a buoyant but ineffective distraction from these fears, and the cycle ends with the ethereal, if unsettled, "Sonnet." Although it makes perfect sense to follow Carpenter and read this as an admission of guilt over illicit love – the "stripling" in the "Pastoral" and "Elfland" in the "Nocturne" point to a childlike innocence to which Britten was aesthetically and sexually attracted – as well as an effort at self-consolation, other readings are possible. For example, the relative innocence of the first two movements might figure a prewar state, which is undone through the immoral choice of taking up arms – though, in such a reading, Britten's ending still attempts to console (or critique?) the British public by narrating their return to slumber. In another possibility, the innocence might figure a prewar state in which moral choices like conscientious objection need not be made (and perhaps even the false freedom from having to make such choices as experienced by Britten and his life partner and musical collaborator, the English tenor Peter Pears, during their American period, 1939–42). The heart of moral darkness expressed in the "Elegy" may then concern guilt over Britten's and Pears's former absence from England and physical safety as conscientious objectors.[1]

CONJUGATING SEX WITH POLITICS IN "NOCTURNE"

To explore how aspects of these interpretations might be articulated on a moment-to-moment basis, let us examine the second song ("Nocturne") more closely. Although few would agree with John Hollander that it is the *Serenade's* "poetic centerpiece" (1981: 130) – the Blake setting ("Elegy") that follows is a better candidate – the "Nocturne" occupies a crucial position in the song cycle's narrative, the moment of (sinful) innocence before the fall. I will discuss the piece's textual source, its generic-stylistic aspects, and its topical and formal materials, in each case suggesting the inter-working of the sexual and the political.

Tennyson's *The Princess* (1847) holds special significance for the composition, given that the Victorian poet's "medley" provided two source texts for Britten while composing the work. Although its critical reputation steadily declined over the course of the nineteenth and twentieth centuries, *The Princess* was one of Tennyson's most popular poems (Killham 1958: 6). The poem itself is a long narrative in blank verse whose main sections are punctuated by lyric poems. It concerns the subject of women's rights, specifically, access to university education, toward which Tennyson adopted a lightly mocking and patriarchal but nonetheless sympathetic view.[2] The plot concerns a prince betrothed from an early age to a princess who, upon growing to adulthood, founds a women's university from which men are barred at risk of death. The prince and two companions nonetheless sneak into the university dressed as women and gain the audience of the princess before they are discovered. The result is chaos, leading to a medieval tournament between the kingdoms of the prince's and princess's fathers, wherein the former are defeated. Feeling terrible guilt because of the wounded men, the princess converts the college into a hospital and personally tends the prince, during which time she yields to his entreaties. The narrative is framed by the story of a house-party game played by seven men, each of whom contributes to the poem while the game is played. Periodically throughout *The Princess* appear short lyric poems – allegedly ballads sung by the women at the party (added to a revised publication in 1850). Britten's "Nocturne" sets one of these ballads from the end of the third section, after which the three cross-dressed men accompany the princess and her two companions on a geological expedition while the sun is setting.

Two points about the poem and Britten's setting are relevant to the overlapping of the "moral" and "national" readings of the song. First, the *place* of the poem is at once mythical and located within a British orbit, with evidence for both attributes sometimes coming from the same source. For example, the reference to "Elfland" clearly evokes a mythical realm associated with fairy tales, but it is also characteristic of the broadly Germanic mythology in English and Scottish folkloric ballads. Similarly, the reference to "castle walls" at once evokes medieval chivalric tales while also pointing to castles, ruins perhaps, in the British landscape. Although the craggy geography of the poem might be read in different ways – John Killham argues that it is alpine (1958: 217), whereas Christopher Palmer claims it is Scottish (1984: 319) – it is clearly northern, that is, not "Oriental." Second, to underscore this aspect of place in the poem and its location within the cycle, Britten's discarded setting of Tennyson's "Now sleeps the crimson petal," which is another ballad from *The Princess* and is influenced by the Persian poetic form *ghazal*, includes the "exotic" imagery of the peacock, cypress, porphyry, and lily. Finally, "The splendour falls" was composed by Tennyson in 1848 after a visit to Killarney, Ireland, where, standing near the "Eagle's Nest" (a mountain of about 1,100 feet), he heard a bugle call from beneath the mountain and "eight distinct echoes" (cited in Tennyson and Ricks 1987: 230). In terms of its imaginary geography, then, the worlds relatively proximate to England would be associated at first glance with ideologies of the "national soil," whereas the moral transgressions of the erotic would be located in more distant, exotic locales, situating this ballad firmly within a "national" problematic. But, in the context of *The Princess*, the geological expedition is also prefaced by a moment in which the smoldering passions of the prince are expressed (though concealed from the princess), and during the expedition he even argues with her in favor of their marital "precontract" – a scene complicated by the queer erotics of a cross-dressed man flirting with a masculinized woman who would, she claims, appear to traditionalist eyes as "a kind of monster." But however important the poetic context might be for the text of the "Nocturne" – and, given the composer's reading habits, we cannot assume that Britten knew *The Princess* well – the poem itself also includes sexually interpretive potentialities realized in their setting (see below).[3]

Like the text, the music-stylistic features of "Nocturne" also reveal the striking intersection of sexuality and politics. In attending to the compositional world that the work inhabits, it is curious that few commentators have paid attention to the sources of its distinguishing features – the quintal-quartal sonorities, the open diatonicism, the sparse textures, a certain folky quality, wide textural stratification, and the appearance of a canon that structures the texture. Greatly affected by his stay in the United States, Britten's music was probably influenced by his encounter with Aaron Copland's "wide-open spaces" style (Lerner 2001: 485–86). One critic at the time of the work's earliest reception noted this connection. In 1945 Arthur Berger stated that the *Serenade* "affords striking evidence that at least one composer abroad is as profoundly conscious of the Copland style as so many young men here are" (cited in Pollack 2000: 74). The possibility that the work is in dialogue with a mid-century American pastoral style suggests that Britten undertook a critical re-examination of twentieth-century British musical pastoralism (Whittall 1993), its associations with the national landscape, and, as a nostalgic or utopian inversion of warfare, the ravaging of that landscape during the First and Second World Wars (Barringer 2011: 159–60). However, the links between Copland and Britten are not only that both exploited critical-nationalist, folk-pastoral aesthetics but also that they occupied parallel formations, both resolutely queer and leftist (Hubbs 2004) – traits that formed the basis of the composers' friendship (Pollack 2000: 73). Copland's populist style, forged in "response to the Depression and Second World War" (Crist 2005: 7), articulated "a sonic representation of American vastness and rugged, simple beauty . . . outfitted with a sentimentalized national heterosexuality" (Hubbs 2004: 10). It might have offered Britten a model for representing the vigorous, mountain-hiking masculinity found in the "Nocturne," with both composers gravitating to implicitly queer variations on the Popular Front's "cult of the virile male working-class body" (Denning 1996: 137). By implication, those seemingly nationalist-heteronormative landscapes and male protagonists evoked by both composers were semantically inflected as a result of these outsiders' representations of imagined communities, reappropriating national belonging during a period of political exclusion or repression of pacifists and homosexuals – and in doing so risked criticisms of a transatlantic gay "conspiracy" in music (Hubbs 2005: 224).

Parallel interpretations of the sexual and political are evident at the more detailed levels of form and topical reference. At the formal level, the "Nocturne" presents a basic opposition between the objective and subjective, dividing cleanly between the text's verses and "blow, bugle, blow" refrain. Britten's song most clearly emplaces the action of the narrator within the song's initial passages (mm. 1–9), which serve as the A material, setting the poetic verses in a two-part (AB) modified strophic form with three stanzas. The mythical, naive quality of the setting might owe something to its entirely diatonic pitch material – particularly given Britten's tendency to use chromaticism to represent moral corruption.[4] Similarly, the string accompaniment has a

EXAMPLE 11.1. Britten, *Serenade,* "Nocturne," mm. 1–2.
*Serenade, op. 31, by Benjamin Britten. © Copyright 1944 by
Hawkes & Son (London), Ltd. Reprinted by Permission.*

refracted, stilted, folk-dance quality, in part because of the "Scotch snaps" in
the upper string parts – which also situate the locale as Scottish by association
and play into its American-pastoral qualities, given that Scotch snaps feature
in much Scotch-Irish folk music in the United States (see Example 11.1). The
bounding character of the melody and accompaniment is partly produced by
their melodic contours. The lower strings consist of short, ascending three-,
four-, or five-chord groups, while the upper strings move against them in
either contrary or similar motion. Cutting against this is a similarly ascending and descending melody that lines up at times with the accompaniment,
with relative peaks in the voice aligning with relative nadirs in the bass (mm.
5, 9). After melodic dips into lower areas ("falls," m. 3) or ascents to higher
ones ("summits old," m. 5), a breakthrough arrival at a root-position E♭-major
triadic center appears in m. 9. The whole effect is one of mountain expedition
and hiking (Whitesell 1993: 103) – a "simple madrigalism" (Monelle 2006: 109),
though it also suggests more strenuous ambulatory "steps" (Monelle 2000:
22–24). The other distinguishing feature of the melody similarly reinforces
the breakthrough arrival narrative: it can be reduced almost entirely to a chain
of descending and then ascending thirds, with the harmonic arrival coinciding with a return to descending thirds in m. 9 in a text-painting of the word
"cataract" (Schoenberg 1975: 405–406; Baker 2009) (see Example 11.2). The
narrative subject, moving through the space mapped out in the A section,
vividly traces that space's physical contours for the listener.

　　If the A section signifies motion through a mythical and/or national
space, the B section brings that motion to a halt and represents a narrative
shift inward, toward a more pointed subjective experience. On the surface,

EXAMPLE 11.2. Britten, *Serenade*, "Nocturne," mm. 2–10 with tertian chains. *Serenade, op. 31, by Benjamin Britten. © Copyright 1944 by Hawkes & Son (London), Ltd. Reprinted by Permission.*

we find a compelling representation of the echoing bugle calls, played on the horn – with Tennyson's eight echoes heard as eight variants of the call in the cadenza at m. 10 (reh. 4). But the harmonic stasis of this passage is animated by an agitated rustling in the strings (trills at reh. 4 and 8, *tremolos* at 6) that signifies both the shimmering, late-daytime light effects in the text ("The long light shakes across the lakes") and an excitement on the part of the narrative subject ostensibly incited by the bugle calls. The actual notes of the first two calls are a direct imitation of the "cataract" vocal line in m. 9, and while these calls reverberate and vary through the cadenza, the voice instead takes the ending tag from the same vocal line (A♭4–F4–B♭4–E♭4, "[leaps] in glory") and reorders the notes for the words "Blow, bugle, blow" (E♭4–A♭4–F4–B♭4). The string accompaniment likewise presents a quintal collection based on the same pitches as the melody (E♭–F–A♭–B♭), whose spare quality differs greatly from the tertian chain found earlier. Goading each other on, the voice and horn seem to be in dialogue – a rhetorical and textural effect reinforced by the matching of ending pitches of each vocal or horn gesture (first B♭3, then F4). The final prominent pitch-matching arrives on G4 – about two-thirds of the way through the cadenza and at the climax of the passage – with the tenor entering on the horn's previous ending pitch with the words "dying, dying" and returning to the chain of descending thirds from which the original "cataract" line and bugle call emerged. At the peak of the song's affective intensity, the

EXAMPLE 11.3. Britten, *Serenade*, "Nocturne," m. 10 (reh. 4), cadenza with note-matching and quintal collections.
Serenade, op. 31, by Benjamin Britten. © Copyright 1944 by Hawkes & Son (London), Ltd. Reprinted by Permission.

singer verbalizes an awareness of the echoes' fragility, and the rush of emotion is subdued – the mutual reinforcement of pitches in the voice and horn is now less overt, and the excitement dwindles to nothingness. Moreover, the "dying, dying" passage tracks through the same chain of thirds that initiated the cadenza (from G5 down to F4). The mutability of the musical material suggests that the bugle call emerges from and returns back to the natural landscape itself (depicted through the tertian chain), whereas the bold quintal material presents a certain distance from that tertian material (and, consequently, the bugle call) – though that quintal material is nearly identical to the pitch material of the rustling strings (Whitesell 1993: 103–104) (see Example 11.3). Thus the explicit object of engagement here is the natural landscape itself, while the experiencing subject is a distinct entity from the landscape.

The song's diptych of bounding motion through a national and/or mythical space and the excitation and subsequent deflation in response to the bugle call can be read several ways, but the crux of the matter hinges on how we interpret the call itself. Britten's bugle topic provides an object lesson in how composers personalize musical topics, transforming an apparent universal into something particular. At least two claims have been made regarding Britten's understanding of the bugle. According to Peter Evans, Britten's "fanfares have . . . less often been military signals in his music than evocations, nostalgic or even ironic, of a natural order, whether sublime or inexorable." Here, the bugle calls and their tertian-chain material (derived from the "cataract" vocal line) are merely a part of Britten's "Nature symbolism" (Evans 1979: 91). Carpenter, in contrast, claims that the bugle "is an instrument evoking boyhood," since for Britten "the bugle's associations were not with the army but school"; Carpenter also notes that the bugle theme in Britten's *Noye's Fludde* (1957) "is a recollection of the school's Officer Training Corps (OTC) practicing in front of the cricket pavilion, where there was a 'grand echo'" (1992: 379–80).[5] In this case, the bugle's referent is not the "natural order" but an idealized linkage between the elite public school (i.e., prep school) and the military, providing an example of Althusser's "ideological state apparatus" (1971: 132–33, 142–45). But a sexual dimension is also relevant to Britten's public school background, given that he may have been sexually assaulted while in school (Carpenter 1992: 20–25) and that his (sexual) conception of himself seems to have been locked in at the age of thirteen, perhaps for related reasons (Bridcut 2006: 1–8). The horn-in-bugle-drag topical technique adds another layer of meaning. The horn's rounded, lower timbre casts a warmth and glow to the bugle calls, rendering it as a shadow or reflection of the tenor voice (Whittall 1993: 371) or even a "complementary" second tenor (Whitesell 1993: 113); it also produces a nostalgic or distancing effect that Lawrence Kramer sees as characteristic of conventionalized musical signs (2002: 157).

Yoking these two perspectives, Britten's bugle has the capacity to represent innocence, whether as a pre-adult stage of development – which Brett characterizes as the Lacanian imaginary or "nescience" (2006: 201) – or as nature itself. In the "Nocturne," the mythical element of this symbolic innocence is amplified when we realize that Britten represents the conflation of the horn and bugle in Tennyson's poem by having a horn play a bugle call, thus affixing the "nature symbolism" of the horn and its childlike, fairy-tale referent in the poem to the bugle's signal. Given the context of the poem within Tennyson's *The Princess*, one could read the rush of feeling in the B section as a projection of (illicit queer and/or pedophiliac) romantic love onto the landscape, hence providing that first, naive budding of erotic love that soon leads to moral corruption and decay in the Blake "Elegy." Peering underneath this naive sensibility, the "blow, bugle, blow" moment also has fairly literal sexual associations – the phallic/fellatio-like symbolism is transparent – and, if we view the bugle itself not only as ersatz phallus but also as a proxy for a male love interest, then the goading effect of the refrain depicts an erotic pursuit and intensification, with the "dying" moment instead figuring orgasm itself in accordance with the long tradition of referring to it as "death."

But although the bugle call "postulat[es] a diatonic chain of thirds rather than a true fanfare" (Evans 1979: 92), its military character, if of a youthful, peacetime nature, remains self-evident. If we tip the balance in favor of a military reading of the call, the affect that stirs in the heart of the narrator could easily be a patriotic or nationalist one, in which the budding of nationalist sentiment emerges from nostalgic attachment to the landscape itself.[6] But, in this reading, the setting of the words "dying, dying," which marks the acoustical death of the echoes and the deflation of patriotism, gains a new irony on account of the wartime period. Here, Britten's pacifism peeks through the song's surface of joyous wonderment, through a half-concealed lamentation of "sighing" two-note figures for dying soldiers (or perhaps citizens) – a poignant moment that, not incidentally, introduces another musical topic.

In reflecting more closely, these two antinomial readings share a dialectical bond, the one producing the other as part of what Brett calls the "double pattern" of Britten's sexual politics (2006: 178). Keeping the sexual and the national/military readings in mind, it is possible to produce a rather literal synthesis of the two, in which the boys and young men who function as the object of the creative persona's desire are understood as future or present soldiers, doomed to early deaths. This dual sonic image of life and death is projected through the poem's youthful, daytime imagery and the looming night of its title and trajectory ("the purple glens" of the second stanza indicating greater darkness than the sunset's "long light" of the first [Barringer 2011: 147]). The expressions of guilt and anguish that follow in the remaining movements of the *Serenade* stem not only from "immoral" sexual desire *for* military youth but also from the nascent pangs of chauvinistic pride *in* them.

The perspectives combining pacifism with queer love were often linked precisely through a personalized understanding of politics within Britten's aesthetic formation. Brett captures one version of this succinctly in describing a line from the novelist Christopher Isherwood, another of the Auden circle's "queer & left & conshies," as Pears described himself and Britten (cited in Brett 2006: 185): "In *Christopher and His Kind*, Isherwood supposes himself in charge of a button that can blow up the entire Nazi army. He reminds himself of his boyfriend Heinz, who was about to become an unwilling part of Hitler's war machine. 'Once I have refused to press the button because of Heinz,' Isherwood writes, 'I can never press it. Because every man in that Army could be somebody's Heinz and I have no right to play favorites'" (Brett 2006: 179). One might identify a similar figure in Britten's life: the young Wulff Scherchen, son of the German conductor Herman Scherchen and living in the UK, with whom Britten had "his first real romance" and who, after being interned because of his German background, served in the British Army (Bridcut 2006: 55, 108–25). Carpenter (1992: 119, 128, 143, 175) and John Bridcut (2006: 90–91) suggest he was the reason Britten felt the need to leave Britain in the first place. Even though Britten's feelings for Scherchen had dissipated by the time he composed the *Serenade* – in part as a result of Scherchen's transformation in internment and the army, in part through Britten's blossoming romance with Pears and encounters with other, younger boys – an inversion of the personal politics described by Brett might have given concrete expression to Britten's anxieties over his pedophiliac inclinations and self-affirmation as English during wartime, both of which contravened his nonviolent morality. Thus, when understood in combination, the moral and national aspects of "Nocturne" and the *Serenade* crystallize in both a concrete figure – the eroticized "soldier boy" (Fussell 2000: 270–309) – and a consistent affective trajectory in response to two different but inextricable aspects of that figure. As such, Britten's sexuality and pacifist politics are indelibly linked, the one *working through* the other, much in the way that in a different context Stuart Hall describes the interaction of race and class: "The structures through which black labour is reproduced . . . are not simply 'coloured' by race: they work through race" (1980: 340).

NARRATING THE "NOCTURNE" AND SERENADE

From the foregoing interpretation, it appears that the sexual-political crisis at the heart of the *Serenade* has its first glimmerings in the "Nocturne," thereby suggesting that the work's dark matter surfaces earlier and may be more pervasive than has been assumed. Yet, despite the *Serenade*'s intimations of negativity, the work consistently deflects attention away from the troubling issues it raises. Most obvious in this regard is the distraction effect of the "Hymn" following the "Dirge." Less apparent is the persistent symmetry and formal enclosures in the work, both within individual movements and the composition as a whole. Regarding the former, the movements of the *Serenade* favor two particular formal types – modified strophic or variation-based forms ("Pastoral," "Nocturne," "Dirge") and rounded-binary or ternary ones ("Prologue"/"Epilogue," "Elegy," and "Hymn"), with the penultimate "Sonnet" being a possible through-composed exception (Whittall 1982: 82). But the two predominant formal types tend to blend into one another: the *da capo* format of the "Hymn" includes a middle section (reh. **23–26**) that is a modified variant of the A material of the movement, and the variation-based forms (including the "Pastoral" and "Nocturne") include middle-section strophes or variations akin to B parts of those movements (reh. **2–3** in the former).

The "Nocturne" is a case in point: the second strophe (reh. **5–7**), which on the surface represents the greatest distance of the bugle's echoes in line with the text's middle stanza ("O hark, O hear! how thin and clear"), comprises the middle section. Differentiation from the other stanzas is achieved primarily through a tonal and modal shift (to C-diatonic Ionian with Lydian and chromatic inflections, in contrast with a more clearly diatonic-Ionian E♭ [Mark 1994: 294]) and through changes in dynamics (much softer) and timbre/texture (thinner, higher in register, muted horn in the cadenza-refrain); the third strophe's registering of the Lydian $\hat{4}$ from the second strophe (especially the A in mm. 25–26) and the new appearance of the Coplandesque learned-style canon in the low strings suggest developmental processes while firmly conveying a return to the material of the first strophe. But the formal roundedness of the "Nocturne" is realized in another way: through the brief return of the verse material at the end (reh. **9**), which provides an incomplete framing effect that helps to divert attention from the implications of the "dying" madrigalisms in the refrain material of the third strophe. Both types of enclosure in the "Nocturne" produce the impression of balance and symmetry, which give the song's narrative a relatively static quality – the narrative movement of greatest import is that of verse to refrain, from objectivity to subjectivity.

The narrative of the *Serenade* as a whole is not nearly as static, but it is contained through similar kinds of formal symmetry and balancing effects. Philip Rupprecht's note that "timbral-dynamic 'distance' frames the immediacy of the inner song cycle" (2001: 307n48) is elaborated in Tim Barringer's commentary on the *Serenade*'s ring-compositional or chiastic form

(Douglas 2007): "Formally, the Serenade is exquisitely balanced, with paired movements giving it a symmetrical shape. Framed by the identical Epilogue and Prologue, the first and sixth sung movements (Pastoral and Sonnet) are meditative and lyrical, the second and fifth (Nocturne and Hymn) are lively, extravert movements . . . and at the core of the piece lie two linked movements of visionary intensity and extreme darkness (Elegy and Dirge)" (2011: 141). Framings and symmetries of this sort in long-form and multimovement works are found elsewhere, including the *Phantasy*, op. 2, *A Ceremony of Carols*, op. 28, numerous stage works like the opera *Billy Budd*, op. 50 (Seymour 2007: 132, 136, 227), and in the church parables like *Curlew River*, op. 71. They have elicited casual comments on the composer's "liking for such frames" (Brett 2006: 145), particularly in contexts involving ritual and liturgical troping (Rupprecht 2001: 187–244), and may involve some connection to Britten's cinematic thinking, such as montage and flashback techniques (Crilly 2009). The "repleteness" of such devices can also provide affective rectitude, compensating for the presence of troubling events (Douglas 2007: 128–29). Lloyd Whitesell's claim that the *Serenade* "includes dark visions, but keeps them well-framed within scenes of light and harmony" (1993: 114), thus may be understood as an evasion of those visions (see also Seymour 2007).

Finally, let us reconsider the problem of the pastoral in the *Serenade*. Drawing on Whittall (1993), Monelle (2006: 107–108), Whitesell (2003: 655), and Barringer (2011), there is a consensus that the *Serenade* is largely a pastoral work, in which the narrative urge toward conflict resolution (Almén 2003) is less central than the working out of various issues within a relatively static framework. If the *Serenade* is understood as aspiring to be a pastoral idyll, a token of a twentieth-century neo-pastoral "expressive genre" (Hatten 1994: 67–90), why does it transgress the boundaries of such idylls, tinged with loss though they may be, and allow its deeper, darker waters almost to break them apart altogether? To answer this question, we should consider the apocalyptic narratives of modernist wartime pastorals in British music (Grimley 2010), upon which Britten implicitly built; we should further attend to the conflict between Britten's interest in a fundamentally placid narrative of childhood – the topos of innocence – and his discomfort with the "immoral" aspects of that experience (including children's sexual desire, his pedophilia, and his own experience of early sexual abuse, but also the violence and cruelty that children are themselves capable of). But whereas Britten was relatively comfortable displaying his aestheticized preferences for young male bodies, his attraction to the demons associated therewith was not typically as com-

fortable a topic of discussion. Britten did, however, elaborate with uncharac-
teristic candor on some related themes in an interview with Donald Mitchell
in 1971: "Night and dreams – I have had a strange fascination by that world
since a very early age. . . . [Night] can release many things which one thinks had
better not be released; and one can have dreams which one cannot remember
even, I find, in the morning, which do colour your next day very darkly. And
it's always very puzzling to me that I can't remember something which has had
such a big emotional effect on the next day, on the next days even" (Britten
1984: 92). Britten's interest in dreaming and dream spaces, which he explored
explicitly in the *Nocturne*, op. 60, is still relevant to the *Serenade* (which, for
Britten, "gets near to" the later work) and is marked as such in the final song's
text, "To Sleep" by Keats. The topos of sleep invokes the unconscious, which
in the *Serenade* is accessed in the process of dreaming, only to be submerged
at the moment of awakening. The "evasion" of the politico-moral quandary
at the heart of the work may then be understood as a psychodynamic act of
repression, expressed within a symmetrically layered dream work.

The narrative agent that induces and dispels sleep appears to be the horn
in the "Prologue" and "Epilogue," the former of which Whitesell describes
as "a kind of portal into the pastoral fantasies of that cycle" (2003: 655). The
music of these twin movements betrays the hallmarks of pastoralism through
their quintal intervallic content (mm. 1–3), through the use of the flat seventh
(the seventh harmonic), which is produced by treating the modern valve horn
like a pre-modern, one-cylinder horn, and through yodel-like figures (m. 9)
that resemble the alpine folk melodies played on the *Alphorn* known as the
ranz des vaches (Monelle 2006: 108). Moreover, the form of the music is in the
rounded-binary layout discussed above, with the B section (mm. 6–10) moving to the dominant of F before the return of the A material and tonic in m.
11. In addition to serving as a sign of the pastoral, these movements provide
a distancing and detached narratorial frame (Abbate 1991: 53) by offering a
pseudo-pre-modern variant of the monophonic, often recitative-like narrator
topic discussed by Michael Klein (2004: 35–38). This narrator seems, at first
glance, to herald the coming (and going) of the pastoral pageant that it frames
and not to register the eerie sentiments and specters that emerge from within
the body proper of the work. Yet we can also understand the "natural" tunings
required by the composer without specifying how they are to relate to the
diatonic pitches given in the score, as disclosing two meanings: a sign of the
fictive pre-modern and a deviation from normative tuning. Paying attention to
these tunings, we can see that non-diatonic tunings occur only in a few spots

EXAMPLE 11.4. Britten, *Serenade*, "Prologue," with non-tempered
natural harmonics identified.
*Serenade, op. 31, by Benjamin Britten. © Copyright 1944 by
Hawkes & Son (London), Ltd. Reprinted by Permission.*

(the B♭4 in m. 4, the E♭4 in mm. 7 and 9, the B♭4 in m. 10, and the D5 in m. 12),
and they appear to intensify as they progress: the B♭4 (the eleventh harmonic
seeming a bit sharp), the E♭4 (the seventh harmonic, somewhat flatter), and
the D5 (the thirteenth or fourteenth harmonic, depending on how it is performed) being the most distant, either sounding like a very sharp D5 (or flat
E♭5) (fourteenth partial) or a minor-modal sharp D♭5 (thirteenth partial) that
foreshadows the opening first-inversion D♭-major chord and D♭–C motive of
the following "Pastoral" (see Example 11.4).[7] However it is rendered, the D5
is strange: it follows upon a triumphant, *fortissimo* return of the A material
in m. 11 and, on account of the dynamic shift to *pianissimo* that undercuts
this return, produces a wan effect, as if the narrator were discomfited by the
shameful secret she cannot avoid revealing over the course of the tale.

The *Serenade* contains a wealth of interpretive complexities; it agonizes and
forgets in response to intersecting crises during a specific historical moment
in Britten's personal life and in British history. The composer's de facto marriage to Pears, already the source of societal disapproval, and his personal guilt
for reasons political and sexual could not "eliminate his powerful feelings for
boys" (Carpenter 1992: 161) and would resonate throughout his creative life.

But the composer's growing self-awareness of his "problems" (128), limited to a small if international circle of individuals, coincided with historical events of monumental magnitude: the end of British global hegemony and the imminent rise of a new, America-centric order, and the violent bloodstains (war deaths, the Holocaust) of the "Thirty Years' War" that decisively marked a new postwar conjuncture (Mayer 1981: 3; Hughes and Stradling 2001: 228). The coincidence of intimate events with those of world-historical proportions should not, however, require that interpretation of musical creations be forced to choose between them. Rather, we should try to think them together, as part of a greater totality of individual and capitalist society, working through what Sartre once called "the problem of mediations" (1963: 35), and think them through the immanent dynamics of form, the aesthetic unconscious of which imposes its own demands on artworks.

NOTES

Thanks to Michael Cherlin, James Dillon, Yayoi Everett, Letitia Glozer, Beth Hartman, Danielle Kuntz, Emily Lechner, Richard Leppert, Patrick McCreless, Severine Neff, Janna Saslaw, and Jason Stanyek for reading drafts of this material and/or offering ideas and references. And special thanks to Philip Rupprecht for generously sharing his expertise on Britten and his astute criticisms of this essay.

1. On the contradictions of Britten's pacifism, see Carpenter (1992: 177, 194–95); Mitchell and Reed (1991: 1176); and McMahon (2009).

2. For more critical treatments of *The Princess*, see Sedgwick (1985: 118–33); Gilbert and Gubar (1988: 6–16); D. Hall (1991); and Denecke (2001).

3. Britten drew the text from a popular anthology, *The Oxford Book of English Verse, 1250–1900* (Mitchell and Reed 1991: 1134), and, as Carpenter notes, "Britten's wide-ranging knowledge of poetry . . . was largely the result of his habit, when experiencing difficulties in his work, of wandering about the house and picking books from the shelves at random" (1992: 185).

4. See Palmer (1984: 319). For a sophisticated discussion of pitch relations in Britten's compositional practice, in which corruption is understood as one type of a broader pitch "discrepancy" in his music, see Rupprecht (1996: especially 321).

5. Britten and his schoolmate David Layton's conscientious objection to participating in OTC training while at Gresham's School (Bridcut 2006: 15) adds another layer of irony and distance to these bugle calls.

6. Britten's own longing for the English landscape during his American sojourn is described in Carpenter (1992: 154–55, 173). And his discovery of Crabbe's work inspired a modest patriotism – in his own words, "I suddenly realized where I belonged and what I lacked" (quoted on 156).

7. For differing perspectives on this pitch, see Tuckwell (1983: 112) and the archived post at http://hornplayer.net /archive/a37.html (accessed July 15, 2011).

WORKS CITED

Abbate, Carolyn. 1991. *Unsung Voices: Opera and Musical Narrative in the Nineteenth Century.* Princeton: Princeton University Press.

Almén, Byron. 2003. "Narrative Archetypes: A Critique, Theory, and Method of Narrative Analysis." *Journal of Music Theory* 47(1): 1–39.

Althusser, Louis. 1971. *Lenin and Philosophy, and Other Essays.* Translated by Ben Brewster. New York: Monthly Review Press.

Baker, Michael. 2009. "Form and Transformation in the 'Nocturne' from Britten's *Serenade* for Tenor, Horn, and Strings." Paper presented at the Music Theory Midwest annual meeting, May 15, Minneapolis, Minnesota.

Barringer, Tim. 2011. "'I Am Native, Rooted Here': Benjamin Britten, Samuel Palmer, and the Neo-Romantic Pastoral." *Art History* 34(1): 126–65.

Brett, Philip. 2001. "Benjamin Britten." In *New Grove Dictionary of Music and Musicians.* 2nd ed. http://www.grove music.com.

———. 2006. *Music and Sexuality in Britten: Selected Essays.* Berkeley: University of California Press.

Bridcut, John. 2006. *Britten's Children.* London: Faber.

Britten, Benjamin. 1984. "Mapreading." Interview by Donald Mitchell in *The Britten Companion*, edited by Christopher Palmer, 87–96. Cambridge: Cambridge University Press.

Carpenter, Humphrey. 1992. *Benjamin Britten: A Biography.* New York: C. Scribner's Sons.

Crilly, David. 2009. "Britten and the Cinematic Frame." In *Benjamin Britten: New Perspectives on His Life and Work*, edited by Lucy Walker, 56–72. Woodbridge, Suffolk: Boydell Press.

Crist, Elizabeth B. 2005. *Music for the Common Man: Aaron Copland during the Depression and War.* New York: Oxford University Press.

Denecke, Daniel. 2001. "The Motivation of Tennyson's Reader: Privacy and the Politics of Literary Ambiguity in 'The Princess.'" *Victorian Studies* 43(2): 201–27.

Denning, Michael. 1996. *The Cultural Front: The Laboring of American Culture in the Twentieth Century.* London: Verso.

Douglas, Mary. 2007. *Thinking in Circles: An Essay on Ring Composition.* New Haven: Yale University Press.

Evans, Peter. 1979. *The Music of Benjamin Britten.* Oxford: Clarendon.

Fussell, Paul. 2000. *The Great War and Modern Memory.* 25th anniversary ed. Oxford: Oxford University Press.

Gilbert, Sandra, and Susan Gubar. 1988. *No Man's Land: The Place of the Woman Writer in the Twentieth Century.* Vol. 1, *The War of the Words.* New Haven: Yale University Press.

Grimley, Daniel. 2010. "Landscape and Distance: Vaughan Williams, Modernism and the Symphonic Pastoral." In *British Music and Modernism, 1895–1960*, edited by Matthew Riley, 147–74. Farnham, Surrey: Ashgate.

Hall, Donald E. 1991. "The Anti-Feminist Ideology of Tennyson's 'The Princess.'" *Modern Language Studies* 21(4): 49–62.

Hall, Stuart. 1980. "Race, Articulation and Societies Structured in Dominance." In *Sociological Theories: Race and Colonialism*, 305–45. Paris: UNESCO.

Hatten, Robert. 1994. *Musical Meaning in Beethoven: Markedness, Correlation, and Interpretation.* Bloomington: Indiana University Press.

Hollander, John. 1981. *The Figure of Echo: A Mode of Allusion in Milton and After*. Berkeley: University of California Press.

Hubbs, Nadine. 2004. *The Queer Composition of America's Sound: Gay Modernists, American Music, and National Identity*. Berkeley: University of California Press.

Hughes, Meirion, and Robert Stradling. 2001. *The English Musical Renaissance, 1840–1940*. 2nd ed. Manchester: Manchester University Press.

Kildea, Paul. 2002. *Selling Britten: Music and the Market Place*. Oxford: Oxford University Press.

Killham, John. 1958. *Tennyson and "The Princess": Reflections of an Age*. London: University of London, Athalone Press.

Klein, Michael. 2004. "Chopin's Fourth Ballade as Musical Narrative." *Music Theory Spectrum* 26(1): 23–55.

Kramer, Lawrence. 2002. *Musical Meaning: Toward a Critical History*. Berkeley: University of California Press.

Lerner, Neil. 2001. "Copland's Music of Wide Open Spaces: Surveying the Pastoral Trope in Hollywood and Beyond." *Musical Quarterly* 85(3): 477–515.

Mark, Christopher. 1994. "Britten and the Circle of Fifths." *Journal of the Royal Musical Association* 119(2): 268–97.

Mayer, Arno. 1981. *The Persistence of the Old Regime: Europe to the Great War*. New York: Pantheon.

McMahon, Brian. 2009. "Why Did Benjamin Britten Return to Wartime England?" In *Benjamin Britten: New Perspectives on His Life and Work*, edited by Lucy Walker, 174–85. Woodbridge, Suffolk: Boydell Press.

Mellers, Wilfrid. 1952. "Recent Trends in British Music." *Musical Quarterly* 38(2): 185–201.

Mitchell, Donald. 1952. "The Musical Atmosphere." In *Benjamin Britten: A Commentary on His Works from a Group of Specialists*, edited by Donald Mitchell and Hans Keller, 9–58. London: Rockliff.

———. 1989. "'Now Sleeps the Crimson Petal': Britten's Other 'Serenade.'" *Tempo* 169: 22–27.

———. 1999. "The Mahler Renaissance in England: Its Origins and Chronology." In *The Mahler Companion*, edited by Donald Mitchell and Andrew Nicholson, 547–64. Oxford: Oxford University Press.

Mitchell, Donald, and Philip Reed, eds. 1991. *Letters from a Life: The Selected Letters and Diaries of Benjamin Britten*, vol. 2. London: Faber and Faber.

Monelle, Raymond. 2000. *The Sense of Music: Semiotic Essays*. Princeton: Princeton University Press.

———. 2006. *The Musical Topic*. Bloomington: Indiana University Press.

Palmer, Christopher. 1984. "Embalmer of the Midnight: The Orchestral Song-Cycles." In *The Britten Companion*, ed. Christopher Palmer, 308–28. Cambridge: Cambridge University Press.

Pollack, Howard. 2000. *Aaron Copland: The Life and Work of an Uncommon Man*. Urbana: University of Illinois Press.

Rupprecht, Philip. 1996. "Tonal Stratification and Uncertainty in Britten's Music." *Journal of Music Theory* 40(2): 311–46.

———. 2001. *Britten's Musical Language*. Cambridge: Cambridge University Press.

Sartre, Jean-Paul. 1963. *Search for a Method*. Translated by Hazel Barnes. New York: Knopf.

Schoenberg, Arnold. 1975. *Style and Idea: Selected Writings of Arnold Schoenberg*. Translated by Leo Black. Berkeley: University of California Press.

Sedgwick, Eve Kosofsky. 1985. *Between Men: English Literature and Male*

Homosocial Desire. New York: Columbia University Press.

Seymour, Claire. 2007. *The Operas of Benjamin Britten: Expression and Evasion.* Woodbridge, Suffolk: Boydell Press.

Tennyson, Alfred Tennyson, and Christopher Ricks. 1987. *The Poems of Tennyson: In Three Volumes,* vol. 2. 2nd ed. Berkeley: University of California Press.

Tuckwell, Barry. 1983. *Horn.* New York: Schirmer.

Watkins, Glenn. 2003. *Proof through the Night: Music and the Great War.* Berkeley: University of California Press.

White, Eric Walter. 1954. *Benjamin Britten: A Sketch of His Life and Works.* Rev. ed. London: Boosey and Hawkes.

Whitesell, Lloyd. 1993. "Images of Self in the Music of Benjamin Britten." PhD diss., State University of New York at Stonybrook.

———. 2003. "Britten's Dubious Trysts." *Journal of the American Musicological Society* 56(3): 637–94.

Whittall, Arnold. 1982. *The Music of Britten and Tippett: Studies in Themes and Techniques.* Cambridge: Cambridge University Press.

———. 1993. "The Signs of Genre: Britten's Version of Pastoral." In *Sundry Sorts of Music Books: Essays on the British Library Collections: Presented to O. W. Neighbour on His 70th Birthday,* edited by Chris Banks, Arthur Searle, and Malcolm Turner, 363–74. London: British Library.

12

Identity, Time, and Narrative in Three Songs about AIDS by the Pet Shop Boys

Fred Everett Maus

NARRATIVE SONATAS OR NARRATIVE SONGS

Discussions of "music and narrative" often center on non-programmatic instrumental music: quartets, symphonies, sonatas, and so on. Such music is central to my own past work on "music and narrative" (e.g., Maus 1988, 1991). It is bold to argue that narrative is central to musical meaning when the musical texts do not seem, in themselves, to ask explicitly for this conceptualization. Interpretive claims about non-programmatic instrumental music and narrative go out on a limb; thus, they may seem exciting, or problematic.

For some other music, involvement with narrative is obvious; the question is not whether a relationship to narrative exists but what the relationship is. Narrative may be overt in the drama of an opera, the verbal language of a song, the program in program music, or the succession of events in a movie. When plot and other aspects of narrative, as understood in non-musical media, appear in these partly dramatic or linguistic forms, the music – the operatic music, film music, and so on – becomes meaningful in relation to narrative. Critical interpretation can ask how the music relates to narrative elements that are undeniably present; theories can generalize about such relationships.

This essay discusses popular songs where the lyrics engage narrative. David Nicholls has recommended study of such songs. For Nicholls, the topic offers a way past the methodological controversies of other "music and narrative" studies. "From a musical point of view the main application of narrative theory may have to be restricted to those instances in which the musical material has been created in response to, or – better – as a setting of, a literary text" (Nicholls 2007: 300). I agree that music in cases such as song and film, where narrative elements may be explicit, rewards critical study. But – briefly and in passing – I want to declare my impenitent attachment to narrative interpretations of non-programmatic instrumental music. Unlike Nicholls, I see no reason to substitute one kind of study for the other or to decide how the "main application of narrative theory" should be "restricted." As I wrote elsewhere, "analogies to narrative can show their value for music criticism by the insights and experiences they produce, the relationships with music that they help to create. The notion of narrative . . . is something to try, one way and another" (Maus 2005: 480–81).

Musicological work on narrative tends toward theory. That is no surprise, since it has often interpreted non-programmatic instrumental music, where conceptual questions seem to require theoretical answers. But Nicholls, too, in turning to examples of popular music with lyrics, proposes, if not a theory, at least a generalized taxonomy. I am fond of theoretical thought, but also of criticism, the attempt to describe experienced qualities of specific songs, compositions, performances, and so on. Sometimes critical interpretation leads to theoretical innovations, as in Anthony Newcomb's (1984, 1987) pioneering essays on music and narrative. But it need not always do so, and the present essay does not take that direction. In this essay, my primary goal is to describe some music that I find fascinating. In working on the essay, my experience and understanding of these songs, and the roles of narrative in their meanings, became richer; I hope this will be the case for my readers as well.[1]

GAY MALE IDENTITY AND NARRATIVE

Political issues of minority sexual identity were prominent in the United States and England during the 1970s, in part through activism after the 1969 Stonewall riots (Duberman 1993). Issues of gender and sexuality, in both hegemonic and dissident forms, were also central to popular music of the time. Rock, for example, was often identified with masculine, heterosexual performers and audiences. Disco, in contrast, carried associations with the newly conspicuous social identity "urban gay male." The sexuality connotations of disco were somewhat muted in the mainstreaming of disco from 1977 on, as in the straight-oriented, homophobic film *Saturday Night Fever* (1977, directed by John Badham). But connections between disco and male homosexuality returned in the homophobic "disco sucks" assault of 1979 and the turn away from disco in mainstream pop music.[2]

From the early 1980s, HIV and AIDS complicated these socio-political issues. AIDS was initially identified primarily as an illness of gay men, especially men in urban centers such as New York City and San Francisco. With growing public awareness of the disease came increased activity in the politics of sexuality, often taking homophobic forms. In this painful atmosphere, popular music remained a crucial medium for the articulation and circulation of images of diversity in gender presentation and sexuality. Sometimes popular songs also responded to HIV/AIDS, with varying degrees of explicitness.

In articulations of sexual identity and sexual politics, time and narrative were crucial structuring factors. Gay male identity was often understood through a number of story lines: discovering one's sexuality, accepting it, and coming out; moving from an unsympathetic environment, perhaps rural or small-town, to the big city; leaving one's biological family and creating a new, alternative family within a gay culture; pre-Stonewall oppression and post-Stonewall openness. All these stories are about beginnings; their lack of narrative closure may feel awkward. They bring their gay male protagonist to the point where identity-defining heterosexual narratives would just be getting under way, but the stereotypical gay male narratives do not carry on past that point. A conventional heterosexual story would continue to love and marriage, a career, children, the empty nest and retirement, aging, grandchildren, and death; the gay narratives just mentioned seem to leave their protagonists in a potentially endless condition of adolescence.[3] In relation to this open-ended narrative, HIV/AIDS could feel like an irrelevant intrusion. Or, in a coherent but hostile narrative, the lack of conventional adult trajectory could feel like a problem, somehow resolved by the arrival of AIDS, perhaps as a punishment for the evasion of adult responsibilities.

These narratives of gay male identity provide reference points for the songs I discuss. As a socially shared repertory of familiar stories, they shape individual songs, somewhat as "plot archetypes" shape individual instrumental works in Newcomb's work on musical narrative.

THE PET SHOP BOYS AND "GO WEST"

The Pet Shop Boys, an English duo, created synthesizer-based pop music from the mid-1980s on. Usually, Neil Tennant sings and writes the lyrics,

Chris Lowe plays keyboards, and both men contribute to the composition of the music. The Pet Shop Boys' first album, *Please*, released in 1986, made them famous.

From the beginning of the Pet Shop Boys' career, gay listeners often heard their songs as insightful articulations of late twentieth-century urban gay men's experiences. But the members of the Pet Shop Boys were slow to accept any public label for their sexuality. In 1994, almost a decade into the duo's high-profile career, Tennant explicitly identified himself as gay: "I'm gay, and I have written songs from that point of view." Apparently, Chris Lowe has never made a direct public statement about his sexuality, though people who follow the Pet Shop Boys' music seem to assume that he is gay.

Up to 1994, in the years of their greatest visibility and commercial success, the Pet Shop Boys seemed to combine a valuable exploration of gay life with the semi-transparent personal discretion of the closet. This could be puzzling. Journalist John Gill, in his well-informed but narrowly conceived book *Queer Noises* (1995), sharply scolded the Pet Shop Boys, and Tennant in particular, for their failure to come out as gay through explicit verbal statements. But if Tennant and Lowe were reticent about verbal self-labeling, theirs was no ordinary closet. Their songs repeatedly thematized discretion, coded discourse, and open secrets (Maus 2001).

The mass-mediated address of the Pet Shop Boys' songs created a public – a very broad one at the height of their career – constituted by individual listeners' shared awareness of belonging collectively to the Pet Shop Boys' audience. The double-voicedness of the Pet Shop Boys' discourse about sexuality created a second, smaller public, a subset of the first one, constituted by listeners' awareness that they, along with the Pet Shop Boys themselves, shared the personal knowledge of urban gay life required for understanding the songs – constituted, too, by this smaller public's awareness that the full meanings of Pet Shop Boys songs were lost on many members of the broader audience.

As mentioned, the Pet Shop Boys became famous in 1986, and they remained particularly successful through their 1993 album, *Very*. Their period of greatest visibility falls within the time between the arrival of AIDS in North American and European gay communities, and the advent in 1996 of effective medications that dramatically changed the nature of the epidemic in those communities.

Walter Hughes (1994), in an essay about disco, depicts disco as a musical and social technology that helped to create the Anglo-American identity "gay urban male." He identifies the Pet Shop Boys' music as a continuation of disco and argues that the effects of AIDS on urban gay life are a central topic of their songs. Hughes argues this not only for a song such as "Domino Dancing," in which the reference to AIDS is plain – "watch them all fall down" – but for many of their other songs, in which Hughes hears the difficulties of redefining gay life after AIDS. Songs about monogamy and infidelity, trust, desire, and sexual danger reflect the new, unwelcome urgency of these issues in urban gay life at the time. I agree about the pervasiveness of AIDS-related concerns in the Pet Shop Boys' songs, evident in their work through the 1996 album, *Bilingual*. The Pet Shop Boys have also recorded several songs that focus on the arrival of the epidemic itself rather than dramatizing its pervasive effects.

I begin with brief comments on the most famous Pet Shop Boys song about AIDS: "Go West," a 1993 cover version. In 1979, when the Village People recorded the song, it praised San Francisco, an urban gay center created by migration. Heard again in the Pet Shop Boys' performance, the song evokes that story but marks a change, commemorating a strong sense of hope and innovation that, by 1993, seemed to belong to the historic past. Still, their performance's reflection of the optimism of the original song signals, ambivalently, a reluctance to abandon earlier aspirations.[4]

Thus, to understand this song, one should relate it to a chronological narrative that extends from the 1970s, when the song was first recorded, to its repetition in the 1990s. The language of the lyrics is not itself a narrative but a series of imperatives and descriptive justifications – a future-oriented exhortation. But the meaning of the Pet Shop Boys' recording is intertwined with the narrative of hope leading to trauma, the narrative in which gay men, before and especially after Stonewall, migrated to urban centers and created a culture of openness and sexual freedom, only to have that community struck with illness and renewed homophobia. The poignancy of the cover version, for some of its listeners, comes from its relation to a narrative that it calls to mind, although the lyrics do not tell this story.

AND THEN IT DID

I shall now comment in more detail on a Pet Shop Boys song that not just evokes, but narrates, the arrival of AIDS.[5] "It Couldn't Happen Here" comes from the Pet Shop Boys' second album, *Actually* (1987). The lyrics are oblique; their lack of specificity comes in part from heavy use of indefinite referring expressions such as "we," "it," "now," "here." The basic narrative is about a change from the past to the present. It is left to listeners – those with appropriate contextual knowledge – to recognize that the song describes the "before" and "after" of AIDS. The song contrasts past and present explicitly, rather than by implication, as in "Go West." The lyrics are in three verses and three slightly varied choruses; these sections are ordered as two verses, followed by a chorus, and a third verse, followed by two choruses.

First, the song describes the past through a present act of narration. The first verse begins with the word "yesterday," and the first two verses are in past tense; the narrator addresses an audience, a "you" evoked in the imperative of the first line – "remember how clear it seemed." The audience could be a friend, or group of friends, with whom the narrator shares memories; it could also be the song's actual listeners, to the extent that they share the narrator's memories. Less obviously, it could be the narrator himself. The song addresses insiders, articulating shared feeling among people already familiar with experiences of the epidemic, rather than attempting to educate an external audience. According to the narrator, in the past everything seemed "clear," and people "knew" they could "go all the way," a phrase with sexual and non-sexual meanings. This shared past belongs to the narrator and his listener or listeners, and implicitly to a past community, created partly through a shared sense of being fashionably up-to-date, wearing "six-inch heels" and referring to "magazines."

The second verse introduces, still within the past, a censorious "someone" who asks aggressive questions: "Who do you think you are?" But the narrator silences this antagonist by closing a door, establishing separation. In the past, the narrator and his community were able to insulate themselves from criticism. These verses remember clarity, knowledge, "going all the way," and a shutting out of skeptics. To listeners familiar with conventional narratives of post-Stonewall gay culture, it is clear that these verses retell that story of liberation.

From the first chorus onward, the song primarily depicts the present. The chorus counters the initial "yesterday" with a "now," when things have changed. The language becomes more elusive, its ambiguities and qualifications expressing the speaker's disorientation. Something, identified only as "it," "almost seems impossible." To say that something *seems* impossible is less certain than saying that it *is* impossible, and the relation to knowledge is weaker still when something *almost* seems impossible. Later, the chorus refers, apparently, to a belief held in the past, but there is no claim to knowledge, as the narrator reports something "we said" in the past, perhaps without having good grounds to believe it. And the narrator seems to express doubt about just what was said: "I may be wrong, I thought we said . . ."

Perhaps the "it" that now almost seems impossible is the confidence and freedom of the past; perhaps "it" is the recent change. The second line of the first chorus is surprising: "We've drunk too much, and woke up everyone." The metaphor, reporting an affronted response from people – "everyone" who slept while others, "we," partied – likens a subcultural generation's explorations to drunken excess, implying poor judgment or adolescent immaturity. At this point, the song raises the issue of attributing guilt, a culpable frivolity, to the urban gay cultures struck by AIDS and fails to take a clear stance on the accusation. In the first verse, the opposition between the speaker's community and the censorious external "someone" seemed clear; in the chorus, the speaker himself seems, perhaps, to take on the perspective of the harsh, formerly external judge.

The reference of the concluding lines of the chorus is also ambiguous: "I may be wrong, I thought we said it couldn't happen here." In the most obvious meaning, "here" is Britain, from where the epidemic and its consequences could initially be seen as American. But the word "we" seems likely to refer to a gay community not included within the "everyone" of the nation. "Here" and "we" can also refer, more metaphorically, to the situation of post-Stonewall gay men and the sense of relative optimism and security discovered by certain urban gay communities in the 1970s.

The "it" that couldn't happen here is the rapid spread of HIV and AIDS but also, perhaps, social phenomena around the infection, including the homophobic antipathy triggered by the disease, the punitive anger of the self-appointed "everyone" or mainstream. *It Can't Happen Here* is the title of a 1935 novel by Sinclair Lewis, imagining a rapid turn to fascism in the United States. The allusion to Lewis is pertinent to the interventionist homophobia that saw mandatory testing and reporting, tattooing, and quarantine as reasonable responses to AIDS.

The third verse, unlike the first two, remains in the present but refers, through mention of "battle scars," to the past. The topic is the appropriate response to AIDS, but there are no conclusions about action. To respond to AIDS and homophobia by making "sense," by claiming "dignity and injured innocence," would be, according to the speaker, to "contradict" wounds that may be reopened. These lyrics reject certain kinds of activism, though the reasoning is not clear. Tennant has associated the lines with the physical ravages of AIDS, but it is not clear why illness should inhibit claims of sense, dignity, and innocence (Pet Shop Boys 2001). Perhaps the speaker is reluctant to reopen psychic wounds of prejudice and political confrontation through the self-exposure of activism. Or perhaps the stigma of the epidemic creates a debilitating shame that precludes an activist response. The song depicts disorientation, pessimism, and fear that lead the speaker to withdraw from an appeal to reason and shared humanity.

"It Couldn't Happen Here" narrates, not explicitly the death of an individual or the widespread death caused by AIDS, but the loss of subcultural confidence and, through multiple ambiguities, the loss of the clarity and certainty of thought that subcultural identity seemed to permit. It expresses a kind of trauma, akin to what psychologist Ronnie Janoff-Bulman (1992) calls the trauma of "shattered assumptions," the destruction of beliefs about security and self-worth. In this story, though, what is shattered is not an "assumption" but self-worth and flourishing community, which were created within recent memory: shattered achievements. The song ends by lamenting that "we've found ourselves back where we started from."

The lyrics are already intricate. But this is a song, and the musical setting further shapes its meaning. The music is slow and serious, with solemn string orchestra sounds, in the style of classical concert music or a classically derived film score, with added percussion. It is a collaboration between the Pet Shop Boys and the film-score composer Ennio Morricone. The music of the chorus comes from a song that Morricone offered to the Pet Shop Boys. According to Tennant, it was "a funny song about a man building an ark" (Pet Shop Boys 2001). The Pet Shop Boys used the music of the chorus but wrote new lyrics, evidently different in tone from those of the original song; they also created new music for the verse.

Tennant sings solo, without backup singers or overdubbing of his voice. The accompaniment uses orchestral timbres, and the textures are those of simple classical music or orchestral film score, at first chordal, later with bits of decorative figuration. There is excessive resonance, as though an orchestra plays in an empty concert hall. The orchestral sound is hollow, as though disembodied. Originally an orchestra was to play the accompaniment, but ultimately it was recorded on Fairlight synthesizer using samples. As Tennant says, "Actually it gives the whole track an eerie quality we would never have got from an orchestra. It sounds tighter, and also more weird. So, ultimately, it was a happy accident" (Pet Shop Boys 2001). The unreality of the orchestral sound matches the disorientation in the lyrics and exemplifies a missing community, the collaborative ensemble of live musicians that is not present.

TABLE 12.1. SECTIONS OF "IT COULDN'T HAPPEN HERE"

0:00	Two-measure intro – exotic percussion
0:08	String intro; two measures of dissonant chord, moving to another dissonant chord and then E minor (Figure 2a)
0:32	Verse 1 moving from E minor to half cadence in C minor
1:04	Verse 2
1:36	Chorus 1, C major, with emphasis on F major
2:08	Verse 3
2:40	Chorus 2
3:12	Instrumental, returning to material of string intro – begins with E-minor chord, leads to C major for chorus
3:42	Chorus 3, at 4:10 cadencing to E minor rather than C major
4:14	Chorus 4, instrumental for first half – cadences to C major
4:47	Intro music again, then alternating E minor and C major

Within this context, the more natural sound of Tennant's voice makes him sound isolated. Through Tennant's sonic separateness in a "weird" environment, the song depicts the narrator's separateness without any consoling representation of the addressees with whom he offers to share his experiences.

As mentioned, the Pet Shop Boys added the verse to the music of Morricone's chorus; the compositional collaboration is superb. Table 12.1 shows the sections of the song. Both the verse and chorus use the eight-measure phrase pattern called a *sentence*, a segmented pattern of 2 + 2 + 4 measures. In a sentence, the first two measures provide a model for mm. 3 and 4; mm. 5 to 8 are more continuous. In many sentences, m. 5 draws on an idea from the first two measures and also provides a model for m. 6, as in both the verse and chorus of this song. This yields a pattern of 2 + 2 + (1 + 1 + 2). In "It Couldn't Happen Here," the parallel phrase patterns of verse and chorus encourage comparison and heighten the effect of contrasts between the two sections.[6]

The song fluctuates between two tonics, E minor and C major. In each key, the F-major triad is prominent, as the Neapolitan ($\flat$II) in E minor and the subdominant (IV) in C major. At several points, a major seventh, or its enharmonic equivalent (the diminished octave), is conspicuous, the upper note of the dissonant interval appearing with strong emphasis in the melody (Example 12.1). These pitch features have expressive potential. Ambivalence between major and minor can express a mixture of positive and negative emotions, though the meaning in this song is more complex. A conspicuous major triad in a minor key, such as the Neapolitan, can suggest a possibility of hope

a.

b.

c.

EXAMPLE 12.1. Diminished octaves and major
sevenths, "It Couldn't Happen Here."

or respite, but one that must be ephemeral because its non-tonic harmony requires resolution. In "It Couldn't Happen Here," F major functions this way in relation to E minor and also, less predictably, in relation to C major, even though the governing tonic is major. Major sevenths or diminished octaves between a melodic note and a lower note can suggest pain, especially when they arrive abruptly. None of these associations is inevitable; these meanings are possibilities that may become relevant in a particular context, as they do in this song.

Given the lyrics of "It Couldn't Happen Here," one might expect the music for words about the past to be strong and confident, the music depicting the present suffering and disorientation to be sad or uncertain. But the reverse is true. The music for the verses, using minor keys, is unstable and ambivalent; the more diatonic, major-mode music for the chorus, beginning and ending in C major, gains greater stability and certainty, though it has its own complexities and conflicts. It is as though the past clarity and confidence described in the first two verses cannot be re-experienced, even as one recalls them, while the present situation seems more real.

An instrumental introduction establishes E minor as tonic. The strings enter on a mysterious dissonant combination; only at the end of two slow measures does this change, subsequently revealing the tonic (see Example 12.1a; the notated examples represent pitch relations but not actual durations of notes). Already, the song introduces an image of sharp, unprepared pain, giving way to dejection.

	Em	F/A	Em	F/A	EbM7	Fm/Ab	D$^{\emptyset}$7	G
E minor:	i	N6	i	N6	?			
Eb major:					I7	ii6	?	
C major:	iii	IV6	iii	IV6	bIII7	iv6	ii$^{\emptyset}$7	V
Roots of chords:	E	F	E	F	Eb	F	D	G
Main bass notes:	E	A	E	A	Eb	Ab	D	G

FIGURE 12.1. Harmonies, verse of "It Couldn't Happen Here."

The music for the verse winds through a confusing succession of chords, with no full cadence, to reach a half cadence at the end (Figure 12.1). In its first four measures, the verse continues in the E minor of the introduction, alternating between two chords, E minor and the Neapolitan F-major chord in first inversion. In the first two measures, with expressive precision, the verse matches the minor chord with the present act of remembering, the major chord with the positive content attributed to the past: the music brightens at the words "how clear it seemed."

M. 5 has a startling new chord, not easy to relate to E minor or, initially, any other tonic; it suggests, if anything, a shift of tonic down to E♭.[7] The major seventh in m. 5 is enharmonically equivalent to the diminished octave in the first chord of the introduction, and the new chord resembles the one in the introduction with a fourth pitch class added. Another new chord in m. 6, perhaps continuing a tonicization of E♭ major, accompanies the same melodic pitch content as in mm. 2 and 4. But the new harmonies are disorienting, and the pitch repetitions are difficult to recognize in their new context. By m. 6, the cumulative music of the verse gives a vivid experience of disorientation and discontinuity, partly because in the succession of chords, one per measure, adjacent chords never have pitch classes in common.

The verse ends more purposefully, with a half cadence in C minor. This clarifies, for the first time, the immediately preceding chords, which may now be heard as III[7] and iv[6] in C minor. However, C minor is not close to the starting point of E minor. Nor is there a clear hierarchy between the keys. E minor sounds first, for a long time, and uses its tonic triad. But it has no dominant-function harmony, except perhaps the first chord of the introduction. C minor is strengthened by the dominant harmony in a half cadence. Having broached two different keys, the verse cadences in neither.

Confusing and fragmentary, this music seems to depict not the positive feelings experienced in the past but a present state of bewilderment as the narrator contemplates a past that now seems "impossible" or "incredible." The combination of words and music creates the audible image of someone trying to remember a past that is accessible, at best, through language but of which the original felt experience no longer returns in memory.

The chorus begins in C major. This clarifies the relationship between E minor and C minor, which now may both be heard as close minor-mode relatives of C major, the first a tonicization of iii, the second the parallel minor. In relation to C major, the verse may be heard retrospectively as a prolonged progression within C major tonic, with a mixture of C minor – iii to ii°⁷ to V.

Compared to the verse, the chorus is harmonically simple, although it is unbalanced in temporal proportions. Its melodic rise and fall suggest a surge of strong emotion. The major mode and harmonic clarity feel affirmative; other aspects, however, complicate this feeling.

The phrase begins with motion from major to minor (C major to A minor, mm. 1–2, and F major to D minor, mm. 3–4), suggesting a move toward sadness. Still, the A-minor harmony occurs within a larger descending motion, and the D-minor harmony belongs, as a vi chord, within a tonicization of F major that takes up most of the phrase: five out of eight measures, mm. 3–7. The continuation in F major, mm. 5–7, is complex, and some features undermine the stability of F major. The first-inversion F-major triad (mm. 5–6) recalls the Neapolitan at the beginning of the verse, another chord that functions within another key. The melodic leap of a major seventh places the leading tone of F major as the highest note in the phrase, ensuring that the F-major passage will sound incomplete despite its cadence; the dissonant leap evokes pain. The major-major seventh harmony recalls the chord at the same point in the verse, the point of maximum instability in that part of the song. The stepwise descent through a third in the melody, E–D–C, beginning with a melodic note that forms a major seventh, recalls the melodic descent in the introduction, an earlier expression of pain (see Examples 12.1a and c).

The return from F major to C major takes place only within the accompaniment. There is conflict between the structure of the vocal melody with accompaniment (mm. 1–7) and the music of the entire eight-measure phrase. As vocal melody, the phrase moves from C major to F major and cadences there. But the accompaniment continues to the C-major cadence, undoing the vocal gesture of cadence and showing C major to be the tonic of this phrase with F major as a locally tonicized IV. The voice tries to reach closure in F major, but the accompaniment contradicts this false ending. In a preliminary version, the chorus ended with additional words, "and then it did," presumably extending the vocal line into the C-major cadence (Pet Shop Boys 2001). The final version, removing these words, is more poignant, as the narrator tries to stop within the memory of a feeling of safety, and within the key of F major.

The concluding plagal cadence, returning to the C-major tonic chord, recalls the conventional harmonic formula for setting the word "amen." The cadence has an eerie assurance, even a sweetness. Does this "amen" reveal an acceptance of catastrophe? Because the cadence to F major was also plagal, the whole chorus has a quality of religiosity or benediction. Despite the complexities I have described, there is a sense of release and affirmation in this major-mode music not easy to understand in relation to the subject of the song. Perhaps, in the music of the chorus, the beauties of a past way of life are allowed to enter consciousness, but this positive meaning is not definite. Adding to the emotional obscurity, the instrumental passages at the beginning, middle, and end of the song ponder, without clear overall outcome, the relation between C-major and E-minor triads, as does the cadence at 4:10 that suddenly substitutes, without clear meaning or consequences, E minor for C major.

"It Couldn't Happen Here" is a troubling song, hermeneutically difficult in its multiple ambiguities and ethically difficult in its indeterminate relation to collective self-blame. It offers a rich articulation of a stunned response to the epidemic, a post-traumatic numbness and incapacity to think or act effectively.

ALWAYS RELY ON A FRIEND

"Being Boring," from the 1990 album, *Behaviour*, revisits the concerns of "It Couldn't Happen Here." In the two songs, one hears the same events narrated, but from radically different perspectives. There are two verses of recollection, and a third verse, beginning with the word "now," takes the perspective of the present. The verses trace the pleasures of being with friends across the years, from early teenage parties, through the legendary post-Stonewall seventies, to

TABLE 12.2. SECTIONS OF "BEING BORING"

0:00	Introduction, G♯ minor
1:24	Chorus (instrumental)
1:50	Verse 1
2:29	Chorus 1
2:57	Verse 2
3:35	Chorus 2
4:09	Instrumental interlude
4:21	Verse 3
4:49	Chorus 3
6:04	Accompaniment continues music of chorus, to cadence in G♯ minor

the present, when these pleasures have been disrupted. To informed listeners, the song offers a community-forming paradigmatic narrative in which a man grows up, leaves home to join an urban gay community, and encounters unanticipated loss. If "Being Boring," like "It Couldn't Happen Here," expresses the loss of adventure and companionship, this time the lyrics and especially the music offer access to the pleasures of the past. The song is free of shame and ambivalence, a radiant depiction of "injured innocence." The vocal performance is hushed, as though the narrator confides in listeners; it is also doubled in octaves, sonically suggesting a shared subjectivity in accord with the pronoun "we." The accompaniment timbres are frankly electronic but use warm string sounds, punctuated by the glamour of the harp. The drumming, a subdued performance of James Brown's oft-sampled "Funky Drummer" pattern, suggests a pensive memory of exuberance. Table 12.2 summarizes the sectional divisions.

Figure 12.2 indicates rhythmic and harmonic aspects of the verse. This music sounds like pleasurable improvisation. Because of the close voice-leading and the lack of definite harmonic and rhythmic direction, it is easy to imagine that someone's right hand is exploring an electronic keyboard in idle fascination, finding intriguingly different ways to drift toward a half cadence through an ample ten-measure phrase. The vocal line rests easily within these harmonies, neighboring a few pitches without any sense of destination.

The chorus is about being so caught up in the moment that one does not think about one's time as limited. It enters with what might be a key change rather than resolving the half cadence of the verse. The music falls into a repeating four-measure cycle, evocative of dance music; it sounds as though

(C# major)

Measures	1 2	3 4	5 6	7 8	9	10
Chords	E#m	D#m7	E#m	D#m7	G#7sus	G#7

C#M:	iii	ii7	iii	ii7	V7	
					4	-	3

Measures	1 2	3 4	5 6	7 8	9 10
Chords	C#	D#m7/C#	B	G#m	G#

C#M:	I	ii2	bVII	v	V

FIGURE 12.2. Harmonies of verse, "Being Boring."

it might go on forever. Figure 12.3 shows the harmonies, ambiguous between the keys of E major and C♯ minor. The latter key would relate the chorus to the C♯-major verse by change of mode, perhaps suggesting sadness. In partial conflict with this, the voice projects the E-major triad, making C♯ a neighbor of B and nudging the harmonies toward a major-mode interpretation.

In the first chorus, at the twelfth measure and on the words "time could come to an end," a tonic cadence arrives with a jolt: the music illustrates all too emphatically the possibility of ending. Up to this point, there has been no tonic cadence in the song, the music instead offering an image of sustained pleasure without a full close, first improvisatory, then dance-like. The second and third choruses respond to this initial jolt of closure by extending the music before cadencing. And the second chorus seems to reverse the meaning of the cadence. The words "time could come to an end" now appear within a musical phrase, and the emphatic cadence comes with the words "you could always rely on a friend." The finality of the cadence reinforces the thought that friendships can last forever.

The third verse, though, reveals that by the 1990s, many friends are gone; AIDS, unnamed in the song but unmistakably its subject for informed listeners, has ended relationships that seemed to extend indefinitely. The chorus, then, repeats the use of a cadence to underscore the past belief in the permanence of friendship, but continues past the cadence without pause, re-entering the ongoing dance music of the chorus. As the singer continues, the song seems almost desperate in its effort to prevent a musical ending by

(C# minor/E major)

	1	2	3	4
	AM7	B	G#m7	C#m

C#m:	VI7	VII	v7	i
EM:	IV7	V	iii7	vi

	5	6	7	8
	AM7	B	G#m7	C#m

C#m:	VI7	VII	v7	i
EM:	IV7	V	iii7	vi

	9	10	11	12	13
	AM7	G#m7	F#m7	EM7	

EM:	IV7	iii7	ii7	I7	

FIGURE 12.3. Harmonies of chorus, "Being Boring."

repetitiously sustaining the evocation of the past. When the vocal line finally stops, it feels as though it is only partway through the music of the chorus, and the vocal ending now suggests a C♯-minor cadence. The instrumental music continues, as though toward another E-major cadence, but suddenly turns to G♯ minor instead, the key of the final instrumental section. As in "It Couldn't Happen Here," the voice breaks off, unable to continue from a memory of the past to a concluding statement about the present. Again, the instrumental music concludes.

The music that ends "Being Boring" also appears in the remarkable introduction, which is almost a minute and a half in length. The unusual texture of this opening music combines an *ostinato* in G♯ minor with plaintive guitar solo, a soulful expression of pain unusual in the Pet Shop Boys' style. Over this, a strange whistling sound outlines an F♯-major triad. These sounds are juxtaposed but not blended, suggesting a layering of unintegrated moods. The prevalent emotional quality is sad or mournful, and one can hear the introduction and conclusion as reflecting the mood of the present moment.

There is a pause at the end of the introduction, with percussion only, before the music takes up the theme of the chorus, as though the change from the present mood to recollection is discontinuous. In contrast, the end of the song leads from recollection back to the present; denial is impossible, although the return to G♯ feels unprepared, like an intrusion.

WE WERE NEVER BEING BORING

The songs I have discussed come from a particular time, when AIDS had become a highly publicized epidemic within recent memory, there were no effective drugs to manage HIV infection, and it was possible to think of AIDS primarily as an event within the First World urban gay male communities that had flourished during the 1970s. We think of HIV and AIDS differently now, as we also think differently about sexual diversity and its various relations to identity and community. These musical narratives, written at a specific moment to tell stories of shared pain and loss, now help to preserve the memory of that moment, making past experience vividly and movingly available for present-day listeners.

NOTES

1. It would be possible, of course, for someone (myself or someone else) to move from the interpretations in this essay to theoretical discussion, for instance of text/music relations, musical depictions of subjectivity, "topics" or "musemes," and so on.

2. For valuable discussion, see Hughes (1994); Lawrence (2004).

3. On the unfinished/adolescent quality of some queer trajectories, see Halberstam (2005: 152–87).

4. Much of what I say about this song draws upon Mark Butler's (2003) excellent essay.

5. To follow my descriptions of "It Couldn't Happen Here" and "Being Boring," readers should have access to the lyrics – included in the albums and widely available online – and the album cuts of the songs.

6. The classic account of the sentence is in Schoenberg (1967: 20–24, 58–81). Caplin offers a lucid contemporary version (1998: 35–48).

7. Here and subsequently, I number measures within either the verse or chorus starting from m. 1; thus, numbers refer to the specific section of the song, not to the numbering for the entire song.

WORKS CITED

Butler, Mark. 2003. "Taking It Seriously: Intertextuality and Authenticity in Two Covers by the Pet Shop Boys." *Popular Music* 22(1): 1–19.

Caplin, William E. 1998. *Classical Form: A Theory of Formal Functions for the Instrumental Music of Haydn, Mozart, and Beethoven.* Oxford: Oxford University Press.

Duberman, Martin. 1993. *Stonewall.* New York: E. P. Dutton.

Gill, John. 1995. *Queer Noises: Male and Female Homosexuality in Twentieth-Century Music.* Minneapolis: University of Minnesota Press.

Halberstam, Judith. 2005. *In a Queer Time and Place: Transgender Bodies, Subcultural Lives.* New York: New York University Press.

Hughes, Walter. 1994. "In the Empire of the Beat: Discipline and Disco." In *Microphone Fiends: Youth Music and Youth Culture,* edited by Andrew Ross and Tricia Rose, 147–57. New York: Routledge.

Janoff-Bulman, Ronnie. 1992. *Shattered Assumptions: Towards a New Psychology of Trauma.* New York: Free Press.

Lawrence, Tim. 2004. *Love Saves the Day: A History of American Dance Music Culture, 1970–1979.* Durham: Duke University Press.

Lewis, Sinclair. 2005. *It Can't Happen Here.* New York: New American Library. First published 1935.

Maus, Fred Everett. 1988. "Music as Drama." *Music Theory Spectrum* 10: 56–73.

———. 1991. "Music as Narrative." *Indiana Theory Review* 12: 1–34.

———. 2001. "Glamour and Evasion: The Fabulous Ambivalence of the Pet Shop Boys." *Popular Music* 20(3): 379–93.

———. 2005. "Classical Instrumental Music and Narrative." In *A Companion to Narrative Theory,* edited by James Phelan and Peter Rabinowitz, 466–83. Oxford: Blackwell.

Newcomb, Anthony. 1984. "Once More 'Between Absolute and Program Music': Schumann's Second Symphony." *19th-Century Music* 7(3): 233–50.

———. 1987. "Schumann and Late Eighteenth-Century Narrative Strategies." *19th-Century Music* 11(2): 164–74.

Nicholls, David. 2007. "Narrative Theory as an Analytical Tool in the Study of Popular Music." *Music and Letters* 88(2): 297–315.

Pet Shop Boys. 2001. Untitled commentary in compact disk set *Actually/Further Listening 1987–88.* London: EMI.

Schoenberg, Arnold. 1967. *Fundamentals of Musical Composition.* London: Faber and Faber.

Tennant, Neil. 1994. "Honestly." Interview with Paul Burston. *Attitude,* August 10.

13

A Story of Violence: A Guitar Improvisation as a Narrative about Embodied Listening

Vincent Meelberg

Many stories teach us something. Fairy tales educate children about right and wrong, good and bad, safe and unsafe. Adults, too, can learn a great many things from stories. Narratives such as those written by Chaucer, Goethe, and Sophocles – the so-called Great Books (Beha 2009) – have, most would agree, immense educational value. Of course, many would also agree that stories, from children's myths to canonical works of literary fiction, can also be used to control, coerce, and do immense harm to individuals and societies. Can musical stories do the same? Since, in contrast to verbal language, music cannot be explicitly referential, it may seem highly improbable that musical narratives can convey a specific message, let alone teach the listener a valuable lesson. Music might be expressive, but that does not mean it will be able to educate the listener for good or for ill.

Still, I believe that musical narratives can teach us something. As I have suggested elsewhere (Meelberg 2006), some musical narratives have the ability to teach us about listening and musical comprehension. Contemporary non-tonal musical narratives, in particular, can make explicit certain features that are characteristic of musical listening. More specifically, many of these narratives can be considered meta-narratives: they tell the story of the process of narrativization. They are stories about the principles of narrativity, stories that can teach the listener what musical narrativity might be.

In this essay, however, I will discuss a musical narrative that teaches another kind of lesson about listening. More specifically, I will argue that Kevin Eubanks's guitar improvisation in his piece called "Nemesis" can be considered a narrative that foregrounds the fact that listening is embodied and that the embodied nature of listening can often be violent. Moreover, I will maintain that this narrative is indicative of the increasing importance of the trope of violence in post-1900 music. Although, as I will suggest in this essay, music and listening have always had a violent aspect, music from the twentieth century onward progressively emphasizes this characteristic. By making use of dissonance, noise, vocal and instrumental abuses, or wild, agitated rhythms, this music can be considered violent, either because it represents violence or because it actually acts violently on the listener. I will contend that Eubanks's improvisation in "Nemesis" can be interpreted as one such violent sonic act.

First, I will explore the potentialities Eubanks's improvisation has to affect the listener's body. According to theorists such as David Huron (2006) and Marc Leman (2008), listening is always also a bodily experience. Sound does something with the listener's body, and it does this in such a way that it bypasses her conscious awareness. Consequently, music acts on, and violates, the autonomy of the listener's body. This violation is caused by what I call *sonic strokes* (Meelberg 2008, 2009). Sonic strokes are responsible for the preconscious physical arousal of the listener. Exploring the affective potentialities of Eubanks's improvisation necessitates examining the possible sonic strokes in this music.

Next, I will propose that Eubanks's improvisation consists of sonic strokes that gradually increase in intensity and together constitute a temporal development. This means that the music, at least in part, complies with Mieke Bal's (1997) definition of narrative as a representation of a temporal development mapping a succession of events that can be logically or chronologically related. However, sonic strokes are not, in and of themselves, representations. Instead, sonic strokes provoke the listener's body to do something with the sensations caused by these strokes: to enframe the strokes with meaning as gestures and then perhaps to narrativize those gestures as a meaningful temporal succession. The body is motivated kinesthetically to sense the movement of the sounds that caused the arousal and then to enframe that gesture in order to make it meaningful. This enframed, meaningful movement can be called a musical gesture. By regarding a sonic movement as meaningful, one hears it as representation: a gestural sign that stands for the meaning the listener has attributed to the movement. Consequently, I will suggest that in Eubanks's improvisation the actual narrative, the representation of a temporal development, is created by the succession of musical gestures derived from the sonic strokes that caused the initial violation of the listener's bodily autonomy. I will put forward the thesis that this succession of musical gestures can be regarded as a representation that teaches the listener about musical violence. Finally, I will contend that the focus on embodiment and especially violence in this music is indicative of one of the directions in which modernist and postmodern musical aesthetics have evolved.

LISTENING AS BODILY AFFECTION

Almost immediately after listening to the first notes of Kevin Eubanks's improvisation in "Nemesis" (with Steve Coleman on alto saxophone, Dave Holland on double bass, and Kevin "Smitty" Smith on drums, as released in 1989 on *Extensions* by ECM Records, ECM 1410), I can feel their effect on my body. Listening to this music is an electrifying experience for me. The sounds produced in this improvisation affect me in a profound way. The energy of his playing evokes a feeling of excitement: it almost literally fills me with energy. I cannot sit still; I have to move along with the music. I feel as if the music has taken control of my body.

The initial impact of this music is a result not so much of what it represents or means but of how it affects me. First and foremost, I am enjoying the physical reactions the music elicits. Only later might I reflect on the possible musical contents, which can provide additional pleasure. According to Germán Toro-Pérez, this is a general trend in contemporary music. He observes that, during the course of the twentieth century, music underwent a change from an aesthetic of expression to an aesthetic of experience (Toro-Pérez 2010: 34). Moreover, Toro-Pérez asserts that "composition is no longer primarily a matter of bringing something to expression, of revealing something, but rather of opening up opportunities for the experience of sound" (35). This implies that contemporary music in general can be considered as primarily evoking a visceral and bodily, rather than a contemplative and mental, reaction. In the case of contemporary art music, at the very least, this may seem paradoxical, since this kind of music is often stereotyped as one that needs to be approached in a rational manner. On the other hand, even a composer such as Pierre Boulez insists that his music should be regarded primarily as non-representational and immediate.[1]

This focus on immediacy and embodiment is in line with recent findings in cognitive research that confirm the importance of the body in perception. "When interacting with the real world," Rolf Pfeifer and Josh Bongard remark, "the body is stimulated in very particular ways, and this simulation provides, in a sense, the raw material for the brain to work with" (2007: 2). Perception, the manner in which a body comes into contact with the outside world, supplies the perceiving subject with the elements that subsequently can be turned into a genuine percept. According to Pfeifer and Bongard, the activity in which these elements are turned into a percept, which they call *categorization*, is an elementary capacity of the mind. Yet this categorization is determined by embodiment. The morphology and the material properties of a perceiving subject's body determine the formation of categories. In other words, the body regulates the manner in which a subject makes distinctions in the world.

Furthermore, Pfeifer and Bongard remark that human subjects have so-called mirror neurons that fire when a subject performs a movement or observes a movement in another subject. Performing actions and observing actions activate the same brain areas (Pfeifer and Bongard 2007: 191). Thus, watching movement can lead to sensing this movement within the subject's own body, as if the subject is actually performing this movement. This is also the case in the perception of music, as the listener's body is involved in acts of musical listening. The body is literally moved by musical sounds because it kinesthetically senses the movements produced by the music. It feels the music by sensing its dynamic and temporal flow. The body mirrors the musical movement (Overy and Molnar-Szakacs 2009). This is corroborated by Leman (2008), who argues that musical sounds literally do something with the listener's body. The body kinesthetically senses, and subsequently processes, the dynamics, that is, the physical properties of music. The body moves kinesthetically with the flow of musical sounds.

Musical sounds can be highly successful in inducing kinesthetic movement in the observer's body. Synchronization of movement with, say, purely visual rhythm is rare, whereas synchrony with auditory rhythm is far more common. According to Leman, this suggests that there is a particular effect of sound energy on the human motor system. The effect is clearly observable in the tendency to tap along with the beat of the music, which is often done unconsciously (Leman 2008: 112): the beat is the most natural feature for synchronized movement because it appeals to fundamental biomechanical resonances (see also Thaut 2005: 8). Sounds and music can therefore create autonomous reactions of the body by addressing core biological functions. This means that the listener's initial reaction to music is pre-personal, autonomous, and without signification (Huron 2006). Musical sounds can induce a bodily reaction that happens at an unconscious level. I call sounds that elicit such responses *sonic strokes*. Sonic strokes are acoustic phenomena that have an impact on the listener's body. Put differently, a sonic stroke is a sound that produces affect.[2]

According to Gilles Deleuze (2003), affect has no meaning, no signification. It is unqualified emotion. However, it is also bodily, as Brian Massumi (2002) stresses. Affect is energy, resonation, and movement within the body. It is an impetus to thought, to interpretation. Affect motivates the body kinesthetically to sense the entity that produces the affect, thereby inducing motivation to enframe the movement. This interpretation leads to meaning. As soon as there is meaning, affect vanishes. When this occurs, Massumi explains, affect has changed into emotion, which is a subjective content or a *qualified* affect, that is, an intensity that is transformed into "narrativizable action-reaction circuits, into function and meaning" (2002: 28). Affect is pre-personal and meaningless, while emotion is personal, subjective, and meaningful, even though both are bodily phenomena.

According to Deleuze, these bodily changes, these affects, can be so overwhelming that they can actually be called violent (2003: 39). At the same time, affection takes place without the listener having control over it. Sonic strokes do something with the listener, and they do this in a way that bypasses her conscious awareness. Musical affection is thus involuntary and inescapable (Huron 2006: 34). This means that sonic strokes, which induce musical affection, infringe upon the listener's bodily autonomy and therefore do violence to her. In order to further explore the nature of such violent acts, and the possible stories they might yield, it is necessary to examine the manner in which affect is framed.

EXPLORING SONIC STROKES

Since sonic strokes are sounds that affect and do violence to the listener's body, a possible conceptualization of musical narrative is one in which these strokes play a starring role. To an extent, sonic strokes resemble marked musical events. Markedness, Robert Hatten explains, is a theoretical concept that "can be defined quite simply as the valuation given to difference" (1994: 34). Sonic strokes, too, depend on difference. Sonic strokes differ from other sounds in the sense that they affect the listener, as opposed to other sounds that do not have this effect. Both marked events and sonic strokes stand out.

There is, however, an important difference between marked musical events and sonic strokes. Hatten asserts that a marked term has a narrower range of meaning than an unmarked term. A marked term thus has some kind of meaning that is attributed by the listener, a meaning that is in some way more specific, or more pronounced, than that of an unmarked term. A sonic stroke, on the other hand, is meaningless. A sonic stroke is a sound that has an impact on the listener's body. It acts on that body's autonomy and is a motivation that can stimulate interpretation and signification, but the stroke itself has no determinate meaning. A sonic stroke is nothing but an impetus to thinking and reflection. It motivates the listener to reflect on the acoustical phenomenon being confronted.[3]

More specifically, sonic strokes mark gestures in the music. According to Hatten (2004), a musical gesture is a temporal unfolding of a succession of sounds that may be interpreted as significant. Leman adds that the expressiveness of a musical gesture is produced by the body, which, through the firing of mirror neurons, kinesthetically senses the musical gesture and determines the completeness of the gesture (2008: 130–31). In this way the body enframes sound: it gives sonic strokes a reference by interpreting them as constituting a musical gesture. This turns the sounds into an impure, subjective experience of which the exact meaning, as Leman remarks, often remains undefined. As a result, the body is responsible for the listener's ability to structure the music: the body divides the continuous stream of sounds into discrete units, namely, musical gestures. These units can subsequently be related to each other, which results in the listener's creative actualization of a musical structure.

Since sonic strokes are meaningless and cannot be framed, the question arises of how to study these acoustic phenomena. The study of musical affect gives an indication as to how productively to discuss sonic strokes in actual musical works. Studies have been done that attempted to predict musical affect and thus, by extension, sonic strokes (see, e.g., Leman et al. 2005), but these were not entirely successful. Because no clear conceptual distinction between affect and emotion was made, the study was actually about emotion and not about affect. This was implicitly acknowledged in the study itself: since respondents needed to communicate about their musical experiences, the objects of investigation were not only bodily arousal – which, following Deleuze and Massumi, can be called affect – but rather bodily arousal plus cognitive reflection on this arousal, that is, emotion. Just as the occurrence of emotions is an indication of affect (since emotions are a consequence of affect), musical gestures are a result of sonic strokes. Therefore, I propose that sonic strokes can be explored by focusing on musical gestures, the succession of which through time, in turn, can encourage interpretation as a narrative structure. I will focus on musical gestures in my discussion of Kevin Eubanks's improvisation in "Nemesis."

THE SONIC STROKES OF "NEMESIS"

"Nemesis" is a composition in which sections with an $\frac{11}{4}$ time signature periodically alternate with sections in $\frac{4}{4}$ time. The $\frac{11}{4}$ sections are modal (G Phrygian), whereas the $\frac{4}{4}$ sections feature a series of chord changes. Timbre is an important musical parameter in Eubanks's improvisation in this piece, which starts at 5:49 into the composition and lasts until 8:54. Distortion, in particular, gives the solo its distinct shape and structure. By manipulating the volume of the guitar, the amount and intensity of distortion are controlled, which implies that dynamics are an important structuring parameter too. This results in an alteration of sounds that may, at one moment, have an aggressive quality, such as the distorted chord consisting of major seconds and perfect fourths heard at 7:06, 7:20, 7:34, 7:44, 8:36, and 8:54; at other moments, ethereal sounds are faded in. At the beginning of the improvisation, for instance, sounds of this second type are heard when the guitar twice imitates the final, pitch-bent note of the alto saxophone improvisation that precedes the guitar solo.

This sequence of faded in, pitch-bent notes, alongside the distorted chord, can be considered musical gestures, and both have a structuring function. The notes at the beginning of the improvisation connect the guitar solo to the alto saxophone solo, while the chord returns to punctuate different points in the music, indicating closure or musical commas. However, these chords are not always identical in timbre and volume. The final two occurrences, in particular, sound different. The one at 8:36 is faded in, as opposed to the previous occurrences, where the chord has a sharper, more percussive attack. This is noteworthy, in part, because the chord at 8:36 can be regarded as the climax of the improvisation.

The beginning of the improvisation, after the guitar has imitated the final note of the alto saxophone, is fragmentary and incoherent. It consists of staccato motifs, long rests, and muddy, unclear, descending lines. The first time the distorted chord appears (at 7:06) it feels like a comma, since the improvisation continues with incoherent phrases that sound even more frenetic and nervous. At 7:20 the distorted chord sounds again, directly followed by a paraphrase of the *ostinato* bass line, which is played by the double bass throughout the $\frac{11}{4}$ sections. This paraphrase develops into an ascending line that is on the verge of feedback. At 7:34 and 7:44 the distorted chord is played, as if to underline the upcoming change at 8:09, when the chord changes are played. Up until that moment, the guitar again plays paraphrases of the *ostinato* bass line and a repeating motif.

Preparations are now made for the musical climax. Starting on 8:09, the section in $\frac{4}{4}$ time with chord changes begins, with the guitar playing a semi-walking bass line that evolves into eight-note phrases that are faded in. This is followed by feedbacked notes that are almost played *rubato*. At 8:24 a repeating arpeggio is played, one that is on the verge of feedback. This repetition creates a buildup of tension, a feeling that is underlined by the repeating ascending motif that starts at 8:29. This tension is finally resolved at 8:36 by the distorted chord that is faded in. Because this chord is faded in, it evokes a feeling of repressed energy. Instead of ending the phrase on the loud chord that the listener may have been led to expect by the building tension, the reverse is audible. The chord resembles a whisper that screams or, perhaps more accurately, a whispered scream. After this climax, the $\frac{11}{4}$ modal section is played again, the guitar adding the *ostinato* bass line that is characteristic of this section and the composition as a whole. Next, a descending line leading toward the tonic G is played with a feedbacked, howling sound, underlining the feeling that the improvisation is about to end. The actual ending is again the same distorted chord, now played softly.

The most important sonic strokes in this improvisation are those that enable the sensation, and thus potentially the recognition, of the distorted chord that is repeatedly, and in different guises, played throughout the music. The chords always have an element of surprise, either because they appear at an unexpected moment or because they have a timbral quality that seems out of place at that point in the music. According to Huron, these kinds of musical surprises act at an unconscious level, causing autonomous reactions of the listener's body (2006: 269). The sounds that cause the sensation of these chords act violently toward both the listener and the musical continuity. At the same time, these violent sounds help the listener to create a sense of the structure of the music, because the chords made up by these sounds, these sonic strokes, act as closures and commas as well as the climax and final musical event of the improvisation. The surprises induced by the chords' sonic strokes incite the listener to interpret them structurally.

The improvisation's sonic strokes also constitute a temporal development. Tension and resolution are produced by the fading in of notes and phrases, acting as mini-*crescendos* that create suspense, as well as the particular use of distortion, in which relatively clean notes alternate with heavily distorted ones. This interplay of tension and resolution results in a temporal development starting from relative softness and heading toward distortion. The distorted chord frequently interrupts the interplay, and eventually this chord becomes the climax of the music. Yet this climax is at the same time an anticlimax, since the expected eruption of energy does not arrive. Instead, a restrained – almost frustrated – version of the chord is played.

NARRATING THE VIOLENCE OF EMBODIED LISTENING

The fact that Eubanks's improvisation can be regarded as a temporal development does not automatically make it a narrative. In order for an object to be narrative, it should be a representation of a temporal development: a representation of a succession of events that are in some way logically and chronologically related (Bal 1997). Therefore, a narrative cannot consist of sonic strokes alone, for sonic strokes are not representations. Instead, in Eubanks's improvisation, the actual narrative is composed of a succession of musical gestures – the enframed, meaningful, musical movements – derived from the sonic strokes that caused the initial violation of the listener's bodily autonomy. The resulting interplay of tension and resolution is what amounts to a temporal development: a succession of musical gestures that can be regarded as a narrative about the violence that is induced by the sonic strokes in the music. This narrative is an explication of what musical violence might entail. The musical gestures that make up the narrative foreground the often violent corporeality of listening, that is, the violence created by the violation of the listener's bodily autonomy. All music violates this autonomy to a certain extent, but the Eubanks improvisation is an example of one of the many forms of contemporary music that make this aspect of music more explicit.

Twentieth-century music and art progressively thematized violence. The Italian futurists proclaimed in their 1909 founding manifesto that art needs to be violent in order to be original and innovative and that art can be nothing but violence, cruelty, and injustice (Bowler 1991: 763). Many artists in the twentieth and twenty-first centuries adapted versions of this idea. The futurists, the Dadaist movement, many forms of performance art, cinema, Igor Stravinsky's *Le sacre du printemps* (1913), the music of Edgar Varèse, Krzysztof Penderecki's *Threnody to the Victims of Hiroshima* (1960), Steve Reich's *Come Out* (1966), and examples of musical genres such as rock, hip-hop, free jazz, and electronic music – all have explicitly violent aspects (Goodman 2010; Johnson and Cloonan 2008). Eubanks's guitar improvisation is another example of such music. It is also an example of musical narrativity. Although it is beyond the scope of this essay to discuss the meanings of violence in recent music, it nevertheless seems pertinent to explore the possible stories this particular narrative of violence might tell and what we can learn from them.

In this improvisation, musical violence is expressed through distortion and, more specifically, through the distorted chord that acts as the main musical gesture in the music. Distortion is in itself already a figure of violence: it is literally the disfiguring of a purer tone. And distortion, or at least the kind employed by Eubanks, has a tactile quality. Listening to distortion is thus, at the same time, a haptic sensation comparable to, say, the physical effect that the sound of nails scratching on a blackboard can have on a perceiver. Particularly when it concerns the distorted chord, the listener of "Nemesis" cannot but undergo the sensations and the reactions this sound elicits. Her autonomy is infringed by the violence of the haptic sensation and the element of surprise invoked by the recurrent appearance of the distorted chord. In "Nemesis," a temporal development is constituted from mild toward severe affection, caused by the gradually intensifying use of distortion and the increasingly unexpected occurrences of the chord.

The main musical parameters that constitute the particular character of this chord are timbre (which gives the chord its distorted quality), dynamics (which control the intensity of the distortion), and texture (which determines the density of the chord and enables the distinction between it and the monodic musical phrases). Timbre and dynamics are also the main parameters that I characterized above as being responsible for the sonic strokes in this music. As these three parameters foreground the physical aspect of musical listening in relation to this piece, it is not surprising that they also act as the main musical actors in the narrative about musical violence constituted by this music. An actor in a narrative is an agent that causes or experiences events. A musical actor, therefore, can be the musical parameter or parameters that create or undergo musical events or gestures (Meelberg 2006: 83), in this case, timbre, dynamics, and texture. These actors feature in Eubanks's musical narrative, that is, the representation of a temporal development constituted by musical gestures, which tells a story about the potentialities the music has to violate the listener's bodily autonomy.

Apart from this musical narrative, "Nemesis" is capable of establishing at least one other kind of story. This narrative is created by the listener's interpretation of her succession of actual physical reactions while listening to the music. As Richard Menary explains, human subjects tend to turn embodied, physical experiences into a narrative: "Narratives arise directly from the lived experience of the embodied subject and these narratives can be embellished and reflected upon if we need to find a meaningful form or structure in that sequence of experiences" (2008: 76). So "Nemesis" also provokes an embodied narrative – a narrative that is constructed via the interpretation of bodily experiences. These musical and embodied narratives are closely related. The musical narrative told by "Nemesis" can be regarded as the cause of the embodied narrative. It is an account of the possible ways the music addresses the listener's body, whereas the embodied narrative is a story constructed around the actual bodily affections "Nemesis" elicited.

What might that musical narrative have to tell us, then, about our experiences of musical violence? For one thing, it can teach us about the importance of violence when it concerns musical pleasure. As Reinhold Friedl (2002) explains, tension, including musical tension, always includes a kind of "pain" and thus can be considered an act of violence. At the same time, tension is felt as pleasure, as long as there is the promise of resolution. There can be no joy without pain, no pleasure without violence. This is what the sonic strokes in "Nemesis" exemplify: that musical pleasure has a definite sadomasochistic quality, comparable to the process of catharsis, of undergoing suffering until a form of resolution or cleansing has been achieved. Without the distorted chords, and the way in which they are arranged in the musical narrative, there would not have been such powerful disturbances and tensions in the unfolding of this piece. At the same time, these disturbances constitute the haptic and pleasurable sensations the narrative can elicit exactly because they are disturbances – and thus violations of the musical logic *and* of the listener's bodily autonomy – that eventually will be resolved in one way or another. In this way, they create musical tension that can be pleasurable, albeit in a sadomasochistic way. The guitar improvisation in "Nemesis" – a musical narrative that ends with a whispered scream – teaches us that always getting exactly what we expect cannot yield musical pleasure. Musical pleasure can be attained only when a certain measure of violence and pain has been experienced.

This is just one of many possible interpretations of the narrative told by "Nemesis." Like all musical narratives, its expressive potential bears many stories, contains truths, confirms none of them. And although both musical and embodied narratives can be intersubjective, in the sense that their stories can be shared verbally, even these accounts are necessarily partial and fallible. The embodied narrative is literally subjective: it is a personal account of the way the music has actually affected and violated the autonomy of a particular listener. The analysis recounted above explores the extent to which listening to Eubanks's improvisation in "Nemesis" felt violent to me and considers ways in which the musical narrative constituted by that improvisation could teach listeners about the potential violence of the music, and the narrative potential of violence.

NOTES

1. In the documentary *Sur incises – a Lesson by Pierre Boulez* (in Scheffer and Sommer 2006), for instance, Boulez stresses the importance of the physical, intuitive aspect of experiencing his music.

2. See Meelberg (2008) for a more detailed discussion of sonic strokes.

3. See Meelberg (2009) for an elaboration of the distinction between sonic strokes and musical gestures.

WORKS CITED

Bal, Mieke. 1997. *Narratology: Introduction to the Theory of Narrative*. 2nd ed. Toronto: University of Toronto Press.

Beha, Christopher R. 2009. *The Whole Five Feet: What the Great Books Taught Me about Life, Death, and Pretty Much Everything Else*. New York: Grove.

Bowler, Anne. 1991. "Politics as Art: Italian Futurism and Fascism." *Theory and Society* 20: 763–94.

Deleuze, Gilles. 2003. *Francis Bacon: The Logic of Sensation*. Translated by Daniel W. Smith. London: Continuum.

Friedl, Reinhold. 2002. "Some Sadomasochistic Aspects of Musical Pleasure." *Leonardo Music Journal* 12: 29–30.

Goodman, Steve. 2010. *Sonic Warfare: Sound, Affect, and the Ecology of Fear*. Cambridge: MIT Press.

Hatten, Robert S. 1994. *Musical Meaning in Beethoven: Markedness, Correlation, and Interpretation*. Bloomington: Indiana University Press.

———. 2004. *Interpreting Musical Gestures, Topics, and Tropes: Mozart, Beethoven, Schubert*. Bloomington: Indiana University Press.

Huron, David. 2006. *Sweet Anticipation: Music and the Psychology of Expectation*. Cambridge: MIT Press.

Johnson, Bruce, and Martin Cloonan. 2008. *Dark Side of the Tune: Popular Music and Violence*. Aldershot: Ashgate.

Leman, Marc. 2008. *Embodied Music Cognition and Mediation Technology*. Cambridge: MIT Press.

Leman, Marc, Valery Vermeulen, Liesbeth de Voogdt, Dirk Moelants, and Micheline Lesaffre. 2005. "Prediction of Musical Affect Using a Combination of Acoustic Structural Cues." *Journal of New Music Research* 34: 39–67.

Massumi, Brian. 2002. *Parables for the Virtual: Movement, Affect, Sensation.* Durham: Duke University Press.

Meelberg, Vincent. 2006. *New Sounds, New Stories: Narrativity in Contemporary Music.* Leiden: Leiden University Press.

———. 2008. "Touched by Music: The Sonic Strokes of *Sur Incises.*" In *Sonic Mediations: Body, Sound, Technology,* edited by Anthony Enns and Carolyn Birdsall, 61–76. Newcastle: Cambridge Scholars Publishing.

———. 2009. "Sonic Strokes and Musical Gestures: The Difference between Musical Affect and Musical Emotion." In *Proceedings of the 7th Triennial Conference of the European Society for the Cognitive Sciences of Music (ESCOM),* edited by Jukka Louhivuori, Tuomas Eerola, Suvi Saarikallio, Tommi Himberg, and Päivi-Sisko Eerola, 324–27. Jyväskylä: University of Jyväskylä.

Menary, Richard. 2008. "Embodied Narratives." *Journal of Consciousness Studies* 15: 63–84.

Overy, Katie, and Istvan Molnar-Szakacs. 2009. "Being Together in Time: Musical Experience and the Mirror Neuron System." *Music Perception* 26: 489–504.

Pfeifer, Rolf, and Josh Bongard. 2007. *How the Body Shapes the Way We Think: A New View of Intelligence.* Cambridge: MIT Press.

Scheffer, Paul, and Andy Sommer. 2006. *Pierre Boulez: Éclat, Sur incises.* DVD. Nieuw Ensemble, Ed Spanjaard and Ensemble Intercontemporain, and Pierre Boulez. Paris: Idéale Audience.

Thaut, Michael H. 2005. *Rhythm, Music, and the Brain: Scientific Foundations and Clinical Applications.* London: Routledge.

Toro-Pérez, Germán. 2010. "On the Difference between Artistic Research and Artistic Practice." In *Art and Artistic Research,* edited by Corina Caduff, Fiona Siegenthaler, and Tan Wälchli, 30–39. Zurich: Scheidegger und Spiess.

14

Ives and the Now

Matthew McDonald

At the conclusion of his 1927 essay "Photography," a critique of the photographic medium and its purchase on fidelity and truthfulness, Sigfried Kracauer asserted the potential of film to invest photographic images with a contextual meaning they lack: "If the disarray of the illustrated newspapers is simply confusion, the game that film plays with the pieces of disjointed nature is reminiscent of *dreams* in which the fragments of daily life become jumbled. This game indicates that the valid organization of things is not known" (1993: 436). According to Kracauer, isolated photographs lack context and hence significance. Film can remedy the situation not simply by setting photographic images in motion (i.e., by restoring their temporal context) but by "fragmenting" and "jumbling" the moving images – in other words, by editing shots into a narrative. The model for film editing, Kracauer implies, is memory, where images are retained and arranged according to their significance and meaning. That the "valid organization" of these images is indeterminate is to be regarded positively: truth is found not via faithful technological reconstructions of events from the past but by representing the past as we make sense of it in our minds. Kracauer's essay dates from the end of the silent-film era, when many of the now-familiar conventions of narrative cinema had already been codified. These conventions generally service the illusion that films represent real life. Kracauer seems to suggest, however, that at a fundamental level films represent not life so much as our *recollections* of life and that the organization of shots in films is best understood in terms of indeterminate psychological processes or cognitive structures.

The notion of memory and film as sites where "the fragments of daily life become jumbled" is useful for conceptualizing Charles Ives's music, another such site. The subject of memory and the techniques of fragmentation and collage are well-known features of Ives's music, which he wrote during the same years that film was emerging as an artistic medium. For these and other reasons, the cinema provides one of the most useful models for understanding the organization of Ives's fragmented musical textures and their meanings. In the first part of my essay, I will offer a close interpretive analysis of "The Things Our Fathers Loved," a familiar song and a concise and provocative example of how Ives used fragmentation to represent memory (the complete song is reproduced at the end of this essay; see Example 14.4). Ives's song is fundamentally about bringing the past to life in the present moment, an imperative that is inherently modernist and is shared with the cinema, where the dead images of photography are animated in front of the spectator. Thus, in the second part of my essay, I will consider my analysis in the context of modernist ideas about time and temporality, particularly as these ideas were shaped and reflected by the cinema. In so doing, I hope to shed light on the oft-cited problem of how to reconcile Ives's decidedly modernist compositional techniques with his defiantly anti-modernist worldview.

"THE THINGS OUR FATHERS LOVED": TWO ANALYSES

"The Things Our Fathers Loved," completed in 1917, has been frequently discussed in scholarly literature on Ives (see Burkholder 1995: 306–11; Feder 1990: 249–66; Hepokoski 1994; Metzer 2003: 25–27; Morgan 1997; and Starr 1992: 57–67).[1] Often cited as exemplary of the composer's style, it highlights numerous definitive characteristics, all in a mere twenty-two measures: borrowing, attenuated tonality, fragmentation, open-endedness, and the subject of memory. Ives himself (perhaps with some help from his wife, Harmony) wrote the text, further distinguishing the song as quintessentially Ivesian. The vocal persona begins with a reflection: "I think there must be a place in the soul all made of tunes, of tunes of long ago." A string of four memory fragments follows, each but the third identified as an *aural* memory and distinguished as such by the presence of at least one borrowed tune. The text and music together give a sense of "being there," of the past materializing before us:

I hear the organ on the Main Street corner,
Aunt Sarah humming Gospels;
Summer evenings,
The village cornet band, playing in the square.
The town's Red, White and Blue, all Red, White and Blue.

Finally, amidst a whirlwind of musical activity, the persona returns from these daydreams to the reflective mode of the song's opening, her emphatic words undermined somewhat by a musical ending that is distinctly open and questioning: "Now! Hear the songs! I know not what are the words / But they sing in my soul of the things our Fathers loved."[2]

As in many of Ives's works, the text clearly refers to a real-world situation, a person engaged in recollection and contemplation. But the temporal status of the situation is fundamentally ambiguous: Does the text simply refer to a chronological series of events (a reflection followed by a series of memories followed by another reflection), or does it jump back and forth in time between the present of the persona's reflections and the past to which they refer? Any attempt to resolve this ambiguity would diminish rather than enhance our understanding of the song; instead, I will point to musical features that support each interpretation, offering first a linear hearing of the music and the events it represents and then a non-linear hearing. In semiotic terms, each hearing weaves together accounts of the "temporality of the signifier" and the "temporality of the signified" (Monelle 2000: 83). A "temporally polyphonic" hearing (as Steven Rings [2008: 202] has recently dubbed it) will ultimately emerge, where the linear and non-linear hearings are allowed to coexist. Whereas the linear hearing will have some conceptual similarities with previous studies of this song, the non-linear hearing will offer an entirely new analytic entry point and means of addressing the song's potential meanings.

1. Linear Hearing

Ives's musical setting depicts the persona's shift into memory with a high degree of subtlety. C major is often an emblem of truth in Ives's music, and the bald C-major triad of m. 1 prepares the opening lyric as a statement of utmost sincerity while additionally (and more importantly) providing an initial glimpse of "the soul" and the idealized images of the past within it. This clarity is maintained in the vocal line and the accompaniment of the piano's left hand in mm. 2–3 (I–IV in C major) but slightly eroded by the melodic echoes of the piano's right hand, whose transpositions of the vocal line up a major third gesture toward the whole-tone collection and its characteristic lack of tonal focus: the daydream is beginning. The right hand's countermelodies gently pull upward at their diatonic equivalents (G–F–E, C–B♭–A), and the C♯ of m. 3 in particular instigates a more decisive tonal shift in m. 4, as the F-major triad of m. 3 proceeds to F♯ major in m. 4. The effect is of a harmonic slide (not to be confused with the neo-Riemannian "slide relation"), with parallel semitonal voice leading in the piano's left hand and motion from A to B♭ in the voice; furthermore, the vocal line of mm. 3–4 paraphrases Stephen Foster's "My Old Kentucky Home" in F major, but with the final two pitches (D♯–C♯) shifted one semitone too high (Burkholder 1995: 307). The F♯ chord (functioning as its enharmonic equivalent, G♭) leads to an E♭ dominant ninth chord in mm. 4–5, the latter poised to progress to A♭ as an applied dominant and thereby to chromaticize a stepwise ascent from the F♯ harmony of m. 4. But rather than an A♭ chord, an A-minor eleventh chord arrives in m. 6, a second disorienting harmonic event.

In sum, mm. 1–6 feature two upward, semitonal harmonic shifts: the F-major triad of m. 3 slides to F♯ in m. 4, and the normative resolution of the E♭ dominant to A♭ is displaced to A in m. 6. The overall effect is of a gradual shifting of consciousness, from reflection in the present to reflection on the past: the persona is drifting into a dream.[3] This effect is enhanced by an ongoing sense of harmonic blurriness, generated first by the countermelodies of mm. 2–3 and then by the overlap between the F♯ and E♭ harmonies beginning at m. 4.2.[4] The semitonal shifts of mm. 4 and 6 can be understood to disrupt the normative progression C–F–D⁷–G: F and D⁷ are displaced by one semitone (mm. 4–5) and G by two (m. 6). This progression would have confirmed C major as a tonal center, a key that evaporates completely from the song after the opening measures. The second half of this progression (D⁷–G) is obscured by the harmonic shifts in mm. 4–6, and the subsequent measures are fixated on this loss and all it represents – namely, the tonal path back to C major and the "place in the soul" it signifies. The melodic motive G–D dominates mm. 6–9, grafted over the A-minor and F-major harmonies of these measures – another example of harmonic blurriness that contributes to the dreamlike quality of this portion of the song. The motive appears first in the piano's right hand of m. 6, an anticipation of the vocal line in m. 7, the apparent source of the motive: a fragment of the tune "On the Banks of the Wabash" borrowed by the voice in mm. 6–7 (see Burkholder 1995: 307–10 for a convenient overview of borrowed tunes in the song). The motive lingers in mm. 8–9, modifying the voice's brief reference to the tune "Nettleton," which properly would end G–G, not G–D. The attempt to regain the tonal motion D⁷–G, as we shall see, is greatly intensified later in the song.

The upward harmonic shifts of mm. 4 and 6 are balanced by reciprocal semitonal shifts *downward* corresponding to the vocal persona's emergence out of memory in mm. 14–15. First, the F-major tonality of mm. 11–13 abruptly gives way to an E dominant on the downbeat of m. 14. The proper resolution of this dominant to A major is delayed until m. 14.3. In turn, this A-major triad progresses to the D dominant of m. 15; thus, a "middleground" descending-fifths progression, E⁷–A–D⁷, lends coherence to the relatively chaotic harmonic activity of mm. 14–15 and provides momentum toward the desired (but ultimately unrealized) resolution of the D dominant to G major. Yet, coexisting with these elements of harmonic continuity is an unmistakable harmonic breach at the downbeat of m. 15. The A-major triad of m. 14.3 does not lead directly to the D⁷ of m. 15 but first initiates an octatonic sequence, consisting of a descending octatonic bass (A–G–G♭–F♭), with every other note functioning as the root of a major triad (A major, G♭ major; these triads ascend in the right hand). The next chord in the sequence would be an E♭-major triad in root position, as opposed to the D⁷ that arrives on the downbeat of m. 15. The sense of disjunction here is compounded by the vocal line, which, after a stepwise ascent spanning a minor sixth in m. 14, jumps from B♭ to D, the vocal apex of the song (aside from ornamental D♯s in mm. 4 and 5).

Thus, the shift into memory at the beginning of the song, evoked by two upward semitonal shifts, is reversed later in the song by two downward semitonal shifts. The return to the "here and now" in m. 15 is marked by a return to the overriding pitch level of mm. 1–3, while the D dominant lost in m. 5 is regained. This mirroring of departure and return is enhanced by the nature of the two pairs of semitonal shifts. Just as the first pair features a harmonic slide (F to F♯) followed by a harmonic substitution (A for A♭), the second pair likewise features a slide (F to E) followed by a substitution (D for E♭). Tellingly, each pair of shifts commences from F and traverses a diatonic third within F major (F to A, F to D). The overall result is a symmetrical design spanning the song's memory section (mm. 3–15.1). The reciprocal pairs of semitonal shifts frame seven measures that are quasi-symmetrical with respect to tonality, enhancing the overall symmetry: mm. 7–9 and 11–13 are firmly anchored in F major, whereas m. 10 ("Summer evenings") sits ambiguously in the center. Thus, F is not only the point of departure for each pair of harmonic shifts but the central tonal area of the memory section as well.

EXAMPLE 14.1. "The Things Our Fathers Loved,"
displaced connection from m. 5 to m. 15.

2. Non-linear Hearing

The critical moments of entering and leaving the realm of memory, as we have
seen, are the downbeats of m. 6, where the first memory commences ("I hear
the organ on the Main Street corner"), and m. 15, the return to the present,
the "Now." As explained above, each moment features a semitonal harmonic
substitution that arrives with a jolt, as though the tonal surface has shifted.
An alternative hearing, however, is that the music's *temporal* surface shifts
at these moments, that in each case a musical succession has been fractured
and its component parts separated from one another. Examples 14.1 and 14.2
propose these temporally displaced successions. In Example 14.1, m. 5 is juxtaposed with m. 15, showing how the E♭ dominant can be interpreted as a
German sixth chord leading to the D dominant of m. 15. Highlighted in the
example is the standard resolution of the augmented sixth to an octave, articulated by the bass and vocal line; C♯ is the focus of the vocal line in mm. 4–5,
intensifying its need to resolve. The example also highlights the G–F dyad of
the piano's right hand in m. 5, echoed by F♯–E in m. 15, as though grafted on
top of the bass's descending semitone. These associated dyads form part of a
larger textural correspondence that helps bind mm. 5 and 15 together across
the intervening music: in both measures the piano part features sustained
basses, arpeggiated textures in the mid-register, and rhythmically similar
figures in the upper register.

EXAMPLE 14.2. "The Things Our Fathers Loved,"
displaced connection from m. 14 to m. 5.

In Example 14.2, m. 14 is juxtaposed with m. 5, demonstrating how the
E♭ harmony of m. 5 might continue the octatonic sequence initiated at m.
14.3. As shown in the example, my proposed realignment of these measures
is supported by the retention of common tones between the G♭ triad of m. 14
and the E♭ harmony of m. 5 as well as quasi-symmetrical octatonic motions in
the bass and vocal lines within the ambitus A to E♭/D♯, together comprising
a complete octatonic collection. The A to E♭ motion in the bass can be understood as a reversal of the E♭ to A bass motion in mm. 5–6, one that supplies
a harmonic logic missing in these measures. Thus, whereas in mm. 14–15 an
actual progression from A (m. 14.3) to D displaces a motion to E♭, in mm. 5–6
an actual motion from E♭ to A displaces a motion to D: both moments revolve
around the same constellation of three chordal roots.

The initiation of another displaced harmonic progression appears in m.
10 ("Summer evenings"). Although the essential harmonic succession in this
measure, A^7–C_2^4, forms part of a chromaticized progression in F major (I–
III^7–V$_2^4$–I), it is isolated in many ways from the measures that precede and
follow (see, e.g., the awkward voice leading into A^7 and away from C_2^4), and
the succession itself has a similar flavor to the jarring semitonal shifts on
the downbeats of mm. 4 and 14. This quality stems from the semitonal bass
motion (A to B♭), the non-normative resolution of the A dominant, the vocal
leap B to F♯ within an otherwise stepwise line, and the A appoggiatura in the
upper melody of the piano, which disrupts an otherwise chromatic ascent. In
all of these respects, a smoother and more logical continuation is provided

G major: V7/V————————   V7

EXAMPLE 14.3. "The Things Our Fathers Loved,"
displaced connection from m. 10.2 to m. 15.

once again by m. 15 (Example 14.3). In this recomposition, the A dominant
resolves to a D dominant, with strong root motion in the bass and a characteristic resolution of the tritone C♯–G to C–F♯ (see the lower portion of the
piano's right hand). The C♯ octave in m. 10 actually splits, resolving downward
to C in the piano (the seventh of D⁷) and upward to D in the voice (the root);
this dual motion forms a counterpart to the German sixth resolution shown
in Example 14.1, which features chromatic contrary motion *toward* an octave
and the identical C♯–D motion in the voice. Finally, the piano's G♯ in m. 15
can be heard as the goal of the ascending upper piano line of m. 10, concluding
an elaborated E–F♯–G♯ motion, a reversal of the countermelody in m. 2: note
that in both mm. 2 and 15, the presence of G♯ alludes strongly to the "even"
whole-tone collection.[5]

   Thus, the two dominants of m. 10, A⁷ and C♯⁴₂, rather than merely functioning within the F-major context of mm. 7–13, are oriented toward two
different tonal areas: A⁷ pushes toward D⁷ and thus ultimately toward G
major, the unattainable goal of the song's final measures, whereas C♯⁴₂ leads
back to F major, the tonal core of the dream sequence. In other words, the
two dominants initiate opposite trajectories in tonal space, with C major (the
point of departure in mm. 1–2) as the point of equilibrium. G major is one
step on the circle of fifths to the sharp side of C major, whereas F major is
one step to the flat side, and the crucial A and E♭ harmonies are extensions of
these steps: A is three steps to the sharp side, E♭ three steps to the flat side.
The tonal motion A⁷–D⁷–(G) pushes back toward C, whereas the motion C♯⁴₂
–F pushes away from it. These opposite motions in tonal space suggest op-

posite motions in time: A^7 pushes away from the past and toward the present, ultimately approaching the imagined future of G major, whereas C^4_2 pulls the persona back into the past.

These trajectories between past and present provide an interpretive context in which to understand the displaced connections proposed in Examples 14.1–3. The E♭ "German sixth" of m. 5, like the A^7 of m. 10, finds its harmonic fulfillment in the D^7 of m. 15. And thus, whereas in the linear hearing m. 5 is fully subsumed within the drift into memory, in the non-linear hearing it fights against this drift, striving forward in the opposite direction, toward the "Now." The octatonic sequence initiated in m. 14, on the other hand, like the C^4_2 of m. 10, is harmonically oriented toward the memory section, pushing back to the E♭ harmony of m. 5. Once again, my linear and non-linear hearings of m. 14 suggest opposite temporal trajectories: whereas in the linear hearing this measure initiates a decisive return to the present, in the non-linear hearing it pulls the persona back toward psychological absorption in the past. Viewed in tandem, my non-linear hearings of the framing moments of the memory sequence (as modeled in Examples 14.1 and 14.2) effectively bracket off the entire section as a self-enclosed unit that might exist entirely outside of the flow of "real time" experienced by the persona in the present. In one interpretation, the persona's reflections in the present (mm. 1–5 and 15–22) proceed uninterrupted, as implied by the linear connection between mm. 5 and 15, whereas the memories of mm. 6–14 cycle in an endless loop within the persona's soul, as implied by the potential of m. 14 to circle back to m. 5.[6] The A dominants of mm. 10 and 14, as alternative paths of return to m. 15, are portals linking past and present.

The "Now" of m. 15 in this interpretation is a loaded moment: it not only emerges climactically from the *crescendo* and *accelerando* of m. 14 (and is set up harmonically by the A dominant of m. 14.3) but also satisfies the harmonic urges of mm. 5 and 10; each of these measures (mm. 5, 10, and 14) is associated with a different memory or stage in the process of remembering. With all of this musical motion and corresponding psychological activity directed in one place, it is no wonder that the persona seems overwhelmed by memory in mm. 15–20, as the dynamic reaches *fortissimo* and the piano figuration becomes hyperactive. Meanwhile, the recollections of mm. 5–14 spill over into the present moment and pile upon one another: the upper layer of the piano part in mm. 15–18 and 20 (played by the left hand) recalls the piano's reference to "The Battle Cry of Freedom" in mm. 11–13; the rapid figuration in the piano's mid-register emerges as an accelerated variant of the left-hand arpeggios in mm. 5–6; and in m. 18, the voicing of the A-minor ninth chord recalls the harmony of m. 6, which provided a backdrop for the first distinct memory (the organ on the Main Street corner). Simultaneous with all of these memory traces or recollections of recollections, the refrain from the gospel hymn "In the Sweet By-and-By" emerges in the vocal line – yet another tune of long ago but one that is no longer consigned to the realm of memory. This tune from the past is brought to life, surfacing in m. 15 as a port within the emotional storm represented by the piano. The song is an artifact from the past, one of those very songs of which the persona sings ("Now! Hear the songs!"), but it is now fully present *in* the present. Indeed, to bring the past to life in the present may have been the fundamental project of Ives's music, and the persona seems on the verge of success at this moment.

But this is a project that Ives repeatedly exposed as not fully realizable. In "The Things Our Fathers Loved" a negative judgment is rendered by the end of the song, when the voice's quotation of "The Sweet By-and-By," sung in G major and largely faithful to the original, disintegrates just as it should cadence on G (see mm. 21–22). Instead of the hoped-for G-major triad, the song ends on a sustained *pianissimo* chord anchored on D♯, apparently an unconsummated chromatic move back to D initiated by the E-minor harmony of m. 20. The lower dyad of this chord, D♯–A♯, gestures back to the E♭–B♭ dyad of m. 5 (the exact same pitches, enharmonically respelled), whereas the upper three pitch classes, F♯–B♯–G♯, reactivate the whole-tone-tinged dominant of mm. 15–17 (two of these pitch classes, G♯ and C, occur in the same register): in other words, the final chord refers back to the primary portals by which the persona passes between the past and present. But whereas the dominants of mm. 5 and 15–17 are dynamic and forward-directed, the final chord of the song is completely inert, devoid of tonal tension, and therefore devoid of direction or possibility. This final harmony contains exclusively sharped notes (see mm. 21–22), which provide the best indication of how far the music has strayed from the C-major triad of m. 1: the voicing of the lower D♯-minor triad mimics that of the opening C-major triad (inviting the comparison), but the root of D♯ suggests an insurmountable distance on the sharp side of the circle of fifths (specifically, nine steps on the circle, as opposed to the two steps required to travel from the D dominant back to C). The gulf between past and present, nearly overcome in the preceding measures, is ultimately reopened. This regression is reinforced by Ives's invocation of the song's title as its final lyric, the only instance of the past tense in the song. Whereas each memory is sung in the present tense, as though the past has been transported into the present, and the climactic "Now" reinforces this effect dramatically, all of this is undermined by the final chord and the final word.

MODERNISM AND THE PRESENT MOMENT

Whereas the ending is unmistakably Ivesian, the representation of memory in "The Things Our Fathers Loved" and the song's apparent desire to bridge the gap between past and present is best understood as more than an Ivesian concoction: it is a quintessentially modernist formulation that has numerous points of contact with contemporaneous ideas about time, memory, and their representation. For example, the idea that memories exist outside of our lived experience of time evokes Freud's (1955a: 577–78; 1955b: 187) notion of the unconscious as atemporal, a site of permanent storage where memories, rather than fading, retain their original fullness over time.[7] Or the experience of Ives's persona might bring to mind the narrator of Proust's *Remembrance of Things Past* and his *"moments bienheureux,"* in which memories flood the narrator in extended moments triggered by specific non-visual senses.[8] Proust represented such an experience most famously in the madeleine episode from *Swann's Way* (1913), the first volume of *Remembrance*, where the taste of a small cake ultimately unlocks for the narrator numerous visions of his childhood (2006: 63–64), memories similar to those of Ives's persona in "The Things Our Fathers Loved," whose recollections are linked to a particular sense (hearing) and experienced as a single instant of great intensity.[9] Proust's novel is frequently linked to the philosophy of Bergson, and indeed Bergson's notion of *durée* provides a related means of conceptualizing the intermingling of past and present in Ives's song. Bergson described the concept using an often-quoted musical metaphor: "[The ego] forms both the past and the present states into an organic whole, as happens when we recall the notes of a tune, melting, so to speak, into one another" (1910: 100).

Such conceptions of memory and time are relevant to an understanding of Ives's music, part of a much larger constellation of ideas and strategies for making sense of the modern world. In the space remaining, however, I will focus on what I view as an especially enlightening point of contact, the emerging medium of film. The beginning of Ives's compositional career roughly coincided with the arrival of the cinema (Ives was a student at Yale when the Lumière brothers debuted their films in 1895–96), and Ives was maturing as a composer during the first decade of the twentieth century, when film was evolving from a "cinema of attractions," whose primary aim was to "show" images rather than to "tell" stories, into a predominantly narrative medium (see Gunning 1990). The primary technical development that made this evolution possible was the cut: the editing of film strips gave filmmakers access to narrative techniques previously unavailable and largely unimagined in the context of cinema. In my analysis of "The Things Our Fathers Loved," displaced musical successions function in a similar way, signifying jumps forward and backward in time in the manner of filmic montage. And thus it is useful to conceptualize Ives's music in relation to narrative models (a view I have elaborated elsewhere; see McDonald 2004).

This feature of Ives's music is not demonstrably the result of any direct influence of narrative cinema on Ives, as is the case with Debussy (see Leydon 2001), but rather evidence of how early narrative cinema and Ives's music are mutual artistic responses to certain key questions and problems posed by modernity. In her book *The Emergence of Cinematic Time*, the film theorist and historian Mary Ann Doane has argued persuasively that the cinema provides the best means of understanding modernist ideas about temporality. Prominent among these ideas is an obsession with defining and capturing the present moment: "The present . . . acts as a zero or placeholder for something outside of what is perceived as a more and more rigorously ordered social system, organized by technological, industrial, economic, and political determinants – the intricate web of commodity capitalism. . . . The present . . . marks the promise of something other, something outside of systematicity" (Doane 2002: 106). This fixation on the present moment is a feature of the work of Freud, Proust, and Bergson, and Doane demonstrated its centrality in the thought of a wide range of artists and intellectuals, including Charles Baudelaire, Charles Sanders Peirce, Paul Souriau, and many others. Most importantly, Doane traced this modernist preoccupation as it was reflected and shaped by technology, beginning with its roots in photography, continuing through the exercises in chronophotography by Étienne-Jules Marey and related attempts to depict movement via photography, and culminating with the invention and early development of the cinema. In this historical narrative, the arrival of cinema signals a crucial shift in thinking about the present moment. A photograph captures the moment; however, when we view the photograph, this moment seems to be frozen in the past. The cinema, on the other hand, offers a fundamentally different experience: it takes a series of photographic images and creates from them the illusion of motion and presence; it takes events from the past and brings them to life in the here and now. This point of view was rendered concisely by Roland Barthes, who theorized that photographs are perceived as being in the past, the "having-been-there," whereas film is perceived as being in the present, the "being-there" (1977: 44–45; see also Doane 2002: 103).

Implicit in Barthes's categorizations, *motion* is the feature that distinguishes cinema from photography. For Kracauer, as indicated at the beginning of this essay, the key element that differentiates the temporality of these two media was not simply the illusion of movement manufactured by film, however, but film's ability to create narratives via editing, to combine "parts and segments to create strange constructs" (1993: 436; see also Doane 2002: 102–103; Gaudreault 2009: 81–89). For Doane, it was the cinema's very basis in the succession of still images – that is, its basis in photography – that determined the central importance of editing: "The cut is the most exemplary cinematic operation. For the cut is the haunting echo of the frameline – its reiteration at a different level" (2002: 217). And thus, like Kracauer, Doane emphasized the importance of cinematic editing in establishing a distinct temporality: "[Time] becomes something that can be held or possessed in a metaphorical sense. This is why the cut as ellipsis is a crucial figure. Time becomes delimitable, commodifiable, objectlike" (217–18).

This packaging of time into discrete units via editing is, of course, a defining feature of narrative cinema (many have theorized that it is *the* defining feature), the most important means by which films achieve narrative status (see McDonald 2004: 276–77). Among the earliest editing conventions to gain currency was "parallel editing," what Tom Gunning identified as "the key figure of the narrative system"; Gunning placed its origins in the years 1906–1908 (1991: 110, 76–77). Parallel editing involves cutting back and forth between two zones of activity as a means of representing actions that are separated in space but simultaneous in time; to cite a cliché, think of the hero rushing to rescue the heroine tied to the train tracks. Today's film viewer understands the temporal signification of such sequences effortlessly, and thus it is easy to miss the inherent contradiction of the convention: as Doane noted, for parallel editing to function effectively, "succession must be accepted as the signifier of its opposite, simultaneity" (2002: 189). This apparent incongruity no doubt initially confused filmgoers, and indeed the widespread adoption of this and similar editing strategies by filmmakers appears to elude rational explanation. But parallel editing was not an awkward practical solution to a representational problem but an artistic strategy shaped by modernist ideas about temporality: the question of "sequence versus simultaneity," as the cultural historian Stephen Kern has shown (citing parallel editing as one of many examples), was a defining problem of modernity (2003: 68, 70–72).[10] Just as important, however, parallel editing was a means of entertainment. As characterized by Doane, "Parallel editing successfully eroticizes time, injects it with desire, expectation, anticipation, and displaces the spectatorial time of viewing by contributing to the construction of a 'lived,' imaginary temporality" (2002: 193).

All of this provides a helpful context for conceptualizing Ives's treatment of temporal relations in "The Things Our Fathers Loved." As I have suggested, at many points in the song, succession signifies simultaneity: the images of the memory sequence, although they may be understood as part of an ongoing chronological representation of events (as in my linear hearing of the song), also may be understood as occurring in a timeless instant, as though the dotted barline of Example 14.1 has been pulled open to reveal an infinite space (as in my non-linear hearing). Pushing the analogy further, we might identify two cross-cut stories around which the song is organized, one characterized by descending fifths (the "middleground" progression E^7–A–D^7 of mm. 14–15, and the displaced progression A^7–D^7 shown in Example 14.3) and one by descending semitones (the $E\flat^7$–D^7 progression shown in Example 14.1, extended to include the E–D$\sharp$ bass motion in mm. 20–22).[11] Borrowing Doane's words, Ives's splicing of these tonal motions "injects [time] with desire, expectation, anticipation": A^7 and $E\flat^7$ strive toward D^7, but in each case the dominant arrival is delayed; when it does arrive in m. 15, the climactic energy is unmistakable.

But this analogy is limited: the two tonal motions are not clearly differentiated, nor do they "parallel" one another, and while they may come together at the D dominant of m. 15 (hero and heroine united in the same frame), this union is undermined as the G-major resolution slips away in the final bars. Rather than the relentless linear logic and goal achievement that define parallel editing, Ives's musical montage is founded on the free-associational logic of memory or dreaming, a quality Kracauer associated with the cinema and attributed to the possibilities of editing, as we have seen. But whereas parallel editing is too orderly to serve as a conceptual model for Ives's song, Kracauer's notion of "jumbled fragments" is too chaotic: behind Ives's fragments is the suggestion of something continuous, evoked by the sustained "Now" of the song's climax and more subtly by the displaced connection that frames the entire memory sequence ($E\flat^7$–D^7).

There is good reason to assume that this implied continuity amidst chaos was deeply meaningful to Ives, here and in the many other works that evoke a similar condition. In the *Essays before a Sonata*, first published in 1920, Ives wrote:

> There may be an analogy . . . between both the state and power of artistic perceptions and the law of perpetual change, that ever-flowing stream, partly biological, partly cosmic, ever going on in ourselves, in nature, in all life. This may account for the difficulty of identifying desired qualities with the perceptions of them in expressions. Many things are constantly coming into being, while others are constantly going out – one part of the same thing is coming in while another part is going out of existence. (1961: 71)

Ives's image of life as an "ever-flowing stream" is remarkably Bergsonian, although it is no doubt more directly related to the philosophy of Ralph Waldo Emerson, particularly the notion of an "over-soul" uniting all of human existence. (Ives likely borrowed the stream metaphor directly from Emerson; see Emerson 1990: 152–53.) In Ives's music, the image finds its most characteristic musical depiction in the coda of the "Emerson" movement of the *Concord Sonata*. The above quotation also provides a hint of how Ives sought to evoke an idealized experience of the present moment in "The Things Our Fathers Loved": the future "comes in" while the past "goes out," and they commingle in the present – in this case, over a prolonged dominant that never resolves.

Ives's song seeks desperately to hold on to the present moment, and so, as I have suggested, did many modernists. For Doane, the primary impetus was the desire to escape the industrialized world: "The subject is no longer immersed in time, no longer experiences it as an enveloping medium. Through its rationalization and abstraction, its externalization and reification in the form of pocket watches, standardized schedules, the organization of the work day, and industrialization in general, time becomes other, alienated" (2002: 221). Ives's anti-technological sentiments are well established, and the notion of Ives's music and its various experiments with musical time responding to the alienation of time in the industrialized world is compelling. As Leon Botstein wrote in an essay comparing the modernism of Ives and Mahler, "One easily might hear in the music of both composers the clash between an idealized world and culture associated with an embattled rural landscape of the past and the urban, industrial, and technological facts of modern times" (1996: 43).

More concretely, the modernist fixation on the present can be understood as a confrontation with mortality. Industrialization created for many the sensation of time's acceleration; the duration of one's life felt increasingly calculable and hence the specter of death more palpable. The unprecedented bloodshed of World War I and the unfathomable number of premature deaths it claimed fed into these feelings, and certainly it was at the forefront of Ives's mind when he composed another song from 1917, "Tom Sails Away," which is explicitly about America's youth going to war. At one stage, Ives conceived of these two songs as a miniature collection called "Two Songs" (Sinclair 1999: 657), and the same basic narrative structure that defines "The Things Our Fathers Loved" – reflections in the present framing a central memory – characterizes "Tom Sails Away" as well. In a passage that closely parallels the return to "Now" in "The Things Our Fathers Loved," the persona of "Tom Sails Away," after recalling Tom's idyllic childhood, sings: "But Today! In freedom's cause Tom sailed away for over there." As the final two words are repeated, the vocal line evokes the melody of "Taps," and the implications for Tom are clear. The connection between these two songs sheds light on Ives's quotation of the refrain from "In the Sweet By-and-By" in mm. 15–22 of "The Things Our Father Loved," a tune about eternal rest ("we shall meet on that beautiful shore"). Ives's persona, though apparently immersed in the present, has an eye toward a future reunion with her "fathers"; but although the tune she paraphrases looks forward to a peaceful reunion, the ending of Ives's song belies a profound unrest.

Gayle Sherwood Magee interpreted the quotation of "In the Sweet By-and-By" as a reflection of Ives's anxiety about the war: "[Ives's] placement of a unified, complete American melody in opposition to a European-styled accompaniment that threatens to overwhelm it embodies the contemporary reality of national unity in the face of a foreign war" (2008: 127). Alongside Sherwood Magee's reading, I would suggest a parallel metaphor in which the persona sings one of her (our) fathers' tunes, pulling it into the present in order to brace herself from the onrush of *memories* that threaten to overwhelm her, memories that call attention to time's passing and thus serve as harbingers of mortality. Kracauer explained the impulse to preserve the past in photographs and on film in similar terms: "That the world devours [photographs] is a sign of the *fear of death*. What the photographs by their sheer accumulation attempt to banish is the recollection of death, which is part and parcel of every memory-image" (1993: 433). Ives's use of memory fragments might be understood, then, as palliatives against mortality – his fellow citizens', and perhaps his own.

In 1933 Ives made the first of a series of recordings in which he played and sang his own music. (These have since been made available on the disc *Ives Plays Ives: The Composer at the Piano in Four Recording Sessions, 1933–1943* [1999], which contains surely the most essential and entertaining performance of Ives's music on record, the composer's own rendition of his song "They Are There!") After his initial sessions at Abbey Road studios, Ives jotted down his reactions in a rant whose manic energy makes it well worth quoting in full:

> Machinery! – and what everything else is, and the other side of life as machinery, or as a result of its influence and fixtures – all of this, whatever the above means, I saw this a.m. I wanted to record (for my own observation) certain passages of piano things of mine. In the first place you have to be there at a certain time – so does Paderewski when he gives an 8:31 concert. How do you know at 8:31 that you are going to feel like playing note #92? Then you have to play what you have to play, which may not be exactly what you have to play. A bell rings – two bells – and a nice red light starts – and you start. You get going, going good maybe the first time, as I did this a.m. Then the nice engineer comes back and says you took over four minutes, and the last part was not recorded. As I remember, the last part was the only part of the above "going good" part. Then he played it over – it happened to be one of the best [times] that I've played it – so I told him that was just o.k., and I'd play some of the other passages. Then he says – "What? – that recording is all gone – we didn't keep [it] – it was only to get the time" – !! So I had to play it again – and it was awful this time – sweaty fingers, short of breath, everything going wrong, wrong notes, rhythm dying, mad inside, cussing under your breath. Then the man comes in and says "This is all recorded" – even the cuss words. Then just as I was going good again, the red light [goes out] and the buzzer sounds, and the time is up. The next record has to start in the beginning of the last measure – but how can you dive off a rock when you're in the middle of the pool? So I told him I'd start all over again, and this time I got started going wrong and kept it up perfectly, and it was recorded perfectly! Now what has all this got to do with music? – this is the business of music as it is today! It's all just music to make business, rather than the business to make music. A man may play to himself and his music starts to live – then he tries to put it under a machine, and it's dead!
> (1972: 80–81)

In this remarkable tirade, Ives provides us with a vivid image of the modern artist virtually dehabilitated by anxiety about technology and its control over time. He went so far, in the final sentence, as to equate audio recording with death, and he perhaps hinted at this association metaphorically as well: "the red light [goes out] and the buzzer sounds, and the time is up." Ironically, whereas mechanical reproduction was heralded by many as a means of immortality, a way of preserving sounds and images for eternity, it was also saddled with opposite connotations. For Ives, to record music was to take the life from it. In the early cinema, the absence of a character in the frame brought connotations of death, a key element in generating suspense via parallel editing: when the film cuts away from the heroine, her absence within the frame implies her impending death.[12]

Ives produced very few new compositions after 1918, and this lack of productivity over the last thirty-five or so years of his life has been the subject of much speculation. The most convincing explanation has been provided by Sherwood Magee, who claimed that Ives suffered from what was known as "neurasthenia," a nervous condition that stemmed from "a fear of modernization . . . in the social, economic, and industrial spheres" (2001: 574). As Sherwood Magee concluded, "When viewed through the lens of neurasthenia, Ives's relationship to the modern world is redefined as one of anxiety, a fear of change and upheaval" (577) – a conclusion powerfully supported by Ives's account of his experiences at Abbey Road. But even years earlier, when composing "The Things Our Fathers Loved," Ives was on the verge of what, according to Sherwood Magee, was his second neurasthenic breakdown in the fall of 1918. And thus this song and its troubled ending can be heard as the work of a composer with profound and pressing concerns about the status of his music, his life, and humanity in the modern world.

NOTES

1. Unless otherwise noted, all references to "The Things Our Fathers Loved" are from the original 1922 edition of *114 Songs*, published by Ives himself. In 2004 a critical edition of these 114 songs (plus fifteen others) was published, correcting what the editor H. Wiley Hitchcock referred to as the original edition's "obvious problems: palpable musical errors, idiosyncratic and ambiguous music notation, puzzling textual inconsistencies and irregularities of punctuation" (Ives 2004: xviii). In the case of "The Things Our Fathers Loved," virtually all of the discrepancies between the two editions amount to notational details. Although Hitchcock's edition is an invaluable resource, my preference is for the original, both because it contains inscrutable notational anomalies that hold potential symbolic value and thus might be best left uncorrected, and because these anomalies strike me as sympathetic with Ives's ideas about the written text's lack of authority and the value of contingency in the creative process.

2. Although the gender of the vocal persona is not indicated, I will use feminine pronouns in this essay for the sake of consistency.

3. Ives's use of *ascending* semitonal shifts to represent the onset of memory suggests an understanding of memory and dreaming as heightened states of consciousness. An opposite (and more intuitive) strategy in the music of Debussy is outlined in Rings (2008: 203).

4. The nomenclature "m. 4.2," as used here and elsewhere, refers to the second beat of m. 4.

5. The progression A⁷–D⁷ suggested in Example 14.3 is particularly meaningful in light of a correspondence noted by Robert P. Morgan between the "Summer evenings" measure and a passage from Wagner's Prelude to *Tristan und Isolde* (1997: 14). Morgan observed that the upper melody of the piano in the first half of Ives's m. 10 is a rhythmically altered version of the melody from the *Tristan* Prelude, mm. 16–17 (the famously tortured deceptive motion), transposed down a major second. Probing further, we can see that Wagner's deceptive progression B⁷–E⁷–F (mm. 13–17), transposed down a major second, becomes A⁷–D⁷–E♭. The latter progression comprises Ives's constellation of chordal roots discussed above, and it is realized in mm. 10, 15, and 21–22 of Ives's song, with A⁷ of m. 10 proceeding to the D⁷ of m. 15, as suggested in Example 14.3, and the final D♯ harmony of mm. 21–22 thwarting D⁷'s resolution onto G.

6. In many works, Ives signified timelessness and eternity more directly via codas featuring static textures, typically built around one or more layers of *ostinati*; see, for example, the ending of the "Thoreau" movement that concludes the *Concord Sonata*.

7. Freud writes: "A humiliation that was experienced thirty years ago acts exactly like a fresh one throughout the thirty years. . . . As soon as the memory of it is touched, it springs into life again and shows itself cathected with excitation" (1955b: 578). Similarly, the sudden rush of memories that overtakes Ives's persona correlate to Freud's notion of *Nachträglichkeit* (deferred action), which, like Ives's song, is founded upon the idea of communion between past and present.

8. The Proust-Ives connection is often alluded to but rarely explored in depth. See, for instance, Hepokoski (1994) and Block (1997), both of whose titles make unmistakable references to *Remembrance*, but neither of which ever refers to Proust or his novel by name.

9. Rings invoked Proust and the *"moment bienheureux"* recently in a related musical context, a parenthetical passage in Debussy's piano prelude *Des pas sur la neige* (2008: 203–205).

10. Kern weaves into his account Ives's representation of clashing marching bands in the "Putnam's Camp" movement of *Three Places in New England* (2003: 75).

11. See Ives's choral work *Psalm 14* (ca. 1912–13) for a much more straightforward musical analogue of parallel editing: verse 7 cross-cuts the music of verses 2 and 3 (transposed) and unites the ending of each verse with the bitonal cadence in the piece's final four bars.

12. This connotation is not merely metaphoric; rather, it was part of the way early filmgoers grappled with the new conventions of narrative film. Anecdotal evidence is provided by my two-year-old son, Leo, who has recently been coming to terms with these conventions himself. While watching *The Muppet Movie*, during a scene in which Kermit and Miss Piggy take leave of their Muppet companions to enjoy a romantic dinner together, he suddenly began to sob: "What happened to Fozzie??"

EXAMPLE 14.4. Ives, "The Things Our Fathers Loved."

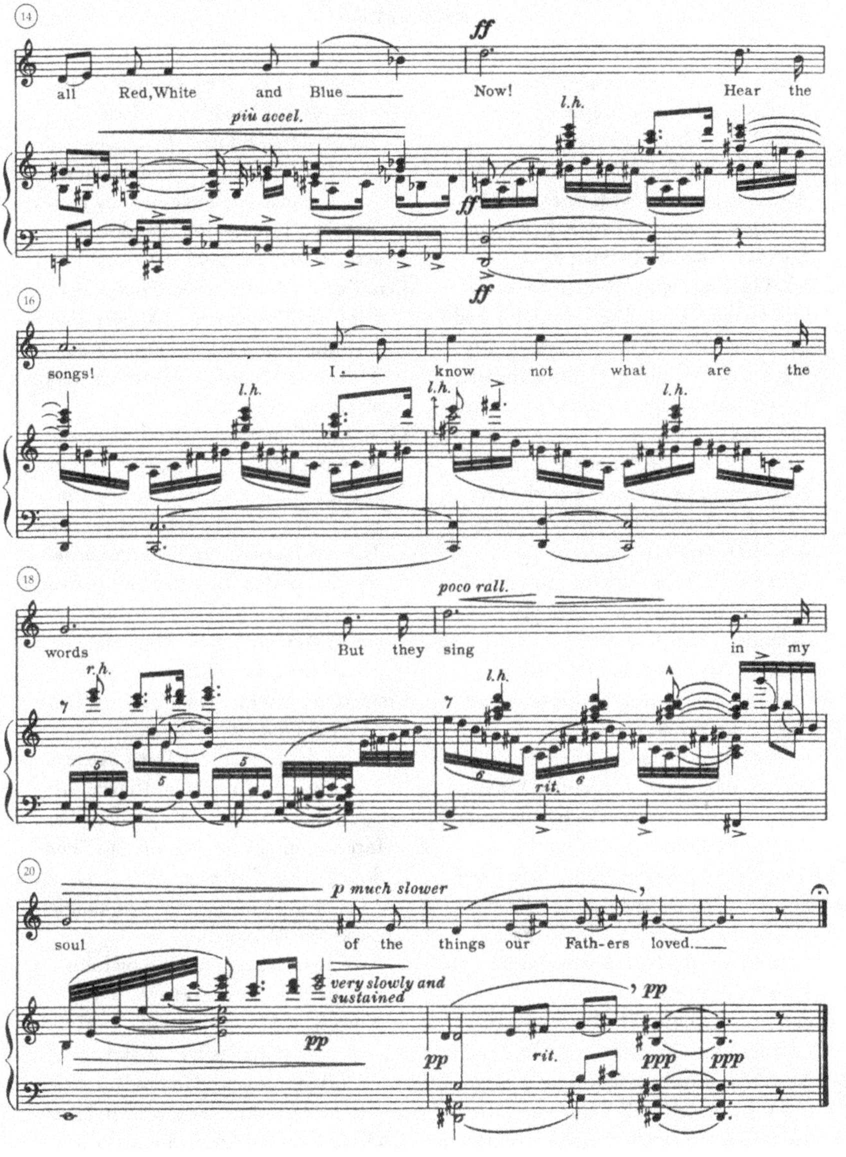

EXAMPLE 14.4. *(continued).*

WORKS CITED

Barthes, Roland. 1977. *Image, Music, Text.* Translated by Stephen Heath. New York: Hill and Wang.

Bergson, Henri. 1910. *Time and Free Will: An Essay on the Immediate Data of Consciousness.* Translated by F. L. Pogson. London: Allen and Unwin.

Block, Geoffrey. 1997. "Remembrance of Dissonances Past: The Two Published Editions of Ives's *Concord Sonata.*" In *Ives Studies,* edited by Philip Lambert, 27–50. Cambridge: Cambridge University Press.

Botstein, Leon. 1996. "Innovation and Nostalgia: Ives, Mahler, and the Origins of Twentieth-Century Modernism." In *Charles Ives and His World,* edited by J. Peter Burkholder, 35–74. Princeton: Princeton University Press.

Burkholder, Peter J. 1995. *All Made of Tunes: Charles Ives and the Uses of Musical Borrowing.* New Haven: Yale University Press.

Doane, Mary Ann. 2002. *The Emergence of Cinematic Time: Modernity, Contingency, the Archive.* Cambridge: Harvard University Press.

Emerson, Ralph Waldo. 1990. "The Over-Soul." In *The Oxford Authors: Ralph Waldo Emerson,* edited by Richard Poirier, 152–65. New York: Oxford University Press.

Feder, Stuart. 1990. "The Nostalgia of Charles Ives: An Essay in Affects and Music." In *Psychoanalytic Explorations in Music,* edited by Stuart Feder, Richard L. Karmel, and George H. Pollock, 233–66. Madison: International Universities Press.

Freud, Sigmund. 1955a. *The Interpretation of Dreams.* Vols. 4–5 of *The Standard Edition of the Complete Psychological Works of Sigmund Freud.* Translated and edited by James Strachey. London: Hogarth Press. First published 1900.

———. 1955b. "The Unconscious." In *The Standard Edition of the Complete Psychological Works of Sigmund Freud,* translated and edited by James Strachey, 14: 166–204. London: Hogarth Press. First published 1915.

Gaudreault, André. 2009. *From Plato to Lumière: Narration and Monstration in Literature and Cinema.* Translated by Timothy Barnard. Toronto: University of Toronto Press.

Gunning, Tom. 1990. "The Cinema of Attractions: Early Film, Its Spectator and the Avant-Garde." In *Early Cinema: Space, Frame, Narrative,* edited by Thomas Elsaesser and Adam Barker, 56–62. London: British Film Institute.

———. 1991. *D. W. Griffith and the Origins of American Narrative Film.* Urbana: University of Illinois Press.

Hepokoski, James. 1994. "Temps Perdu." *Musical Times* 135: 746–51.

Ives, Charles E. 1922. *114 Songs.* Redding: Published by the author. Reprinted by Associated Music Publishers, Peer International Corporation and Theodore Presser Company, 1975.

———. 1961. *Essays before a Sonata.* New York: W. W. Norton.

———. 1972. *Memos.* Edited by John Kirkpatrick. New York: W. W. Norton.

———. 1943. Charles Ives, piano and voice. Liner notes by James B. Sinclair, Vivian Perlis, Richard Warren Jr., and David Gray Porter. Composers Recordings. CRI CD 810.

———. 2004. *129 Songs.* Edited by H. Wiley Hitchcock. Music of the United States of America, vol. 12. Middletown: A-R Editions.

Kern, Stephen. 2003. *The Culture of Time and Space: 1880–1918.* Cambridge:

Harvard University Press. First published 1983.

Kracauer, Siegfried. 1993. "Photography." Translated by Thomas Y. Levin. *Critical Inquiry* 19(3): 421–36.

Leydon, Rebecca. 2001. "Debussy's Late Style and the Devices of the Early Silent Cinema." *Music Theory Spectrum* 23(2): 217–41.

McDonald, Matthew. 2004. "Silent Narration? Elements of Narrative in Ives's *The Unanswered Question*." *19th-Century Music* 27(3): 263–86.

Metzer, David. 2003. *Quotation and Cultural Meaning in Twentieth-Century Music*. Cambridge: Cambridge University Press, 2003.

Monelle, Raymond. 2000. *The Sense of Music: Semiotic Essays*. Princeton: Princeton University Press.

Morgan, Robert P. 1997. "'The Things Our Fathers Loved': Charles Ives and the European Tradition." In *Ives Studies*, edited by Philip Lambert, 3–26. Cambridge: Cambridge University Press.

Perlis, Vivian. 1974. *Charles Ives Remembered: An Oral History*. Urbana: University of Illinois Press.

Proust, Marcel. 2006. *Remembrance of Things Past*, translated by C. K. Scott Moncrieff, vol. 1. Hertfordshire: Wordsworth Editions.

Rings, Steven. 2008. "*Mystères limpides*: Time and Transformation in Debussy's *Des pas sur la neige*." *19th-Century Music* 32(2): 178–208.

Sherwood Magee, Gayle. 2001. "Charles Ives and 'Our National Malady.'" *Journal of the American Musicological Society* 54(3): 555–84.

———. 2008. *Charles Ives Reconsidered*. Music in American Life. Urbana: University of Illinois Press.

Sinclair, James. 1999. *A Descriptive Catalogue of the Music of Charles Ives*. New Haven: Yale University Press. Available online at http://webtext.library .yale.edu/xm12html/music/ci-d.htm.

Starr, Lawrence. 1992. *A Union of Diversities: Style in the Music of Charles Ives*. New York: Schirmer.

15

Narrativity, Descriptivity, and Secondary Parameters: Ecstasy Enacted in Salvatore Sciarrino's *Infinito nero*

Rebecca Leydon

Post-tonal: the term axiomatically implies a casting off of the syntactical richness and implicative entailments of common-practice tonal structures. Rejecting the rhetoric of tonal trajectories and cadential closure became an emblematic device of musical modernism, one facet of a broader anti-narrative turn across the arts in the twentieth century. For many artists in this lineage, narrative has been understood as fixed *fabulae*, as already scripted, coercive, and an impediment to authentic expression. "Stories hide the truth," claims experimental theater director Richard Foreman; with narrative works, he argues, "people are led on a journey that reinforces the emotional habits of their lives" (quoted in Coleman 2007). Anti-narrative works, in contrast, persuade us to resist our own compulsions to narrativize and thereby achieve a greater intimacy with the "whatness" of what is immanently present to our senses. A central strain of avant-garde music in the twentieth century has had to do with escaping the perceived prison-house of narrative coherence by seeking out uncontaminated sound worlds, sonic landscapes not yet colonized by narrative associations. Viewed from this anti-narrative position, the truth of musical sound lies in its "thingness." Even as temporality continually erodes that status, musical sound is configured as basically static – a *picturing* rather than a *telling*.

Reciprocal with the waning of tonal rhetoric is the inexorable rise of secondary parameters. Leonard Meyer (2000) characterized the contrast between primary and secondary parameters in terms of their "syntactical" and "statistical" capacities, respectively: melody, harmony, and rhythm are "pattern forming," while timbre, texture, tempo, and loudness simply intensify or abate. Primary parameters are understood in a relational sense to other sounds within a sound stream (e.g., the leading tone, the subdominant key, the pick-up to m. 5), whereas secondary parameters are immediately grasped in an instantaneous bodily fashion (e.g., cymbal choke, flutter-tongue, *andante*). Meyer expressed doubts about the possibility of a legitimate syntax of, say, timbre or dynamics (except within some willfully imposed intra-opus system, such as integral serialism), for "in order for syntax to exist . . . successive stimuli must be related to one another in such a way that specific criteria for mobility and closure are established. Such criteria can be established only if the elements of the parameter can be segmented into discrete, non-uniform relationships so that the similarities and differences between them are definable, constant, and proportional" (1989: 14).

Arguably, nineteenth- and twentieth-century composers' growing reliance on secondary parameters is not merely ancillary but central to the demise of the common-practice idiom. Meyer traces a shift in emphasis over the course of the nineteenth century from syntactical to statistical elements, as composers become increasingly preoccupied with the repudiation of convention and the corresponding embrace of nature. Paradoxically, Meyer shows how processes of texture, density, dynamics, and timbre – processes that "may cease, but cannot *close*" – came to serve as "natural signs" (1989: 15). Secondary parameters "seem able to shape experience with minimal dependence on learned rules and conventions. . . . For many listeners, the power of sheer sound – as music slowly swelled in waves of sonic intensity, culminating in a statistical climax or a plateau of apotheosis – in a very real sense shaped experience 'naturally'" (Meyer 2000: 218).

Put another way, while primary parameters make possible a set of criteria for coherent narrative trajectories and closures, secondary parameters, in their role as anaphones for aspects of the natural world, enhance music's capacity for vivid *description*. Like narrativity, descriptivity may be considered a transmedial attribute – not exclusively tied to verbal media but rather a "semiotic macro-mode," as Werner Wolf (2007) has argued, expressed across diverse media, including literature, film, visual art, and music. In one sense, description and narration are antipoles: picturing versus telling, *mise-en-scène* versus action, stasis versus process. But the two modes are in fact closely entangled in the notion of a story. As Wolf explains:

> A typical effect of the experience of "good narratives" both in everyday
> situations and in the arts and media is the impression of becoming part
> of the narrated world and becoming re-centered in the storyworlds even
> to such an extent as to feel suspense. . . . While "good" narratives (besides
> other functions, such as making sense of temporal experience) often allow
> us to become immersed in the eventful facets of the represented worlds and
> to witness the actions and fates of anthropomorphic beings, descriptions
> generally confront us with the sensory aspects, the "whatness" of individual
> phenomena and world-facets. They are usually described in order to convey
> a vivid idea of them, to "re-present" or evoke them to the imagination of the
> recipients. (2007: 14)

By enhancing music's capacity for vivid description, secondary parameters
immerse listeners in a more vivid and sensuous musical present. Viewed in
this way, the surge of secondary parameters in post-tonal music could serve
as a means of liberating musical narrativity from the strictures of common-
practice processes. In a manner comparable to the effects of cinematic editing
on traditional presentational modes of storytelling, extra-syntactical musical
sounds made possible a whole range of new narrative types.

Admittedly, in some post-tonal practices this wealth of narrative possibilities remains untapped—for instance, Darmstadt's post-traumatic modernism, where the anti-narrative impulse seemed to reach its apex. But many
post-serial composers expressed a renewed interest in narrative concepts. Jann
Pasler remarks on this trend, which she tentatively identifies as "postmodern
narrative":

> Because people's experience and understanding of time has changed in this
> century, artists of all kinds, particularly composers, have sought to give
> form to other processes that are not necessarily goal-oriented, dramatic, or
> organic. . . . The return to using narrative concepts, perhaps in response to
> the crisis over a lack of norms in this century, signals a renewed desire on
> the part of composers to have their audiences participate in the aesthetic
> experience by bringing their own knowledge of life's processes to the music;
> however, as life has changed, the events that are signified and organized by
> those narratives has changed. (2007: 44)

The rehabilitation of musical narrativity is closely connected with an
expansion of the repertory of secondary parameters, as new sounds opened
up new prospects for musical signification. Since the mid-twentieth century,
this expanded palette comprises not only the wealth of novel electronic possibilities but also new approaches to playing conventional instruments, such as

the techniques explored in the music of Helmut Lachenmann. With his *musique concrète instrumentale* Lachenmann insists that musical sounds are tied to the materiality of sound making: his compositions foreground the fleshy, breathy, and tactile aspects of acoustic sound production. Referring to his *Air: Musik für grosses Orchester mit Schlagzeug-Solo*, Lachenmann explains how "energies that were basic to instrumental sound, as the trace of its mechanical production, were consciously incorporated into the composition and played a crucial role in the work's sonic and formal structure. This was my own way of breaking away from what I felt to be a falsely abstract and increasingly sterile structuralism" (2004: 46). These instrumental sounds "describe or denote the concrete situation: listening, you hear the conditions under which a sound- or noise-action is carried out, you hear what materials and energies are involved and what resistance is encountered" (Lachenmann et al. 2008).

While Lachenmann insists that his music remains "nonfigurative," his techniques nevertheless open up the possibility for a particular kind of *heard agency* in his music. To hear the physical labor of sound production and "the resistance encountered" is to hear vivid corporeal agents – not simply iconic musical signs but virtual personae. Naomi Cumming's concept of the "musical subject" is pertinent here. For Cumming, all hearing is "hearing as," and music most engages us precisely when it enables us to identify with an expressive virtual agency. Cumming asserts that the voice-like aspects of timbre, the kinesthetic movements of rhythmic and melodic gestures, and the "willfulness" of directed harmonic processes all come together to catalyze this "musical subject," or "sonic self." The unambiguously visceral quality of *musique concrète instrumentale*, with its powers to evoke certain kinds of embodied experience, seems to offer an especially conspicuous interface with a sonic agent.

So while it is often tacitly assumed that the disappearance of a universal harmonic syntax and cadential rhetoric at the end of the common-practice period deprived post-tonal music of a great deal of its power to communicate intelligible stories, the concomitant ascendance of secondary parameters ultimately liberated two components crucial to musical narrativity: sensuous musical spaces and tangible musical agents. In their capacity to serve as natural signs, effects of timbre and texture, especially those created through extended instrumental techniques, can sculpt especially vivid musical story worlds. Consequently, they can act as narrative triggers: enveloped in a palpable sonic space populated by viscerally perceived subjectivities, listeners may be more inclined to hear the unfolding of musical events as narrative transformations, independent of any scripted syntactical processes.

TABLE 15.1. *INFINITO NERO*, TEXT AND ENGLISH TRANSLATION

L'anima si trasformava nel sangue, tanto da non intendere poi altro che sangue, non vedere altro che sangue, non gustare altro che sangue, non sentire altro che sangue, non pensare altro che di sangue, non poter pensare se non di sangue. E tutto ciò che operava la sommergeva e profondava in esso sangue	The Spirit was transforming into blood, understanding nothing but blood, seeing nothing but blood, tasting nothing but blood, feeling nothing but blood, thinking nothing but blood, unable to think anything but blood. And everything it did, submerged and sunk it into that very blood
influirsi influssi influiva rinfluiva e il sangue influiva rinfluiva influssi rinfluire rinfluisce rin fluisce influssi rinfluivono influsii rinfluivono superesaltando	Flowing in in-flowing influx flowing out and the blood flowed in flowed out flows out flows out out-flowing influx outflowing overexalting
allora il Santo mi versò sul capo un vaso e il sangue mi coperse tutta. Anche la Santa versò. Il latte mescolandosi col sangue mi fa una bellissima veste. Obumbrata la faccia	then the Saint poured his cup over my head and the blood covered all of me. And so did the woman Saint. The milk mixed with blood makes a beautiful gown for me. Covering my face
o, o, o (silenzio) o, o, o (sil.)	oh, oh, oh (silence) oh, oh, oh (silence)
o se le piante potessino avere amore, non griderebbero altro	oh if the plants could have love, they would shout of nothing else
o, io non lo so (sil.)	oh, I do not know (silence)
timui timore amoris. Timui timore amoris. Timui timore amoris (sil.)	timui timore amoris. Timui timore amoris. Timui timore amoris (silence)
ma dillo, ma dillo	but say it, but say it
mors intravit per fenestras.	mors intravit per fenestras.
Ma tu perché figure immagini e facce, aspirazione, inspirazione e respirazione in te. (sil.) vieni sul corpo tuo aperture a noi incognite. Usci, finestre, buche, celle, forami diccielo, caverne. Senza fondo stillanti. Sono le piaghe dentro cui mi perdo vieni, vieni con la corona: le sue spine, lunghe, trapassano il Padre Eterno in cielo egli scrive su di me con il sangue. Tu con il latte della Vergine. Lo Spirito con le lagrime vieni non si aprino le nuvole, si bene il vergineo ventre (sil.) si ma	But because figures, images and faces, aspiration, inspiration and respiration in you (silence) you come openings on your body unknown to us. Doorways, windows, holes, cells, apertures in the sky, caverns. Bottomless trickling. They are the wounds in which I lose myself come, come with the crown: its long thorns pierce the Eternal Father in heaven he writes on me with his blood. You with the Virgin's milk. The Spirit with tears come the clouds do not open, but the virginal womb does (silence)
vieni, vieni, deh, vieni, o, vieni vieni (sil.)	yes but come, come, ye, come, oh, come come (silence)
ohimé, vivendo muoio (sil.) o, o, o (sil.)	alas, I die living (silence) oh, oh, oh (silence)
(stando un poco si pone a sedere)	

orsù eccomi in terra (sil.) non posso ir più giù io (sil.) e sì (sil.) o savia pazzia (sil.)	now here I am on earth (silence) I can no longer go further down (silence) and yes (silence) oh wise madness (silence)
(aprendosi nelle braccia tutta sirilassa, ferma ferma. E poi comincia a divincularsi: gesti e moti che pare si consumi, per un pezzo)	
io non intendo (sil.) è meglio il tuo, sì. si (sil.) ohimé (sil.) tu sei senza fine, ma io vorrei veder in te qualche fine	I don't understand (silence) yours is better, yes, yes (silence) alas (silence) you are endless, but I would like to see an end in you

Source: Reproduced with kind permission of Universal Music MGB Publications.

HOW DO YOU SOLVE A PROBLEM LIKE MARIA? A VIABLE NARRATIVITY OF TIMBRE IN SCIARRINO'S *INFINITO NERO*

These onomatopoeic narrative triggers feature prominently in the music of Italian composer Salvatore Sciarrino. Sciarrino closely resembles Lachenmann in his approach to instrumental writing: both composers create instrumental works wholly based on extended techniques. Like Lachenmann, Sciarrino puts tremendous energy into sculpting these unusual sounds, and he is fastidious in his directions to performers as to how, precisely, to produce the sounds on conventional instruments. Sciarrino's *Infinito nero, estasi di un atto* (1998) utilizes an expanded Pierrot ensemble of flute, oboe, clarinet, violin, viola, cello, percussion, and mezzo-soprano. A variety of carefully specified techniques are required of the instrumentalists: key slaps, tongue stops, flutter-tongue, multiphonics, breath- and whistle-tones on the wind instruments (the flute part is especially intricate), harmonics with *glissandi, tremolo,* and unusual bowings in the strings. These techniques produce fine gradations of delicate timbres, often at the threshold of silence.

But perhaps the most striking aspect of the work is Sciarrino's treatment of the voice. The mezzo is asked to declaim the text in short paroxysmal bursts, so hectic and cramped that individual words can scarcely be made out. This vocal tachyphrasia serves to depict the principal character in the drama, Saint Maria Maddalena de' Pazzi, a sixteenth-century Florentine nun whose mode of pressured speech was recorded by her fellow Carmelite sisters during her fits of ecstasy. Throughout her life, Maria succumbed to these recurring raptures, which sometimes compelled her to hurl herself bodily toward sacred objects but which, more typically, caused her to channel the words of the

Holy Spirit. To cope with the explosive speed with which Maria's (often gory and erotic) utterances burst forth, her fellow nuns developed a sophisticated system of real-time dictation and transcription: as Maria spoke, some of the nuns were assigned the task of repeating her words aloud, while others put text to paper. Maria herself objected to the translation of her essentially oral experiences into written inscriptions and even threatened to destroy the resulting manuscripts. They survive, however, published as her *Colloquies*, from which Sciarrino has taken a segment as his text for *Infinito nero* (Table 15.1).

David Metzer calls Sciarrino "the contemporary composer most devoted to silence" (2006: 364). Metzer's study of *Infinito nero* enumerates a range of types of silence in the work with which Sciarrino orchestrates the *silenzio* inscriptions in the text, from the breath-like sounds of the opening measures to the final ethereal clusters of string harmonics. For me, attending closely to these exquisite silences reveals a distinct process of narrative unfolding. Sciarrino's meticulously crafted instrumental textures tell a strange story from multiple points of view: from the perspective of Maria herself, as she slips into her cataleptic trance and encounters the divine, and that of the stenographers, as they struggle to seize hold of and accurately record her fleeting and bewildering ululations.

MARIA'S VOICE

If we consider the form of the work as projected by the vocal part, the piece falls into four main segments. The first eleven minutes of the approximately twenty-five-minute work consist primarily of faint instrumental sounds. The voice itself appears only very briefly, at mm. 44 and 45 (about five minutes in), where the singer utters two fragments of text: "l'anima si trasformava nel-" and "sangue, tanto da non in-." The vocal line is carved out of the framing silences by attacks in the extreme registers of the piano at the onset and termination of each utterance. Here and elsewhere, a composite vocal timbre is formed by fusing together instrumental articulations with the torrent of vocal sounds. After this initial eruption of text, the singer falls silent until m. 90, where her febrile utterances resume, each fractured gesture punctuated by silences. Like the initial utterances, these remain confined to narrow pitch bands, each outlining a small set of micro-chromatic pitches lying mostly in the range of B4 to E5 (Example 15.1).

This mode of declamation continues until m. 105 (exactly halfway through the piece), where, at the word "profundava," the voice drops in register: the

EXAMPLE 15.1. *Infinito nero, m. 45, Maria's initial utterances.*
Reproduced with kind permission of Universal Music MGB Publications.

next several outbursts unfold in the range F3–G3 before inaugurating a new mode of vocal declamation: rapid alternations between the low and high registers. Here the piano becomes unfastened from the vocal line. While still delivered with impenetrable rapidity, the singer's phrases now extend for longer periods of a full measure or pair of measures, separated by more extensive instrumental passages.

At m. 124 (about fifteen minutes in) the singer switches to a third mode of declamation, producing long, sustained tones – the first such instances in the piece and, as Siglind Bruhn has noted, the only elements in the work that "generate vocal beauty" (2003: 486). The sustained pitches act as anacruses to further short bursts of text. At m. 150, fragments of pressured speech continue, with the Latin wordplay "timui timore amores"; a few isolated chordal skips appear with the words "ma dillo, dillo."

The final section, from the perspective of vocal modes, begins at m. 180. Here, the sporadic bouts of tachyphrasia, the sudden registral shifts, and the

EXAMPLE 15.2. *Infinito nero*, mm. 182–83, the combined modes of vocal delivery. *Reproduced with kind permission of Universal Music MGB Publications.*

sustained pitches are combined, along with a new, fourth element: a childlike melody outlining the pentatonic fragment D5–E5–D5–B4, which gradually effloresces in the vocal part. In the final minutes of the piece, the singer returns to the original mode of pressured speech, each interjection occupying a narrow micro-chromatic range in the lowest register of the singer's voice (Example 15.2).

Bruhn observes that the different modes of vocal delivery express different aspects of the text: the initial micro-chromatic telegraphese describes the engulfing presence of blood; the registral shifts describes the narrator's submission to the pouring of blood over her head; the sustained pitches and pentatonic melody signal her complete and rapturous surrender. Beyond

EXAMPLE 15.2. *(continued)*.

these broad outlines, however, it is difficult to follow any narrative thread by examining the vocal part alone. There are only tenuous connections linking one vocal state to another. To understand the narrative transformations that unfold across the work it is necessary to attend to certain details of rhythm and timbre in the instrumental ensemble – the passages that fill out the *silenzi*. In particular, we can focus on a recurring rhythmic motive: a rhythmic *ostinato* comprised of two attacks on the first and sixth sixteenth notes of a measure of slow $\frac{3}{4}$ (Figure 15.1).

While the specific sonorities vary with the statements of the *ostinato*, the position of the onset of attacks within the bar remains constant, consistently articulating time intervals of five and seven sixteenth notes. The *ostinato* is

time-point 1   time-point 2

FIGURE 15.1. The *ostinato*.

projected by different instruments and composite timbres; it never appears in the vocal line; it disappears entirely for segments but reappears in new guises, sometimes elaborated with slurred melodic figures and echoes filling the gaps between the two attack points, or with a slight widening of the agogic fringe of the attacks. Since meter and tempo remain constant throughout the piece, however, tracking the varied appearances of this rhythmic pattern is relatively straightforward. Complete statements of the *ostinato* occur in 126 of the work's 220 measures, with partial, emergent, or deteriorating forms in additional measures. The clearest course through Sciarrino's narrative can be followed by attending to this single rhythmic feature.

The *ostinato* appears in five distinct timbral versions. I summarize these below, showing representative measures from the score, and I provide each version of the *ostinato* with a programmatic label. I then trace these iterations of the *ostinato* through the work, exploring how they interact with the other musical elements and how they function as cardinal episodes within a narrative process.

THE FIVE FORMS OF THE *OSTINATO*

1. The *respiratory* version: The source of the *ostinato* is the rhythmic breathing in the flute that opens the work. The opening is marked *respiro dentro la testata,* and the flutist's exhaling and inhaling of breath mark out each of the two time points. This form of the *ostinato* appears in mm. 1–6 and again in mm. 54–70 (Example 15.3).

EXAMPLE 15.3. *Infinito nero,* m. 1, the respiratory form of the *ostinato.*
Reproduced with kind permission of Universal Music MGB Publications.

2. The *pilomotoric* version: The bass drum and the cello *tremolo* articulate time point 1; *flautando* strings and the clarinet's *colpo di lingua* project time point 2. This version of the *ostinato* occurs in only two places in the work, at mm. 6 and 46 (Example 15.4).

EXAMPLE 15.4. *Infinito nero*, m. 6, the *pilomotoric* version of the *ostinato*.
Reproduced with kind permission of Universal Music MGB Publications.

3. The *hæmic* version: The *ostinato's* time points are articulated by *colpo di lingua* techniques on the wind instruments, suggestive of the sounds of dripping fluids. This version of the *ostinato* occurs in mm. 7–43 and 47–70 (Example 15.5).

EXAMPLE 15.5. *Infinito nero*, flute and clarinet at m. 7, the *hæmic* version of the *ostinato*.
Reproduced with kind permission of Universal Music MGB Publications.

4. The *spiracular* version: Here an aeriform sound is created by having the violinist produce harmonics that sound beyond the audible pitch range. The violin forms a composite timbre with the bass drum and clarinet's *colpi*. This form of the *ostinato* emerges tentatively at m. 75, decisively in mm. 83–90 (Example 15.6).

EXAMPLE 15.6. *Infinito nero,* clarinet, bass drum, and violin at m. 84, the *spiracular* version of the *ostinato*.
Reproduced with kind permission of Universal Music MGB Publications.

5. Finally, the *numinous* version: Distinct high pitches in the viola articulate the *ostinato* time points using a variety of slurred melodic figures, including the three examples shown in Example 15.7. This more elastic and fluctuating form of the *ostinato* emerges and retreats at three points in the piece: mm. 96–107, 153–78, and 189–210. It becomes increasingly diatonic in its later incarnations, finally settling onto a major second, A–B.

The initial association of the two time points with the outflow and uptake of breath, respectively, inculcates a physical logic of continuity in the *ostinato* – a viscerally felt necessity for continuation. Because each respiratory event entails the next, all subsequent iterations of the *ostinato* – its hæmic, pilomotoric, spiracular, and numinous forms – are imbued with an implicative quality typically unavailable within the realm of secondary parameters. On a large-scale level, the transformations from one form of the *ostinato* to another are an invitation to follow a thread of narrative connections as Maria Maddalena gradually makes contact and begins to dialogue with her divine interlocutor.

EXAMPLE 15.7. *Infinito nero,* viola at mm. 107, 193, and 208, *numinous* versions of the *ostinato.*
Reproduced with kind permission of Universal Music MGB Publications.

NARRATIVIZING MARIA'S TRANCE

The work opens with the source of the *ostinato,* which at first hardly yields to analysis as a musical object at all: the flutist simply re-creates the sound of slow regular breathing by a single person, someone possibly asleep or in a state of deep meditation. The explicit corporeality of the sound is a transparent narrative cue to imagine a human agent. It draws us into a fictional space where

Maria herself lies before us: we are in the position of her Carmelite sisters, leaning in close to her body and ready to attend to her rapturous speech.

As the breathing rhythm continues, the flute's second *inspirando* is joined by a soft *colpo di lingua* "pop" in the clarinet – a sound suggesting a droplet of fluid – following which the flute's exhalation is postponed, momentarily shifting time point 1 forward in the measure by three eighth notes. Let us imagine this is Maria herself, literally holding her breath as she attends to the intrusive sound. Perhaps she becomes conscious of water dripping in the stone passageways of the Florentine convent, and the sound suggests to her the image of Christ's wounds. Her breathing pattern resumes, with another bated breath on the third quarter-note beat of m. 5 in anticipation of the shuddering string *tremolos* in m. 6. This statement of the *ostinato* in its pilomotoric form suggests a brief convulsion of Maria's quiescent body.

Maria's shudder initiates a prompt transformation of the *ostinato*: it is now projected in the sounds of trickling fluid. Beginning at m. 7, alternating *colpi* in the flute and clarinet map out the two time points of the *ostinato*. The rhythmic pattern, associated initially with the breathing rhythms, now suggests something liquiform – an image that Maria's first textual interjections will soon make explicit: "The Spirit was transforming into blood."

Let us imagine that Maria, in her spiritual trance, begins to sense the proximity of her divine interlocutor through this apparition of blood. Maria's breathing persists intermittently as a discrete element in the music, but the *ostinato* in this, its hæmic form, is now foregrounded. As listeners, we are the sisters gathered around her; at first we, too, hear only the faint sound of water dripping. But as we attend closely to the rhythmic *ostinato*, we are gradually drawn into Maria's perspective, crossing a boundary between perspectival modes of narration until, like her, we are seeing, tasting, feeling, and thinking "nothing but blood."

What provokes this hallucinatory shift in perspective is a third element that enters the texture at m. 8, the oboe's *colpo di lingua* articulations. These articulations initially appear in rhythmic unison with the clarinet but begin to lag behind time point 2, shifting forward in the measure by increments of quintuplet sixteenth notes. At m. 12 the oboe adds a second pulse that shadows the incremental shifts of the first. A gradual phasing process unfolds over the following thirty-six measures, the pulses disappearing again when they realign with time points 1 and 2. At m. 42 the piano's highest B♭ and a simultaneous *inspirando* in the flute mark the final re-engulfing of the oboe articulations by the hæmic *ostinato*.

What is this third, shifting, liquiform layer, with its quasi-minimalistic process? Some other fluid, perhaps, like the milk of the woman saint mixed with blood to which Maria will refer in her textual outbursts? The phasing process projects a glacially paced breathing rhythm of its own, as the oboe's droplets separate from and are reabsorbed into the fixed articulations of the *ostinato*. Steve Reich has described his own use of gradual processes: "One hears the details of the sound moving out *away from intentions*, occurring for their own acoustic reasons" (Reich and Hillier 2002: 35, emphasis added). With Reich's words in mind, we can hear this protracted passage as a relinquishing of intentionality; it enacts the surrendering of Maria's will as she edges closer to her spiritual interlocutor. The liquiform layers separating and realigning, like the shift from the respiratory to the hæmic forms of the *ostinato*, track a perspectival shift, from the position of the eavesdropping sisters to Maria's own. More accurately, we move into an ambiguous third-person place wherein what is audible to Maria is phenomenologically accessible to us but remains semantically opaque.

The *ostinato* vanishes with the first entrance of the voice – the burst of micro-chromatic tachyphrasia at m. 44. It resumes again, however, at m. 46 with the pilomotoric "shiver" and then at m. 47 in its hæmic form, articulated by *colpi* in the oboe. The flute's respiratory sounds reappear as well, intermittent and rhythmically discrete at first and then gradually fusing with the *ostinato*'s rhythms. The two sonic elements become fully synchronized at m. 54, as the *ostinato* is articulated simultaneously by the flute's respirations and the oboe's *colpi*. The synchronized pattern continues for seventeen measures.

We can understand this fusion of breath and blood as an intensification of Maria's trance. The next key step toward her contact with the divine agent occurs at m. 75: here the flute's respiratory rhythms are joined by a stratospheric violin harmonic, so high that it is merely a hiss of air. Because of Sciarrino's intricate placement of dynamic markings, the effect here is not of a fused, composite timbre with the breathing flute but rather of a *second breather* entering the space, one that begins to dominate the sonic texture over the next fifteen measures. While not literally breathing, the association of time points 1 and 2 with exhalation and inhalation, respectively, color these sibilant violin impulses as breaths; the exhalations are reinforced by bass drum pulsations, the inhalations by the hæmic clarinet droplet. As this spiracular form of the *ostinato* materializes, the effect is of a portal opening to the supernatural world, a conduit through which the divine being infuses Maria's trance space with its breath. In this shifting soundscape we hear a transformation of the supernatural presence from fluid to breath, a process that will lead to manifest orality.

Three events now signal the increasing vividness of Maria's interlocutor. First, at m. 90, her febrile utterances begin anew, resounding with new composite timbres of piano and winds. Second, the violin's hissing breaths become more irregular, slipping off the *ostinato* time points and accelerating at m. 94. Finally, from within this layer of aeriform violin harmonics, discernible pitches begin to materialize: descending viola harmonics – reinforced by oboe *colpi,* bass-drum pulsations, and the breathing flute – emerge like a trail of supernatural whispers, gradually transforming as the pitches descend into something like palpable vocalizations. At m. 106 slurred groups of viola harmonics lock on to the *ostinato* time points: this numinous form of the *ostinato* can be heard as the supernatural voice, the Word fully present to Maria in the deepest moments of her trance. From this point forward, we can understand instances of this sound quality – the penetrating viola harmonics and, later, the diaphanous crotales, bells, and dobachi – as addresses from the divine voice.

M. 109 initiates the singer's second vocal mode of rapidly shifting registers as she delivers her tongue-twisting text: "influirsi influssi influiva rinfluiva . . ." There is a confounding double dialogue here: at the level of Maria's individual utterances, the registral shifts make a virtual polyphony of her voice; and at the level of the phrases, Maria's passages are repeated, inaccurately, by the breathy flute contours at mm. 111, 112–13, 114–15, and 120. Ought we to hear this passage as a dialogue between Maria and her spiritual interlocutor? Or, rather, does the flute transmit the voices of the Carmelite sisters as they struggle with their transcriptions, heard now from Maria's perspective, muffled and distant, as if coming from somewhere outside the consecrated space of her divine communion? Crucially, the numinous sound quality associated with the divine utterances and the rhythms of the *ostinato* itself remain concealed throughout this passage: the intake and outflow of breath and blood are instead rendered purely abstractly through Maria's verbal descriptions of them. Maria's more sustained phrases here suggest a greater effortfulness as she tries to overcome the obstinacy of language and to thwart its textual transliteration.

Slicing through this tangle of text and repetitions comes an extraordinary sound: the steep *crescendo* of the descending violin slide and the *fortissimo* snap at the end of m. 115 – perhaps the most striking instrumental effect of the entire work. The sound cuts off Maria's text in the midst of a word; pulsating bass-drum heartbeats fill the ensuing silence for several measures. The singer resumes her flow of words again at m. 120 but shortly settles into her third declamatory mode: the vocal beauty of sustained pitches. At m. 127 she is accompanied by a shimmering F♯ in the strings for two measures (an effect created by having each instrument execute the same pitch with a different technique: *sul tasto* in the cello, a micro-tonal *glissando* in the violin, and a releasing and reapplying of finger pressure in the viola), a sound that returns again at mm. 135–38 and 149–50. The numinous form of the *ostinato* at last begins to resurface at m. 153. In the midst of its re-forming, at m. 155, the crotales ring out a major second D–E. The same pitches are picked up by sustained cello and violin harmonics at m. 160. Then, as the singer initiates her final, composite mode of vocal delivery, her newly blossoming pentatonic melody seems to latch onto and grow from these same celestial crotales pitches. The chiming bells and dobachi at m. 183 reinforce the connection. Initially, Maria's utterances alternate with bursts of breathy multiphonics in the flute and convulsive piano figures in a manner similar to the confounding dialogue of the previous section. Finally, however, an unambiguous exchange develops between Maria and the numinous presence when her pentatonic tune begins to propagate in the violin harmonics at mm. 192, 197, and 200. In the final measures of the piece, the singer falls silent while the numinous *ostinato* settles into its final diatonic and reverberant forms.

A MUSICAL SEMIOTICS OF TRANSCENDENCE

This journey through Maria's trance moves from the tangible corporeality of breath and blood to a realm of transcendent orality. The sonic materials, represented by the transformations of the *ostinato*, trace a path from a kind of abject fleshy noise to sinusoidal diatonic purity. In this respect, Sciarrino's techniques of signification are similar to those used by a number of other avant-garde composers. His use of ethereal diatonicism and string harmonics as signifiers for spiritual transcendence resembles similar techniques in George Crumb's *Black Angels* and, in an even more striking parallel, the music of the Russian composer Sofia Gubaidulina. Gubaidulina's *In Croce*, for cello and organ (alternatively, for bayan and cello), similarly exploits the contrast between inharmonic noise and sinusoidal purity and enacts a similar, if much less subtle, journey from abject corporeality to spiritual transcendence. *In Croce* is a meditation on the crucifixion, considered as a kind of ritual purification, a transcending of the body itself as abject. Organ and cello are assigned distinct dramaturgical roles, and the opposition between the abject and the transcendent is mapped onto the distinction between agitated micro-chromaticism in the low registers and static, wispy pentatonicism in the high registers. The organ begins with high, ethereal arpeggiations of an A-major triad, accompanied by a long E–F♯ trill. The cello begins on its lowest E, wavering around that pitch with expressive swells and slippages, obscuring the boundaries between notes. Over the course of the piece, the cello gradually makes its way up to the register initially occupied by the organ, is gradually purged of its micro-chromatic and fragmented motives, and finally attains a *legato*, pentatonic stasis as it takes over the A-major triads and E–F♯ trills. The organ, meanwhile, reaches down into the rumbling, abject low register; and as the performer holds a final subterranean cluster chord, the organ's motor is shut off.

Both Gubaidulina's and Sciarrino's narrative trajectories depend upon their techniques for arranging distinct timbres and textures in a series of fine gradations. Their compositions require a scaling of events along continua that run from the micro-chromatic to the diatonic, from noisiness to purity, from sounds that can be readily mapped onto the embodied experience of the listener to those with an increasingly alien spectro-morphology. The sophistication with which these artists handle the parameters of timbre, texture, dynamics, articulation, and sheer pitch height allows them to create, if not a strict Meyerian syntax, a clear sense of directed processes with real implicative entailments. They demonstrate how the expanded world of secondary parameters generates viable new musical narrativities within the post-tonal practice.

POST-TONAL NARRATIVITY

Ultimately, a definition of musical narrativity should comply with criteria that most listeners understand as central to musical storytelling. My view is that such criteria comprise a small set of essential elements: musical *spaces*, musical *agents*, and musical *transformations*. I am adopting the position of narratologist Marie-Laure Ryan that it is useful to conceive of narrativity as a fuzzy set of attributes:

> Rather than regarding narrativity as a strictly binary feature, that is, as a property that a given text either has or doesn't have, the definition proposed . . . presents narrative as a fuzzy set allowing variable degrees of membership, but centered on prototypical cases that everybody recognizes as stories.

In a scalar conception of narrative, definition becomes an open series of concentric circles which spell increasingly narrow conditions and which presuppose previously stated items, as we move from the outer to the inner circles, and from the marginal cases to the prototypes. (2007: 28)

First among Ryan's set of criteria is that a narrative must take place in "a world populated by individuated existents" (she marginalizes scenarios involving aggregates such as "the human race" or "matter"). Second is that the fictional world must "be situated in time and undergo significant transformations" caused by "non-habitual" events. Further criteria in her list serve to distinguish prototypical narratives from other sorts of accounts (such as recipes, sets of instructions, horoscopes, reports of causally unconnected events, or simply "bad stories" that fail to communicate meaningfully to an audience). Ryan emphasizes that different kinds of narratives may include some but not all of these elements and that certain narrative genres emphasize some criteria over others. Spatial features may be privileged over processive ones (e.g., as in fantasy and sci-fi genres), or goal-oriented action may be stressed over vivid portrayal of the fictional entities.

Post-tonal music may downplay the notion of a unified causal chain leading to cadential closure yet still retain other powerful narrative features, such as expressive agents and vivid spaces. In a work like Sciarrino's *Infinito nero*, with so much silence and muddled repetition, the lack of overtly syntactical features is itself a descriptive facet of a particular kind of agent inhabiting the story world – one who relinquishes her agency to the divine. But in any case, the parameters of timbre and texture, through their careful scaling and arrangement in the composition, have a capacity to project their own robust narrative logic of continuity and succession.

WORKS CITED

Bruhn, Siglind. 2003. *Saints in the Lime-light: Representations of the Religious Quest on the Post-1945 Operatic Stage.* Hillsdale: Pendragon Press.

Coleman, David. 2007. "At Home before and behind the Curtain." *New York Times,* March 4, 2007; Permalink: http://www.nytimes.com/2007/03/04/fashion/04possess.html (accessed January 26, 2010).

Lachenmann, Helmut. 2004. "Composing in the Shadow of Darmstadt." *Contemporary Music Review* 23(3): 43–53.

Lachenmann, Helmut, et al. 2008. "Music concrete instrumentale." Slought Foundation Online Content http://slought.org/content/11401/ (accessed June 27, 2010).

Metzer, David. 2006. "Modern Silence." *Journal of Musicology* 23(3): 331–74.

Meyer, Leonard B. 1989. *Style and Music.* Chicago: University of Chicago Press.

———. 2000. "Exploiting Limits: Creation, Archetypes, and Style Change." In *The Spheres of Music: A Gathering of Essays,* 189–225. Chicago: University of Chicago Press.

Pasler, Jann. 2007. *Writing through Music: Essays on Music, Culture, and Politics.* New York: Oxford University Press.

Reich, Steve, and Paul Hillier. 2002. *Writings on Music 1965–2000.* New York: Oxford University Press.

Ryan, Marie-Laure. 2007. "Toward a Definition of Narrative." In *The Cambridge Companion to Narrative,* edited by David Herman, 22–35. Cambridge: Cambridge University Press.

Sciarrino, Salvatore. 1998. *Infinito nero.* Milano: Casa Ricordi.

Wolf, Werner. 2007. "Description as a Transmedial Mode of Representation: General Features and Possibilities of Realization in Painting, Fiction, and Music." In *Description in Literature and Other Media,* edited by Werner Wolf and Walter Bernhart, 1–90. Amsterdam: Rodopi.

16

The Tropes of Desire and *Jouissance* in Kaija Saariaho's *L'amour de loin*

Yayoi Uno Everett

What I have in mind here is not a rigid opposition but a constantly negotiated tension between speech and music. For if it is possible as I have said, to
speak of a progression from speech to the cry, this progression is anything
but linear because it is ceaselessly caught up in the dialectic of the production of *jouissance* and its mastery, of attempting to transgress a limit and at
the same time to reaffirm it.

MICHEL POIZAT, *THE ANGEL'S CRY*

What if we conceive *desire* not simply as an object that seeks fulfillment in
the Other but rather as something that unleashes its own seeds of disruption, leading to a realm that Roland Barthes calls *jouissance*? Barthes defines
jouissance as being far more radical than bliss or pleasure in its orientation
toward the unknown, a trans-sensual experience characterized by disruption,
fragmentation, and loss of ego (1975: 51). In musical terms, Michel Poizat in
The Angel's Cry locates *jouissance* in the sustained high notes in tragic operas,
where verbal articulation dissolves into a primal cry; he points out that the
path leading to *jouissance* is nonlinear, marked by a dialectical process of af-
firming and transgressing the limit of vocal utterance. In this essay, I argue
that the narrative trajectory of Saariaho's *L'amour de loin* (2000) is governed
by a musical trope of desire that culminates in a state of *jouissance* precisely
in this manner. The opera revolves around the troubadour Jaufré, Countess
Clémence, who lives in exile in Tripoli, and the Pilgrim, who tries to bring
the lovers together. Unable to withstand the harsh journey at sea, Jaufré arrives in Tripoli but dies in Clémence's arms as soon as they are united. Clé-

mence blames herself for Jaufré's death and resolves to give her life to serve God. However, her final prayer to a "love far away" is filled with tension and ambiguity; in shouting out "J'espère, mon Seigneur!" over and over again, she transgresses into a mystical realm where it is no longer certain to whom she addresses her cry. The unity between lovers is established through their desire for the unattainable Other in the spiritual realm prior to their encounter in the phenomenal one, where desire unravels into the disruption of identity associated with *jouissance*.

Generally speaking, *jouissance* denotes "pleasure" or "enjoyment" in French; from a Lacanian perspective, however, it describes a condition that moves beyond the Freudian pleasure principle by "breaking off negotiations with the reality principle, that it [*jouissance*] bypasses the (unconscious) moderating, mitigating influence of the ego on the drives" (Johnston 2005: 234). Simply put, when the subject attempts to transgress the limit imposed on his or her enjoyment, pleasure turns to pain; the act of transgression, which is unable to control the subject's limit, pushes the subject into the dysphoric pole of *jouissance*. In Seminar XX (*Encore*), Lacan posits a specifically feminine form of *jouissance* that has to do with the *jouissance* of the Other; the feminine form differs from the masculine form, which is associated with bodily pleasure.[1] In the plot of *L'amour de loin*, the target of the two lovers' desire becomes displaced from the idealized Other to each other. Clémence is the enactment of Jaufré's fantasy, his search for the ideal woman – the Other displaced onto a woman who is, in actuality, consumed with self-doubt. Clémence's desire for the Other (displaced onto Jaufré) and the cause of desire (i.e., alienation from her homeland, union with God) become intertwined and lead her toward a crisis of identity associated with *jouissance*.

In my reading of *L'amour de loin*, Saariaho's music conveys the trope of desire and *jouissance* through the interplay of three types of music. The first involves textures based on sound masses, such as the fluid orchestral overture and electronic sounds that symbolize water and impermanence, which I argue convey the idea of desire as an *emergent* entity expressed in the Imaginary domain.[2] The second involves rhythmic chants and musical forms that index aspects of medieval culture, such as references to the troubadour song ("Lanquan li jorn"), open fifth chord, and medieval dance rhythm. The troubadour song encapsulates the pleasure and despair associated with the lovers' desire for the Other in the Symbolic domain: music is fused with the sung text and accompanying gestures to co-articulate the conflicting elements of desire. The last involves chords of rupture – dissonant, explosive chords that echo the lovers' fears and doubts. Notably, these chords are sounded at first as musical pronouncements detached from the characters' texted utterance; they later appear in the form of a *jouissance* attained, that is, when Clémence crosses over the vocal threshold, where her speech dissolves into a primal cry.

The powerful role music plays in *L'amour de loin* is especially vivid in a live production. In attending the 2003 production of the opera in Amsterdam, I was immediately struck by Saariaho's use of wordless choir and electronic effects to generate a timbral wash of sounds that resonated throughout the hall. The overture emerges from the a-metric, fluid texture, which simulates the vastness of the ocean separating the lovers and out of which concrete gestures emerge one by one to signify the material world. In response to a colleague's remark that the "music goes nowhere," I defended the music's deliberate absence of teleology as an essential feature of the musical drama. The music's circularity creates a hypnotic effect that embodies the ephemeral quality of desire, undercut by the ruptures created by the pounding, dissonant chords that seem to come out of nowhere. The ensuing analysis demonstrates how musical gestures, coupled with the libretto and performative components, embody the essence of desire and crisis of identity in both semiotic and symbolic terms.[3] To this end, I will refer to the DVD of the operatic production featuring Dawn Upshaw (Clémence), Gerald Finley (Jaufré), and Monica Groop (the Pilgrim), with the Finnish National Opera conducted by Esa-Pekka Salonen and the operatic production directed by Peter Sellars (Saariaho 2005).

NARRATOLOGICAL ANALYSIS

Saariaho became interested in the legend of Jaufré Rudel (1125–48), the prince of Blaye who fell in love with the countess of Tripoli, whom he never met. Through a pilgrim who came from Antioch, he sent his songs with beautiful melodies to her. Saariaho thought that the simplicity of this history suited the operatic subject she was looking for (Mallet 2002: 2). Taking the medieval troubadour Jaufré's poem "Lanquan li jorn son lonc en mai" (When the days are long in May), she used it as a source for *Lohn,* a piece for soprano and electronics (1996), and then incorporated the poem (with a melodic setting distinct from *Lohn*) into the full-scale opera. While the lovers' brief union before Jaufré's death may call to mind the final scene from Wagner's *Tristan und Isolde,* this narrative altogether avoids the romantic notion of transcendence. Here, the term *loin* (distance) is the key to understanding the irony of the dramatic narrative. *Loin* refers foremost to the physical distance that separates the lovers. However, the psychological separation of the lovers speaks to a deeper and more profound distance between them.

Amin Maalouf's libretto centers on the thoughts and mental states of the two lovers, who discover their longing for each other and communicate through the androgynous character of the pilgrim, who also serves to mediate between the Orient (Tripoli) and the Occident (Blaye). Liisamaija Hautsalo (2008) regards the story as influenced by multiple sources: Christian Crusades in the twelfth century, the troubadour tradition, Persian love poetry, and biblical and operatic texts. From a biblical perspective, Hautsalo sees the pilgrim as an angel, Clémence as a symbol of mercy, and Jaufré's journey into death (his Via Dolorosa) as a move toward resurrection. But is the narrative truly redemptive in the Christian sense? According to Pirkko Moisala, Saariaho regards this story as having relevance to how lovers relate to one another in today's world. Moisala claims that the lovers create illusions about one another but are afraid to confront reality; thus, Jaufré's death ultimately results from his lack of strength to face reality (2009: 97–98).

My reading builds on Moisala's perspective by focusing on the element of irony, which emerges in the narrative trajectory. Expressed through Greimas's semiotic square, a character's role (*actant*) and the course of action (*function*) each one undertakes in the narrative can be illustrated as shown in Figure 16.1. As with other semiotic squares, S_1 and S_1' (S_2 and S_2') are related via contradiction, S_1 and S_2 (S_1' and S_2') via contrariety, and S_1 and S_2' (S_2 and S_1') via complementation. If we were to reduce the actants to S_1 = hero/heroine, S_1' = anti-hero, S_2 = victim, and S_2' = helper, and if the accompanying functions were F_1 = love, F_1' = fear/despair, F_2 = death, and F_2' = life, then we could understand the narrative as follows: Jaufré (S_1) falls in love with the idea of Clémence (F_1), confronts fear of the sea or the unknown (F_1'), and succumbs to death (F_2). Clémence (S_1) falls in love with the idea of a troubadour who worships her (F_1), confronts fear and hate within herself and her relationship to God (F_1'), but in the end chooses to live (F_2'). While the Pilgrim assumes the role of the helper (S_2'), the lovers' doubt and fear are manifest as their nemesis (S_2). Their positions mirror one another on this schematic diagram, as shown by the arrows that point in different directions. They are united in their desire for one another, but desire as an object is tossed back and forth, *mise en abyme*, between the lovers, who communicate through the Pilgrim. And desire for the unattainable Other manifests itself differently within each of the three characters: Jaufré yearns for spiritual love that moves beyond the material domain, Clémence for her childhood and her homeland (Toulouse),

Actants   Functions

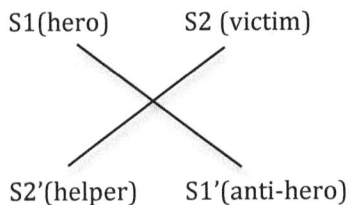

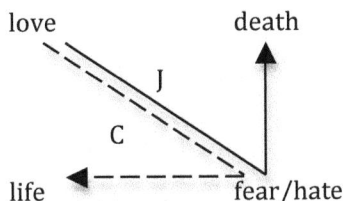

FIGURE 16.1. Actantial progression.

and the Pilgrim for the Holy Land (Iitti 2002: 11). It is only when their desires move beyond the Imaginary into the phenomenal realm of the characters' existence that those desires elicit fear and pain.[4]

This progression from desire to *jouissance* can be broken down into more specific phases: there is a tropological shift that takes place as desire gives way to doubt, then to a dream, followed by death and despair. The formal scheme of the opera divides into five acts, and the dramaturgical structures of acts 1 and 2 mirror one another in such a way that the Pilgrim serves the pivotal function in establishing contact between Jaufré and Clémence. The desire for the Other crystallizes in act 2, when the Pilgrim sings Jaufré's song to Clémence and the latter echoes the first phrase by singing it back to herself in Occitan. In act 3 fear and doubt begin to manifest themselves in the lovers' reaction to the Pilgrim's news about the other: Jaufré is initially angered by the fact that the Pilgrim sang his song and revealed his identity to Clémence, while Clémence is plagued by the thought of loving the poem more than the troubadour himself. From here onward, the mirroring structure dissolves, giving way to discontinuity. In act 4 the Pilgrim takes Jaufré on the journey at sea, where the lovers' desire comes to fruition in a dream where the two meet. Act 5 provides the scene where the lovers finally meet, only to confront Jaufré's death. As the narrative progresses, the lovers fall sway to the excesses of desire; caught up in the euphoric and dysphoric states of *jouissance,* they can no longer see the world as it once stood. It is in the dream (act 4) that Jaufré experiences the highest state of bliss, where desire reaches its point of culmination for him; awakening from the dream, he is consumed by the fear of death at sea. With Jaufré's death, Clémence is pushed into a trans-sensual realm of *jouissance:* her cry to God is at first excessive and primal, filled with anger and remorse, before it eventually passes into resignation.

And the concluding situation is ironic precisely because the context fails to support what is claimed. It is unclear whether Jaufré is in love with Clémence or in love with the idea of the unattainable Other. Likewise, Clémence is at first enraged with God for the death of Jaufré, then she asks for forgiveness as she resigns herself to living out the rest of her life in a convent. But when she speaks of love at the end, it is uncertain whether her utterance is directed at Jaufré or God.

MUSICAL ANALYSIS

There are a number of scholarly publications that have uncovered the stylistic and structural aspects of this work with sufficient clarity. For example, Liisamaija Hautsalo's book explores the medieval notion of courtly love by uncovering various musical topics in *L'amour de loin*, which include the pastoral, *pianto*, lullaby, chorale-lament, tarantella, and resurrection. She classifies them according to types based on icon, index, and genre (Hautsalo 2008: 82). Her analysis is particularly useful in illustrating the intertextual dimensions of the music and how they relate to operatic conventions from the past. The function of the chorus is particularly important in filling out an atmosphere of medieval times. As Jaufré's friends at the court of Blaye, the members of the male chorus interact with the troubadour; in the "tempest" scene, they sing a song about the warrior who feared the sea in the style of a tarantella (act 4, scene 3). In contrast, the members of the female chorus represent Clémence's women at the court of Tripoli and interact with the countess in a number of distinctive ways: notably, they sing a chorale lament in consoling Clémence after Jaufré dies and, at a later point, assume the voice of God in silencing Clémence's rage.

Spencer Lambright's dissertation complements Hautsalo's work by focusing on the harmonic and textural structure of Saariaho's opera. Notably, in tracing Saariaho's treatment of harmony influenced by techniques of the French spectral school, Lambright introduces the concept of *harmonic field* to refer to a series of harmonic units, characterized by smaller intervals clustered in the higher register over the bass, to which the surface musical gestures are anchored. Although Saariaho does not use spectral harmonic techniques per se in *L'amour de loin*, many of her harmonic fields are modeled on the distribution of pitches that resemble the structure of the harmonic overtone series. Lambright illustrates the progression in the harmonic fields based on a B♭ pedal, as shown in Example 16.1: Field I constitutes the main chordal complex

EXAMPLE 16.1. Harmonic fields based on B♭ pedal (Lambright 2008).

that contains the open-fifth sonority of F♯/C♯ (omitting the bass B♭); Field II shifts the F♯ to the highest register, while the intervening voices support the troubadour melody in the Aeolian mode; Field III shows the chordal forma-tion at the climax of the orchestral interlude, whose intervallic constitution resembles the overtone series most closely;[5] and Field IV appears at the end of the opera (Lambright 2008: 64–67). Notice how the harmonic fields expand in register, while the density of the chord thins down to three notes by the end. Lambright further provides detailed analyses of harmonic changes within acts 1 and 2, illustrating the local fluctuations of harmonic fields within the opening scene from act 2, as shown to the right of Example 16.1. Notice how the harmonic progression oscillates back and forth between chords built on E♭3 and the "pillar" chords built on B♭1.

Overall, Lambright's analysis illustrates how a sense of distended time emerges through the gradual and organic changes in harmony and texture (2008: 65). And this compositional strategy is essential to creating and sus-taining the static, circular sense of temporality one experiences in hearing the opera live. Adding to Hautsalo's and Lambright's findings, I offer a her-meneutic reading that brings the stylistic and structural elements together in exploring the musical trope of desire and its manifestation into *jouissance*.

MUSICAL TROPES OF DESIRE

Saariaho introduces two opposing musical expressions that materialize into the trope of desire; that is to say, desire is initially expressed as an ascending motive that signifies positive engagement (yearning), on the one hand, and as a descending motive that signifies negative engagement (resignation), on the other. In the opera's unfolding, these motives emerge to signify desire through cyclical repetition and correlation with the sung text. The idea of

Translation: "the woman I desire is so far, so far away."

EXAMPLE 16.2. Jaufré's "desire" motive (act I, reh. N1).

desire is manifested symbolically in the troubadour song that the Pilgrim sings to Clémence, which embodies desire in the forms of longing and resignation. Desire reaches its fulfillment in the dream Jaufré has on his voyage to Tripoli, where he sees a vision of Clémence. Their brief encounter prior to Jaufré's death pushes Clémence into a state of *jouissance*, fraught by disruption, rupture, and a loss of identity.

For an example of the former category, the ascending quintuplet motive that accompanies Jaufré's articulation of desire for a woman far away is shown in Example 16.2; it is characterized by a cyclical repetition of an ascending four-note motive (*x*) that accords with Jaufré's expression of desire on a D-Lydian mode, with a slight modal clash between A (voice) and A$\sharp$ (vibraphone). This motive is introduced in the vibraphone in the overture (m. 3), the first scene that introduces Clémence (act 2), and appears in various configurations transferred to the harp before and after the decisive point where it correlates to Jaufré's expression of desire for the woman; since he does not know yet whether she exists or not, the motive is emblematic of desire for the imaginary Other. Later in act 3, when Jaufré learns the woman's name from the Pilgrim, a series of ascending motives in the piano is introduced (Example 16.3); here the melodic contour is neither cyclical nor static but is distinguished by an upward linear motion that ascends to a higher register. Jaufré's vocal contour also aims toward the melodic apex on D4, the focal pitch of the desire motive (*x*) shown in Example 16.2. The lilting triple meter here also anticipates the musical ode he will sing to Clémence during his brief encounter with his beloved before his death.

In contrast, a descending melodic contour is used to express desire in the form of resignation. The most prominent of these motives is the three-

Translation: "Clémence, Clémence, like the sky is merciful!"

EXAMPLE 16.3. Jaufré's recognition of Clémence's name (act 3, mm. 369–74).

part phrase played successively by piccolo, flute, and alto flute, which is associated with the Pilgrim in the opera.[6] The falling semitone *glissando* (sigh
motive) provides an important marker of the Pilgrim's own yearning in her
life spent as a nomadic seafarer. When Clémence expresses her longing for
her homeland (Toulouse), her vocal utterance similarly takes the form of a
descending line (motive *y*) that extends from B♭5 to F♯4, as shown in Example
16.4. Although the Pilgrim speaks passionately of many who aspire to visit
Tripoli and other countries that comprised the Orient during the medieval
period, Clémence responds with remorse and a touch of melancholy, unable
to finish her train of thought. She utters the same phrase two more times,
with slight variations in contour and rhythm; in her final extended utterance,
she confesses her desire to leave Tripoli: "So many people dream of coming to
the Orient, while I dream of leaving it." This passage segues into Clémence's
painful memory of being uprooted from her homeland at the age of five to live
in Tripoli, never able to see her homeland again.

The same descending line from B♭ to F♯, anchored to harmonic Field I
(Example 16.1), is expanded into a longer sequence to signify the sense of resignation and despair in the final act.[7] As Clémence realizes that she has lost
Jaufré, she initially pleads to God, expressing that she "still hopes" for his pity,
compassion, and goodness. As the female chorus joins in with a solemn chant,
Clémence's spirit begins to unravel, and her sorrow gradually turns to anger
and despair. The melodic incipit, an ascending D–F♯–G–A that accompanies
her utterance "J'espère encore," is heard in direct opposition to the descending
sequence based on motive *y*.

s'adressant à lui, mais également au Ciel, ainsi qu'à elle-même:

Translation: "So many people dream of coming...."; "Constantinople, Babylon, Antioch, the oceans of sand...."

EXAMPLE 16.4. Clémence's longing for her homeland.

The troubadour's song, sung by the Pilgrim and Clémence, encapsulates both aspects of desire (longing and resignation), bringing them together into a coherent utterance. The lyrics are partially drawn from Jaufré Rudel's "Lanquan li jorn son lonc en mai." The Pilgrim sings three stanzas in French, then Clémence echoes part of the first stanza in Occitan. The act of mirroring the Pilgrim is an important process by which Clémence begins to acknowledge desire for the Other within herself. The English translation appears below.

The Pilgrim:
Never shall I delight in love
If I delight not in this distant love,
For a nobler nor a better love I know not of
Wheresoever, neither near, nor far.
Its worth so great is, and so true,
That over there, in the kingdom of the Saracens,
For her sake, I would a captive be.

I hold faith with Our Lord
That by his grace I shall see my distant love.
Yet through this one piece of fortune
My ills are doubled, since she is so far away.
Ah, that I were there, a pilgrim
So that my staff and my robe
Could fall beneath the gaze of her beautiful eyes.
He who calls me greedy speaks aright
For wishing for a distant love,
For no joy would please me as much
As to delight in this distant love,

But what I wish for is denied me.
Such was my godfather's decree,
That I should love and be not loved.

Clémence:
Never shall I delight in love
If I delight not in this distant love,
For a nobler nor a better love I know not of
Wheresoever, neither near, nor far.

The melody of this song is structured so that the phrases end alternately on the focal pitch A4 and its dominant E5 above. As shown in Example 16.5, the vocal phrase makes ample use of ornamentations such as the upward semitonal *glissando*, melisma, and trills. The word "loin" (far) is always placed on the melodic apex, E5, on the alternate phrase to accentuate the sense of longing. While the antecedent phrase features a falling contour, the consequent phrase rises to the melodic apex. The mode is primarily Aeolian, although the occasional use of B♭ infuses it with a Phrygian inflection. When Clémence echoes this melody in the final verse, she sings it a whole step higher, beginning on C5, and her melodic phrase extends the contour upward as if to project her desire more forcefully onto her psyche. This is the pivotal moment when Clémence passes from the Imaginary ("mirror-play") to the Symbolic domain: she takes ownership of this song as the embodiment of desire by singing it back in her own dialect (Occitan). After she concludes her last utterance, "loin," on the melodic peak, B6, the orchestra strikes the chord of rupture; the dissonant constitution of this chord presages the turn toward the dysphoric pole of *jouissance*.

Ultimately, the lovers' expression of their desires takes place in the dream state (act 4, scene 2). As Jaufré embarks on a journey at sea, he overcomes his fear of the sea in a dream in which he has a vision of Clémence singing to him: "Your love fills my mind, waking and dreaming. But it is dreaming that I prefer, because in dreams you are mine!" He, in turn, sings to himself about his fear: "Then she turned around and opened her arms, but I dared not go to her."[8] Thus in this very dream where they appear to be addressing one another, there is a profound physical separation of the lovers. As soon as he wakes up from the dream, Jaufré confesses to the Pilgrim his fear of dying at sea – the fear to which he eventually succumbs. In the actantial progression, the dream provides the pivotal moment in which the positive pole of desire (S1) shifts toward the negative pole of fear and despair (S1').

Translation: "Never will I enjoy love, if I don't enjoy this distant love."

EXAMPLE 16.5. Troubadour's song (the Pilgrim).

JOUISSANCE: CHORDS OF RUPTURE AND THE PRIMAL CRY

Anne Sivuoja-Gunaratnam, in her analysis of Saariaho's *Lohn*, suggests that the disruptive processes in the last stanza of the song characterize Barthes's *jouissance*, a trans-sensual experience in which the subject is led beyond language (2003: 79). Most importantly, Barthes argues that *jouissance* differs from the principle of pleasure, which obeys cultural codes, such as literary or stylistic conventions, in pushing beyond established modes of signification, seasoned by erotic desire. As Barthes himself describes the characteristics of *jouissance* in terms of fragmentation ("Pleasures in pieces, language in pieces, culture in pieces"), Sivuoja-Gunaratnam argues that the treatment of the final stanza of the text testifies to this state of *jouissance* through fragmentation. As Saariaho's music for *Lohn* progresses, she uses fewer lines from Jaufré's stanzas and recombines fragments of words in such a way that the linearity and semantic meaning dissolve and give way to sheer vocality (77).

In *L'amour de loin*, Clémence crosses this vocal threshold when she cries out to God over the loss of Jaufré. And while the lovers are not conscious of this development at first, dissonant chords are interpolated into the earlier scenes (acts 1 and 2) to foreshadow the shift that will take place from the initial state of bliss to doubt and despair. The main sequence of chords (rhythm and instrumentation omitted) appears in Example 16.6. Compared to the relatively consonant "pillar" harmonic fields discussed by Lambright, these chords are much more dissonant, including microtonal deviations at times; see, for example, the C5 with a quarter-tone flat in the first harmonic field shown under Example 16.6. As Saariaho herself identifies them as chords of "destiny," their sporadic appearances in act 1 cast an ominous shadow over the course of events to come.[9] In the earlier scenes, these chords of rupture

EXAMPLE 16.6. Chords of rupture.

index doubt and a shift in mood (melancholy) in the Imaginary domain – that is to say, often following an action or verbal utterance, the chords "mirror" the characters' internal response, which is yet to be integrated into their conscious thought. Although the density and range of each chord varies from context to context, they are most often anchored to the bass note B♭. Other occurrences of this chord (omitted from Example 16.6) include Jaufré's fear of going to Tripoli by sea (act 2, scene 2), his fear of the sea (act 4, scene 1), and his convulsions (act 5, scene 1).

The articulation of these chords *becomes* symbolic only when they converge with the enunciated text in the final act. Clémence's ecstasy in receiving the news of Jaufré's arrival in Tripoli dissolves quickly into frenzy as soon as she realizes that he is dying. Her cry to God verges on the point of madness; her repeated outcry to God, "Seigneur," is sung *Sprechstimme*, punctuated by the most dissonant harmonic field played *tutti* (Example 16.6, fifth chord). Later, when the women of the chorus warn her ("Woman, you are letting your passion lead you astray!"), their repeated outcry on the word "Silence!" is accompanied by a series of pounding, dissonant harmonies anchored to B♭1 (Example 16.6, sixth chord). These chords build up to a peak of dynamic and gestural intensity, forcing Clémence (in Sellars's production) to cover her head in sheer pain and agony. These chords of rupture signify *jouissance* by articulating the positive and negative poles of desire and despair in tandem. And this process manifests itself differently for the lovers. For Jaufré, it is the fear of the unknown – the long journey at sea – that breaks him down. He nonetheless dies blissfully in Clémence's arms as he finds fulfillment in their brief encounter. For Clémence, it is the realization that Jaufré died in his attempt to be united with her that catapults her into this fused state of bliss and despair. As a constitutive experience for the listener, the final two scenes are filled with dramatic excesses that signify Clémence's fall into an irrational, disorienting state of *jouissance*. In Sellars's production, one wonders what is signified by the static and reverberating final scene, where Clémence sinks into the water and sings to God, "I only adore you." From Lacan's psychoanalytic perspective, this excess represents the surplus that resists integration into the Symbolic Order of her material existence. With Clémence's repeated cries to God followed by her eventual resignation, she gives in to the fluid, pre-symbolic realm of the Real. As the chords of rupture reverberate in the electronic soundscape that envelopes her, her final words are about the distance (*loin*) that separates her from God – that the unattainable Other is God, not Jaufré, after all.

CONCLUSION: DESIRE AND THE TRANSITIVITY OF LOVE

Jann Pasler suggests a new kind of narrative in contemporary works that "borrow the most important attributes of traditional narratives – the use of signifieds, well-defined structures, configuration, unifying reference points, transformation, and memory. But they continue to respond to the modern desire for expressing the multiplicity of existence, fragmentary and seemingly irrational orders, and meanings that go beyond those that are known" (1989: 252). Saariaho and Maalouf's *L'amour de loin* fits Pasler's notion of a new kind of narrative that explores the fragmentary and irrational order of existence as a manifestation of desire from a thoroughly modern perspective. Departing from Freud's notion of desire as "an internal, subjective force distorting the external, objective order of the space of social reality," Lacan's desire of the Other "encircles" the topographical space by "being co-extensive with an external order" (Johnston 2005: 212). The musical trope of desire in this opera is articulated not through a diametric opposition of forces that propels the motion forward but rather through the *encircling* musical elements that shape the distended sense of narrative time.[10] Through cyclical and non-developmental procedures, the melodic elements (with upward or downward contours) project desire and resignation, while the chords of rupture evolve into the signifier of *jouissance* as vertical sonorities that disrupt stable harmonic fields (anchored to B♭1). What consumes Clémence at the end of the opera is the feminine form of *jouissance* or the *jouissance* of the Other: she relinquishes the suffering incurred from her pursuit of worldly love through the metaphysical union she wishes to achieve with God. Her immersion in water at the end of this production is especially telling: through this quasi-baptismal rite, she returns to the undifferentiated domain of the Imaginary as she points her finger to the sky. Her final utterance, which dissolves into the reverberating electronic soundscape, suggests that God is her "l'amour de loin" (love far away).

One could argue that the primary functions (i.e., love vs. fear) that drive the narrative trajectory of the opera are fused as both cause and effect: Jaufré fears death and thus succumbs to death for the love of Clémence; Clémence fears suffering and suffers for love as she finds refuge in God. To reduce the narrative trajectory of this opera simply to a tragic or romantic archetype fails to confront the essential questions it raises: What is the nature of human desire? Is it a projection of our own lack? Could we fathom Clémence and Jaufré as constituting different elements of our own divided psyche? What this opera delivers in the end are messages about the transitivity of love, its plural and fragmented nature, and the *jouissance* of the listener in experiencing his or her own dissolution of boundaries in identifying with the characters' journey.

NOTES

1. Lacan discusses how the feminine form moves beyond the masculine form of *jouissance* precisely because woman is "not-whole" and "has a supplementary jouissance compared to what the phallic function designates by way of jouissance." I interpret this to mean that woman is not confined to the "phallic" *jouissance* with a signifier that can be sustained by a discourse but rather to an all-encompassing form of *jouissance* that can be experienced, however ultimately unsignifiable. Lacan mentions the state of ecstasy associated with mystics such as Saint Theresa and Hadewijch as examples of the feminine form of *jouissance* (see Miller 1998: 74–76).

2. For Lacan, the Imaginary is the preverbal domain in which opposite expressions are brought together without cohering into a meaningful totality. The Symbolic takes place in the linguistic domain characterized by differentials: "The identity of each of the moments consists in its difference to the opposite moment," and a verbal utterance "embodies what is lacking in the other" (Žižek 1989: 193–94). In my hearing of this opera, the musical trope of desire emerges first in the Imaginary ("mirror play" of musical expressions without concrete signification) before it passes into the Symbolic domain (where the sung text and music are fused into a meaningful totality).

3. By drawing a distinction between the semiotic and symbolic, I refer to Julia Kristeva's notion that the semiotic embodies the performative dimensions of tone, rhythm, and gestures that shape a musical utterance: emergent, signifying processes that precede and exceed the syntactical dimensions of musical structure (1984: 26). Furthermore, Suzanne

Gruss argues that Kristeva conceived the semiotic as founded "not on a lack, but on a form of plenitude" that precedes and exceeds the structure of language. In contrast to Lacan, Kristeva views the symbolic as unstable due to "the constant pressure of the excessive semiotic," leading to her thesis that the constitution of a subject is never finished (Gruss 2008: 112).

4. From a Lacanian perspective, fear and pain are the traumatic residues of the Real; while these residues resist definition by symbolic discourse, they take shape in the symbolic discourse in the form of ruptures (Žižek 1992: 39).

5. The third harmonic field comes from an orchestral work, *Oltra mar* (Across the sea), which Saariaho composed prior to the opera; this work is based on a cyclical structure in which the textural density builds up slowly to cover the full range of the harmonic field. She incorporated it into the opera as the prelude to act 4, where Jaufré embarks on a journey across the ocean.

6. Based on an interview with Kaija Saariaho on June 10, 2010.

7. See DVD track 14 for act 4, scene 4, where Clémence (played by Dawn Upshaw) directs her anger at God for the death of Jaufré.

8. See DVD track 10 for act 4, scene 2.

9. Based on an interview with Kaija Saariaho on June 10, 2010.

10. Pasler claims that transformation, particularly in music, involves "a creative manipulation and integration of the three senses of time – past, present and future." Quoting Paul Ricoeur, who refers to Augustine's concept, she argues that one can only really experience distention "if the mind acts, that is, expects, attends, and remembers" (Pasler 1989: 243).

WORKS CITED

Barthes, Roland. 1975. *The Pleasure of the Text.* Translated by Richard Miller. Oxford: Basil Blackwell Publishing.

Gruss, Susanne. 2009. *The Pleasure of the Feminist Text.* Amsterdam: Editions Rodopi BV.

Hautsalo, Liisamaija. 2008. *Kaukainen rakkaus: Saavuttamattomuuden semantikka Kaija Saariahon oopperassa.* Helsinki: Yliopistopaino.

Iitti, Sanna. 2002. "*L'amour de loin*: Kaija Saariaho's First Opera." *International Alliance for Women in Music* 8(1–2): 9–14.

Johnston, Adrian. 2005. *Time Driven: Metapsychology and the Splitting of the Drive.* Evanston: Northwestern University Press.

Kristeva, Julia. 1984. *Revolution in Poetic Language.* New York: Columbia University Press.

Lambright, Spencer N. 2008. "*L'Amour de loin* and the Vocal Works by Kaija Saariaho." DMA diss., Cornell University.

Mallet, Franck. 2002. "Kaija Saariaho de subtiles connexions entre lumière et son." *Le monde de la musique* June–August, 1–3.

Miller, Jacques-Alain, ed. 1998. *On Feminine Sexuality, the Limits of Love and Knowledge, 1972–73: Encore (The Seminar of Jacques Lacan, Book XX).* Translated by Bruce Fink. New York: W. W. Norton.

Moisala, Pirkko. 2009. *Kaija Saariaho.* Chicago: University of Illinois Press.

Pasler, Jann. 1989. "Narrative and Narrativity in Music." In *Time and Mind: Interdisciplinary Issues,* edited by J. T. Fraser, 232–57. Madison: International Universities Press.

Poizat, Michel. 1992. *The Angel's Cry: Beyond the Pleasure Principle in Art.* Translated by Arthur Denner. Ithaca: Cornell University Press.

Saariaho, Kaija. 2005. *Kaija Saariaho: L'Amour de loin.* Deutsche Grammophon DVD B0004721-09.

Sivuoja-Gunaratnam, Anne. 2003.

"Desire and Distance in Kaija Saariaho's *Lohn.*" *Organised Sound* 8(1): 71–84.

Žižek, Slavoj. 1989. *The Sublime Object of Ideology.* London: Verso.

———. 1992. *Looking Awry: An Introduction to Lacan through Popular Culture.* Cambridge: MIT Press.

17

Expressive Doubling and the Narrative of Rebirth in Shostakovich's String Quartet No. 3, op. 73

Sarah Reichardt Ellis

I would like to begin in the middle, which is also an end. The second movement of Dmitri Shostakovich's five-movement String Quartet No. 3 (1946) ends with a *morendo* marking and a dissonant tetrachord created by E2, G2, G3, C4, and E♭4 (Example 17.1). Judith Kuhn describes this final chord as having an "eerie ambiguity" that sounds "more like an ellipses than a conclusion" (2010: 117).[1] *Morendo* markings are a bit of a cliché in Shostakovich's works; ten of his fifteen quartets close with that performance instruction. Yet, most often the marking appears at the end of a work; a *morendo* marking concluding a middle movement is a rarer occurrence. Shostakovich uses internal *morendo* markings in only six of his string quartets, the first four and Nos. 10 and 15. But not all of these uses of the performance marking are as straightforward as they initially seem. In the First Quartet the movement with the *morendo* marking was originally the final movement and thus, at least when first composed, was not an internal *morendo* (see Kuhn 2010: 37). The internal *morendo* in the Fifteenth Quartet is part of a contradiction in performance instructions, as the first movement ends with both a *morendo* and an *attacca* marking. In addition, it is not Shostakovich's standard practice to end on a dissonant harmony. When he does, it usually occurs along with an *attacca* that launches the music directly into the next movement.[2] Couple the dissonant tetrachord with the internal *morendo* marking and this becomes a very unusual end to a movement. The close raises multiple questions with

EXAMPLE 17.1. Shostakovich, String Quartet No. 3, final measures of the second movement.
String Quartet No. 3 in F Major, op. 73. By Dmitri Shostakovich. Copyright © 1947 (Renewed) by G. Schirmer, Inc. (ASCAP). International Copyright Secured. All Rights Reserved. Reprinted by Permission.

regard to the eerie dissonance and a marking that instructs the music to "die" in the midst of a piece.

The fading dissonant harmony of the second movement leaves the Third Quartet in an ambiguous state; in the space between the second and third movements, the quartet seems to be at an expressive crossroads. With the opening of the third movement, any notion of a non-tragic narrative trajectory instantly disappears; in Richard Taruskin's words, "thereafter things turn serious" (2009: 351). What follows is a brutal scherzo, a keening lament, and a haunting finale, all of which defy standard formal definitions. Instead, the third and fourth movements seem to be a negative mirror of the initial movements, presenting the issues at stake in the opening movements from a

dysphoric perspective. In doing so, these movements create a dialectical response to the first and second movements, which can be interpreted through
the concept of expressive doubling.

EXPRESSIVE DOUBLING

In *Music as Cultural Practice*, Lawrence Kramer explores the structural
trope of expressive doubling in Beethoven's two-movement piano sonatas
(1990: 21–71). Kramer defines expressive doubling as "a form of repetition in
which alternative versions of the same pattern define a cardinal difference
in perspective" (22). He relates expressive doubling to Derrida's concept of
the supplement, where the initial term presents something that is presented
as a whole; the second term, the double, is "an extra, a discontinuity, that
displaces – but does not nullify – the original term" (24). The supplement,
in short, is something that completes what was thought to be complete in
the first place. The result is a dialectical engagement between terms, as the
second term responds to problematic aspects of the first, transposing them to
a different expressive plane. Kramer notes that an expressive double should
not be perceived as mandatory, stating, "It is a trope of the possible, the extra,
the unforeseen" (36). Inherent in a doubling is a hierarchy of terms, where one
term often "represents the transposition of the other to a higher or deeper
plane, a more brilliant or profound register" (30). Whereas most expressive
doublings involve a utopian master plot moving from a low term to one on a
higher plane, which Kramer identifies as transfiguration, the reverse, travesty,
is also possible.

Robert Hatten uses Kramer's conceptualization of expressive doubling as
a means of understanding the dramatic content of Beethoven's String Quartet
in B♭ Major, op. 130 (2004: 35–42). Hatten argues that Beethoven's design for
the inner movements involves two pairs of contrasting movements, with each
coupling composed of a scherzo and slow movement, creating a six-movement
amplification of the more traditional four-movement structure. In each of
these pairs, the slow movement responds to the scherzo that precedes it. Specifically, Hatten argues that the dysphoric plenitude of the Presto movement
is countered by a euphoric plenitude of the Andante and that the Andante is
better understood through this relationship than through its formal structure, which is rather ambiguous. In Hatten's words, "an expressive interpretation may be more to the point in capturing the relevant dramatic trajectory of
its [the Andante's] form" (50).

I suggest that in his Third Quartet Shostakovich composes a work in which the five-movement form can be interpreted through a framework of movement doublings, similar to Hatten's discussion of op. 130. Specifically, the third and fourth movements present alternative versions of the first two movements, as each of the later movements is structured out of the earlier movement's points of dissolution. As noted, a clear rhetorical break occurs between the second and third movements. On closer inspection, though, the opening movements show signs of fraying; in the first movement, the exposition is suddenly interrupted and the recapitulation aborted, leading to an unexpectedly "dying" second movement. The points of dissolution in the comparatively non-tragic first set of movements then create doubles that express a sense of inescapable brutality and intense sorrow. Yet the quartet does not end on this dysphoric note. Shostakovich adds a fifth movement, with which he moves beyond the tragic narrative of the expressive doubles toward a sense of rebirth and transcendence.

THE FIRST AND SECOND MOVEMENTS

With the opening pair of movements, Shostakovich places the Third Quartet firmly within the lineage of the first Viennese school by referencing traditional conceptions of Classical forms. The first movement, in F major, is clearly in sonata form. In addition to sharply delineated primary- and secondary-theme zones and a Beethovenesque fugue for a development, he includes what is by 1946 an anachronistic repeat of the exposition. (Shostakovich would write one other expositional repeat in his quartets in the first movement of the Fifth Quartet.) The second movement also follows convention as a scherzo and trio form.

Still, both movements have ruptures in form, rhetoric, and key. On the formal level, both movements have issues with respect to closure. In the first movement, near the end of the secondary area, the musical flow is forcefully cut short by a three-measure interruption (mm. 81–83), which is rhetorically marked on several levels (Table 17.1). With the interruption, the dynamics increase from *piano* to *forte*, the three-voice texture in the low registers contrasts with the interruption's high melody with accompanimental multi-stop chords, and the movement's first change of meter occurs. Motives from the interruption are taken from the themes of the Primary (P) and Secondary (S) zones.[3] The initial descending sixteenth-note run is outlined in the opening theme, and the descending trill-figure first appears earlier in the S zone. Prior to the

TABLE 17.1. FORM OF THE FIRST MOVEMENT

SECTION			MEASURES	KEY
Exposition				
	Primary (P) zone		1–45	F d V/F
	Transition		46–53	V/F e
	Secondary (S) zone			
		S1 S2	54–80	(C?) e
		Interruption	**81–83**	
		S2 S1	84–92	e♭
	(Re)transition		93–102	e F
Development			103–81	
(fugue)				
Recapitulation				
	P zone		177–89	F
	Transition		190–98	
	S zone		199–225	b
		Interruption	**226–50**	b
Coda			251–72	F

interruption, the music had begun to wander away from its already tenuous tonal moorings, and the interruption further muddies the harmonic situation. After three measures, the second melody from S returns, but not without residual effects – the melody enters in the first violin at an octave higher than it was prior to the interruption, and the cello follows in a dissonant canon, now over two octaves higher (Kuhn 2010: 112). The dynamics, dissonant imitation, and high range all combine to indicate that the tension created by the interruption does not dissipate as quickly as it appeared.

The recapitulation does not function as a structure of accomplishment, as it lacks both large-scale harmonic and rhetorical resolution. The return of P occurs in the midst of developmental tension and is truncated after its initial phrase. The S material returns in B minor, a tritone removed from the home key, to which it never manages to return. In addition to the failure to create harmonic closure, the S zone is not allowed to conclude rhetorically. In the exposition, the interruption disrupts the S zone; in the recapitulation, this music takes control of the conclusion of the movement. Instead of briefly suspending the course of the S theme, the music of the interruption, which is both metrically and harmonically unstable, expands to twenty-five measures (mm. 226–50) and leads directly to the coda (based on P material). It is not until the end of the coda, outside the sonata space, that the tonic key, F, is reestablished. Thus, what occurs is a severely truncated recapitulation in which the S material never returns in the tonic and is cut short by the music of the interruption. While the movement does return to the home key, it only does so in the coda.

The second movement, in E minor, is in a scherzo and trio form, although the large-scale return of the scherzo never fully takes shape, and music from the trio bleeds into the final section (see Kuhn 2010: 114). The descending scalar motion of the interruption reappears in this movement (initially in m. 6) and is developed into a quintuplet turn (see m. 44), which plays a role in the first significant fissure in the movement's structure (in m. 147), during the return of the scherzo. Prior to m. 147, the material of the scherzo had wandered off any stable harmonic course, resulting in the violins performing parallel tritones. This music leads to m. 147, where the lower three instruments hold a dissonant trichord (increasing dynamically from *forte*) while the first violin performs the quintuplet turn. The turn itself begins at *fortissimo* and is marked with a *crescendo*. After this forceful dissonance, a quarter rest and a fermata over the barline follow, creating a moment of echoing silence. With the compound ternary return of the scherzo material failing to bring the movement to a close, the music turns to material from the middle of the trio, which is itself interrupted by a brooding, ascending solo in the first violin. The violin reaches up to E5, with which it reintroduces the main theme of the trio in E major, setting the stage for another potential closure in the home key. Yet the trio's music also dissolves into a moment of silence (see m. 173), followed by a return of the scherzo's opening theme in the cello, which soon fades off into a four-octave, E-minor arpeggio that creates a beautiful rhetorical, harmonic, and structural close (see Example 17.1, mm. 183–86). But the quintuplet turn reappears in the next measure, now in the viola, again disrupting the antici-pated closure. After this best attempt at closure is frustrated, the music gives up, fading away on the dissonant tetrachord.

In retrospect, the dissonant tetrachord points to harmonic conflicts left unresolved in the opening movements. In the first movement, tensions arise with the key of the S zone. In comparison to the primary material, the S zone is a more loosely defined structure, and initially its key is unclear. Denise Elshoff has shown that the opening phrase of the S1 theme is tonally ambiguous and initially could be interpreted as in either C major or E minor (see mm. 54–61). Eventually, a linear wedge to E at m. 61 begins to weight the music toward E minor; this is confirmed by an authentic cadence at mm. 68–69. Thus, the S zone seems to vacillate between a traditional, diatonic move to the dominant and a non-traditional, chromatic slip down a half step from the home key to E minor (Elshoff 2007: 78–79, 182; see also Kuhn 2010: 109–11).

The opening measures of the second movement dash any thoughts that the first movement's coda had resolved the F versus E tension, as the second movement begins with E-minor arpeggiations in the viola, announcing the key for the movement. The half-step dissonance is amplified with the opening theme of the movement, where the first violin's melody outlines both F and F♯ major, creating a disorienting period of polytonality. As noted, while the first movement's recapitulation is abruptly cut short and forced to an end, the second movement spends almost fifty measures trying to conclude, and three times the music disintegrates into silence before it fades away on the dissonant tetrachord. The chord has at least two potential interpretations: (1) as a split third chord with a root of C; (2) as a momentary instance of polytonality where E minor is defined in the lower instruments and C minor in the violins (recall the polytonal opening of the movement). If the chord is polytonal, it expresses the two potential tonics of the first movement's S zone (E and C). If it is a split third chord, the movement as a whole moves from E minor to C, thus wavering between the S theme's two potential tonics. Determining a definitive label for this chord is not important, as what is interesting is the correlation between the harmonic instabilities of the close of the second movement and those of the first movement's secondary space.[4]

In the first movement, the expositional S zone was able to overcome its internal harmonic tension and cadence on E minor, ultimately creating a large-scale tension between F and E. The three-measure interruption then introduces motivic instabilities that eventually force an end to the movement before the recapitulation can complete its rhetorical and structural function. The second movement, immediately weakened by polytonality, cannot force a close, instead disintegrating thematically before stalling on an unstable harmony. With the final, dissonant chord the second movement references the point where the first movement began to go off course. The first aggressive *fortissimo* double-stop chords of the third movement irreversibly push the work toward a tragic narrative.

THE THIRD AND FOURTH MOVEMENTS

As discussed earlier, the third and fourth movements present a negative image of the opening movements by reflecting their formal and harmonic instabilities and using motives that originally marked moments of rupture. In the first movement, the interruption begins as three measures before expanding in the recapitulation. The motives of the interruption spread again, to the third movement, and provide the basic elements from which the movement is formed. The third movement opens with an accompaniment in the lower instruments created out of double-stop chords and a constant alternation of the two meters of the interruption. In addition, the basic motives from the melody of the interruption, the descending sixteenth notes followed by a leap and the downward scalar motion with a trill, are both integral motivic elements of the third movement, now altered to contain more dissonance (for examples, see mm. 18 and 124–25, respectively).

The general sense of instability in the interruption is emphasized throughout the third movement through harmonic and metrical means. Over the G♯-minor tonic harmony, the melody initially implies E major but expands into a twelve-note theme. In addition, the movement makes significant use of second-inversion chords; a root-position tonic triad does not appear until twelve measures before the movement ends. The changing meter undercuts any consistent downbeats, giving the multi-stop chords a mocking irony. Most importantly, the forceful character of the interruption returns. The dynamics open at *fortissimo*, as the lower three instruments tear away at double-stop chords. In effect, the violence latent in the two interruptions of the first movement becomes the defining aspect of the third.

While the opening movements clearly took pains to reference conventional sonata form, the third and fourth movements do not adhere to standard formal types. Whereas most scholars label the third movement a scherzo, the term is used as a catchall phrase to describe any brutal interior movement in Shostakovich's repertoire. While sectional boundaries are somewhat definable, none of the sections take on a stable function. For example, while the section beginning at m. 96 changes texture and, to a lesser extent, style, it is not obvious that this section is a trio. Just as the three-measure interruption did not fit comfortably within the confines of sonata form, the third movement exists outside conventions of both formal design and harmonic structure. The fourth movement, an Adagio, is a strange passacaglia, where the first phrase of the theme, a funereal passage with dotted rhythms and parallel octaves, repeats with only minor alterations. The second phrase of the theme, on the other hand, is contrapuntal and varies greatly. Thus, both the second and fourth movements open with normative formal constructs before diverging in unconventional directions.

The Adagio's theme starts with the same $C_\sharp$ to $C_\natural/B_\sharp$ motion as the open-ing melody of the second movement, and its first phrase contains a quintuplet turn. The quintuplet turn performs a similar function in both the second and fourth movements, as it aids in frustrating attempts at closure. The fourth movement reaches its rhetorical climax with the sixth repetition of the theme. With the seventh iteration the rhetoric calms considerably, as the theme en-ters in the viola at *piano* (and *espressivo*). Yet, after four measures, when the viola reaches the quintuplet turn, the music stumbles. Initially, the viola tries again, repeating the turn down a second, but to no avail; it seems incapable of moving beyond the quintuplet. Not able to finish its thematic charge, the viola moves directly to a cadence, eschewing the second part of the theme. After a modified repetition of the cadential motion, the viola peters out on $C_\sharp$, echoing the anapest rhythm in the cello and eventually expanding the anapest metrically to create a written-out *ritardando*. The movement never reaches a conclusion but flows directly into the finale with an *attacca*. Thus, in the fourth movement, the quintuplet turn motive, which marks where the second movement becomes lost in its search for closure, becomes an integral element in a theme that symbolizes loss via the fourth movement's intense lament and again marks the spot where the music stumbles in its quest to close, leading to disintegration.

Previously, I stated that at the end of the second movement, which is marked with a fermata and *morendo*, the quartet is at a narrative crossroads. As we have seen, the journey taken after this moment propels the work on a tragic course. If we take the word *morendo* literally, we might ask why the music "dies" at the end of the movement, in the midst of the work. I suggest the *morendo* marking plays a role in the signifying layers created by expres-sive doubling. Functioning as a form of supplement, the expressive doubling becomes coupled with the concept of death. In Derrida's words, death is "the master-name of the supplementary series" (1974: 183).[5] Perhaps, then, the *morendo* at the end of the second movement truly signifies a kind of death, as after the *morendo* the narrative trajectory of the work turns decidedly tragic. The quartet's third and fourth movements, as doubles of the first two, pres-ent alternate, dysphoric versions of the earlier movements. Kramer describes those works that move from a high term to low term as depicting travesty. In these works, he notes that in the second movements "a decidedly physical, performative energy impels the music" (Kramer 1990: 45). Indeed, all of the movements classified as the low term by both Hatten and Kramer are in a vig-orous style. Initially, the doubling in the Third Quartet follows this blueprint

TABLE 17.2. FORM OF THE FIFTH MOVEMENT

SECTION		MEASURE	KEY
Exposition			
	A (refrain)	1	F
(tenuous)			
	B	71	d
	A	111	F
	C	139	A
Development			
	A	196	F
	passacaglia theme	246	c♯
Recapitulation			
	C	292	a A
	B	322	f
Coda			
	A material	353	F

with the entrance of the physically violent scherzo. Yet, with the addition of the keening lament of the Adagio, the range of the expressive doubling is extended as Shostakovich takes the sheer physicality of the travesty and expands it into a psychological tragedy.

Shostakovich does not end here, as one movement still remains: the finale. With the Third Quartet, Shostakovich composed one of his first cumulative finales. This movement moves beyond the tragic narrative formed by the expressive doubling, working to create an admittedly mediated sense of transcendence.

FINALE

The fifth movement's form is a kind of expanded sonata rondo (see Table 17.2). The opening section routinely returns in the tonic key, functioning like a refrain, and a development section helps define the sonata aspect of the movement. What is unusual is that the C section is not the developmental space; the development emerges from the refrain material, which should be the most stable music. Kuhn notes that the C section is by far the most harmonically stable (2010: 128). The tonic key, F, is very tenuously established in the opening of the movement through a melody full of half-step resolutions of accented dissonances. Elshoff shows that with each recurrence of the theme, the harmony becomes more stable, as over the course of the movement the tonic key is established in a slow, deliberate manner (2007: 23–27, 120–23).

The finale is still haunted by the issues of the previous movements, however, and for a time it seems as if it will fail on all levels. At the finale's developmental climax the tragic theme of the Adagio returns, as the continuous variations, which never reached a conclusion in the penultimate movement, resurface. In the finale, the theme returns in a violent, dissonant canon in its original key of C♯ minor and with *fortissimo, fortississimo,* and *espressivo molto* performance markings, creating a forceful and emotional climax to the movement.[6] But, as in the previous movement, the theme breaks down; the music fragments and reduces to a solo violin holding a trill on G♯. The cello enters with a solo recitative, which also peters out to almost nothing, sporadically playing an E4.[7] Thus it is the Adagio's theme that is the significant melodic idea of the climactic dissonance that precedes the disintegration of the musical fabric and once again causes the music to fragment and decay. In contrast to the first movement, where the end of the development and the beginning of the recapitulation overlap, in the finale, after the climax, the development disintegrates, eventually decaying to the cello's sporadic playing of an E (with markings of *piano* and *diminuendo sempre*), the pitch that has created tension with the tonic F through the work.

At this point, sound (and the piece) nearly fades away. But it doesn't. Instead, with the anacrusis to m. 291, the first violin, quickly joined by the rest of the quartet, enters with a new beginning, resolving the cello's E as the dominant to the key of A. While the move to A provides a resolution of the E for the entrance of the recapitulation, this resolution is only local, as the work's overriding F/E tension remains. From its onset, the recapitulation is restrained by *piano* dynamics and mutes. The music that opens the recapitulation is evocative not only due to the performance instructions but also because it is a thematic allusion to the opening of the quartet. Being only an allusion, though, much has changed. The theme that enters after the gesture of disintegration is a recapitulation of the C section of the finale's exposition. When it returns to begin the recapitulation, it is re-orchestrated, through which Shostakovich lays bare the connection between the C section's theme and the quartet's opening. Examples 17.2 and 17.3 compare the beginning of the quartet to the start of the recapitulation in the finale, showing the correspondence in orchestration between the opening of the two themes and that the theme of the C section is an inverted allusion to the opening theme. Instead of descending like the quartet's opening, the melody of the C section

EXAMPLE 17.2. Shostakovich, String Quartet No. 3, opening measures. *String Quartet No. 3 in F Major, op. 73. By Dmitri Shostakovich. Copyright © 1947 (Renewed) by G. Schirmer, Inc. (ASCAP). International Copyright Secured. All Rights Reserved. Reprinted by Permission.*

ascends; moreover, it has moved from the cello in the exposition to the first violin in the recapitulation. Moving upward, the theme opens the musical space, reaching toward a new height. As the theme progresses, the quartet builds strength; by m. 307 the music reaches the original tempo and, at the same time, the mode shifts from minor to major. In short, the original theme now appears to be reborn, rising in a new, ascending form from the destruction that preceded it.

Twice in the work, then, the Adagio's theme leads to a near disintegration: once at the end of the fourth movement and a second time at the end of the development in the finale. The question that arises is how the near disintegration, as an expressive effect, contributes to the dramatic trajectory of

EXAMPLE 17.3. Shostakovich, String Quartet No. 3, recapitulation of
the C section in the finale.
*String Quartet No. 3 in F Major, op. 73. By Dmitri Shostakovich. Copyright
© 1947 (Renewed) by G. Schirmer, Inc. (ASCAP). International Copyright
Secured. All Rights Reserved. Reprinted by Permission.*

the finale and the quartet. At the end of the fourth movement, the rhetorical
gesture of disintegration also seems to mark a disintegration of the dysphoric
narrative created by the doubling of the first four movements, as the move to
the finale creates a shift in discourse (see Hatten 1994: 174–88). The quiet,
atmospheric music that opens the finale gives the impression of an aftermath.
In the finale's development, the fourth movement Adagio theme wells up a
second time in the dissonant *stretto* at the climax of the finale's development,
leading to another near disintegration. The response is a return of material
not only from the third section of the exposition but also from the opening
of the work in a new, ascending form.

In the coda to the first movement of his Fifth Symphony, Shostakovich makes use of an inverted version of the main theme, about which Michael Mishra writes: "The use of inversion here creates the effect of a theme rising from the ashes of past catastrophe into the rarefied air from which it originally came" (2008: 365). In the Third Quartet, the rebirth after the development's near disintegration creates the air of a new beginning that resides in an altogether otherworldly time and place. The opening of the work appears in the guise of the material from the C section, creating the effect of a rising spiritual form. Initially, the rising form is muted, but it gains power as it moves forward. The recapitulation, while replaying aspects of all the themes of the exposition, is short (87 measures in a 377-measure movement), presenting an image of a transient, ephemeral existence. This evanescent existence is epitomized by the final melodic line of the work. With the coda, the opening phrase of the refrain returns in the first violin. Initially in the C4–C5 register, it floats upward, eventually reaching into harmonics, while the rest of the instruments perform an F-major drone four octaves below. The tension between F and E never resolves, as the violin's final pitch is a ghostly E7, which fades away. Thus the Third Quartet does not present a full, overflowing transcendence but an atmospheric, ephemeral one overshadowed by the dysphoric narrative that precedes it and a lack of absolute resolution.[8] It is a transcendence fashioned by Shostakovich for the twentieth century. Created out of a tragic destruction, it is presented in an ethereal form, floating away from the ruins from which it came, perhaps reflecting the realities of postwar life in the Soviet Union during the time in which the quartet was composed (1946).[9]

Kramer argues that in the late eighteenth century, expressive doubling "gives the utopian project of art a concrete lyric or dramatic shape. It inscribes the sought-for historical progress from the actual to the ideal within a definite temporal frame" (1990: 30). Thus Beethoven's music typically moves from low to high. When inverted, Kramer states that it "implies that the higher term has failed to master a transferred ambivalence and offers the lower term as an unorthodox alternative" (37). Shostakovich's Third Quartet expands the narrative concept of expressive doubling to go beyond travesty to unqualified tragedy. At the same time, the quartet moves beyond a simple doubling by circling back yet again to its beginning, though on a new expressive plane. Instead of continuing a cycle of destruction, the finale presents an alternative, a cycle of rebirth. The Third Quartet offers a twentieth-century version of transcendence in which the sense of renewal is ephemerally soft, muted, and overshadowed by the extreme brutality that precedes it, but is there.

NOTES

1. Kuhn's book is a necessary point of departure for scholarship of the first seven quartets. In addition to analytical discussions, Kuhn places the works within Shostakovich's biographical context and presents the quartets' reception history within the Soviet Union. Our technical analyses of the Third Quartet often overlap; I have not cited every correspondence but have acknowledged when her discussion has informed mine.

2. See the close of the first movement of Quartet No. 5 and of the second movement of Quartet No. 7.

3. Formal terminology follows James Hepokoski and Warren Darcy's system for labeling sections of sonata form. For a general overview and discussion, see Hepokoski and Darcy (2006: 14–22).

4. For a discussion of the E/C polarity with respect to Joseph Straus's concept of axis tonality, see Brown (2009).

5. I discuss Derrida's connection of the supplement to death in Reichardt (2008: 48).

6. Kramer interprets another, albeit different, form of doubling with the return of the Adagio's theme in the Third Quartet's finale, as he states: "The mourning song [the theme] breaks out anew, a double of itself at double its 'original' intensity" (2002: 273–74).

7. We see the same pitches emphasized, here in reverse order, as the keys of the middle movements, C♯, G♯, and E. It is as if the music tries to go back to before conflict entered the musical discourse, only to fail again. These pitches, allowing for enharmonic equivalency D♭, A♭, and E, are introduced as chromatic pitches in the opening theme.

8. In Michael Talbot's words, the refrain "soars upwards into celestial transfiguration." Talbot continues: "Final redemption through escape to a (literally) higher sphere is a motif Shostakovich will employ again in quartets 4, 5, 10, 11, and 13" (2001: 211). For a discussion of plenitude as a means of creating transcendent fulfillment in late Beethoven, see Hatten (2004: 249–66).

9. At this time the Soviet state, although a "superpower," was struggling to recover from the death and devastation of World War II. In addition, the quartet shares many compositional features with two of Shostakovich's war symphonies, the Eighth and Ninth. Both Kuhn (2010: 106–107) and McCreless (2009: 9–10) go into detail regarding the similarities between the works. It is often thought that Shostakovich gave the individual movements of the Third Quartet formal subtitles. Kuhn (2010: 105–106) presents solid evidence to the contrary.

WORKS CITED

Brown, Stephen C. 2009. "Axis Tonality and Submediant in the Music of Shostakovich." *Music Theory Online* 15(2). http://mto.societymusictheory.org/.

Derrida, Jacques. 1974. *Of Grammatology.* Translated by Gayatri Chakravorty Spivak. Baltimore: Johns Hopkins University Press.

Elshoff, Denise. 2007. "Melody, Counterpoint, and Tonality in Shostakovich's String Quartets Nos. 1–8." PhD diss., Yale University.

Hatten, Robert. 1994. *Musical Meaning in Beethoven: Markedness, Correlation, and Interpretation.* Bloomington: Indiana University Press.

———. 2004. *Interpreting Musical Gestures, Topics and Tropes: Mozart, Beethoven, Schubert.* Bloomington: Indiana University Press.

Hepokoski, James, and Warren Darcy. 2006. *Elements of Sonata Theory: Norms, Types, and Deformations in the Late-Eighteenth-Century Sonata.* New York: Oxford University Press.

Kramer, Lawrence. 1990. *Music as Cultural Practice, 1800–1900.* Berkeley: University of California Press.

———. 2002. *Musical Meaning: Toward a Critical History.* Berkeley: University of California Press.

Kuhn, Judith. 2010. *Shostakovich in Dialogue: Form, Imagery and Ideas in Quartets 1–7.* Burlington: Ashgate.

McCreless, Patrick. 2009. "The String Quartets of Dmitri Shostakovich." In *Intimate Voices: Aspects of Construction and Character in the Twentieth-Century String Quartet.* Vol. 2, *Shostakovich to the Avant-Garde,* edited by Evan Jones, 3–40. Rochester: University of Rochester Press.

Mishra, Michael. 2008. *A Shostakovich Companion.* Westport: Praeger Publishers.

Reichardt, Sarah. 2008. *Composing the Modern Subject: Four String Quartets by Dmitri Shostakovich.* Burlington: Ashgate.

Talbot, Michael. 2001. *The Finale in Western Instrumental Music.* New York: Oxford University Press.

Taruskin, Richard. 2009. *On Russian Music.* Berkeley: University of California Press.

18

Afterlife of an Archetype: Prokofiev and the Art of Subversion

Gregory Karl

❦

Western musical scholars of the last few decades have vigorously debated the existence and nature of a so-called narrative dimension in music.[1] Soviet composers under Stalin didn't have this luxury, for under the prevailing doctrine of socialist realism such a dimension was taken utterly for granted, and they could be denounced or praised, their careers dashed or advanced based on – or at least rationalized by – narrative interpretations of their work. The criticism greeting the 1937 premiere of Shostakovich's Fifth Symphony is a vivid case in point. At stake was the composer's rehabilitation after nearly two years of official censure following the denunciation of his opera *Lady Macbeth of Mtsensk District* and his ballet *The Limpid Stream* in 1936. What was the ideological standard against which Shostakovich's work was measured? According to Richard Taruskin, socialist realism "has always been an occult subject, especially when applied to music" (1995: 25). Nevertheless, by the mid-1930s "the idea had been roughly defined in practice" as a "recipe [of] heroic classicism" (25). It took its models of interpretive criticism from the literary traditions surrounding revolutionary works of Beethoven, like the Fifth and Ninth Symphonies, and those of Tchaikovsky while assimilating the fundamental premise of romantic-expressive aesthetics: that music expresses the experience, internal states, or mental life of its composers and subjects. Thus we find Shostakovich's Fifth parsed in quasi-biographical terms as "the formation of a personality" and as an "optimistic tragedy" in which the composer's recent personal struggles can be heard (34).[2] In these reviews, the tense and tragic moments of the first three movements ultimately are redeemed because, as in the archetypal plot pattern of Beethoven's Fifth, they are resolved in a heroically triumphant finale.[3]

From the beginning, however, some found this finale suspect, hearing sarcasm in its overwrought tone and mockery in its triumph (Taruskin 1995: 34–38). This line of interpretation, in which the finale subverts the struggle-to-victory archetype, has more recently been trumpeted by revisionists like "the author of *Testimony*" (see Shostakovich 1979) and Ian MacDonald (1990), who seek retrospectively to cast Shostakovich in the role of dissident.[4] The Tenth Symphony, too, has been heard as a subversive statement, organized by a hidden program in which the composer and Stalin are represented by characteristic themes (see Shostakovich 1979; Fanning 1988; Karl and Robinson 1997). In both symphonies, however, the instantiation of subversive content depends on strictly observing the conventions of the plot type. The Fifth merely adds (putatively) a sarcastic inflection to the expected triumphant conclusion; the otherwise conventional plot moves of the Tenth only yield subversive meaning when heard in light of an extra-musical key.

The subject of this essay, Prokofiev's Sonata in F Minor for Violin and Piano, perpetrates a more radical form of subversion, drawing its formal and expressive coherence from the conventional plot moves of the archetypal pattern while in the end undoing them. As we will see, this sonata, too, has been interpreted as a subversive political statement. I will argue, however, that its subversive tendencies are of an order and nature different from those attributed to Shostakovich's Fifth and Tenth Symphonies, based not on ideology but on aesthetic principle. Prokofiev, I suggest, having sketched the first three movements, simply recognized that a heroic, optimistic, or otherwise conventional conclusion was aesthetically untenable. The gravity and power of the remarkable first movement, the *Andante assai*, proved inescapable, and the finale's ecstatic dance was pulled inexorably back into its orbit. Prokofiev's unintended transgression against socialist realism is understood as a gloriously perverse aesthetic act: he managed to create a deeply depressing finale in the major mode. The conclusion, *tranquillo* and in F major, seems to grant the last word to peace and optimism and, in so doing, to make a concession to the ideals of socialist realism. But for anyone who comprehends the sonata's plot, it is a mere fig leaf over utter desolation. Before analyzing the sonata's plot, however, it is necessary to explain what, in my view, such comprehension might entail.

ON MUSICAL PLOT

The sub-discipline of musicology devoted to the study of plot-like teleology in instrumental music is shot through with deep fault lines practical and philosophical. The one I find most critical is between two diametrically opposed views on plot's ontological status. Is plot an interpretive construct by which one mediates between human experience and abstract musical structure (structure with a life and coherence of its own based on "purely musical" principles), or is it conceived as part of the fundamental substance of musical works? Is it something we read into or project onto musical works to imbue them with human significance, or is it actually woven into the musical fabric in the act of composition and in the historical evolution of musical form? The former position, which we might designate as formalist or conservative, is one end of a continuum. The latter position, the radical one, is the one I embrace.

On this view, and from an historical perspective, plot designs based on the systematic development of thematic and motivic oppositions arose as a particularly flexible and potent solution to a fundamental problem of musical form first addressed in a sustained fashion by Beethoven: how to create and maintain the tension necessary to fuel the dramatic teleology of vastly expanded movements in sonata form and in other forms, and how to create tensions that can persist beyond and in sharp distinction to the tonal tensions resolved within individual movements, thereby allowing the unification of multi-movement cycles into integrated arcs of dramatic force. These innovations, I suspect, were the essence of the "new path" Beethoven chose for his compositional efforts beginning in the first few years of the nineteenth century.[5] In "Structuralism and Musical Plot" (Karl 1997), I show how such plot designs might be constructed and analyzed using the first movement of the "Appassionata" Sonata as an illustration. The methodology is similar to that developed in 1928 by structuralist literary theorist Vladimir Propp in his pioneering work *Morphology of the Folktale* (1968). Propp demonstrated that fairy tales can be broken down into a small inventory of component elements in two categories, called *roles* and *functions*. Roles are standard character types that account for the entire active population of the genre. They include hero, villain, princess (or sought-for person), false hero, and so on. Propp defines a function as "an act of a character, defined from the point of view of its significance for the course of the action" of the tale as a whole (1968: 21). Functions "serve as stable, constant elements in a tale, independent of how and by whom they are fulfilled" (21). Despite their amazingly multiform, picturesque, and colorful surfaces, at a deep level, fairy tales are remarkably uniform and recurrent (19).

In the structuralist system I propose, themes and motives cast in a small number of generalized dramatic roles set and develop the terms of their evolving relationships through plot functions analogous to but more abstract than those Propp finds in fairy tales. For sonata-allegro movements, the basic roles often include three with counterparts in Propp's system. But where Propp uses the terms *hero*, *sought-for person*, and *villain*, musical themes, because they normatively have no specific extra-musical referents or meanings, are better served by more abstract terms. As substitutes I prefer *protagonist* (P), *goal* (G), and *antagonist* (A). Support for ascribing this system of roles to themes in sonata-form movements can be found in the critical and historical literature as well as in the extra-musical referents of themes in programmatic music and opera overtures.[6] Together these sources established a broadly influential interpretive tradition with which most Soviet composers were familiar, consciously or unconsciously. Other standard roles include *initial state* (I) and *final state* (F) and some strongly associated with specific functions, such as *counteraction* (C). In addition, further roles often emerge as binary opposing pairs idiosyncratic to a particular work. Among the common functions enacted by thematic and motivic agents are *enclosure, disruption, subversion, counteraction, subsumption, integration, withdrawal, interruption, anticipation, divergence, bifurcation*, and *transfiguration*. There is no need for lengthy definitions of these terms here; their meanings in this system are close to the literal ones, and any exceptions will be explained as needed.

ANALYSIS

The speed and facility with which Prokofiev composed are legendary. Yet he was stumped after sketching most of the material for the first three movements of the F-Minor Violin Sonata in 1938 (see Nestyev 1960: 385). Five years later, in a letter to Nickolai Miaskovsky, who was then composing one of his own, Prokofiev wrote: "It will be interesting to see how you deal with the sonorities of a violin sonata: I began one a long time ago already, but cannot seem to figure out how to continue" (Robinson 1998: 330). The breakthrough wouldn't come for another three years, in the summer of 1946. Prokofiev doesn't specify the nature of the impasse he was facing, but since the sketches from 1938 find the other movements well under way, we must suspect the finale to have been the problem. The solution the composer finally settled on suggests that the difficulty may have been finding a satisfactory way of tying together loose threads from the earlier movements. Each of the first two movements exhibits a pattern of progressively intensifying contrasts. The first starts in monolithic unity and only teases out a striking contrast of related material in its last minute. The second is a movement in sonata form in which two opposing themes are drawn into a spiral of ever-intensifying conflict. The movement ends at its highest peak of tension with nothing resolved. Thus the early portions of the sonata leave hanging a number of plot threads that must be taken up again in the finale. Because these threads are tied to the trajectories of developing relationships among the movements' themes and motives, the resolution of the work's dramatic problems requires the reprise and further interaction of these elements later in the cycle. Thus nearly every melodic element in the finale is a quotation, transformation, or allusion to a theme of the first or second movement. The resulting surfeit of contrasting material, tempi, and moods defies traditional formal schemes. There is, of course, a musical logic to the movement's unique formal pattern, but it is musical logic dictated by the demands of narrative coherence. In short, the finale must discharge all of the residual dramatic tensions and pay all of the outstanding obligations accrued by the earlier movements – and these movements, particularly the opening Andante assai, are profligate in their dramatic logic.

In a laconic overview of the sonata, Prokofiev describes this opening movement as "severe in character – a kind of extended introduction to the second movement" (Nestyev 1960: 385). It does have an open-ended, rhapsodic quality, failing to resolve the tensions and issues it raises, only reaching its essential questions at the very end after slowly unfolding a striking contrast of texture and expression from the monochrome opening. This process of intensifying contrast, or bifurcation, proves critical to the sonata's plot because the opposing elements emerging from it are juxtaposed to greater effect in the work's final pages. Opening this bifurcation is one of the movement's essential contributions to the sonata's plot. Another is establishing the dark starting condition from which the archetypal progression toward the light proceeds.

The movement is idiosyncratic and brilliant in its simplicity, combining a symmetrical key scheme based on equal division of the octave (F minor–B minor–F minor) with a free process of variation on a single theme. It is also some of the most unrelentingly dark music Prokofiev ever wrote, mining the extreme low register of the piano in all but ten of its measures and touching on

EXAMPLE 18.1. Prokofiev, Violin Sonata, principal themes, first and fourth movements.

six different minor keys without the least whiff of major modality. In half of the movement's one hundred–odd bars, the piano maintains the stark texture of bare octaves characterizing the opening phrase.

The theme unfolds in a quaternary pattern over about two minutes, the contrasting material offering no relief from the downward pressure of the principal phrase (henceforth, the motto) and its ubiquitous falling fifths (Example 18.1a). Then, starting from E♭ minor, a slow, harrowing crescendo over seven measures to *fortissimo* begins a tense transition. At the high point the violin begins to weave chromatic counterpoint in double-stops over the piano's octave Ds. After six measures in G minor the dynamic level relaxes to *piano*, the violin settling into what is ostensibly diatonic counterpoint in E♭ minor, still over the pedal Ds, now elaborated by lower neighbors on C♯. The tension is excruciating and the subsequent collapse into B minor a blessed relief.

The variation on the motto that follows is remarkable for what it accomplishes with the barest of means (Example 18.2). Chromatic language and harsh dissonance have given way to pure diatonic strains. The soft dynamics and caressing double-stops of the violin, soon joined by the piano,

EXAMPLE 18.2. Prokofiev, Violin Sonata, first movement, B-minor variation.

weave a tender, diaphanous texture, all elaborating the tonic harmony. But the sense of repose is short-lived. After six measures, the motto's initial rising and falling fifth-figure tolls beneath like deep mournful bells, sounding the movement's lowest pitches. Their elemental power is answered by a delicate quotation of the motto's third and fourth measures in the high register of the piano. In these two measures, for the first time in the work, the low bass register clears, imparting a sense of weightlessness to the fleeting crystalline vision above. Thus the motto's two memorable motives sound in their original rhythmic disposition, preserving the lyric flow of the original phrase, but the second has been transposed so that its final falling fifth (C♯ to F♯ in m. 60) outlines the dominant rather than the tonic. Sounding at the end of a four-measure *crescendo*, this dominant is elaborated by a crushing descent in double-stops, shadowed a ninth lower by the piano. The devastating power of this climax lies, I believe, in the way it juxtaposes diametrically contrasting images – highest versus lowest registers, powerful tolling versus delicate chiming – introducing a bifurcation into the originally monolithic theme, creating two contrasting voices where there was one. It is precisely by silencing the delicate voice of mm. 59–60 that the crushing descent and tolling of mm. 60–61 attains its bitter intensity. But this voice and the caressing accompaniment that introduced the variation are not forgotten, and soon the momentary bifurcation is expanded and embodied in a larger opposition: the two competing variations with which the movement closes.

Echoes of the climax persist through m. 68, where the transition back to F minor begins with two halting half-statements of the opening phrase in C minor. The piano alone then spirals down to the tonic, and the final section of the overall ternary design begins in m. 79 with a third variation on the principal theme. With the fleeting exception of the six bars opening the B-minor section, this variation (Example 18.3) is the only significant deviation from the movement's nearly monochromatic affective palette. After nearly five minutes of unremitting gloom, low sonorities, stark, hollow textures, lugubrious quarter- and eighth-note motion, and concentrated emotional intensity, the lush seventh and ninth chords, relatively high register, and soaring passagework speak of consolation and release, fulfilling the fleeting vision of the B-minor variation. And yet there are troubling incongruities: the lush and sonorous warmth of the piano's chords, for example, contrast sharply with the coldness and emotional distance suggested by the *freddo* marking in the violin part and evoked by the icy, metallic sonority of the muted violin at *pianissimo*. Then there is the energy and blurred velocity of the violin's passagework rendered insubstantial by the *pianissimo* dynamic level and muting. In sum, if there is consolation in this passage, it is a cold one, and if there is release, it is not the kinesthetic release of physical motion or dance, nor the release of overt expression, but more like an inward-turning flight of pure contemplation or imagination. There is even something of exultation in this passage, especially in mm. 83–84, where a four-octave ascent leads to a piercingly beautiful high C. In the terms of my structuralist system, this variation is a *withdrawal* to an interior realm – cold and beautiful, but terrible in its loneliness and isolation.

The moment of release, the movement's lightest image, is followed by another that is perhaps its grimmest: the motto, once again in bare octaves in the piano below an angular chromatic line in brittle, muted *pizzicato* (Example 18.3). The two passages are immediately repeated in varied form and followed only by a brief coda. Thus, the only significant contrast above the motivic level is reserved for the final section, where the escape into pure contemplation is

EXAMPLE 18.3. Prokofiev, Violin Sonata, first movement, mm. 79ff.

interrupted by reminders of the movement's darkest moments. The heightening of contrast at the end raises issues and poses questions only to leave them hanging, creating a state of dramatic tension that necessitates the reprise of these elements in the finale.

Three of the basic roles one might expect in a first-movement sonata-allegro, *antagonist* (A), *protagonist* (P), and *goal* (G), are taken by themes and motives of the Allegro brusco, though not in the most common order. Prokofiev's typically colorful expression markings confirm the roles I suggest. The opening theme, *A*, when it returns in the finale, is marked *feroce*; the second theme, *P*, is marked *eroico* at its first sounding. But the character and antithetical relationship of the themes become clear enough without extramusical clues.

The rough-hewn and brutal first theme comprises three versions of a single sentence. They are built up from terse, disjointed fragments, which, however, are broadly unified by the opening three-quarter-note and two-quarter-note motives and by pervasive harsh minor-second/major-seventh dissonances. But unity does not entail order or rationality, and the brutality of the theme seems arbitrary and senseless for two reasons. First is the unpredictable manner in which two-stroke and three-stroke motives follow one another, occasionally expanded or elided. The result is a shifting, irregular meter and an impression of clumsy jostling. Second is the way diverse motivic chunks are beaten into unity literally by rhythmic pounding, resulting in a nearly incoherent series of gestures with little linear continuity. Overall the theme is jarring, unstable, and charged with harsh dissonance.

The heroic second theme contrasts in every way with its adversary. The first theme's stark two-voice counterpoint and harsh dissonance are replaced by a firm triadic texture. Rather than rough and competitive interaction on the same motives, we find the instruments in cooperation and with a clear division of function into soaring melody and chordal accompaniment. The meter of the second theme is regular, and instead of the first theme's brutal, disjointed motivic chunks, we find a sustained and purposeful arch of melody with frequent bold, decisive leaps. These features of the second theme, along with the clear F-major tonality and *forte* dynamic level, are all consistent with Prokofiev's expression marking, *eroico*. Together they establish the kind of stark contrast required in a plot built on dramatic opposition.

In the closing, the protagonist takes action, as heard through increased rhythmic activity in the violin and a single-minded, octave-doubled line in the piano, which covers a broad ambitus through its simple arpeggiations. The violin's pervasive ascending motion and spiky leaps into the upper register at *forte* (mm. 89, 92, and 99) are like an angry, defiant railing that finally expends itself against an impenetrable wall of dissonance in mm. 100–101. These measures recall the harsh dissonance of the first theme, suggesting that the protagonist has fought its way back to near parity by the end of the exposition before meeting this unbreachable barrier.

A bizarre, increasingly dissonant crescendo opens the development (mm. 103–14) – like a demented sawing or a parody of tuning the open fifths of the violin. The first two motives of *A* then enter *marcato* and sinister. These stealthy intrusions of the antagonist are countered immediately by the action

EXAMPLE 18.4. Prokofiev, Violin Sonata, transformations across the sonata.

of the protagonist – developments of the defiant closing (mm. 129–38) that win a temporary respite in the *Poco più tranquillo* section of mm. 139–52.

The *Poco più tranquillo* is the second link in a chain of transformation beginning with P and ending with the sonata's final phrase (see Examples 18.4a and 18.4d, respectively). It anticipates the second theme of the finale, the sonata's only light-hearted melody (Example 18.4c). Because the work's dark-to-light progression culminates in this single bright moment, the designation of *goal* (G) is appropriate. The anticipatory passage in the second movement becomes *g* (anticipation of G) by association (Example 18.4b).

The *Poco più tranquillo* theme sounds twice, both times followed by motives from the antagonistic principal theme, which build to a violent, dissonant climax on A's head motive. Beginning in m. 196, the conflict begins in earnest as the thematic protagonist enters at *fortissimo* in the violin, the original multi-phrase theme telescoped into a single extended sentence. The piano's accompaniment derives from the brutal motivic chunks of A, signaling that the dramatic opposition has escalated to explicit conflict. The opposing ideas sound as unfused and incompatible voices working at cross-purposes, and the harsh dissonances of the accompaniment (e.g., mm. 197, 206) are like a physical assault – blows thrown to impede P's progress. The conflict is decided in favor of the antagonist: a third and more intense climax on the head motive of the principal theme is the upshot of the struggle, and this passage (mm. 216–27) is ingeniously elided in mm. 227–28 with the powerful return of A at *fortissimo*. Thus, in the final section of the development and the retransition, the protagonist is *subverted* and *enclosed* by its rival.

The recapitulation follows the order of the exposition, though both principal themes are shortened significantly, and the closing material has been considerably expanded. The result is an intensification of contrast, as opposing images follow one another more closely than in the exposition. After its *subversion* and *enclosure* in the development, P begins in a subdued manner at *mezzo piano* and only gradually regains its usual momentum. Appropriately, its railing against fate in the closing is intensified as well; spectacular virtuosity is demanded in the violin's second assault on the highest register, but, as in the exposition, the spiky upward leaps meet a wall of dissonance. But in the recapitulation the antagonistic underpinnings of this resistance are made explicit, the head motive of A sounding continuously through mm. 289–96, the forward momentum bogging down in a morass of dissonance. The last four measures are P's violent attempt at extrication, which, though perhaps successful, leaves the protagonist exhausted.

The third movement, Andante, has no explicit thematic links to the other movements and so no overt or central structural role in its plot. But by passing over it lightly here, I in no way discount its essential contribution to the sonata as a whole. The violent conflict with which the second movement ends and the ecstatic dance that opens the finale are worlds apart expressively. The unquiet dream of the Andante mediates seamlessly between them.

The opening theme of the finale, Allegrissimo, transfigures the motto of the Andante assai (Example 18.1b). While the motto was in the minor mode, slow, enervated, dark, grim, and sinking, the finale theme is in the major mode, fast, energetic, light, joyous, and buoyant. The underlying motivic relationships linking the themes cast their contrasting formal and expressive qualities in special relief. By placing these themes in a relationship of simultaneous identity and contrast – making them foils – Prokofiev defines the teleology of the work not just as a progression from one condition to another but also as the transformation of a single subject from within. The finale theme is an index of improved prospects for the work's persona, closing the overall minor-to-major-mode, dark-to-light progression with an allusion to the material with which it began. Because it derives from the motto while rejecting every feature of its source's physiognomy, the finale theme willfully defies the oppressive and brooding state the motto had spread throughout the opening movement. In structuralist terms, the finale theme is a *counteraction*. This move is the essence of the archetypal plot pattern at the basis of the sonata.

Like an ecstatic dance, the finale theme leaps through irregular steps in four-measure phrases of twenty-seven beats (the meter is marked $\frac{5}{8}, \frac{7}{8}, \frac{8}{8}$). Overall the theme is ternary: the first part is solidly doubled in octaves; the second is light and nimble, with *pizzicato* violin over a *staccato* piano line; and the third breaks all restraints, bristling with energetic counterpoint and driving through a pounding, frenetic transition toward the dominant. But the theme may have a tragic flaw: it has no long-term goal or sense of sustained linear process; it is a string of equal phrases, energetic and exuberant, but never much more than the sum of its parts. Its effort at counteraction does accomplish one thing, however. By overtly rejecting the brooding state of the motto and declaring the ascendancy of a new and optimistic condition, it clears the way for the C-major theme of the *Poco più tranquillo*, beginning in m. 53. As noted earlier, this theme is the goal state anticipated from the midst of conflict in the second movement. It is the work's only moment of untroubled joy.

EXAMPLE 18.5. Prokofiev, Violin Sonata, fourth movement, mm. 181ff.

The central developmental section begins in m. 114 in a manner consistent with the continuation of a light sonata-rondo design – a free treatment of the principal theme and its motives. A significant new motive derived from the first theme (marked Z in Example 18.5) is introduced in m. 128, and immediately afterward events begin to take a more serious turn: the proceedings are interrupted in m. 133 by three ferocious strokes on octave Bs at *fortissimo* in the lowest register of the piano. A moment later there is a second interruption (mm. 140–41), where the ferocious pounding is harshly dissonant against the prevailing harmony. The three strokes are reminiscent of the head motive of the second movement set in augmentation, but as yet its return is only rumor. After this second interruption, motive Z moves into a high register and is repeated five times, giving an impression of hysteria, like incessant squeals of fear. The sentiment proves to be well founded; the third interruption by the *feroce* motive is followed four measures later by the second motive from the second movement. Now it is clear that the work's primary antagonistic element is gaining a foothold in the finale, disrupting material derived from the opening theme.

As soon as the antagonistic role of the interruptions is confirmed in mm. 157–58, the first theme enters to offer resistance (mm. 159–63) but fails to attain any momentum. After five bars it fragments, giving way to motive Z's shrieks of fear. In mm. 170–71, the three ferocious strokes sound yet again, now on C, the original pitch at which they were heard in the second movement. Soon after, tension reaches its peak as the incessant wailing of motive Z is pushed to its highest pitch, and a complete statement of the first three motives of the second movement sounds in the bass in mm. 181–88 (Example 18.5). This forceful statement overwhelms the thematic protagonist, and in mm. 189–90 there is a plummeting from on high, an ignominious collapse toward the original tonic key of F minor. It is in this passage that Prokofiev subverts the expected sonata-rondo design, but, more important, it is here that he undercuts the archetypal plot pattern and begins to apply his own tragic twist.

Immediately after the finale's first theme is overthrown by the return of A, the final F-minor section, which takes the place of a recapitulation, begins by quoting the darkest variation from the first movement, the angular figure originally set in muted *pizzicato* in mm. 89–91. The significance of this thematic return in the sonata's opening key of F minor is clear: the downfall of the thematic protagonist has opened the door to dark forces and grim impressions from the past, which, it seems, have proved inescapable in the end. This painful passage soon runs its course, however, dissipating in a *diminuendo* (mm. 206 ff.) where motive Z repeats and loses all rhythmic definition (m. 210), as if washed out or exhausted. It gives way to the last of three passages from the preceding movements revisited in reverse chronological order; the moment of release or sublime resignation from the end of the first movement (mm.

80–88 and 92–97) whose inward-turning flight of imagination has returned as consolation – but not as the final word.

The last seven measures (Example 18.4d) contain the only recapitulation of material from the sonata-rondo exposition, a setting of the second phrase of the second theme, which is ostensibly in F major. In fact, the melody is the same as in the exposition, but the crawling chromaticism of the accompaniment has at least as much allegiance to the minor mode as to the major. In the slower tempo of the final pages, and with the naively cheerful version in the exposition as a foil, the effect is one of utter desolation, an agonized acknowledgment that the sonata's fleeting moment of joy can never be recaptured. The sonata thus ends with a lament for lost hopes. However, the third missing from the final tonic sonority is unequivocally major, and this phantom third somehow mitigates the desolation of the final passage by sweetening the oblivion into which it dissolves.

INTERPRETATIONS AND INTENTIONS

Some five decades after the sonata received a Stalin Prize First Class in 1947, Daniel Jaffé (1998), echoing trends in the reception of Shostakovich's music, interpreted it from a revisionist perspective. He focused on the passage for muted violin I have read as an inward-turning flight of imagination (Example 18.3), citing the composer's own description of it as evidence of a subversive program. Prokofiev told David Oistrakh, who was preparing the premiere performance, that it should sound "like wind in a graveyard" (Oistrakh 1978: 202). Leaping over more mundane and reasonable interpretations of these words, Jaffé characterizes the passage as "a literal allusion to the several million Russians arrested and hundreds of thousands shot in the late 1930s when the sonata was originally conceived" (1998: 192). He believes it significant that this passage follows not long after the return of a "bullying" three-note motive, which, as we have seen, quotes the principal theme of the second movement (193). Jaffé identifies this as a "Stalin motif," drawing a causal connection between its violent action and the graveyard passage (193).

Jaffé's interpretation is ill conceived on at least two grounds. First, it fails to account for why the graveyard scene sounds in the first movement as well, before the "Stalin theme" makes its entrance. More important, he fails to explain what the tyrant is doing throughout the second movement and who his heroic opponent might be. The larger problem with Jaffé's position, however, is the assumption that Prokofiev had intended any specific meaning

at all – indeed, that intention is important on any level. I would suggest that
for a Soviet composer in Prokofiev's day, having a good ear for musical design
on the grand scale entailed an intuitive grasp of abstract plot structure in
something like the terms proposed here. This is because in the style in which
he was composing, a coherent structure, it happens, is necessarily a coherent simulation of human experience. Did Prokofiev hear something like an
inward-turning flight of imagination in the final pages of his sonata? For all
we know, he may merely have wanted something flashy yet restrained for the
soloist to do during the slow endings of the first movement and finale. But his
ears told him it worked, and others find it profound. Did he set out to write a
daring, tragic variant of a traditional plot pattern when he sketched the first
three movements in 1938? Surely not. But when faced with the monumental
task of pulling their disparate threads together, his ear for dramatic structure
led him to it. Faced with a choice between an unconvincing optimistic conclusion and a successful but wrenching tragedy, Prokofiev had the aesthetic
integrity and musical sense to choose the latter. To have executed the sonata's
profoundly tragic reversals in a movement starting and ending in the major
mode is evidence of a singular and perverse genius.

Was the *tranquillo* ending in the major mode a bone thrown to the com-
pulsory optimism of socialist realism? Or a taunt? If it was a concession, it
was an isolated one. In his large instrumental works of the 1940s, Prokofiev
often embraced dark expression and dangerous complexity, as in the Sixth
and Eighth Piano Sonatas and the Sixth Symphony. He spent his considerable political capital in composing what he wished so that when the cold
wind of cultural repression blew again in 1948, he suffered as much as anyone,
dying with pain in his soul, never to see the thaw.[7] Works like Prokofiev's
First Violin Sonata reanimated a heroic-classical tradition that was all but
moribund in the West, and his countrymen appreciated his achievement. He
might have taken special comfort in the words of his younger contemporary,
Shostakovich, who, long after his death, standing transfixed on a wooded road
and hearing the strains of this sonata coming from the terrace of a nearby
cottage, was moved to say: "What wonderful music Sergei Sergeyevich wrote,
wonderful music" (Wilson 1994: 313).

NOTES

1. The early skeptics included Abbate
(1989), Nattiez (1990), and Kramer (1992).

2. "The formation of a personal-
ity" quote is from A. Tolstoy, *Izvestiiya,*

December 28, 1937, 3, quoted in Fay (2000: 102).

3. Newcomb (1984) was largely responsible for bringing the term *plot archetype* into common usage in the critical theory of music.

4. Taruskin's construction, "the author of *Testimony*," neatly and humorously solves the issue of how to address the book's problematic attribution to the composer.

5. Carl Czerny writes: "About the year 1800, when Beethoven had composed his Opus 28 he said to his intimate friend, Krumpholz: 'I am far from satisfied with my past works: from today on I shall take a new way.' Shortly after this appeared his three sonatas Opus 31, in which one may see that he had partially carried out his resolve" (1968: 143). The original quotation of Beethoven reads: "Ich bin nur wenig zufrieden mit meinem bisherigen Arbeiten. Von heute an will ich ein neuen weg einschlagen." See major essays on this topic by Philip G. Downs (1970) and Carl Dahlhaus (1991). Ludwig Misch (1953) anticipates some of Dahlhaus's thinking by two decades.

6. Carl Maria von Weber's *Der Freischütz*, for example, is essentially the setting of a fairy tale. Three themes of its overture are associated with characters playing the roles of hero (Max), sought-for person (Agathe), and villain (Samiel). As per the model outlined above, Max is associated with the first theme (*P*), Agathe the second (*G*), and Samiel, a motive sounding at the end of the introduction (*A*).

7. In his last year, when his second wife asked if he had pain anywhere, Prokofiev sometimes responded: "My soul hurts" (Robinson 1987: 492). He died on March 5, 1953, on the same day as Stalin.

WORKS CITED

Abbate, Carolyn. 1989. "What the Sorcerer Said." *19th-Century Music* 12(3): 221–30.

Czerny, Carl. 1968. *Erinnerungen aus meinem Leben*. Edited by W. Kolneder. Strasburg: P. H. Heitz.

Dahlhaus, Carl. 1991. *Ludwig van Beethoven: Approaches to His Music*. Translated by Mary Whittall. Oxford: Oxford University Press.

Downs, Philip G. 1970. "Beethoven's 'New Way' and the *Eroica*." In *The Creative World of Beethoven*, edited by Paul Henry Lang, 83–102. New York: W. W. Norton.

Fanning, David. 1988. *The Breath of the Symphonist: Shostakovich's Tenth*. Royal Musical Association Monographs 4. London: Royal Musical Association.

Fay, Laurel E. 2000. *Shostakovich: A Life*. New York: Oxford University Press.

Jaffé, Daniel. 1998. *Sergei Prokofiev*. London: Phaidon Press.

Karl, Gregory. 1997. "Structuralism and Musical Plot." *Music Theory Spectrum* 19(1): 13–34.

Karl, Gregory, and Jenefer Robinson. 1997. "Shostakovich's Tenth Symphony and the Musical Expression of Cognitively Complex Emotions." In *Music and Meaning*, edited by Jenefer Robinson, 154–78. Ithaca: Cornell University Press.

Kramer, Lawrence. 1992. "Musical Narratology: A Theoretical Outline." *Indiana Theory Review* 12: 141–62.

MacDonald, Ian. 1990. *The New Shostakovich*. Boston: Northeastern University Press.

Marx, A. B. 1859. *Ludwig van Beethoven: Leben und Schaffen*, vol. 2. Berlin: Janke.

Misch, Ludwig. 1953. "The Problem of the D Minor Sonata." In *Beethoven Studies,* translated by G. I. C. de Courcy, 39–53. Norman: University of Oklahoma Press.

Nattiez, Jean-Jacques. 1990. "Can One Speak of Narrativity in Music?" *Journal of the Royal Music Association* 115(2): 240–57.

Nestyev, Israel. 1960. *Prokofiev.* Translated by Florence Jones. Stanford: Stanford University Press.

Newcomb, Anthony. 1984. "Once More 'between Absolute and Program Music': Schumann's Second Symphony." *19th-Century Music* 7(3): 233–50.

Oistrakh, David. 1978. *"In Memoriam."* In *Sergei Prokofiev: Materials, Articles, Interviews,* 199–205. Moscow: Progress Publishers.

Propp, Vladimir. 1968. *Morphology of the Folktale.* Translated by Laurence Scott, edited and revised by Louis A. Wagner. Austin: University of Texas Press.

Robinson, Harlow. 1987. *Prokofiev.* Boston: Northeastern University Press.

———, trans. 1998. *Selected Letters of Sergei Prokofiev.* Boston: Northeastern University Press.

Shostakovich, Dmitri. 1979. *Testimony: The Memoirs of Dmitri Shostakovich.* New York: Harper and Row.

Taruskin, Richard. 1995. "Public Lies and Unspeakable Truth: Interpreting Shostakovich's Fifth Symphony." In *Shostakovich Studies,* edited by David Fanning, 17–53. Cambridge: Cambridge University Press.

Wilson, Elizabeth. 1994. *Shostakovich: A Life Remembered.* Princeton: Princeton University Press.

19

Identity Formation in Webern's Six Pieces for Large Orchestra, op. 6

Alan Street

What kind of story is inscribed in Webern's Six Pieces for Large Orchestra, op. 6? As is typically the case with musico-fictive interpretation, immediate legibility is at best partial. In the first instance, the set is supported by a prose program whose avoidance of vulgar mimetic cues and evident, if attenuated, causal sequence is nonetheless conveyed sonically without the consistent guidance of individual piece titles or the presence of sung vocal texts. Further, the tracing of a defined temporal progression, although ostensibly linear, is plainly more episodic than dynamic in kind; as conceded by the composer himself, the nature of his work at least through to the adoption of serialism was "almost exclusively lyrical [in] nature" (quoted in Shreffler 1994: 18). The fact that contemporary narrative studies in music have a contested history, however, gives cause for a more flexible mode of appraisal. For Fred Everett Maus, for instance, a pragmatic reading by analogy is altogether preferable to the alternative prospects associated with either ontological evangelism or epistemological skepticism (2005: 466). More precisely, Maus suggests, our mutual reliance on transpersonal norms of musical narration can be taken to amount to a tangible poetics of humanizing involvement: in short, a form of affinity struck between observer and observed whose degree of investment in narrative communication is itself a prime index of musicality, broadly conceived (475–76).

By comparison, an altogether more encompassing strategy for aesthetic interpretation can be seen in the recent work of Karol Berger. Far from dismissing narrative as a casual metaphor, his argument in favor of a general theory of art proposes both it and lyric "as the most general and fundamental kinds of form which artworlds may possess" (Berger 2000: 190). Following Gérard Genette and Paul Ricoeur, Berger acknowledges that the showing-telling distinction that separates drama and epic on the modal level can be thematically disregarded through their shared reliance on narrative emplot-ment. The primary structure of narrative is in turn determined by time; it is thus "nothing other than the temporal form" (194). Lyric, conversely, is the atemporal form in which time plays no essential role. Because if narrative is shaped by actions and events that are inherently time-bound, then lyric makes present human sentiments – "mental states, thoughts, emotions, situ-ations" – that are not dependent on "necessary or probabilistic causality" (195).

Having established this foundation, Berger advances a strongly program-matic assertion in respect of narrative and lyric such that their interplay "not only maps the complete field of artistic forms [but because] . . . of the correla-tion of these forms with kinds of content, with action and passion (or mental state) . . . also maps the complete field of human ways of being in the world, that is, of everything that one might want to represent in art if one treats art as an instrument of human self-revelation" (2000: 204). Passion in this respect is at the same time a passive condition; the unchangeable state of affairs that humans often find themselves in whereby they are powerless to act and thus experience, most characteristically, suffering. Indeed, it is for this reason that the "form of the lyric and the content of suffering humans go together" (203). From this standpoint, then, it would seem that the dichotomy of narrative and lyric might prove unusually robust as a conceptual mainspring capable of pro-pelling hermeneutic inquiry. Nevertheless, Berger takes pains to stress that its interpretive import is ontologically rather than empirically determined. Critical application thus necessitates recognizing narrative and lyric first and foremost as "fundamental poetic forms of composition, not genres." Conse-quently, while actual works of literature "may represent these forms in their pure state," ordinarily the two forms will tend to coexist "in various, often unexpected proportions" (196). It is with these strictures in mind, therefore, that the following heuristic narrativization will seek to tease out some of the fabular threads that bind the six orchestral pieces comprising Webern's op. 6. In this context, *prosopopoeia*, much as for Carolyn Abbate (1991: 13) or J. Hillis Miller (1990: 75), will form a central, if necessarily illusory, narrative trope. Yet keeping faith with Maus, the analogical function of agency will be acknowl-edged as a means to an end: specifically, the belief that all narrative may be in essence obituary insofar as "the retrospective knowledge that it seeks, the knowledge that comes after, stands on the far side of the end, in human terms on the far side of death" (Brooks 1984: 95).

❧

The op. 6 pieces were written in the summer of 1909 during the composer's annual stay at the Preglhof, the family estate located a few miles from the town of Bleiburg near the Austrian border with Slovenia. Completed sometime before the end of August, the set was composed more or less contemporaneously with Webern's teacher's own Five Orchestral Pieces, op. 16. First mentioned to Schoenberg in a letter of June 16 the same year, the op. 6 pieces were subsequently described by Webern on August 30 as a cycle ("rather, I should say, it just happens to turn out this way") whose instrumental character would feature "almost entirely pure colors. Just as it comes about" (quoted in Moldenhauer and Moldenhauer 1979: 126). Schoenberg was latterly made the set's dedicatee when Webern had two hundred copies of the score published at his own expense prior to the first performance in the Great Hall of the Vienna Musikverein on Monday, March 31, 1913. The set was programmed as his op. 4, and Webern must have invested considerable faith in its favorable reception under Schoenberg's direction. What took place, however, was a hostile confrontation between conservative public and aesthetic modernism that, through its familiar designation as the *Skandalkonzert*, has come to emblematize the cultural tensions evident in pre–First World War Viennese society.

For Webern himself, already recovering from a breakdown in health during January of the same year, the experience proved particularly traumatic. Nonetheless, fifteen years later, in August 1928, the composer began to rescore the Six Pieces for a more normal-sized orchestra, a revision that, given that it followed almost immediately on the completion of the Symphony op. 21, seems to have indicated a sustained belief in the set, a conviction that prevailed despite the intervening technical developments that had led to the adoption of serialism. In truth, the set had already been felt to overlap with a much earlier work, the Five Movements for String Quartet, op. 5. Considered a supplement to what had previously been said using this chamber medium (as reported to Schoenberg on May 31, 1911; see Moldenhauer and Moldenhauer 1979: 130), the impression of creative continuity that the Six Pieces were taken to represent was, as Julian Johnson has affirmed, less motivated by formal concerns than by programmatic association (1999: 105). Johnson's identification of a music that resounds ultimately as nature might seem calculated to support an aesthetic turn that renders detailed sociohistorical interpretation immaterial. But in point of fact, he argues persuasively that both biographical material and musical substance are held to attain objective significance only on account of their mediated correspondence within a wider social milieu. The cultural construction of nature in this context thus entails a complex of tropes associating the natural not only with light and landscape but also with the effects of memory, a conflux that finds its most coherent expression in the Germanic concept of *Heimat*. For Webern, this sense of geographical identity, of belonging, was powerfully centered on the family estate in Carinthia. And infused with the recollections of childhood and familial loss, its topography repeatedly led back to the maternal grave in the tiny village of Schwabegg. As confirmed in a letter to Berg of July 12, 1912, Webern acknowledged that, aside from a few exceptions, all of his recent works had referred to the death of his mother, Amelie, in September 1906 (Johnson 1999: 84). Yet in truth, Johnson concludes, virtually all of Webern's pieces written between 1906 and 1945 "relate to the death of his mother in some way" (85). Hence a consistent lexicon of topical devices drawn from the history of Austro-German music is made to figure the effects of this event subject to the further metamorphoses wrought by the various stages of his individual stylistic development. But while the effect upon the composer of the death of his mother can hardly be understated, Johnson adds, the significance of this "for Webern's work *as art* . . . has nothing to do with Amelie Webern, . . . who died in 1906, but everything to do with a cultural concept of the maternal by which Webern's thought was deeply informed" (86).

Overall, Johnson positions the composer very convincingly as an heir to eighteenth- and particularly nineteenth-century musical tradition. But presented as the outcome of an extended culture-nature dialectic, it might be wondered whether this creative course does not actually invite a familiar charge leveled against aesthetic modernism. Put simply, faced with the heterogeneous effects of gender and sexuality, not to mention race and class, modernism sought either to suppress or to sublimate the circumstances of its socially-situated condition. Johnson himself is plainly well aware of the ideological relationship between art's concrete context and its autonomous processes. All the same, the worldly associations that formed Webern's creative identity are arguably far more diverse than the primary trope of nature otherwise suggests.

TABLE 19.1. WEBERN'S PROGRAMMATIC OUTLINES FOR OP. 6

(1913)		(1933)
The first piece is to express my frame of mind when I was in Vienna, already sensing the disaster, yet always maintaining the hope that I would find my mother alive. It was a beautiful day – for a minute I believed quite firmly that nothing had happened. Only during the train ride to Carinthia – it was on the afternoon of the same day – did I learn the truth. The third piece conveys the impression of the fragrance of the Erica . . . which I gathered at a spot in the forest very meaningful to me and then laid on the bier. The fourth piece I later entitled marcia funebre. Even today I do not understand my feelings as I walked behind the coffin to the cemetery. I only know that I walked the entire way with my head held high, as if to banish everything lowly all round. I beg you to understand me properly – I am myself trying to gain clarity about that peculiar state. I have talked to no one as yet about it. The evening after the funeral was miraculous. With my wife I went once again to the cemetery and there straightened out the wreaths and flowers on the grave. Always I had the feeling of my mother's bodily presence – I saw her friendly smile, it was a blissful feeling that lasted moments. Two summers after that . . . I was at our estate again for an extended period; this was the time when I wrote these pieces at summer's end. Daily, towards evening, I was at the grave – often in deep dusk.	1 expectation [2] fulfillment 3 contrast 4 funeral march [5] remembrance [6] resignation	The pieces originated in 1909. . . . They represent short song forms, in that they are mostly tripartite. A thematic connection does not exist, not even within the individual pieces. I consciously avoided such connections, since I aimed at an always changing mode of expression. To describe briefly the character of the pieces (they are of a purely lyrical nature): the first expresses the expectation of a catastrophe; the second the certainty of its fulfillment; the third the most tender contrast; it is, so to speak, the introduction to the fourth, a funeral march; five and six are an epilogue: remembrance and resignation. In 1928 the pieces received a new instrumentation, which, compared with the original version, represents a substantial simplification and is to be considered the only valid one.

Source: Moldenhauer and Moldenhauer 1979: 126, 128.

EXAMPLE 19.1. Webern, op. 6, no. 3, analytical outline.
Webern, 6 Stücke für Orchester, op. 6, ursprüngliche Fassung. © 1961 by Universal Edition A.G.,
Wien/PH433. © Renewed. All rights reserved. Used by permission of European American
Music Distributors, LLC, U.S. and Canadian agent for Universal Edition, A.G., Wien.

To expand on the range of association encoded within Webern's Six
Pieces, it will be helpful first of all to examine the two programmatic outlines
provided by the composer, reproduced in translation in Table 19.1. The more
detailed version on the left (reproduced in Moldenhauer and Moldenhauer
1979: 126) was originally conveyed to Schoenberg in a private communication
of January 13, 1913; the version on the right (reproduced on 128) was compiled
for public consumption in connection with a performance of the revised score
given in Dortmund in June 1933. The central annotation draws together the
order of the pieces as first identified (those not specifically designated are

enclosed in square brackets) with the single-word descriptions that form the main substance of the publicly sanctioned summary. As Johnson remarks, the music is not programmatic in a literal sense but rather assumes a narrative quality on account of the sequential effect established by the overall succession of pieces (1999: 105). Referring to the 1933 synopsis, it is also worth noting that the composer understood the avoidance of thematic connection across the individual song forms to be offset by a series of paired relations between pieces 1 and 2, 3 and 4, and 5 and 6. If the expressive continuum was felt to be in constant flux, however, it is also important to observe that the 1913 scenario identifies a number of physical locations that in turn may be grouped according to a range of experiences associated with the public sphere (1–2–4) as opposed to those connected with a more private domain (3–5–6).

Example 19.1 shows how the tripartite formal outline proposed by the composer pertains to op. 6, no. 3.[1] Thus mm. 1–4, 5–8, and 9–11 form a larger A–B–A' sequence underpinned by a series of smaller subsections (six in total). Simply put, the piece is articulated through a sequence of textural contrasts involving either a solo line plus static chordal support (e.g., mm. 1–2) or a descending monophonic strand (e.g., mm. 3 and 9, these latter occurring exactly one-quarter and three-quarters of the way through the piece). An equally straightforward gesture also connects the first and second main sections such that the homophonic platform that appears in mm. 1–2 played by the trumpets is immediately reiterated, a feature that is then recalled in mm. 5–6 by the clarinets. Plainly, this association is intended to reinforce a number of tetrachordal pitch connections, since while the sustained clarinet and solo violin elements reproduce the opening trumpet chord a tone lower, the same harmony is also restated in its original transposition as a kind of disconnected bass line distributed among French horn, harp, and bassoon across mm. 5–7.[2]

The consolidation of a $\frac{6}{8}$ meter through defined downbeats at this same juncture points forward as well as backward within the piece as the explicit $\frac{6}{8}$ of m. 3 is itself presaged by an implied compound patterning in the viola line in mm. 1–2 that is latterly recalled by the trumpet in mm. 10–11. These features are then further bound together by an array of motivic pre- and post-echoes whereby the upper neighbor-note figure of the opening viola line is compressed into a compound melody in the flute and glockenspiel in mm. 5–6 that also presages the trumpet's half-step valediction. An additional harmonic resonance is also created by the string chord in m. 3, one-third of the way through the piece, whose upper and lower pitch classes, F and A♭, form the harmonic frame for the chromatic sequence that concludes m. 8 and, in retrograde, mm. 9–10. Such details do not, however, obscure the most striking gesture of this compositional miniature: the implied I–IV–I tonal progression in A♭ that imposes itself in mm. 5–6. The deliberate naïveté of this allusion seems in turn to invoke a generic marker for the piece as a form of *Wiegenlied*. The sense of a compound ⁶⁄₈ grouping that bleeds through from the previous piece in the sequence is thus made more poignant by its initial embedding in the ⁴⁄₄ meter that will dominate the following funeral march. Yet perhaps there is also a wider point of intertextual resonance to be perceived in connection with the Prelude to act I of *Parsifal*, whose sacramental connotations are reinforced by a number of pitch-class-specific references unfolded as a rising minor third together with a succession of neighbor-note figures in the opening melodic line (m. 2, F4–A♭4; mm. 2–3, G4–A♭4–G4; and mm. 4–5, C4–D♭4–C4) that were first made meaningful to the composer on his initial pilgrimage to Bayreuth in 1902.[3]

Despite the composer's stated disavowal of thematic development, a range of precise pitch associations can nonetheless be traced across the surface of the Six Pieces. One such instance, the appearance of 6-Z44, the Schoenberg hexachord, in identical forms in m. 2 of op. 6, no. 3 (see again Example 19.1) and mm. 1–4 of op. 6, no. 6 (harp and cellos only) will need to suffice as an exemplar. Significantly, as James Baker notes of Webern's remark on the use of the chromatic B–A–C–H tetrachord in the op. 28 String Quartet, literal inscriptions might be thought too ostentatious (1982: 27). However, as his additional 1912 disclosure to Berg that compositional craft and experiential detail were often intimately entwined implies (see Johnson 1999: 84), any distinctive correlation is unlikely to be the product of happenstance. Consider then the vivid correspondence that arises between the piccolo line, which presses toward the climactic point of the second piece over mm. 19–22, and the accumulating timpani line that shapes a similar structural high point at the end of the funeral march in mm. 33–41. Both strands stress the same trichordal element involving identical pitch classes (B, C, and F). The potential for reading this component as a signifier for loss is strengthened if the solo viola line from mm. 1–2 of op. 6, no. 3 is reintroduced. Here the same three pitch classes form the termination of the line. Yet the sense of commencement and closure, of animation and extinction, is dramatically intensified by noting the multiple projection of this same harmonic fragment across each of the solo lines that unfold over mm. 1–4, primarily through their initial and concluding pitch classes (Example 19.2).[4]

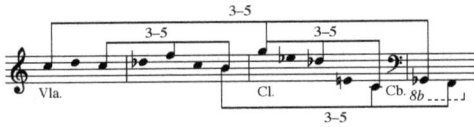

EXAMPLE 19.2. Webern, op. 6, no. 3, trichordal projection.

What kind of memorial function is intended by Webern's Six Pieces given this form of structural braiding? Admittedly, the set might fulfill the function of a *tombeau* if technique and aesthetic are taken to be paramount, albeit without a declared figurehead. In Johnson's view, the most convincing appraisal of Webern's individual compositions at this time is as static tableaux comparable to the individual scenes depicted in his 1911 stage play, *Tot* (1999: 105). This said, the Six Pieces may still be interpreted in part as a traditional elegy. Hence private grief is transmuted into public performance as a means of assuaging suffering while achieving a lasting memorial to the deceased figure. Indeed, creative rebirth thus confers eternal life in established humanistic terms. Further, the fact that Webern's synopses neglect to elaborate on features of maternal physical association beyond a single beatific image can be readily aligned with the Christian conception of death as the afterlife and the purpose of human existence. Responding to the visual connotations connected with instrumental types, Johnson supposes that the grouping of celesta, harp, and bells deployed in *ostinato* formations throughout the later pieces of the op. 6 set is intended to convey the impression of bright light in a manner similar to that exploited by Mahler. Indeed, the instrumental complex of harp, celesta, glockenspiel, and solo violin evidently intersects with the topical elision of landscape, death, and Marian imagery associated with the Mater Gloriosa passage of Mahler's Eighth Symphony and the final movement ("Der Abschied") of *Das Lied von der Erde* (Johnson 1999: 159–61).

Correspondences of this type are made more compelling by the synaesthesic reaction op. 6, no. 3 is meant to capture: the scent of heather placed on the funeral bier was surely felt to mimic the impression of incense and thus function as a sign of subservience to the salvation granted through divine grace. Yet as Jane Silverman Van Buren observes, the wider class of creativity myths that describes the rebirth of plant life from mythic personae also serves collectively to embody the antithetical implications of the maternal through an immanent poetics of existence and extinction (1989: 45). This confluence of the anthropological and the filial domestic itself correspondingly turns back toward infant identification of the most intense emotional experience with the partner of earliest symbiosis. Any genuinely empathetic reading of Webern's op. 6 pieces ought thus to proceed perhaps from a more intimate point of orientation, one that records its most compelling insights through the charting of interior psychic space. For David Schwarz (2006), maternal object loss as mediated through the op. 6, no. 4 funeral march establishes palpable correspondences between Viennese musical modernism and the birth of psychoanalysis. In Schwarz's view, attempts to register the effects of traumatic pathology, traceable from Plato but codified more systematically throughout the nineteenth and twentieth centuries, can be understood to furnish a valid interpretive framework for the composer's affective and technical idiolect.

While this genealogy is unquestionably pertinent, it can be profitably expanded with reference to more contemporary psychoanalytic reflections on the bond between mother and child, most notably issuing from the field of feminist critical thought. In this regard, psychoanalytic tracing of what happens when bodily needs become subject to the mold of culture finds no shortage of critical models by which to register the beneficent qualities of maternal association. Consequently, the sonic impression of childlike security conveyed by the third of the Six Pieces warrants comparison with the pre-Oedipal modes of attachment linking the male child with the maternal body, as described by Julia Kristeva (see Roof 1991: 162–64). This choric fantasy too is of necessity a retroactive construction of fundamentally irrecoverable, ineffable experience. Yet in appropriating Kaja Silverman's elegant formulation made in the context of film soundtrack study now more than twenty years ago (1988: 73), it is actually her advocacy of Guy Rosolato's tropes of the acoustic mirror and maternal vocal envelope that seems most fecund for the further interpretation of Webern's op. 6 (72, 79–80, 84).

Assembling what he acknowledges to be a number of fairly undefined, even crude musical topics in order to decode the cultural import of the Six Pieces, Johnson focuses his attention on the way that registral expansion at the close of the fifth piece represents a moment of spiritual presence and hence transcendental fullness (1999: 111–12). Having elsewhere noted the otherworldly, angelic character of the solo violin, along with the utopian quality of triadic formations in Webern's chromatic language (121, 98), he nonetheless disregards the A-major/minor fluctuations in the solo violin line of op. 6, no. 5 that might refer directly to Amelie Webern (mm. 21–26). This allusion is apparent at least as early as the fourth measure of op. 6, no. 3, where the second-inversion A-major trichord forms part of a sonority that, as Allen Forte remarks (1998: 99), is otherwise highly discordant in relation to its prevailing harmonic surroundings. Explaining the state of plenitude bound up with the trope of the maternal vocal envelope, Rosolato also likens it to the earthly equivalent of the celestial womb and consequently the paradigm for all musical gratification (cited in Silverman 1988: 84–85). Here, the Lacanian Imaginary is re-envisaged as a dream of recovery born out of the sense of division and loss. Testimony to the experience of lack attendant on symbolic Oedipal castration, the mother's voice is recognized as an instance of the *objet petit a*,[5] a perceived element of the self forever displaced following the initial stages of individuation. For Rosolato, its aesthetic realization comes to represent the condition of interiority transformed into *jouissance* through substitution of the mother's singing voice for the father's prohibitive voice (cited in Silverman 1988: 99). Significantly, then, the generic framing of op. 6, no. 3 as a *Wiegenlied* is supported by additional features that may be shown to possess empirical validity. Remarking on the cross-cultural characteristics of lullabies, for instance, Anna M. Unyk, Sandra E. Trehub et al. have observed not only that simplicity is the prototypical quality that defines the type (Unyk et al. 1992: 20) but also that this is a determinant that distinguishes the caregiving vocal contributions of mothers as opposed to fathers (Trehub et al. 1997: 506). In this regard, maternal preference for a stereotypical approach to aspects of form and content can also be linked to the essential function of lullabies – their soothing capacity (Trehub et al. 1997: 506). Melodies that mimic the descending contours of infant-directed speech are most successful in achieving the desired end of pacified contentment (Unyk et al. 1992: 22). Hence, not only does the sequence of melodic descents in mm. 3, 8, and 9 of op. 6, no. 3 seem calculated to replicate a distinctive generic cue, but its wider echoes also reaffirm a defining familial bond, because the composer, as his sister Rosa Warto later wrote, was initially schooled as a musician by listening to and playing along with his mother, an amateur pianist and singer (see Moldenhauer and Moldenhauer 1979: 34).

In sum, the idyllic naïveté of op. 6, no. 3, despite its premonitory relationship to the piece that follows it, seems incontrovertible. And if one might recall a familiar poetic conceit by which the offspring momentarily suppose themselves to have become parent to the deceased forebear at rest in the coffin prior to entombment, the overall effect is made still more touching. The necessity of exposing private grief to the constraints of public ritual depicted in op. 6, no. 4 thus appears to make eminent sense both of Webern's program and of the extreme affective contrast employed to convey its meaning. Yet, rather than assuming abject desolation to be the cause of such subjective protest, the details recorded in the composer's 1913 description may be taken to reveal a significant measure of equivocation (see again Table 19.1). True, the state of depressive confusion to which Webern refers is matched by a musical language whose distorted features seem incapable of communicating the effects of grief other than through hysterical excess – a point that Schwarz develops insightfully at length. However, the fact that the declared focus shifts from the deceased to the stoic sacrifice of the composer as mourner is indicative of an underlying ambivalence.

As Van Buren relates, the recognition of a more defined life-cycle that developed in the wake of modernist secularization succeeded a lengthy historical shadow that had previously aligned motherhood far more closely with mortality (1989: 20). Indeed, for Freud, male cultural hegemony tied to the primacy of the visual faculty as the locus of abstraction was predicated over human olfactory capability – the sense of smell – as a menstrual mark indicative of somatic regression (12). The paired conjunction of op. 6, nos. 3 and 4 thus seems to effect a form of psychological splitting involving good and bad maternal images associated with annihilation anxiety. Here, Melanie Klein's thesis of part-objects by which the pre-Oedipal infant negotiates its relationship with the external world appears most convincing, based as it is on an association with the body of the "real" mother (see Walker 1998: 141–44). Initially a paranoid-schizoid fantasy summoned by the rudimentary ego as an agonistic response to the developing awareness of alterity, its status as a position rather than a temporal phase denotes a state of infant reorientation, which, in Klein's view, remains pertinent throughout adult life. The eventual shift toward wholeness that subsequently takes place permits the infant subject to achieve a degree of regretful reparation for its polarized dissemination. Nonetheless, it is prior immersion in acts of absorption and expulsion that crucially engenders this process.

In noting the preliminary function of the acoustic mirror by which the maternal voice facilitates subject-object confluence and thus infantile introjection and projection, however, Rosolato once again relates this agonistic relationship not to Kleinian psychology but rather to the Lacanian Imaginary (cited in Silverman 1988: 80, 85). Prior to assuming the condition of the gendered subject inserted into language, the pre-Oedipal infant continues to perceive the maternal voice as the auditory equivalent of the mirror stage in that desire by and for the mother is immediately satisfied. Nonetheless, haunted, as Michel Chion supposes, by an increasing awareness of the maternal voice as the primary axis of otherness, this same vocal continuum begins to turn from the locus of plenitude and bliss into a malign signal for impotence and entrapment (cited in Silverman 1988: 74). For Silverman, Chion's evocation of the terror of the uterine night sustains its most convincing effect at the level of textual performance (77). All the same, she acknowledges that the cultural resonance of such formulations is sufficiently compelling as to denote the mother's voice not only as that which the male subject transcends through language but also as the signifier for all that it finds culturally intolerable (86). Significantly, then, it is instructive to compare the benign tonal implication of A major/minor that occurs in op. 6, no. 5 with the prior appearance of these same pitch classes as the registral boundary points (m. 35, $C\sharp2$ and C4 moving to m. 39, A2 and $C\sharp7$) of the harmonic progression that concludes op. 6, no. 4.[6] Here the constricting force of Chion's umbilical net – eliciting the effect of a "stifled, musical scream" for Schwarz (2006: 76) – is made all the more oppressive by the articulation of the entire sequence on wind instruments, themselves a giant prosthesis of the voice as interpreted by Rosolato (cited in Silverman 1988: 96).

What occasions this traumatic shift? Assuming that any speculative cause could be posited, it might be thought to reside in the state of indebtedness that is symbolized by the third of the Six Pieces. Thus the virtual merging of identities that is accomplished by the deployment of A major/minor (not only Amelie but also Anton) may be supposed to trigger a violent ambivalence caught between idealized homage, on the one hand, and the irrational anger provoked by unresolved mourning, on the other. And yet, as Deborah Rubin writes in her commentary on the subject of literary commemoration, if one social code for understanding the dissolution of such boundaries between mother and child is corporeal in kind, then its nearest equivalent is unmistakably carnal (1994: 22–23). In short, is it incestuous anxiety that impels the composer to supplant his mother's memory with her corpse in both op. 6, nos. 3 and 4 and then to ventriloquize it?

At this point, however, it is also vital to consider the degree to which the counter-transferential effects of the text begin to implicate the hermeneutic interpreter in the circuit of desire. Seduced by the promiscuous quest for meaning, it is additionally tantalizing, for instance, to recall the tonal strand in the French horn that emerges in mm. 5–6 of op. 6, no. 3 (see again Example 19.1). Again a rudimentary tonal progression, this time of $I–V^7–I$ in B, the gesture confirms a pervasive correlation of pitch classes F, A♭, and B that

Octatonic ←—————————→ *Tristan*

G♯

(D)   (D♯)

B

F

EXAMPLE 19.3. Webern, op. 6, nos. 3 and 4, pitch-class coalescence and attendant harmonic duality.
Webern, 6 Stücke für Orchester, op. 6, ursprüngliche Fassung. © 1961 by Universal Edition A.G., Wien/PH433. © Renewed. All rights reserved. Used by permission of European American Music Distributors, LLC, U.S. and Canadian agent for Universal Edition, A.G., Wien.

also finds a fragmentary expression in the instrumental solos of the funeral march shown in Example 19.3. For Schwarz, writing previously on Lacan, a withheld (or at least deflected) pitch class in the setting of Heine's "Der Doppelgänger" from Schubert's *Schwanengesang* serves to exemplify the inherent impediment of the *objet petit a* and hence the traumatic loss that is central to the formation of subjectivity (1997: 69–72). Heard in relation to the octatonic harmonic perspective that Forte identifies throughout the op. 6 pieces, the missing pitch class is arguably D, the component that would round out an expanded diminished-seventh cycle [0,3,6,9]. But perceived a different way, as part of a supplementary intertextual allusion, the all-pervasive structure of desire epitomized by the *Tristan* chord makes D♯/E♭ the withheld object.

Indeed, it is also possible to advance a pitch-class-specific reference to the chromatic F–A♭ "Desire" tetrachord immediately preceding the climactic point of the *Tristan* Prelude itself (violins 1 and 2, mm. 80–81).[7] Seeking to gloss Lacan's thinking on the consequences of irreducible disjunction, Slavoj Žižek argues that, far from disabling the circuit of gratification, this split is precisely what enables the symbolic self to experience the perverse pleasure of displeasure (quoted in Schwarz 1997: 69). Repeated circulation around the unattainable, always-missed object is what induces *jouissance*. Hence, to the extent that Webern may be thought to communicate this same irretrievable lack more or less reflexively as an invitation to the listener not to compete in desire but rather to sustain the mutual renunciation of a fantasy, he thereby enables an encounter with the ground of alterity wherein new meanings are created through the shifts of desire that take place not only in musical but also in critical language.

This said, the enhanced awareness advanced by any such compact between composer and listener arguably does little to resist that sequestering of the female voice that Silverman identifies as the cultural politics of the cinema soundtrack (1988: 77–78). Indeed, the disavowal of the maternal as the source of corporeal excess and discursive impotence that became partially constitutive of the historical self in early twentieth-century Vienna finds its encapsulation, as Žižek (1999: 139) and Schwarz observe, in the defining concept of hysteria. Read against this ground in its gendered guise, therefore, masculine desire thwarted by the impossibility of discovering a stable subject beneath the multiple masks of feminine performance assumes a paradigmatic importance in relation to the traumatic birth of Viennese modernism. By comparison, Webern's extended *Fort-Da* relationship with the effects of maternal legacy seems a somewhat restricted recounting of the vicissitudes experienced by the modernist voyager. Taken literally, his sentiments stress maternal empathy as the precondition for creative growth; read conversely for their gendered predispositions, however, the belief in patriarchal religion as the necessary fulfillment of maternal spirituality, not to mention the underlying dichotomy by which female nature is regarded as the inspiration for male cultural activity, together reinforce an unquestioning acceptance of biology as destiny.

From this position, it might be possible to open out the terms of Webern's seeming repetition compulsion in order to establish its psychotic motivations:

less a strategy for coping with the damage inflicted by maternal loss than the libidinal wish to fulfill the hallucinatory impulse of self-engendering by reaching the Real in the other.[8] However, all that has gone before could simply be thought to place an impossible interpretive burden on Webern's op. 6 pieces. To provide something of an epilogue, therefore, I would like to consider a more consistently applicable thesis as outlined in 2004 by Abbate. Put simply, Abbate poses the question as to whether music should be approached according to a drastic or gnostic inclination. Drastic comprehension she defines as musicology in real time: an immediate response to live performance as a material acoustic phenomenon, an irretrievable experience. Gnostic interpretation, by comparison, is what we have now: an acculturated, metaphysical predilection for displaced reflection grounded in an abstract notion of the musical work. The general assumption of sociocultural embedding is still to be welcomed, she argues; yet it takes a fundamental wrong turn by supposing performance to equate to nothing more than a delivery system over and above which true significance can be rendered not only legible but also specifiable. As Abbate reinforces the assertion, "Faith in specificity and legibility means believing that musical artifacts at later points can be read for exact localizable traces, that once upon a time something left a mark, and that reading such traces for the facts they reflect accesses the proper meaning that one should attach to musical sounds" (2004: 515).

Hermeneutics, whether "low" (i.e., historically validated) or "soft" (i.e., critically reflexive) in character, effectively assume the same status by invoking an enlightened perception that is otherwise predicated on a clandestine mysticism that seeks to invest music with heightened meaning. Anticipating instead a counter-argument in favor of music's unique signifying nature, Abbate proceeds to attribute this to a codicological faith in what is termed the "cryptographic sublime" – in sum, a hieroglyphic mode of mechanical inscription wherein the truth of music is held to be the more authentic the more deeply it is hidden (2004: 524–26). A source of ambivalence even for figures such as Adorno who sought to implement it as a means of achieving critical distance from the tradition of nineteenth- and early twentieth-century hermeneutics, its romanticized origins nevertheless find contemporary support in the guise of psychoanalytic interpretation. Listening to the sound of the subconscious in this way may appear to acquire a level of beguiling semiotic sophistication. All the same, its tendency to reduce music to a form of cinematic soundtrack is undeniable and all too readily absorbed into the sphere of cinematic kitsch.

Ostensibly, at least, the present commentary is thoroughly circumscribed by the terms of Abbate's analysis. Put succinctly, it stands revealed as an exercise in allegorical retelling whose objective mode engenders an act of clairvoyant communing that could scarcely seem more emblematic of the critical predilection for sonic disembodiment. Seeking sanctuary in the synthetic materiality of the dead letter only thus encapsulates the ideological shortcomings of English-speaking musicology across the past two decades. Yet in supposing formalism and hermeneutics to be mutually antagonized by the corporeal nature of "performed music's action" (2004: 530), Abbate might ironically be thought to have singled out her own critical performance for combined censure. Hence Craig Ayrey (2006), already skeptical of the need to denounce discursive communication precisely by employing it, is moved to align Abbate's negative responses not only to codes and systems but also to intellectual and creative labor with an exclusive attachment to staged music that is ultimately incapable of discriminating between musicological interpretation and media commentary on organized sport. Less ludicly inclined, Berger (2005) concedes that there may indeed be a plethora of physical, spiritual, and moral-political virtues to be accounted for in the course of forming experiential contact with phenomenalist performance. Nonetheless, no temporal art can render itself available to unmediated experience, since the fugitive present moment must forever be inflected by the horizons of both past and future.

Like Ayrey, Berger ultimately declares himself impatient with Abbate's self-dramatizing heroism, electing to repudiate the risks putatively bound up in real-time, point-blank confrontations with acoustic alterity as evidence of a solipsistic infatuation with ecstatic-aesthetic individualism. Yet before becoming a mark for the ennui that has curiously settled on a post–New Musicological elite, it is worth recalling that an ethic of affirmation in the face of historical dispossession was, as François Cusset has written (2008: 334–35), the motivating call to action that originally led, more than forty years ago, to the North American assimilation of postwar French intellectual thought in the service of engaged critical readings, enabling cultural identification and articulate symbolic contestation. Death too, as Sandra M. Gilbert has recently reminded us (2006: xxi), manifests itself only through a refracted array of emotional, societal, and aesthetic attachments, themselves overcoded by affinities of class, ethnicity, and faith, not to mention once more the male-female dialectic that was in turn so constitutive of artistic modernism. Indeed, if the twentieth century became the epoch whose denial of mortality suspended the moment in which life becomes transmissible, it was at the same time the era whose procedures of medicalization, bureaucratization, and mechanization effectively transformed death into a cipher that is at once ubiquitous and unlocatable. Exploring the poetics of bereavement from a century ago cannot of course reverse this historical lineage, much less redeem the perennial social solecism of grief. But to adopt and marginally adapt Gilbert's tentative conclusion (2006: 463), even listening, just listening to the polarized void that spans emptiness and transcendence in respect of human evanescence may itself be understood as a nascent form of victory. To what extent programmatic awareness is essential in order to enable listeners to participate meaningfully in the performative social practice surrounding a surrogate victim whose death might function as a restorative rehearsal for their own must remain moot. Yet in foregrounding the intensity of feeling that informs Webern's op. 6 pieces, it can at least be attested, contra Lawrence Kramer, that narrative is not solely a vehicle that "addresses the living but empowers only the dead" (1995: 117).

NOTES

1. This reduction, along with the analytical remarks made throughout the present commentary, is based on the original 1909 score as the version most contemporary with the composer's impressions of maternal bereavement. I should like to thank Kathryn Puffett for her very kind assistance in typesetting Examples 19.1–3 for inclusion in this volume.

2. This pitch-class-specific extension of the initial 4-Z15 collection is noted in Kabbash (1984: 241); see also his comments on the exact proportional articulation of op. 6, no. 3 (237–39).

3. The opening page of the composer's diary entry, showing a handwritten incipit drawn from the score in its upper-right corner, is reproduced in Moldenhauer and Moldenhauer (1979: 50).

4. The illustration is based on Crotty (1979: 31, Ex. 8). Crotty's short commentary includes many insightful observations, particularly with regard to the

recurrence of whole- and half-step neighboring motions throughout op. 6, no. 3.

5. Schwarz develops this point more directly with respect to Freud's reflections on the *Fort-Da* game (2006: 81–82).

6. Schwarz draws specific attention to the pitch-class $C\sharp$, associating it with Forte's suggestion of a reference to the Christian cross and to a prevailing sense of D-centeredness that spans the original version of op. 6, no. 4 in its entirety.

7. The way in which both harmonies figured in the development of Wagner's depiction of libidinal desire has recently been explored by Laurence Dreyfus (2010: 73–116). Significantly, perhaps, the [2,5,8,11] tetrachord is the one that complements the complete octatonic [0,1] collection formed by the opening trumpet chord and descending clarinet line over mm. 1–3.

8. Schwarz hears the final repeating sonority as representing immobility and hence a marker for a missed encounter with the Real (2006: 81).

WORKS CITED

Abbate, Carolyn. 1991. *Unsung Voices: Opera and Musical Narrative in the Nineteenth Century*. Princeton: Princeton University Press.

———. 2004. "Music – Drastic or Gnostic?" *Critical Inquiry* 30(3): 505–36.

Ayrey, Craig. 2006. "Jankélévitch the Obscure(d)." *Music Analysis* 25(3): 343–57.

Baker, James A. 1982. "Coherence in Webern's Six Pieces for Orchestra Op. 6." *Music Theory Spectrum* 4(1): 1–27.

Berger, Karol. 2000. *A Theory of Art*. Oxford: Oxford University Press.

———. 2005. "Musicology According to Don Giovanni, or: Should We Get Drastic?" *Journal of Musicology* 22(3): 490–501.

Brooks, Peter. 1984. *Reading for the Plot: Design and Intention in Narrative*. Oxford: Oxford University Press.

Crotty, John. 1979. "A Preliminary Analysis of Webern's Opus 6, No. 3." *In Theory Only* 5(2): 23–32.

Cusset, François. 2008. *French Theory: How Foucault, Derrida, Deleuze and Co. Transformed the Intellectual Life of the United States*. Translated by Jeff Fort. Minneapolis: University of Minnesota Press.

Dreyfus, Laurence. 2010. *Wagner and the Erotic Impulse*. Cambridge: Harvard University Press.

Forte, Allen. 1998. *The Atonal Music of Anton Webern*. New Haven: Yale University Press.

Gilbert, Sandra M. 2006. *Death's Door: Modern Dying and the Ways We Grieve*. New York: W. W. Norton.

Johnson, Julian. 1999. *Webern and the Transformation of Nature*. Cambridge: Cambridge University Press.

Kabbash, Paul. 1984. "Aggregate-Derived Symmetry in Webern's Early Works." *Journal of Music Theory* 28(2): 225–50.

Kramer, Lawrence. 1995. "Musical Narratology: A Theoretical Outline." In *Classical Music and Postmodern Knowledge*, 98–121. Berkeley: University of California Press.

Maus, Fred Everett. 2005. "Classical Instrumental Music and Narrative." In *A Companion to Narrative Theory*, edited by James Phelan and Peter J. Rabinowitz, 466–83. Oxford: Blackwell.

Miller, J. Hillis. 1990. "Narrative." In *Critical Terms for Literary Study*, edited by Frank Lentricchia and Thomas McLaughlin, 66–79. Chicago: University of Chicago Press.

Moldenhauer, Hans, and Rosaleen Moldenhauer. 1979. *Anton von Webern: A Chronicle of His Life and Work*. New York: Alfred A. Knopf.

Roof, Judith. 1991. "'This Is Not for You': The Sexuality of Mothering." In *Narrating Mothers: Theorizing Maternal Subjectivities*, edited by Brenda O. Daly and Maureen T. Reddy, 157–73. Knoxville: University of Tennessee Press.

Rubin, Deborah. 1994. "The Mourner in the Flesh: George Herbert's Commemoration of Magdalen Herbert in *Memoriae Matris Sacrum*." In *Men Writing the Feminine: Literature, Theory, and the Question of Genders*, edited by Thaïs E. Morgan, 13–28. Albany: State University of New York Press.

Schwarz, David. 1997. "Music and the Gaze: Schubert's 'Der Doppelgänger' and 'Ihr Bild.'" In *Listening Subjects: Music, Psychoanalysis, Culture*, 64–86. Durham: Duke University Press.

———. 2006. "Music and the Birth of Psychoanalysis: Anton Webern's Opus 6, No. 4." *In Listening Awry: Music and Alterity in German Culture,* 58–82. Minneapolis: University of Minnesota Press.

Shreffler, Ann C. 1994. *Webern and the Lyric Impulse: Songs and Fragments on Poems of George Trakl.* Oxford: Oxford University Press.

Silverman, Kaja. 1988. *The Acoustic Mirror: The Female Voice in Psychoanalysis and Cinema.* Bloomington: Indiana University Press.

Trehub, Sandra E., Anna M. Unyk, Stuart B. Kamenetsky, David S. Hill, Laurel Trainor, Joanna L. Henderson, and Myra Saraza. 1997. "Mothers' and Fathers' Singing to Infants." *Developmental Psychology* 33(3): 500–507.

Unyk, Anna, Sandra Trehub, Laurel Trainor, and Glenn Schellenberg. 1992. "Lullabies and Simplicity: A Cross-Cultural Perspective." *Psychology of Music* 20(1): 15–28.

Van Buren, Jane Silverman. 1989. *The Modernist Madonna: Semiotics of the Maternal Metaphor.* Bloomington: Indiana University Press.

Walker, Michelle Boulous. 1998. *Philosophy and the Maternal Body: Reading Silence.* London: Routledge.

Žižek, Slavoj. 1999. "Otto Weininger, or 'Woman Doesn't Exist.'" In *The Žižek Reader,* edited by Elizabeth Wright and Edmond Wright, 127–47. Oxford: Blackwell.

Contributors

BYRON ALMÉN is Associate Professor of Music Theory at the University of Texas at Austin. He is author of *A Theory of Musical Narrative* (Indiana University Press, 2008) and co-editor (with Edward Pearsall) of *Approaches to Meaning in Music* (Indiana University Press, 2006).

SARAH REICHARDT ELLIS is Associate Professor of Music Theory at the University of Oklahoma. Her research focuses on issues of musical meaning. Her main project concentrates on understanding the hermeneutics of Dmitri Shostakovich's music through his manipulation of the post-Beethovenian semiotic space. She is author of *Composing the Modern Subject: Four String Quartets by Dmitri Shostakovich* (2008).

YAYOI UNO EVERETT is Associate Professor in Music Theory at Emory University in Atlanta, Georgia. Her research specializes on the analysis of postwar art music through the perspectives of cultural studies, film studies, literary theories, semiotics, and East Asian aesthetics. In addition to her book, *The Music of Louis Andriessen* (2006), her publications include "Counting Down Time in John Adams' Doctor Atomic" (*Musical Semiotics: A Network of Signification*, forthcoming), "Toru Takemitsu's Film Music for *Double Suicide*" (*Journal of Film Music*), and "György Ligeti's Opera *Le Grand Macabre*" (*Music Theory Spectrum*).

EMMA GALLON completed her PhD thesis in 2011 at Lancaster University on narrativity in the music of Thomas Adès between the operas *Powder Her Face* and *The Tempest*. She now works at Ashgate Publishing and intends to continue her research into contemporary music, opera, and narrativity independently. Emma also carries out freelance editorial work for the journal *Ethnomusicology Forum*.

SUMANTH GOPINATH is Assistant Professor of Music Theory at the University of Minnesota. He is currently working on two book projects, one on the politics of race and ethnicity in the music of Steve Reich and another on the global ringtone industry. He is also editing, with Jason Stanyek, a volume provisionally titled *The Oxford Handbook of Mobile Music Studies*.

MÁRTA GRABÓCZ is Professor at the University of Strasbourg (France). Her main publications concern narrativity in eighteenth- and nineteenth-century instrumental music and contemporary (mostly electroacoustic and computer) music. Her books include *Musique, narrativité, signification* (2009), *Morphologie des œuvres pour piano de F. Liszt* (1996), and *Zene és narrativitàs* (Music and narrativity) (Jelenkor, Pécs, 2004). She has also edited a number of books, including *Sens et signification en musique* (2007) and *Gestes, fragments, timbres: La musique de György Kurtág* (co-edited with Jean-Paul Olive, 2009).

ROBERT S. HATTEN is Professor of Music Theory at the Butler School of Music, the University of Texas at Austin. He is the author of *Musical Meaning in Beethoven: Markedness, Correlation, and Interpretation* (1994, co-recipient of the Wallace Berry Publication Award from the Society for Music Theory) and *Interpreting Musical Gestures, Topics, and Tropes: Mozart, Beethoven, Schubert* (2004), both from Indiana University Press in the series he edits, Musical Meaning and Interpretation.

GREGORY KARL holds a doctorate in musicology from the University of Cincinnati. His publications include essays on the music of Shostakovich, Prokofiev, Rachmaninoff, King Crimson, and others as well as articles in music theory and aesthetics. He has taught at several colleges and universities; worked in the libraries of the Boston Symphony, the Metropolitan Opera, and the New York Philharmonic; and composed a number of orchestral and chamber works. He currently runs a music library and copying service. His home is in the Adirondack Mountains, where he explores the untracked wilderness.

MICHAEL L. KLEIN is Professor of Music Studies at Temple University. He is author of *Intertextuality in Western Art Music* (Indiana University Press, 2005). In 2004 his article "Chopin's Fourth Ballade as Musical Narrative" (*Music Theory Spectrum*) earned a Publication Award from the Society for Music Theory. He serves as an associate editor of the journal *19th-Century Music*.

LAWRENCE KRAMER is Distinguished Professor of English and Music at Fordham University. He is editor of *19th-Century Music* and author of ten books on the cultural meanings of classical music, including most recently *Interpreting Music* (2010) and a twentieth-anniversary edition of *Music as Cultural Practice* (1990). He is also a composer whose works have been performed internationally; his contribution to this volume includes a brief discussion of a work for solo piano performed at the conference from which the volume took wing.

REBECCA LEYDON is Associate Professor at Oberlin Conservatory, where she teaches music theory. She has published on a range of twentieth-century music topics, including the music of Debussy, science-fiction film music, mid-century popular music, minimalism, and the avant-garde. Her work appears in *Music Theory Spectrum, Popular Music, Perspectives of New Music, Music Theory Online,* and several anthologies.

JOSHUA BANKS MAILMAN (AB, philosophy, University of Chicago; MA, PhD, music theory, Eastman School of Music) teaches at Columbia University and NYU. He has presented papers on the music of Carter, Crawford-Seeger, Ligeti, Brahms, and Schoenberg and on topics such as temporal dynamic form, narrative, electroacoustic music, binary-state Generalized Interval Systems, and octave-equivalence with atonal melodies in the context of long-term memory. His publications appear in *Music Analysis, Psychology of Music,* and *Music Theory Online.*

FRED EVERETT MAUS teaches music at the University of Virginia. He has published essays on drama and narrative in relation to classical instrumental music, gender and sexuality in relation to musical analysis and aesthetics, popular songs by R.E.M. and the Pet Shop Boys, and other topics in music theory and criticism.

MATTHEW MCDONALD is Assistant Professor of Music and a member of the Cinema Studies faculty at Northeastern University, where he teaches courses in music theory, music history, and film music. His published writing focuses on early modernist music and music in film. In 2010 he was awarded an ACLS Fellowship to complete his book on the music of Charles Ives, which will be published by Indiana University Press.

VINCENT MEELBERG is Senior Lecturer at Radboud University Nijmegen, the Netherlands, Department of Cultural Studies, and researcher and lecturer at the Academy for Creative and Performing Arts in Leiden and The Hague. He is author of *New Sounds, New Stories: Narrativity in Contemporary Music* (2006) and *Key Themes in Music Studies* (in Dutch, 2010). He is founding editor of the *Journal of Sonic Studies* and editor in chief of the *Dutch Journal of Music Theory.*

NICHOLAS REYLAND is Senior Lecturer in Music, Film Studies, and Media, Communications, and Culture at Keele University. His research interests include Polish music, screen music, narrative theory, and music analysis.

Recent publications include papers on Witold Lutosławski, music and narrative in *Music Analysis* (for which journal he serves on the editorial board)
and *Music & Letters* (joint winner of the Westrup Prize); an essay (forthcoming) on music narratology and film scoring for the journal *Music, Sound, and
the Moving Image*; and a monograph on Krzysztof Kieślowski's *Three Colors*
trilogy, *Zbigniew Preisner's "Three Colors" Trilogy: A Film Score Guide* (2011).

ELISHEVA RIGBI is Adjunct Professor of Musicology at the Hebrew University of Jerusalem and a music critic. She also serves as a programs producer
at Israel's public radio's art music channel. She is currently finishing a book
on the history and reception history of *fin de siècle* music and musical thought.

PHILIP RUPPRECHT is Associate Professor of Music at Duke University.
His publications include *Britten's Musical Language* (2001) and a chapter on
thematic drama in *Peter Maxwell Davies Studies* (Cambridge University Press,
2009); he is co-editor, with Felix Wörner and Ullrich Scheideler, of *Tonality
1900–1950: Concept and Practice* (2012).

ALAN STREET is Assistant Professor of Music Theory at the University
of Kansas and editor of the journal *Music Analysis*. He is author of numerous
articles on aspects of musical and critical theory, and his recent published
work includes essay contributions to *The Philosophical Horizon of Composition
in the Twentieth Century* (2003) and the *Cambridge Companion to Twentieth-
Century Opera* (2005).

ARNOLD WHITTALL is Professor Emeritus of Music Theory and Analysis, King's College, London. While his recent books – *Exploring Twentieth-
Century Music* (2003) and *Introduction to Serialism* (2008) – interweave technical analysis with cultural-historical perspectives, his recent articles balance
extracts from his book-length study *The Wagner Style* against hermeneutic
analyses of contemporary composers – among them Jonathan Harvey, Harrison Birtwistle, Elliott Carter, and Pierre Boulez.

Index

Musical Meaning & Interpretation

Robert S. Hatten, editor